WE
WHO
BELIEVE
IN
FREEDOM

SWEET HONEY IN THE ROCK...
STILL ON THE JOURNEY

BERNICE JOHNSON REAGON

AND

SWEET HONEY IN THE ROCK

ANCHOR BOOKS

DOUBLEDAY

NEW YORK LONDON TORONTO SYDNEY AUCKLAND

AN ANCHOR BOOK
PUBLISHED BY DOUBLEDAY
a division of Bantam Doubleday Dell Publishing Group, Inc.
1540 Broadway, New York, NY 10036

ANCHOR BOOKS, DOUBLEDAY, and the portrayal of an anchor
are trademarks of Doubleday, a division of Bantam Doubleday
Dell Publishing Group, Inc.

Acknowledgments for individual works appear on pages 365–67.

Library of Congress Cataloging-in-Publication Data

Reagon, Bernice Johnson, 1942–
    We who believe in freedom : Sweet Honey In The Rock—still on the journey / Bernice Johnson
Reagon and Sweet Honey In The Rock.
        p.   cm.
    Includes bibliographical references (p.   ).
    1. Sweet Honey In The Rock (Musical group) 2. Gospel musicians—United States—Biography.
I. Sweet Honey In The Rock (Musical group) II. Title.
ML421.S9R4 1993
782.25—dc20   93-20308
                                                                                          CIP
                                                                                          MN

ISBN 0-385-46861-X (hardcover)
0-385-46862-8 (paperback)

BOOK DESIGN BY SIGNET M DESIGN, INC.

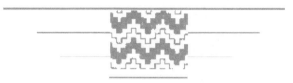

TO OUR MOTHERS . . .

*Marcella Robinson Barnwell, Gwendolyn Cray Harris, Beatrice
Wise Johnson, Mary Magdalene Johnson, Thomasina Johnson,
Rosalind Jordan, Shirley Elizabeth Maillard, Mary Vivian Robinson,
Gladys E. Weaver-Williams*

**WITHOUT YOU THERE WOULD NOT BE A JOURNEY OR SONGS
TO SING**

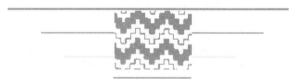

CONTENTS

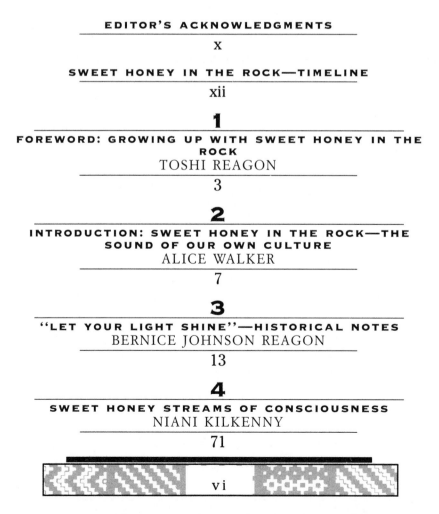

CONTENTS

CONTENTS

CONTENTS

EDITOR'S ACKNOWLEDGMENTS

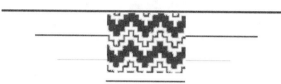

I am humbled and bow in thanks and gratitude to the community chorus called together through the work of creating this book.

When I presented the idea of a book to Sweet Honey in 1991, Ysaye Maria Barnwell, Evelyn Maria Harris, Aisha Kahlil, and Nitanju Bolade Casel (this host group would be joined later by Carol Maillard), I thought that if at least five of us wrote personal statements, with a history chapter and a photo essay we had a book. We decided to go ahead and drew up an ideal plan. We invited women who had been in the group over the past almost two decades who had maintained contact and identity with the group to contribute chapters. We wanted those people you never see from the stage—the producer, artist representative, sound engineer, members of our team who are our support structure—to be present. We wanted the audience in the number. It seemed that in book form we could have the real Sweet Honey chorus visually heard.

Then we wondered if anybody would publish this concert. I turned to my daughter Toshi who through her network introduced me to Faith Childs who as our agent introduced the idea of this concert in literature to Martha Levin and Sallye Leventhal at Doubleday who said let's do it! Without this hovering entourage the curtain would still be down on this event.

My ability to perform as senior editor was based on creative, consistent work rendered by Judith Ann Moore as publication coordinator and Kathy Anderson as

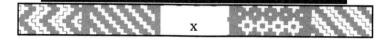

copy editor. At strategic times, Adisa Douglas stepped in as counsel, reader, and clerical support. Madeleine Remez of Roadwork helped organize the project's photo archives and locate photographers, as well as create the data base for Ann Rall, who created the group's time line.

Jim Deerhawk and our team at Earthbeat!, with managerial intercessions by John Telfer, production assistance by Toshi Reagon and yours truly, audio mix mastering by Mike Zook at Bias Studios, and digital mastering by Dave Glasser at Bias Studios resulted in the Earthbeat!–Sweet Honey–Doubleday extra surprise collaborative CD in the first-printing hardcover issue.

Then there are those of you who agreed to write your Sweet Honey melodies, rhythms, and harmonies on these pages, standing in for twenty-one women, thousands of volunteers, and millions of audience members who keep us alive because they keep coming and checking on us—and we keep singing . . . still on this tedious journey.

In gratitude and service
BERNICE JOHNSON REAGON

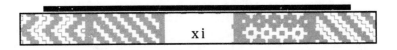

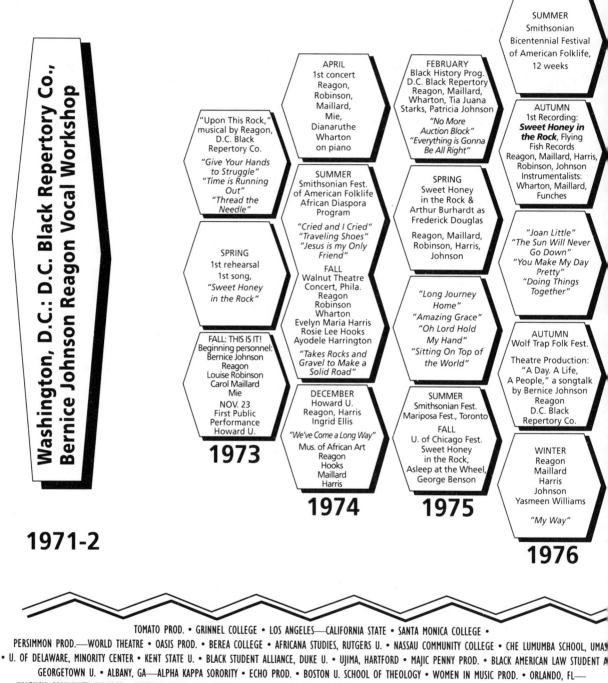

Washington, D.C.: D.C. Black Repertory Co., Bernice Johnson Reagon Vocal Workshop

1971-2

"Upon This Rock," musical by Reagon, D.C. Black Repertory Co.

"Give Your Hands to Struggle"
"Time is Running Out"
"Thread the Needle"

SPRING
1st rehearsal
1st song,
"Sweet Honey in the Rock"

FALL: THIS IS IT!
Beginning personnel:
Bernice Johnson Reagon
Louise Robinson
Carol Maillard
Mie
NOV. 23
First Public Performance
Howard U.

1973

APRIL
1st concert
Reagon,
Robinson,
Maillard,
Mie,
Dianaruthe Wharton
on piano

SUMMER
Smithsonian Fest. of American Folklife African Diaspora Program

"Cried and I Cried"
"Traveling Shoes"
"Jesus is my Only Friend"

FALL
Walnut Theatre Concert, Phila.
Reagon
Robinson
Wharton
Evelyn Maria Harris
Rosie Lee Hooks
Ayodele Harrington

"Takes Rocks and Gravel to Make a Solid Road"

DECEMBER
Howard U.
Reagon, Harris
Ingrid Ellis

"We've Come a Long Way"
Mus. of African Art
Reagon
Hooks
Maillard
Harris

1974

FEBRUARY
Black History Prog.
D.C. Black Repertory
Reagon, Maillard, Wharton, Tia Juana Starks, Patricia Johnson

"No More Auction Block"
"Everything is Gonna Be All Right"

SPRING
Sweet Honey in the Rock & Arthur Burhardt as Frederick Douglas

Reagon, Maillard, Robinson, Harris, Johnson

"Long Journey Home"
"Amazing Grace"
"Oh Lord Hold My Hand"
"Sitting On Top of the World"

SUMMER
Smithsonian Fest.
Mariposa Fest., Toronto
FALL
U. of Chicago Fest.
Sweet Honey in the Rock,
Asleep at the Wheel,
George Benson

1975

SUMMER
Smithsonian Bicentennial Festival of American Folklife, 12 weeks

---

AUTUMN
1st Recording:
Sweet Honey in the Rock, Flying Fish Records
Reagon, Maillard, Harris, Robinson, Johnson
Instrumentalists:
Wharton, Maillard, Funches

"Joan Little"
"The Sun Will Never Go Down"
"You Make My Day Pretty"
"Doing Things Together"

AUTUMN
Wolf Trap Folk Fest.

Theatre Production:
"A Day. A Life, A People," a songtalk by Bernice Johnson Reagon
D.C. Black Repertory Co.

WINTER
Reagon
Maillard
Harris
Johnson
Yasmeen Williams

"My Way"

1976

THE ROCK—TIMELINE

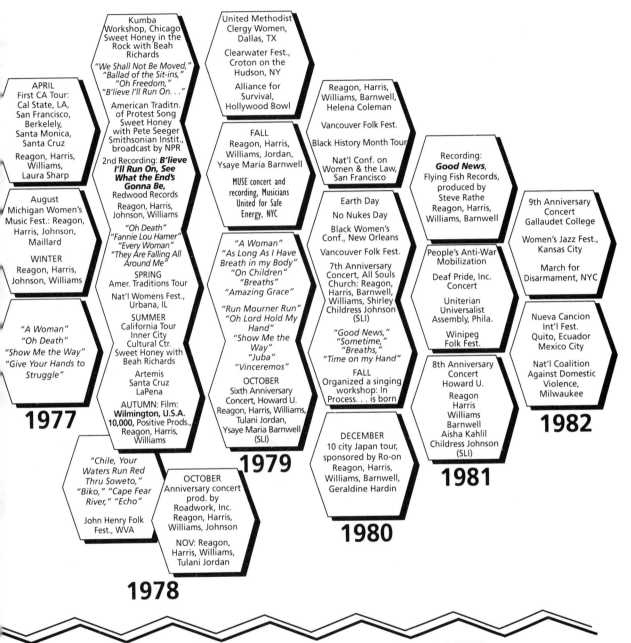

APRIL
First CA Tour:
Cal State, LA,
San Francisco,
Berkeley,
Santa Monica,
Santa Cruz

Reagon, Harris,
Williams,
Laura Sharp

August
Michigan Women's
Music Fest.: Reagon,
Harris, Johnson,
Maillard

WINTER
Reagon, Harris,
Johnson, Williams

"A Woman"
"Oh Death"
"Show Me the Way"
*"Give Your Hands to
Struggle"*

1977

Kumba
Workshop, Chicago
Sweet Honey in the
Rock with Beah
Richards

"We Shall Not Be Moved,"
"Ballad of the Sit-ins,"
"Oh Freedom,"
"B'lieve I'll Run On. . ."

American Traditn.
of Protest Song
Sweet Honey
with Pete Seeger
Smithsonian Instit.,
broadcast by NPR

2nd Recording: **B'lieve
I'll Run On, See
What the End's
Gonna Be,**
Redwood Records
Reagon, Harris,
Johnson, Williams

"Oh Death"
"Fannie Lou Hamer"
"Every Woman"
*"They Are Falling All
Around Me"*

SPRING
Amer. Traditions Tour

Nat'l Womens Fest.,
Urbana, IL

SUMMER
California Tour
Inner City
Cultural Ctr.
Sweet Honey with
Beah Richards
Artemis
Santa Cruz
LaPena

AUTUMN: Film:
**Wilmington, U.S.A.
10,000,** Positive Prods.,
Reagon, Harris,
Williams

*"Chile, Your
Waters Run Red
Thru Soweto,"*
*"Biko," "Cape Fear
River," "Echo"*

John Henry Folk
Fest., WVA

1978

OCTOBER
Anniversary concert
prod. by
Roadwork, Inc.
Reagon, Harris,
Williams, Johnson

NOV: Reagon,
Harris, Williams,
Tulani Jordan

United Methodist
Clergy Women,
Dallas, TX

Clearwater Fest.,
Croton on the
Hudson, NY

Alliance for
Survival,
Hollywood Bowl

FALL
Reagon, Harris,
Williams, Jordan,
Ysaye Maria Barnwell

MUSE concert and
recording, Musicians
United for Safe
Energy, NYC

"A Woman"
*"As Long As I Have
Breath in my Body"*
"On Children"
"Breaths"
"Amazing Grace"

"Run Mourner Run"
*"Oh Lord Hold My
Hand"*
*"Show Me the
Way"*
"Juba"
"Vinceremos"

OCTOBER
Sixth Anniversary
Concert, Howard U.
Reagon, Harris, Williams,
Tulani Jordan,
Ysaye Maria Barnwell
(SLI)

1979

Reagon, Harris,
Williams, Barnwell,
Helena Coleman

Vancouver Folk Fest.

Black History Month Tour

Nat'l Conf. on
Women & the Law,
San Francisco

Earth Day
No Nukes Day
Black Women's
Conf., New Orleans
Vancouver Folk Fest.

7th Anniversary
Concert, All Souls
Church: Reagon,
Harris, Barnwell,
Williams, Shirley
Childress Johnson
(SLI)

"Good News,"
"Sometime,"
"Breaths,"
"Time on my Hand"

FALL
Organized a singing
workshop: In
Process. . . is born

DECEMBER
10 city Japan tour,
sponsored by Ro-on
Reagon, Harris,
Williams, Barnwell,
Geraldine Hardin

1980

Recording:
Good News,
Flying Fish Records,
produced by
Steve Rathe
Reagon, Harris,
Williams, Barnwell

People's Anti-War
Mobilization

Deaf Pride, Inc.
Concert

Unitarian
Universalist
Assembly, Phila.

Winipeg
Folk Fest.

8th Anniversary
Concert
Howard U.

Reagon
Harris
Williams
Barnwell
Aisha Kahlil
Childress Johnson
(SLI)

1981

9th Anniversary
Concert
Gallaudet College

Women's Jazz Fest.,
Kansas City

March for
Disarmament, NYC

Nueva Cancion
Int'l Fest.
Quito, Ecuador
Mexico City

Nat'l Coalition
Against Domestic
Violence,
Milwaukee

1982

• ROXBURY PRESBYTERIAN CHURCH • KAREN GORDON FUND, FT. WASHINGTON, MD • U. OF ARKANSAS
• PENN STATE • CRESP, CORNELL U., ITHACA, NY • WOMEN'S RESOURCE & ACTION CTR., U. OF IOWA • U. OF PUGET SOUND • WOMEN'S STUDIES, SUNY BINGHAMTON
• SWEET BRIAR COLLEGE, VA • ALBANY EMPIRE, LONDON • ST. PAUL CHURCH, PHILADELPHIA • CARIBBEAN CULTURAL CENTER • TEMPLE UNIVERSITY, PHILA. • FLORIDA STATE
J. WOMEN'S CENTER, TALLAHASSEE • STAMFORD, CT • CONCERNED CITIZENS FOR MINORITY HEALTH SERVICES, BALTIMORE • BALTIMORE MUSEUM OF ART • ST. PAUL • AVA PROD.,
MINNEAPOLIS • KENTUCKY COMMISSION ON WOMEN, LEXINGTON • MANCHESTER FESTIVAL, ENGLAND • CHRIST CHURCH, POUGHKEEPSIE, NY • WOMEN'S STUDIES, WEST
VIRGINIA U. • STRAND THEATRE, DORCHESTER, MA • EBUSHA FOUNDATION, FLORENCE, SC • LANGSTON HUGHES CENTER FOR ARTS, PROVIDENCE, RI • PEACE & HARMONY
ESTIVAL, GETTYSBURG, PA • RUTGERS U. ORG. OF BLACK FACULTY STAFF • YWCA OF UTICA • STEINMAN ARTS FESTIVAL, CANTON, NY • WESLEYAN COLLEGE • NAT'L AFRO-AMERICAN
MUSEUM, COLUMBUS, OH • NAT'L COUNCIL OF THE AGING, INC. • BEACH PLUM MUSIC FESTIVAL, PROVINCETOWN, MA • HOPKINS CENTER, HANOVER, NH
• MADISON URBAN LEAGUE, INC. • MT. HOLYOKE COLLEGE • MCKINLEY MEM. BAPTIST, ABINGTON, PA • MOUNTAIN STAGE

FEBRUARY
Film, "Gotta Make This Journey," PBS
"More than a Paycheck"
"Down by the Riverside"
"Understand It Better By and By"
JUNE
Nat'l Black Women's Health Conf., Atlanta

NOVEMBER
Recording, **We All... Everyone of Us**, prod. by Evelyn Harris
Reagon, Harris, Williams, Barnwell, Kahlil
"Listen to the Rhythm," "I'm Gon' Stand," "Crying for Freedom in South Africa," "Battle for My Life"

NOVEMBER
10th Anniversary Reunion Concerts, prod. by Roadwork
Bernice Reagon, Evelyn Harris, Yasmeen Williams, Ysaye Barnwell, Aisha Kahlil, Carol Maillard, Louise Robinson, Tulani Jordan-Kinard, Dianaruthe Wharton, Tia Juana Starks, Helena Coleman, Geraldine Hardin, Rosie Lee Hooks, Ayodele Harrington, Shirley Childress Johnson

DECEMBER
Smithsonian Instit. Rev. William Herbert Brewster, Song Journey
Accompanied by Pearl Williams-Jones
"Where are the Keys to the Kingdom," "Leaning and Depending on the Lord," "Old Landmark," "Jesus is All"

1983

Sisterfire prod. by Roadwork, Inc.
"Oughta be a Woman"
"Ella's Song"
"Fannie Lou Hamer"
"This Little Light of Mine"

D.C. Women's Network, Jesse Jackson Campaign
"Sweet Bird of Youth"
"What a Friend We Have in Jesus"
"Hallelu"
"Balm in Gilead"

11th Anniversary Concert Warner Theatre
Reagon, Harris, Barnwell, Kahlil, Childress Johnson (SLI)

1984

Decade of Women conference in Kenya
Harris, Barnwell, Kahlil, Yasmeen

Sweet Honey demonstrates in front of South African Embassy: Reagon, Barnwell arrested

12th Anniversary Concert, Warner Theatre: Reagon, Harris, Barnwell, Kahlil, Yasmeen, Tulani Jordan-Kinard, Nitanju Bolade, Childress Johnson, (SLI)

Recording, Flying Fish Records: **Feel Something Drawing Me On,** best gospel album 1985
"Hush Lil' Baby"
"Father I Stretch My Hand to Thee"
"Meyango"
"Waters of Babylon"

Recording: **The Other Side,** prod. by Reagon, Asst. by Toshi Reagon
Reagon, Harris, Barnwell, Kahlil, Yasmeen
"Mae Francess"
"Deportees"
"Mandiacapella"
"Stranger Blues"
"No Images"

1985

"The Dream and the Drum," PBS special on the first federal observance of the Martin Luther King, Jr. holiday, prod. by Ruby Dee & Ossie Davis
Reagon, Harris, Barnwell, Kahlil, Bolade
"Letter to Martin"
"Beatitudes"
"Peace"

England & Germany Tour Berline Festspiele, Berlin
Reagon, Harris, Barnwell, Kahlil, Bolade
Newport Jazz Fest.

1986

Festival des Politischen Liede, East Germany
New Orleans Jazz Festival
Edinborough Festival Scotland & England Tour

Music Feature, CBS Sunday Morning
First Wammies Awards—Best Gospel, Best Ethnic International Group

1987

Galway Fest., Ireland
International Folk Fest., Smithsonian Delegation, Moscow
Australian Tour Sidney, Melbourne, Canberra

Recording, **Live at Carnegie Hall**, prod. by Steve Rathe and Bernice Reagon, 1989 Grammy Nomination for "Emergency," contemporary folk category
"Denko," "Drinking of the Wine," "Our Side Won," "My Lament," "Dream Song of Love"
Recording: **A Vision Shared: Tribute to Woody Guthrie and Leadbelly,** Columbia Records and Smithsonian Folkways Recordings, 1989 Grammy for Best Trad. Folk Recording
Reagon, Barnwell, Kahlil, Nitanju Bolade Casel
Reichold Center, St. Thomas, VI
Women's Coalition of St. Croix, VI

Film: **A Vision Shared: Tribute to Woody Guthrie and Leadbelly,** Ginger Prods.
Reagon, Harris, Barnwell, Kahlil, Casel
"Silvie"
"Old Gray Goose"

1988

PORTLAND PERFORMING ARTS CENTER, ME • COLORADO STATE U. • SEVA FOUNDATION, ST. JOHN THE DIVINE CATHEDRAL, NEW YORK • WOMEN IN MOVEMENT, ALBUQUERQUE • HOWARD U. • WARNER THEATRE • HOPE COLLEGE, HOLLAND, MI • THE ARK, ANN ARBOR • MARY WASHINGTON COLLEGE, FREDERICKSBURG, VA • AUSTIN PEACE & JUSTICE COALITION • MAVEN PRODUCTIONS, BOULDER, CO • THE AIDS SERVICES PROJECT, DURHAM, NC • U. OF CA, DAVIS • MCCARTER THEATRE, PRINCETON • U. OF NEVADA, RENO, NV • CUYAHOGA COLLEGE, CLEVELAND • ST. MARY'S COLLEGE • MADAME C.J. WALKER WALKER CTR.—BRANCHING OUT PRODUCTIONS, INDIANAPOLIS • HELENA FILM SOCIETY, HELENA, MT • BLUES ALLEY • WOODSON FOUNDATION, NEWARK • AFRICAMERICAS FESTIVAL 89, PHILA. • BLACK CULTURAL CTR., SWARTHMORE COLLEGE • BELOIT COLLEGE • ST. LOUIS, MO • NAACP LEGAL DEFENSE FUND, PRINCETON • SISTERVISION, TORONTO • WINSTON-SALEM STATE U. • U. OF WYOMING, LARAMIE • ASSN. OF AMERICAN LAW SCHOOLS • JAMAICA ARTS CENTER, QUEENS, NY • ALVERNO COLLEGE, MILWAUKEE • YOUNGSTOWN STATE U. BLACK STUDIES, YOUNGSTOWN, OH • MOUNT BETHEL BAPTIST CHURCH, FORT LAUDERDALE • WOMEN'S ENERGY BANK, INC., ST. PETERSBURG • DALLAS MUSEUM OF ART • DAVIDSON COLLEGE, NY • U. OF VIRGINIA • VIRGINIA COMMONWEALTH U., RICHMOND, VA • BENISON U., GRANVILLE, OH •

THE ROCK—TIMELINE

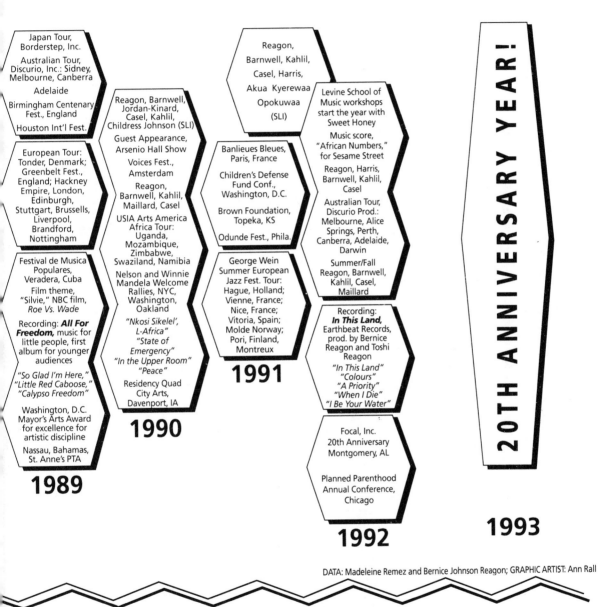

1989

Japan Tour, Borderstep, Inc.

Australian Tour, Discurio, Inc.: Sidney, Melbourne, Canberra

Adelaide

Birmingham Centenary Fest., England

Houston Int'l Fest.

European Tour: Tonder, Denmark; Greenbelt Fest., England; Hackney Empire, London, Edinburgh, Stuttgart, Brussels, Liverpool, Brandford, Nottingham

Festival de Musica Populares, Veradera, Cuba

Film theme, "Silvie," NBC film, *Roe Vs. Wade*

Recording: **All For Freedom,** music for little people, first album for younger audiences

"So Glad I'm Here," "Little Red Caboose," "Calypso Freedom"

Washington, D.C. Mayor's Arts Award for excellence for artistic discipline

Nassau, Bahamas, St. Anne's PTA

1990

Reagon, Barnwell, Jordan-Kinard, Casel, Kahlil, Childress Johnson (SLI)

Guest Appearance, Arsenio Hall Show

Voices Fest., Amsterdam

Reagon, Barnwell, Kahlil, Maillard, Casel

USIA Arts America Africa Tour: Uganda, Mozambique, Zimbabwe, Swaziland, Namibia

Nelson and Winnie Mandela Welcome Rallies, NYC, Washington, Oakland

"Nkosi Sikelel', L-Africa" "State of Emergency" "In the Upper Room" "Peace"

Residency Quad City Arts, Davenport, IA

1991

Banlieues Bleues, Paris, France

Children's Defense Fund Conf., Washington, D.C.

Brown Foundation, Topeka, KS

Odunde Fest., Phila.

George Wein Summer European Jazz Fest. Tour: Hague, Holland; Vienne, France; Nice, France; Vitoria, Spain; Molde Norway; Pori, Finland, Montreux

Reagon, Barnwell, Kahlil, Casel, Harris, Akua Kyerewaa Opokuwaa (SLI)

Levine School of Music workshops start the year with Sweet Honey

Music score, "African Numbers," for Sesame Street

Reagon, Harris, Barnwell, Kahlil, Casel

Australian Tour, Discurio Prod.: Melbourne, Alice Springs, Perth, Canberra, Adelaide, Darwin

Summer/Fall Reagon, Barnwell, Kahlil, Casel, Maillard

Recording: **In This Land,** Earthbeat Records, prod. by Bernice Reagon and Toshi Reagon

"In This Land" "Colours" "A Priority" "When I Die" "I Be Your Water"

1992

Focal, Inc. 20th Anniversary Montgomery, AL

Planned Parenthood Annual Conference, Chicago

1993

20TH ANNIVERSARY YEAR!

DATA: Madeleine Remez and Bernice Johnson Reagon; GRAPHIC ARTIST: Ann Rall

COMM. ON CATHOLIC COMMUNITY ACTION, CLEVELAND • COLLEGE OF WOOSTER • OBERLIN COLLEGE
ENYON COLLEGE • OLD TOWN SCHOOL OF MUSIC, CHICAGO • CLAREMONT UNIVERSITY CENTER • ST. OLAF COLLEGE, MN • THE ATTIC, DETROIT, MI • PEACEWORKS PROD. CO.,
TTLE, WA • MERIDIAN COMMUNITY COLLEGE, MERIDIAN, MS • ALPHA KAPPA ALPHA SOCIETY, CHARLESTON, SC • HIGH POINT COLLEGE, NC • BENNETT COLLEGE, GREENSBORO
• 3 RIVERS ARTS FESTIVAL, PITTSBURGH • UME KILN ARTS, LEXINGTON, VA • ANN ARBOR SUMMER FESTIVAL • NATIONAL COUNCIL OF NEGRO WOMEN, JACKSONVILLE, FL •
FOUNTAIN STREET CHURCH, GRAND RAPIDS • ELKHART CONCERT CLUB, ELKHART, IN • EASTERN MENNONITE COLLEGE • FUND FOR SOUTHERN COMMUNITIES • THE MEMPHIS
ACK ARTS ALLIANCE, MEMPHIS, TN • THE HULT CENTER, EUGENE, OR • MEYERHOFF SYMPHONY HALL, BALTIMORE • KENTUCKY CENTER FOR THE ARTS, LOUISVILLE • WEXNER
CENTER, COLUMBUS, OH • U. OF AKRON • U. OF WISCONSIN • CARVER CULTURAL CTR., SAN ANTONIO • NAT'L COALITION OF 100 BLACK WOMEN, MOBILE • THE AMISTAD
COMMITTEE, NEW HAVEN • COLLEGE OF SAN BENEDICT, ST. JOSEPH, MN • BUCKNELL U., WOMEN'S RESOURCE CENTER, LEWISBURG, PA • FOCAL, INC., MONTGOMERY •
THE U. OF KANSAS PERFORMING ARTS, LAWRENCE • COLUMBUS ARTS COUNCIL, MS • TROY SAVINGS BANK MUSIC HALL, NY • WASHINGTON UNIVERSITY

HERO-IN-TIME

WE
WHO
BELIEVE
IN
FREEDOM

1

FOREWORD:
GROWING UP WITH
SWEET HONEY IN THE ROCK

TOSHI REAGON

N ear the end of a workshop I participated in called "Black Women in Music: 100 Years of Rocking the House," I was asked how I got involved with the subject. How could I not be involved? One, I had a need to know where my voice came from and where I got my songs; and two, I needed to know where this line of Black women in music began. In the conference, as singer Judith Casselberry, poet Hattie Gossett, and I covered Black women's music in America from 1892 to 1992, I found the answers. In each era we covered in our workshop presentation, we used the music of either Bernice Johnson Reagon or Sweet Honey In The Rock.·

I was born in Atlanta, Georgia, in 1964. I've been surrounded by Black women singers all of my life; my mother is Bernice Johnson Reagon, founder and artistic director of Sweet Honey In The Rock. I can't remember a time when my mother wasn't involved in creating music. This need started very early for her in church and then continued with the original Freedom Singers during the Civil Rights Movement and on to the Harambee Singers, a group of Black women doing a cappella singing.

In 1971, when I was seven and my brother Kwan was five, Mom decided to move us from Atlanta to Washington, D.C., to get her Ph.D. at Howard University. We all got into the car and made the trip to D.C. and moved into an apartment complex in Anacostia, Southeast D.C. I liked Washington but remember having

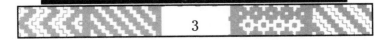

two concerns: who was I going to play football with and who was my mother going to sing with.

As long as I can remember, my mother has sung in churches, at rallies, in concert halls, and at festivals, but it seemed then like we were in Washington a long time before Mom found another group of singers. So I was really relieved when she got a job as musical director for the D.C. Black Repertory Company. It was my first front-row seat to the development and continued career of Sweet Honey In The Rock.

After being in D.C. and getting into the cycle of raising children, going to school, and working at the D.C. Black Repertory Company, Mom wrote the musical *Upon This Rock*. It used songs I had heard all my life. I think it is from this experience that the idea of Sweet Honey grew.

Even from the beginning, I had the sense that Sweet Honey would be around for a while. I will never forget my first impression of Sweet Honey In The Rock performing. It was at the Last Colony Theater, the home of the D.C. Black Repertory Theater on Georgia Avenue (it's closed now). I was particularly struck by Dianaruthe Wharton's original compositions on the electric piano and the group's sizzling version of "See See Rider." I could tell even at the young age of nine that they were special. They were mixing songs from every walk of life! It was intense!

Sweet Honey is so powerful onstage they almost seem indestructible. But as with any good organization, it takes a lot of work, meetings, planning, processing, and rehearsing to come off that cool. Twenty women have passed through the doors of our house for the weekly rehearsals. I listened from my bedroom as the group rehearsed. During these times I would often practice on my guitar. As the group became more popular they had two rehearsals every week—one for singing and one for business. This was a drag, 'cause Mom did not allow my brother and me to cook immediately before or during rehearsals, which took place between 6 and 9 P.M. This rule was made after we cooked pork a few times and the smell of it in the house caused vegetarian-sensitive Evie (Evelyn Harris) to become almost sick.

When I was thirteen and my dreams of becoming the first woman in the National Football League were crushed because of a sports injury, I switched careers and decided to become a musician. I asked my mother for advice. She said, "Learn to produce your own concerts and stay off drugs." So I interned at Roadwork, Inc., the organization that booked Sweet Honey, under Amy Horowitz, and learned about booking and concert production.

One of my jobs was to file the articles and letters that people wrote. I read many of them. People were in love with the group! But I also witnessed firsthand how hard it was to please everyone. I also learned that if you were doing your best, it was crucial to just keep going. I'm happy to say that most of the reviews were great!

Sweet Honey's songs had a wide range: warmth, love, church, and hard-hit-

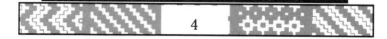

ting. I learned that everybody was not comfortable with everything they sang about. One song in particular was Evelyn Harris' "Battle for My Life." It began:

I'm aware of my condition, because of what's been missing,
Human rights for the people of color
The white man's disease is the same across the seas,
He's full of greed and he'd stab his own mother

The line rang true to me when I first heard it and it still rings true today, but it gave a few people, establishment press included, a little trouble. It was an important lesson for me to watch the group continue to sing a song that had a cutting edge.

I have been going to Sweet Honey shows since I was nine. They have performed in almost every possible music venue from churches to clubs and a variety of music festivals and concert halls all over the world. Sweet Honey has always sung many different musical formats, not shying away from any style based in the Black music tradition, including rap, reggae, and jazz. In the early years you could hear a BJR original, "They Are Falling All Around Me," or the blues song "Stranger Blues" or the powerful song of Black struggle "No More Auction Block for Me," and today those songs are still in the Sweet Honey repertoire. Sweet Honey tries very hard not to lose songs.

I learned many songs by participating in Sweet Honey's August workshops. The group would invite four or five women from the community to participate in their monthlong workshop. I was honored when I received an invitation to join them in the five-day-a-week sessions. Then nineteen years old, I was writing my own songs and fronting bands that I had been putting together since the age of twelve. The workshops were a part of Sweet Honey's need to expand beyond herself and really be in touch with her community. They eventually organized a bigger workshop of Black women singers which became the a cappella group In Process . . .

There are many singers who have gotten the inspiration and, maybe more important, a different model for what an artist can be. I include myself. Music is a mode of communicating to and about my community first, a mode of historical documentation second, and then a mode of entertainment. This philosophy comes from Mom and Sweet Honey In The Rock.

I am a blues-folk-based rock-'n'-roller and I've covered Sweet Honey's songs "How Long" and "The Other Side." One of the first songs I sang in public was my adaptation of their arrangement of "Dream Variations," a poem by Langston Hughes with music by Charles Mann. The reggae folk duo Casselberry-DuPree does a great version of "On Children," a poem by Kahlil Gibran, music by Ysaye Maria Barnwell. The ensemble In Process . . . bases so much of its repertoire and performance style and sound on its early formation as a community-based vocal workshop organized by Sweet Honey. One group of teenage Black women from

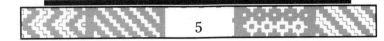

Brooklyn called Revelations . . . sing many of their songs a cappella and they include many Sweet Honey songs in their repertoire, including the very difficult "Denko." I call us all the children of Sweet Honey In The Rock.

Sweet Honey has given us a powerful structure to follow. It is a self-managed group of Black women that has achieved international success through being consistent and persistent. This has given many Black women an alternative image to look to. Sweet Honey has widened the scope of what Black women artists perceive they can be. We don't have to wait to be discovered, we can build the audience and produce the concerts ourselves. We don't have to be naked and act dumb to do it. We can be women of substance and intelligence.

I have always been trying to slip in on my mother's projects. When I was about four, Mom was having a rehearsal for a recording session at our house on Ashby Street in Atlanta with the Harambee Singers. When the singers had gathered around a reel-to-reel to record the song they were singing, I felt the spirit and wanted to contribute, so I ran and got a cardboard box to beat like a drum. When they listened to the recording everyone turned, looking for the one who made the banging sound that accompanied their beautiful vocals. With pride I said, "It was me." I was kindly asked not to participate on any of the other recordings.

Some twenty-three years later I am participating in a more constructive way. My first time in a recording studio was watching Sweet Honey record the song "Doing Things Together" for their first album. Later, singer, guitarist, and producer June Millington taught me a lot about the technical side of record production. Since then, I have co-produced my Mom's solo album *River of Life,* and helped with the studio-mix production on the Sweet Honey recordings *Feel Something Drawing Me On, The Other Side,* and *In This Land.* All of this led me to produce my own album *Justice* in 1990. I am proud to have produced the group's first children's concerts celebrating the release of *All for Freedom.* I was thrilled to be asked to produce their second recording for young audiences, *I Got Shoes.*

I have really liked it when I have rescued the group, for instance when I produced their sixteenth-anniversary concerts in six weeks! It was not difficult to pull off because of Sweet Honey's intense relationship with the D.C. community.

In the last twenty years Sweet Honey's Washington-based community has turned into an international community. Sweet Honey has toured the United States and countries around the world. And since the day Mom gave me her advice, I've traveled throughout the United States, toured Europe, and recorded three albums. There is a direct link between my learning these skills and growing up with Sweet Honey In The Rock. It has been the greatest continued event of my twenty-eight years on planet Earth.

Congratulations to all the women of Sweet Honey In The Rock on twenty years, here's to Tomorrow.

Love,
Your daughter, Toshi

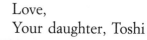

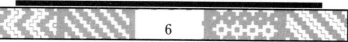

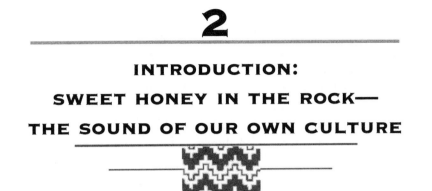

2

INTRODUCTION:
SWEET HONEY IN THE ROCK—
THE SOUND OF OUR OWN CULTURE

ALICE WALKER

My first Sweet Honey concert was in Washington, D.C., in the fall of 1978; Henri Norris, an old friend and a great admirer of Sweet Honey, invited me, saying she had something magnificent to share. I was not disappointed. Although I had heard Bernice Johnson Reagon sing years before as a member of the Freedom Singers, a group that grew out of the Civil Rights Movement of the early sixties, I did not know what to expect, hearing her over a decade later as part of Sweet Honey, the vibrant group of women onstage before me.

Those of us who lived through the Civil Rights Movement and participated in those struggles, can testify that just as there were times when our spirits soared, because of something we experienced by being with our people during a time of major transition—from servant to citizen—there were other times when, because of beatings, bombings, jailings, daily racist humiliations, the loss of loved ones, our hearts were nearly on the ground.

At the time of this particular concert I was just beginning to heal from the dissolution of an interracial, interfaith "Movement" marriage of ten years' duration. I felt my own heart had but a few inches to fall. It was a marriage that had had minimal support from our respective families and communities, yet it had miraculously sustained us through seven years in Mississippi, where my husband worked to desegregate Mississippi's schools and I worked part-time at various Movement tasks, from registering voters to teaching and creating history texts for the fledgling

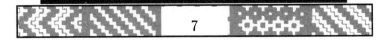

Head Start program. As time went on, however, it had become clear that my real reason for being in Mississippi, one state over from Georgia, where I was born, was to develop myself and my craft so that I might responsibly record, as a writer, the psychic layers of our people's experience at this time.

But where was I going now? Now that I no longer lived among our people in the South. No longer heard the soft courteous cadence of their speech. No longer saw on a daily basis their bright dark faces so full of character, or could observe their sweetly determined, unhurried ways. Yes, as is obvious from this passage, I had fallen in love. What was I to do with it? In New York, where I now lived, I was, for the first time in my life, often afraid of other Black people I encountered on the street. Never had I experienced such poverty, hopelessness, and hostile despair. Just this one reality, which perhaps seems commonplace now, was a staggering blow to my soul. In Georgia, where I had grown up, and in Mississippi, where I had lived, there were few Black strangers whom I physically feared, so completely had the struggle against vicious White racism united us. It was a shock to gaze into the eyes of a Black person on the street and to see myself reduced to the probable contents of my wallet.

And so I sat there, absorbing Sweet Honey's incredible beauty, a part of which was simply her existence, my heart slowly rising to the level of my lap as I heard "This Little Light of Mine," Fannie Lou Hamer's song, and then "We who believe in freedom cannot rest," a line from "Ella's Song." Ella Baker and Fannie Lou Hamer had struggled with us and for us to the very last breath of their lives; softhearted, strong-souled, willful, and heroic visionaries whose fidelity to Black people and to freedom was a single unflagging beat. Now I could really look, through tears of remembrance, at the individual women who comprised Sweet Honey. Except for Bernice, I did not know them. And yet, of course I did. Before my eyes they metamorphosed into my grandmothers; all the way back to the African and the Cherokee; and my mothers, my sisters, my best friends, myself. And I thought: This is what's been missing. The absence of *this* sound in my life is why it is so hard of late to remember who I am, and or what, indeed, the struggle now is. For what was I hearing, experiencing, taking into myself? Soul nurture. That infusion of spiritual carrots and spinach one's own culture can give, and which the dominant culture under which we live cannot.

I thought, sitting there, of the word "culture." And because I am a gardener and grew up under my mother's teachings as a gardener and under my father's teachings as a farmer, I considered what it means literally, in terms of health and growth. "Culture" is something in which one should thrive, the body and spirit simultaneously. But in the United States of America, for so many of our people that is not happening. Instead, like plants whose roots are sunk in poisonous soil, we find ourselves producing generation after generation of blighted fruit. And why is this? It is because the dominant culture, whose values are designed to encourage the full development of only the White and the male, and not even the disadvan-

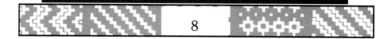

taged of those categories, leaves the rest of us unsupported, except in ways that are frequently injurious to us. It is also because many of us have forgotten or can no longer recognize our own culture at its healthiest. We no longer know that *it* is the soil we need in order to survive, in order to thrive.

By the fifth song I knew why people travel hundreds of miles to attend a Sweet Honey concert. Why people get married to Sweet Honey's songs. Why people give birth with Sweet Honey's music blessing the delivery room. It is inoculation against poison, immunization against the disease of racist and sexist selfishness, envy, and greed. By now my heart had reached my solar plexus, and when I heard the old songs from my grandmother's Hardshell Baptist Church ring out as the freedom songs they always were, I heard all the connectedness that racist oppression and colonial destruction tried to keep hidden. I heard the African beat, yes, and all the African tones. But I also heard the Native American "off-the-note" harmony that used to raise the hair at the back of my neck when my grandmother moaned in church. I heard the White words of the old, nearly forgotten hymns, and felt how the irresistible need of Black people to give contemporary witness to struggle infuses them with life.

These songs said: We do not come from people who have had nothing. We come rather from people who've had everything—except money, except political power, except freedom. They said: Yes, we were captured. They chained our grandmother to the mast of a ship that carried her away from every other face truly reflecting her own; her last view of home being, perhaps, that face resembling her own counting the money from her sale. They said: Yes, they hanged your Indian grandfather from the tree beneath which he worshipped Life. And, Yes, the singers said, it is not over yet. For we are still captive! Look at the lies, the evasions, the distortions of truth with which we live our lives.

Sitting there now, joined by the music with all my ancestors, feeling both my health and my wealth, I think: Yes. How sad it is for us that so often the only mirror we worship is the one in which we do not appear. Nor do we always recognize, with devotion, that which is before our very eyes. Why, for instance, does nobody remind us over and over again that Rosa Parks, the "mother" of the Civil Rights Movement, is as much Indian, and native to this continent, as she is African? And that there is a word, "African AmerIndian," that describes what many of us are? Why are we not constantly reminded, and do not constantly remind ourselves, that James Baldwin, who stood up for us so unflinchingly during the Civil Rights Movement, was a proud example of what a brilliant gay Black brother/father/uncle/lover who loves us can be?

But now—there is a voice rising clear and purposeful from the collective throat of the group. It sings of Soweto. It sings of Chile. It remembers Biko. It recalls Martin. It affirms love between women. It tells us we are wearing clothing that cost somebody's life. It warns us that the jobs we are often forced to take contaminate and destroy us. It tells us we do not own our children. It urges us to

acknowledge the suffering, yes, but to savor the beauty of life and the joy. Under this voice, the world begins to expand, and paradoxically, to grow smaller. We stand on the shore, here in North America, a land that we love through great sadness and pain, and we gaze into the eyes and souls of folks we know in South Africa, Latin America, the Philippines, El Salvador, Israel, and Palestine.

We understand, at last, listening to Sweet Honey, what our freedom songs are for. They show us the way home, which is the whole earth.

My heart is by now in its rightful place, in close proximity to my hands, which are made to reach out, as I write, to all those around me, the living and the ancestral dead, clarifying the struggle for myself and perhaps as well for others. It is close, also, to my brain, which reminds me always to link, as Sweet Honey effortlessly does, intelligence—political and otherwise—to passion.

Sweet Honey is our connection to our roots, as well as strong branches sheltering, blessing our connection to all who labor to create a healthy world. Healthy being another word for just. This is a sacred role—this putting of the heart, the courage, the energy, back in our bodies. There is no way to adequately thank her for being this for us, except to live our culture, which nurtures us, which she so regally represents. And with gratitude acknowledge it is the sight of our own souls' reflection which moves us so profoundly in her song.

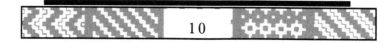

IN THIS LAND, POSTER. EARTHBEAT! RECORDS. 1992. (PHOTOGRAPHER, RICHARD GREEN)

3

"LET YOUR LIGHT SHINE"— HISTORICAL NOTES

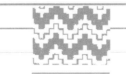

BERNICE JOHNSON REAGON

Let your little light, shine, shine, shine
Let your light, shine, shine, shine
Maybe someone down in the valley,
Trying to get home.

This church song talks about a person's life as a light. If you wake up in the morning and you find that you are not dead—then you can choose to use your life as a light. Maybe some—lost—body can use the reflection to find their way home. Sweet Honey In The Rock is a woman born of a struggling union of Black women singers; she began her journey some twenty years ago. Maybe her light . . .

I NEVER SING A TRADITIONAL SONG UNLESS . . .

I grew up in a region that had developed a strong sacred-music singing tradition, in a Black Baptist community in Doughtery County, Georgia. It is seven miles outside the city limits of Albany, which is located in Southwest Georgia eighty miles north of Tallahassee, Florida and 176 miles south of the capital, Atlanta. For my

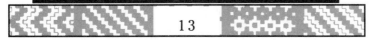

first eleven years, our church, Mt. Early Baptist, located in Worth County, the county next to Dougherty and my mother's birth county, had no piano. Like most of the rural churches in that region, we did all of our singing unaccompanied except for our feet and hands; to this day I am an a cappella singer. I still know the songs I sang as a child and have hundreds of songs I have collected as a scholar.

As a singer, I use songs to keep balance in my life. No matter how old a song is, when I sing it, it should be contemporary for me, if I am to bring honesty in my rendering of it. Otherwise, it becomes a historical relic and is dead.

Usually there is a song running around in my head. Most of the time it is an old song. When it begins to get louder and its presence begins to nudge, I know two things. One, it will stay in my head until I give it life in the air by singing it out loud, and two, I can probably sing it with an understanding of how it applies to my life.

"Sweet Honey In The Rock" was the song running around in my head for weeks before I called the first rehearsal for the group. It was 1973, and I was living in Washington, D.C. with my two children and attending graduate school at Howard University. Before coming to Washington, I had met Vantile Whitfield, who had recently returned to Washington to head up the new Expansion Arts Program at the National Endowment for the Arts. Known as Motojicho, he was the artistic director of a new theater, organized by Robert Hooks (the television and film actor), to train Black actors for professional careers in theater, television, and film. When I got to D.C., Motojicho asked me to work with the actors; so I became the vocal director of the D.C. Black Repertory Company (the Rep). The group Sweet Honey In The Rock was to come out of my vocal workshops.

The first time I had ever faced trying to teach what I knew about singing was as the Rep's vocal director. I used everything I could think of to get the young women and men in my workshops to sing. And this being Black theater, they made use of everything I could come up with, children game songs, funeral songs, lullabies, African songs, new songs, old songs. Although we did a little rhythm and blues and gospel, our major focus was to work out of the musical structures of the older congregational-style songs. I tried to introduce the actors to the spiritual community and power created through that singing.

Because of the democracy in the African American congregational song style (there are no auditions, one has but to enter the congregation and find the courage to sing), I was open to including everybody in the singing. I came to my workshop with my own childhood memory of everybody in the church 'larmed up in full-bodied song. All of them could not have been great singers, yet they sang with as much power as they could muster and it sounded and felt good from inside the congregation. In my workshop session I could lead anybody to the place in themselves where their singing could find the air.

Because of what I felt was a loose approach to time in the Rep's work style, I set up my workshop with strong, clear, rigid structures, so that members under-

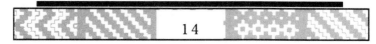

stood that they had an obligation not to waste their time or mine. I believed then, and still do, that being ahead of time is the only way not to be driven by time. If you participated in my workshop sessions, you knew the rules and you met them. I was amazed at the different responses to this kind of discipline. Some simply couldn't cut it; others (who had never really toed any line) pulled up to standard and performed stunning work; and others, who had waited a lifetime for someone to be serious about time, welcomed the structure. If the workshop was scheduled for 6 P.M., the singing began. If you were late, you were not allowed to join the session, and to stay in the workshop you were responsible for material covered. I felt people cleaning cobwebs out of their minds just by gathering the energy to get to my workshops on time. When we began and they were there, they were open and ready.

Some of my students came into the session with a sense that they could sing, but with little awareness of singing as a discipline, as a philosophical guide and a force in one's life. To them, singing was product; any way you got to the sound you wanted was okay. I discovered it was not okay with me. I searched in myself and in the singing that we created in our workshop for an honesty and integrity of sound that many of my workshop participants knew nothing about. They would give me melody, harmony, rhythm, and style, and I kept asking for the rest of it. I wanted to feel and hear their soul in their singing. The talk of older women in church kept coming back to me as a standard, "The child's got a nice voice but I don't feel nothing." To sing and not use it to reveal and work over some aspect of one's internal condition is to miss a major opportunity to bring strength and peace into one's life. I wanted my students to be able to walk this way of singing, to have a way to change their spiritual, physical, and emotional condition by running sound through their bodies.

Besides the monotone singers, relative-pitch singers, and singers told to clap when they were in kindergarten, the strength of the workshop was created by some exciting and experienced singers. Louise Robinson, Carol Ann North, Carlton Poles, Mike Hodge, Lyn Dyson, Carol Lynn Maillard, Smokey, Gaguma (Rafiah), LeTari, Mac, Kenneth Daugherty, and Mie, all made the Rep rock with the sounds of their singing. And what a gift to me, for as I tried to get them to know singing out of this older African American song tradition, I discovered strengths I never knew I had.

IN THE BEGINNING

During my second year as vocal director in 1973, Louise Robinson, LeTari, Smokey, and Maillard began to talk about forming a singing group. I was being asked to organize it and put the music onstage.

After hearing this suggestion a few times, I responded in my usual way. As a

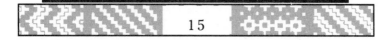

Black girl-child, I grew up being socialized to serve—my family, my community, my people. If someone else needed me to do something, it automatically became my responsibility. This is not always a good thing. Now I take suggestions as suggestions and keep them at a distance until I check to see if they are compatible with my own list. But in 1973, the vision of others had a direct line to my sense of duty and my sense of self. And thus, in response to Louise's nudging (and in my memory Louise was the most adamant in urging me to start a group), I called a rehearsal of about ten of the strongest singers in my workshop.

The first song I taught this group was "Sweet Honey In The Rock." I had never sung the song before in my life. It was a quartet song I had heard as a child and it was time for it to have its way in my life. When the group that first night got the chorus right, I said, "Hum, that's the name of the group, Sweet Honey In The Rock." I heard people trying it out, tasting the phrase on their tongues, under their voices, and then they said, "Yeah, Sweet Honey In The Rock. Yeah, that's cool."

After the rehearsal, I called my father, the Reverend Jessie Johnson, a Black Baptist minister, and asked him about the song and its meaning. He told me that it was based on a religious parable, but that it was not found in the Bible. This parable described a land that was so rich that when you cracked the rocks, honey would flow from them. From the beginning, the phrase—with sweetness and strength in it—resonated in a deeply personal way with me. It was another two years before I understood that for me and for the group, this land where the rocks were filled with honey was beginning to take shape and sound under the shade of that song as the experience and legacy of African American women in the United States of America.

As African Americans and as women, we have had to have the standing power of the rocks and the mountains. This quality often obscures the fact that we are sweet like honey. Inside the strength, partnering the sturdiness, we are—as honey is sweet—sweet. If our world is warm, honey flows, and so do we; if it is cold, honey gets stiff and stays put, and so do we. That first night, I only knew that I had found the name of the group and that I would have to grow into knowing how it would work in my life.

The first rehearsal was a beginning that did not work. We met several times, with new people coming in and others dropping out, but we never found a working chemistry. So after a few efforts and re-efforts during that summer, I let it go. Louise came to me one day and said again that the singing group was a good idea and that we should do it.

So I called another rehearsal of Sweet Honey In The Rock in the fall of 1973. I was there; Louise was there; Maillard was there; and Mie was there. After working with six to ten people, I felt a letdown. But being the strict disciplinarian I was, I started the session. We started the singing and it was good. We sang another song and it was good. I kept calling songs and they were all there, every note! After a while, we stopped—we believed, we looked at each other and said, "This is it!"

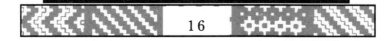

And it was. It was as if Sweet Honey In The Rock, the child, through a prolonged labor, had finally been born.

OUR FIRST PERFORMANCE

Sweet Honey In The Rock gave her first performance at Howard University November 23, 1973. Stephen Henderson, director of Howard's Institute of the Humanities, and his assistant James Early asked me to sing at the opening and closing sessions of the university's conference organized to commemorate the centennial of the composer W. C. Handy's birth. I agreed and for the opening session sang the spiritual "Oh, You Can't Hide Sinner." I also received a lesson that morning in the presentation made by Sterling Brown that figured strongly in the stances I would take later as an artist. I will never forget the venerable Sterling Brown, who questioned whether Handy could be called the "Father of the Blues." He said that Handy was a great composer who used the blues, but he did not have a claim to be father of the blues; his first attraction to the blues was mercenary. Then he read a passage from Handy's autobiography where Handy described witnessing, during his orchestra's break in Mississippi, a local band playing this monotonous crazy tune with a repetitious beat. The audience who had paid to hear Handy's orchestra put more money on the floor for the local band in fifteen minutes than his whole orchestra received for their entire performance. Handy decided then to learn and use this music, and the music was blues.

Sterling Brown was an idol for many of us at Howard. He was a teacher, he was a poet, a scholar, and he counseled many students who left school to participate in the Civil Rights Movement in the South. Here he was directly taking on and critiquing Handy at his centennial. Now, I understood something of his greatness, why he was a legend as a teacher, and how he was an artist in everything he offered that had anything to do with words. Sterling Brown clearly saw teaching as taking great risks to open the way to a usable truth. His stance on that panel seemed compatible with some of the marches I had been in during the Civil Rights Movement. I had studied Paul Robeson and W. E. B. Du Bois, scholars and artists whose offerings had challenged the times in which they moved and worked; but this session with Sterling Brown has stayed with me as a moment of clarity and example. I knew I wanted my work to be cleansing like that. The truth he shared about Handy did not diminish Handy's contribution as a composer and musician, but the corrective analysis was important for those of us trying to understand who he was and how he worked his art in this land.

I told Steve that for the closing session I wanted to use a group I had been working with, and he said, "I trust you, Bernice; however you want to do it, I trust you." It was Sweet Honey's first performance.

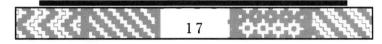

OUR FIRST CONCERT

We produced our first concert at the Rep during the spring of 1974, and people came! I look at photographs of this concert and can still feel the companionship I found from singing with these women—the first Sweet Honey In The Rock. We sang the full range of what would mark the group's performances, such as traditional songs like "No More Auction Block for Me,"gospel songs like "Traveling Shoes," a blues medley of Jimmy Reed's "You got me run/hide, hide/run anyway you want it let it roll," and "See See Rider," and struggle songs, like Len Chandler's "I'm Going to Get My Baby Out of Jail."

Dianaruthe Wharton's composition "Shine on Me" was special, and the spiritual "Let Us Break Bread Together," found new wings as "Let Us All Come Together" led by Louise. One of my strongest memories during that evening was a new blues song, written and sung by Mie as a solo, called "My Man."

My man done walked out of my life
Why I just don't know
My man done walked out of my life
Oh my man
My house done been cold for three days . . .
Oh my man

She sang it with her hand across her stomach like she was having a stomachache, you could feel her emptiness in all the places in you where you have come up wanting and without. . . .

WILL THERE BE A GROUP? AND WILL I LEAD HER?

In the fall of 1974, I faced my first personnel change. The spring before, the Smithsonian traveling artist program had asked us to perform a concert at the Walnut Theater in Philadelphia that September. I remember being scared; the date was six months away! We had never considered a booking with that lead time before. If we took this date, it meant there would have to be a Sweet Honey In The Rock that fall. I clearly did not want to make this decision for the group. *Everyone* said they understood the commitment and that we should take the job, so I signed the contract.

Near the end of the summer in 1974, Mie came to us and said she needed to leave the group to focus on personal issues. Early in the fall we held auditions. We were about to close the discussion on the singers we had heard when another person came in and Louise started hunching me in the side and saying, "Wait! Get

her, Bernice! We've got to get her!" Evelyn (Evie) Maria Harris had walked into the theater.

I remember her height and her head (it was thrown back), her confidence, and how she effortlessly wove a song like it was her breath. No other person in the audition had come close to her artistry. We asked her to join, and she said yes.

By the next rehearsal, Maillard was out of the Walnut Theater job; she had a role in a play. Did I mention that the first Sweet Honey was three actors and me? Theater came first. I looked around and had two of the original singers: Louise and me. So, I asked Dianaruthe Wharton, Ayodele Harrington, and Rosie Lee Hooks to serve as substitutes for the Walnut Theater job and several other performances that fall.

When we went up to Philadelphia on the train, Louise brought her infant daughter Asha with her. It was the first Sweet Honey trip with a baby. I knew then that this group had to be a group that would embrace pregnant women, women with babies, and whatever else women might be carrying as our natural or unnatural load. The only limitations would be whether the woman, the baby, the group, and the system we were evolving could handle the strain, and whether the music would continue to soar. I urged that we just listen to the sound of the music to know if it was all working well enough to keep trying.

We got a great review. . . .

DISCOVERING WHO SHE WAS/WE WERE

Since the beginning, Sweet Honey has been a process, always being defined by whatever part of the path we happened to be traveling at the time, keeping a clear link to our history of struggle and survival. The day-to-day work of being a graduate student, parent to Toshi and Kwan, working at the Rep, and now moving the group kept my gaze closely focused on making the next step steady. If the wider world would ever be open to us, I had to make sure we were turned toward the sun, I did nothing that might limit future opportunities. However, I saw my primary work as deciding what the next move would be. It could be as simple as the next rehearsal, when, where, the next songs to learn, the next performance, what would we wear, who could be present. From its inception, this was a group that came from women who had many other things to do in their lives every day. Sweet Honey would never be the only thing we did. We would always, as we gave her what she needed, also be working to fulfill the other spaces in our lives. . . .

Little about the group was clear to me before it happened. I knew we were a group of Black singers. Being an artist offering songs and singing from the African American struggle was the strongest ground I could stand on and be in the world. However, I did not initially envision that it would be a group of Black *women* singers. I did not know that it would start as four singers or that I would, as a

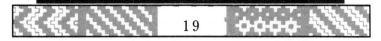

composer, begin to itch because I prefer to have five or six lines to work with in many of my arrangements and compositions. We did not overtly acknowledge that I was the leader (though everybody knew it inside). I did not know at the time that the organized women's movement was going to affect my life and the life that was Sweet Honey In The Rock. I did not know that as years passed it would become clear that Sweet Honey In The Rock was a woman who was always more than the total of the individual women who moved to the stage lending our all so that she could be. All of this was before us as we worked through that rehearsal in the fall of 1973. Maillard, Louise, Mie, and me, the very solid foundation upon which the group was built, willing to follow her wherever her songs and singing would lead.

I walk Sweet Honey In The Rock as a path, a way, a discipline; I do not create the path, which has been carved out by the living and dying of those who walked it before me with their lives, but I make my own tracks in a mountainous road. Sweet Honey is that way, is that path. I must be as true to her as I am true to the spirit of Harriet Tubman, Sojourner Truth, Beatrice Johnson and Mamie Lee Daniels, Septima Clark, Ella Baker, and Mary Johnson, and, and . . . When I am lost and unclear, I turn to these women and draw the lessons their lives wrote for us. And the path and the way unfold, all I have to find is the courage to walk this "narrow" way.

OUR MOTHERS

Ella Baker is my political mother. I had come to honor and work with Miss Baker during the days when I worked in the Civil Rights Movement as a Student Nonviolent Coordinating Committee (SNCC) field secretary and a member of the SNCC Freedom Singers.

She always greeted everyone. In the middle of the most intense Movement crisis, Miss Baker would always ask you about your person, your home, your children, your food, your thinking . . . Through her asking she taught us that no movement could exist without individuals, and that any movement organization had to take care of its people, the ones who made up the movement. So when I began to work with Sweet Honey, I insisted that this community of music also be a community of support, we would not be isolated, but would be a community organization serving and representing our community as a voice, and seeking support from those we served. I also tried to keep before the women singing in Sweet Honey that we were servants and only as strong as our producers, our audience, and our community. We had to return to them a portion of what we received on every level as a group and personally as individuals. I saw Ella Baker act this principle out many times.

Miss Baker was an organizer who loved to sing. One day in 1962, I attended a SNCC meeting in Atlanta, and Ella Baker asked me to sing "Guide My Feet, While

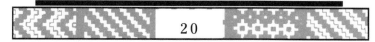

I Run This Race." So when we had the funeral service for Miss Baker in December 1986, almost a year after I last saw her at her birthday party, it was one of the songs I sang. But the most amazing thing happened: the song came out in Miss Baker's key, which was lower than mine. I was in the choir stand of the Abyssinian Baptist Church in Harlem and Miss Baker's body was in the casket. As I sang, I was looking at my voice and smiling because it felt like Miss Baker was using my voice to sing at her own funeral service.

In 1981, when Joanne Grant asked me to write the title song for a film she was making on Miss Baker, called *Fundi,* I wrote "Ella's Song." I created the poem for the song from the text of Miss Baker's speeches; one of the strongest images gave me the choral refrain. It was 1964 and James Cheney, Andrew Schwerner, and Michael Goodman, all Civil Rights Movement organizers, had been killed while driving along a lonely highway in Mississippi. We all believed that it was the presence of Michael and Andrew, two workers, White and Jewish, along with Cheney that forced the search that finally turned up their broken bodies. This suspicion was brought home when, as they dragged the rivers of Mississippi, they began to turn up the bones of Black men killed that no one had ever looked for. Miss Baker's remarks were angry; she was angry about the killing of young men, and about the racism. (When the Goodman and Schwerner families tried to have their sons buried with Cheney, they were blocked, because it was against the law in the state of Mississippi for Blacks and Whites to be buried together.) Miss Baker made it clear that there was to be no rest for those of us who made Freedom our cause!

We who believe in Freedom cannot rest
We who believe in Freedom cannot rest until it comes

Until the killing of Black men,
Black mothers' sons,
Is as important as the killing of White men,
White mothers' sons

That which touches me most
Is that I had a chance to work with people
Passing on to others
That which was passed on to me

Ella Baker believed in young people. She was advisor to SNCC and those of us who count ourselves as her children knew Miss Baker as a leader. She was strong, powerful. She would speak out; she would lead and be in front. But she also led by the way she listened and questioned. In her presence you got the feeling that what you felt inside made sense and could be offered up to the group for discussion as policy or strategy.

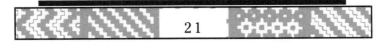

Miss Baker put nothing in front of teaching others to organize for themselves. She urged us as organizers to understand how to create structures that allowed others in our group to also be leaders as well as followers. Her power was in her wanting to increase others' sense of their own power and their access to power. It was a crucial lesson.

Miss Baker was the first executive secretary of the Southern Christian Leadership Conference (SCLC), the group formed by Martin Luther King Jr. out of the Montgomery Bus Boycott. SCLC was primarily an organization of Black ministers. Since many Black ministers (especially Baptist ministers) did not think much of women as leaders in the church (and in many churches women did not take the pulpit except on Women's Day), it must have been an experience for her. During the Movement, I saw many women in the pulpit during the mass meetings because their courage dictated that they should be there. But in the early days, women were helpmates of men—with a proper place and duty—and here was Ella Josephine Baker, who never learned that lesson, helping to build an organization of Black Southern (mostly Baptist) ministers. . . .

There are, too, those women who have come to me in stories passed from generation to generation from our earlier struggle against slavery and for freedom in this land. As an American nineteenth-century leader, the life of Harriet Tubman challenges me every day. The Harriet Tubman story that helped me the most in finding what my singing and Sweet Honey's singing would be about was the one where she finally left the plantation for freedom. She wanted her family to know, but she felt she could not tell her mother, so as she crossed the yard she sang a song to her sister, who was still working in the kitchen:

> *When dat ole chariot comes*
> *I'm gonna leave you*
> *I'm bound for de promised land,*
> *Friends, I'm gonna leave you*

We know Harriet Tubman was a fighter and a conductor on the Underground Railroad, but she was a singing fighter. Her songs were instruments of her struggle to destroy and undermine slavery, to free as many of her people as she could. Her stage for her songs was anywhere she was. Sweet Honey has mostly sung on stages that look like stages, but the image of Harriet as a Moses, as a general, living to fight for change and using song and singing to be clear about her life and work, is the one that I go to, to know what we should be doing in these times.

Sojourner Truth walking away from a New York plantation with her baby in her arms in 1827 challenges me to always be ready to risk in order to change my circumstance. I love working with the stories that come to us about and from her. She seemed to be willing to go anywhere and rise and take the stage before any audience and make herself heard. What is not often shared is that along with her

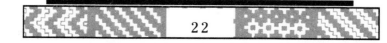

many other talents, she was also a singer and songwriter. She created new lyrics to "John Brown's Body" to honor the Colored Michigan regiment as they prepared to enter the Civil War.

We are Colored Yankee soldiers
Who've enlisted for the war
We are fighting for the Union
We are fighting for the law
We can shoot a rebel further
Than a White man ever saw
As we go marching on

In the first week of January 1991, I had Sweet Honey sing this piece for a film on the songs from the Civil War period produced by Jim Brown and Ken Burns for PBS. We were singing as we read the lyrics, and grinning at Sojourner's fierceness. I thought: We could use this lady in this group! She would fit right in.

OUR FATHERS

Frederick Douglass' stories about his life, coming to us from the middle of the nineteenth century, give us a mighty shaking ground. How important to be able to read his own writing about his life. For me, his living trembled the nineteenth-century ground he walked. His speeches and writing confirm that if you have a voice, you must use it for your people and speak to the world you live in, and if you are alive you should demonstrate it by using the space you occupy. You must help shape the world. He made it clear that freedom would not come without a struggle.

Reading his words on the meanings of our people's songs during slavery helped me to understand why Sweet Honey must continue to sing these songs even as we near the end of the twentieth century; the spirituals create a cultural record of our community being articulate about their plight in bondage.

. . . They told a tale which was then altogether beyond my feeble comprehension; they were tones, loud, long, and deep, breathing the prayer and complaint of souls boiling over with the bitterest anguish. Every tone was a testimony against slavery, and a prayer to God for deliverance from chains. The hearing of those wild notes always depressed my spirits, and filled my heart with ineffable sadness. The mere recurrence, even now, afflicts my spirit, and while I am writing these lines, my tears are falling. To those songs I trace my first glimmering conceptions of the dehumanizing character of slavery. I can never get rid of that conception. Those songs still follow me, to deepen my hatred of slavery, and quicken my sympathies for my brethren in bonds.

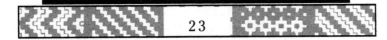

Then there is the intellectual giant of the twentieth century, William Edward Burghardt Du Bois, who seemed to believe that if he thought something, it should be published. This is not a minor lesson for Black and women people. Often when you come up in an oppressive culture, you question the importance of your very existence; you have to search for courage to express yourself. You have to talk to yourself so that when you speak with your voice, it is your heart, your mind, your eyes, your living, that supplies the text. It has been very important for Sweet Honey to use the stage as a forum for sharing the world as we experience it as African people in America, as women people in America. To do this you have to believe that what you feel, the way things come together in your life, in your mind, is worth singing and talking about. Du Bois keeps telling us in his writing that the fact that he was born is important and that the things that came from the labor of his mind should have access to other people's minds.

He also made it clear, with his life and his work, that making room for more than yourself is a requirement and responsibility of all Black men and women who find the way to stand and walk in this world. I have often thought of the singing of Sweet Honey as expanding, solidifying, and nurturing territory for the communities we serve, of which we are a part. Du Bois also believed that the songs created by our people during slavery were important documents for understanding our communities during those awful times. In 1903, in *The Souls of Black Folk,* he wrote:

> I know little of music and can say nothing in technical phrase, but I know something of men, and knowing them, I know that these songs are the articulate message of the slaves to the world. . . . The songs are indeed the siftings of centuries, the music is far more ancient than the words . . .

He spoke to the country as he spoke to us about the richness of our legacy in this land. He believed that it was important that African Americans were in the United States of America and that honest people could not talk about the country, its development, and its legacy without talking about the gifts of her "Negro people."

> Your country? How came it yours, before the Pilgrims landed we were here. Here we have brought our three gifts and mingled them with yours: a gift of story and song—soft stirring melody in an ill-harmonized and unmelodious land; the gift of sweat and brawn to beat back the wilderness, conquer the soil, and lay the foundation of this vast economic empire two hundred years earlier than your weak hands could have done it; the third, a gift of spirit. Around us thrice a hundred years; out of the nation's heart we have called forth all that was best to throttle and subdue all that was worst; fire and blood, prayer and sacrifice, have billowed over this people, and they have found peace only in the altars of the God of Right. . . . Would America have been America without her Negro people?

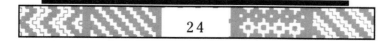

Paul Robeson's voice sounded like a beacon to all young creative souls who would listen. He was an artist, a singer, an actor—one of the most successful in the world during the thirties and forties. Who he was and why he performed the works created by his people called to me in a special way as I tried to understand how to be an artist accountable to my community, my country, and my history. During the thirties, from his base in Europe he wrote of being a Black artist:

> When I first suggested singing Negro spirituals for English audiences, a few years ago, I was laughed at. How could these utterly savage songs interest the most sophisticated audience in the world? . . . These songs are to Negro culture what the works of the great poets are to English culture; they are the soul of the race made manifest. . . .
>
> Sometimes I think I am the only Negro living who would not prefer to be white. . . . I am going back to my people in the sense that for the rest of my life I am going to think and feel as an African—not as a white man.
>
> Perhaps that does not sound a very important decision. To me, it seems the most momentous thing in my life.
>
> Only those who have lived in a state of inequality will understand what I mean—workers, European Jews, women . . . those who have felt their status, their race, or their sex a bar to a complete share in all that the world has to offer. . . .

Sweet Honey In The Rock walked out on hallowed ground. . . .

WOMEN WILL GO AND WOMEN WILL COME

An early hard lesson I had to learn about Sweet Honey was that the women who made up this group would leave. After Mie left, Louise began a two-year period of moving in and out. During this period, I was most unclear about how we would make it, I felt I was walking blind. I worked with other singers, I remember a performance at Howard near the end of the year, with a trio, Evie, Ingrid Ellis, and me. And then Evie stopped making rehearsals and we were looking again.

In early 1975, Pearl Williams-Jones recommended two singers, Tia Juana Starks and Patricia Johnson. I hired them both to do a series of shows we created for schoolchildren at the Rep during Black History Month. The lineup was Dianaruthe Wharton, Carol Maillard, Patricia Johnson, Tia Juana Starks, and me. After the run, Pat decided to stay and work with the group, Tia Juana said we could call if we needed her, and Maillard went to look for Evie, who came back and didn't miss another gig for over eight years.

When we did our spring concert in 1975, we were Maillard, Pat, Evie, and I. With this personnel plus Louise, who was back for a time, we moved into the summer and performed at the Smithsonian Institution's Festival of American Folk-

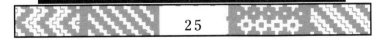

life for two weeks. Over the next year we began to travel. Dianaruthe graduated from Howard and moved to New York, and that ended the occasional piano presence in the group. Louise left around the end of 1975, and I could feel Maillard itching for a change. I asked her near the end of the year to not leave for a while; she said that she would stay as long as she could.

When Louise left, we auditioned Yasmeen and asked her to sing in the group. She had been a part of my workshop and I had begun to know something of her singing abilities, but once she began to work in the group, I learned that I had witnessed only the tip of the volcano. Yasmeen Williams can sing! She has a soprano and lyrical style that gives her astounding flexibility. There are no runs she cannot make. She is both a superb lead and a superb harmony singer, the best singer I have ever sung with in my life.

And her spirit, her capacity for feeling and compassion, seemed endless. It was Yasmeen who after several years said that we should work on how to improve the experiences we had with each other. This led to a retreat system in which we would individually check in with each other, we would talk to the group and to specific women, and in turn we would listen, and then after the circle had been completed we would each have to say whether there was enough in Sweet Honey for us to give her another year. This was new for all of us, and we discovered that some of us made better use of it than others. From the group perspective, we found the quality of life, the way we were together, in meetings, on the road, on the stage, improved; and that individually each of us had an instrument we could make use of when we needed to call the group together to discuss issues that we wanted addressed.

It was Yasmeen who suggested a drug- and alcohol-free policy after a discussion Ysaye and I brought to the group about our discomfort with finding ourselves at a Sweet Honey reception, and witnessing pot being passed around. It was approved unanimously by all present—Yasmeen, Ysaye, Evie, and I. It was a policy that was vigorously debated as new members came in and could not see why you couldn't have a beer if you went to Germany. Smoking was added after a few years.

Yasmeen left the group as a full-time singer in 1985, but she always made it back to the retreats and was always strong on this issue. Yasmeen also showed us that the practice we used when Maillard moved to New York, of bringing her in for specific jobs, could become a pattern within the organization. Singers who left the group could also choose *not* to leave the group. They could remain a part of Sweet Honey if they kept up with the repertoire. This gave us the recipe for survival, because it meant that instead of having only the singers one sees onstage, Sweet Honey would always have two or three additional singers who would go to extraordinary lengths to make a gig if a full-time singer dropped out at the last minute. It also gave me as artistic director the flexibility to book jobs for the group when a full-time singer could not make it. I could always try to fill the position with a substitute singer.

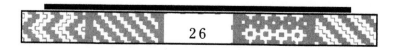

Because of this leaving and continuing to be in the group, I have few scars from the leavings. I initially did not want to face getting a new singer and not knowing where the new singer would come from. I went through the personnel process on automatic, because if I allowed myself to feel, I would not have been able to let people go and then lead the group in receiving the new member.

When it was clear that Carol Maillard was moving to New York, I experienced a big hole in my life. Maillard had become a major strength in the group and the theater. We shared the work of keeping things going. With her in New York, the weight shifted fully back to me.

I began to use Sweet Honey meetings to build the leadership structure of the group. All issues came to the table. I started the practice of asking that everyone be heard on such questions as what political rallies we would sing at, what benefits we would do. If a letter came in from someone requesting the group, it was read at the meeting.

In the early days, it was rough going, it was a new experience and the women had to learn to participate. As the leader, I would orchestrate the process and make the hard decisions, but I grew to understand how important it was to make decisions for the group with the discussion ringing in my head.

We set up a workshop after I left the Rep in 1977. We made sure that each year we would be working with a larger group than the singing ensemble, and we would invite the substitute singers to come in to listen to the new material, and if we needed a new singer, maybe the workshop would provide. . . .

Then the day came when there was no personal stress about personnel, I finally got it inside—in my center—that in Sweet Honey women would come and women would go and women would come, and that that was never a sign that the group was in trouble, it was a characteristic of the group. Sweet Honey was professional, but part-time, it attracted best those women who had family, community, and other career interests and that alone sometimes meant they stayed until they had to leave.

This was not always comforting to our growing audiences, who sometimes became attached to a certain singer. One of my nephews swears he is not smitten with Yasmeen, but nags me about the space she left that can never be filled. I tell him to hold that thought, because it's true. A longtime friend who had been with us in audiences since the first concert told me that she still missed Maillard and Louise. This was ten years after they had left! I looked at her and said, "I know what you mean, I miss them too." And I do. I can hear every voice raised in the name of this woman, Sweet Honey In The Rock. When we bring in a new singer, we do not try to replace the singer who has vacated a position. We bring in the new singer and begin to work to re-create this Sweet Honey statement drawing on the contribution that this new congregant ensemble can make. Often the repertoire is the same, the new singer learns old parts, but no one can replace a line woven in the

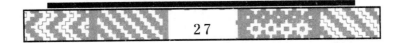

heart of another artist. You have to look at the whole composition, learn the notes and timing of your line, and find your own way of weaving it into a new life when it is called in a concert.

SWEET HONEY AND THE WOMEN'S MOVEMENT

Sweet Honey is a group of Black *women* singers and I grew to understand what that could mean to me, to the other women, and to the voice we try to raise in this land. Our beginnings in 1973 evolved in the midst of a period of heavy organizing in this country by and about women. Initially the group seemed outside or peripheral to this activity, because so much of the work reaching the national media was identified with White middle-class women.

I received a phone call one day from a woman's consciousness-raising group in Atlanta, inviting me to come to a session and share from my experiences as an activist, cultural organizer, and progressive singer. I asked them what women's liberation meant, since I had heard about it but didn't know much about the theory. The women explained that they were working on ways in which women could go beyond conventionally held stereotypes. She broke it down further, explaining, "It's like when you don't have to wash diapers and dishes. Women want and can do more than housework." I remember my face gettin' hot. I felt she was talking down to me, underdefining, simplifying her answer. Did she think I couldn't handle more complexity? Her example struck me as wrong! At the time I was the sole support of my family with two small children. I told her I would love to have someone sit me down so that I could wash dishes and clean the house.

The truth is, I was feeling that the work I had to do outside the home to get money to sustain my family had little to do with a personal calling. I saw looking for work as a kind of prostitution. I was offering myself daily on a market corner to the highest bidder, which then was $75 a week tops. I was also sole housekeeper, dishwasher, and parent. I felt deeply that being a part of a team, so that I could get a break and do less, would make me feel more normal in my day. Today I know more about why those women, primarily White from middle-class backgrounds, were gathering in those rooms. They were trying to rewrite the definition of who and why they were. In 1970, their search was not mine.

At the same time many Black women were also getting together. I was already a part of a group of Black women meeting in Atlanta around the issues that were central to our lives. We talked about our children, our people, the sense of unsafety living as a Black person in the United States, the need to be able to protect ourselves. . . .

A few years later, for the first time a friend of mine talked to me about feminine and masculine responses in women and men—I became alarmed. She was

describing something, but I did not know what she was talking about. I asked, "What do you mean, feminine? Masculine?" I had known the terms as external conditions, issues of style and choice. A person's inner being was genderless to me; it just was. I had no sense that the way I felt inside and operated in the world was feminine and that that was different from the way men felt inside. I believed that you were taught to be feminine and that you were taught to be masculine and that those characteristics did not tell you much about who you were.

The women I'd known in Southwest Georgia were adult females who carried their weight and any weight they had to carry to get through the world and not break. After a while of digging in my memory I started to come up with broken adult females. I discovered females who broke under the weight of oppression, sexism, and their responsibilities. Were they not women? I had left them out! And in my contemporary life, I was drawn to women who could carry the weight, theirs and everybody else's. I had little time for people who seemed to operate only in their own space and in their own individual interest. They were adult females, but they were not included when I tried to sort out "woman" in my mind. To be a woman like my mother and the women I knew growing up: like Mrs. Daniels, like my Aunt Fannie, like Mrs. Helen Lee, like Mrs. Lula Logan, and Mrs. Young, you had to be covering and holding up more territory than the ground you personally needed to stand on—and you had to be successfully holding up this broader ground for yourself and everybody else.

Then I began to let into myself and my psyche those women in my history and in my contemporary experience who carried heavy scars in their spirits from the full force of abuse this society unleashes on women. Joan (pronounced "Joanne") Little and her struggle to survive jail, rape, and North Carolina was a great help to me in that part of my search. She had been arrested on a burglary conspiracy charge in 1975. During a forced rape by her jailer, she managed to take his knife, kill him, and escape. North Carolina put out a dead-or-alive warrant on her head. When I heard about Joan Little, I thought: Oh! They Die! Rapists can be killed! In school and growing up I was told by my counselors and the police that if you are raped, you shouldn't fight back, because they might kill you. Joan Little taught me at my center that in the greatest danger, at your lowest point, you can fight back with the life you have. And sometimes, rapists die. An important addition to my sense of being whole came when I was open to letting in, as women, adult females from places I had not acknowledged before.

While they searched for Joan Little, I went into a barbershop with my son Kwan and my daughter Toshi, to have our Afros cut. The barbers, all Black men and my friends, were laughing and talking about Joan Little. They were alluding to the moment that so distracted the jailer that she could get his knife. I did not say a word. I could see that they did not feel what I felt when I thought about Joan Little. They talked around and about only a sex act, not as rape, not as violence, but a sex

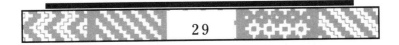

29

act as a known experience that they could connect with—the man's climax! Could these be my friends? I left the barbershop enraged, forming the chorus to my next song.

> *Joan Little, she's my sister,*
> *Joan Little, she's our mama,*
> *Joan Little, she's your lover,*
> *Joan's the woman who's going to marry your child*

As the verses began to form, I backed up from the barbershop scene to my growing-up years, and recalled the way I heard older people, women and men, talking about people who got into trouble. If a student was put in jail, or became pregnant, there was an effort by the elders to put a distance between us and that student lest we also suffer the same and wander down the same road. I started the song speaking to the women and men who loved me and raised me and shaped me and who would have had problems with the fact that Joan Little was in jail. I needed them to know how much I knew inside about Joan. I wanted them to know that Joan was a member of my family. Anything anybody said about her, they also said about me.

> *I've always been told since the day I was born*
> *Leave those no-good women alone*
> *Keep your nose clean, keep your butt off the street*
> *You gon' be judged by the company you keep*
> *I always walked by the golden rule*
> *Steered clear of controversy, I stayed real cool*
> *Along came this woman not even five feet tall*
> *Charged and jailed with breaking the law*
> *The next thing I heard as it came over the news*
> *Was first-degree murder, she was on the loose*
> *Tell me who is this girl?*
> *And what is she to you?*

> *I ain' talking about the roaring West*
> *This was 1975 at its most oppressive best*
> *North Carolina state, oh! the pride of this land*
> *Made her an outlaw hunted on every hand*
> *What did she do to deserve this name?*
> *Killed a man who thought that she was fair game*
> *When I heard the news, child, I screamed inside*
> *I lost all my cool, my anger I could not hide*
> *'Cause now Joan is you, Joan is me*

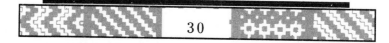

Our prison is this whole society
'Cause we live in a land that brings all pressure to bear
On the head of a woman whose position we share
Tell me who is this girl?
And what is she to you?

Sweet Honey premiered the song in 1976, in a concert with Lucha, a group of women (all White, radical, and fluent in Spanish) also based in Washington, D.C., who had worked in South America and who used their singing to do organizing work around Central and South American issues. We also sang it at a benefit for Joan Little. Both concerts were held at the All Souls Church Unitarian in Northwest D.C., a home and center for so many of our gatherings during the sixties and seventies. At the rally for Joan Little (she was out on bail in 1976), we listened to her testimony as she talked about running and hiding under a mattress while the police searched the house for her. We listened as her lawyer related the story of how the judge in her case said that he did not believe you could rape a Black woman, because of our nature!

"Joan Little" was also the first song of Sweet Honey In The Rock that played on the radio—and it was on a news broadcast. That should have given me some clues about how we would fare on Top 40 Black radio. Kojo Nnamdi, who did the news for WHUR Howard University radio, invited us to the station to sing and record it for his introduction and ending of the Joan Little story on the news hour at the station.

Opening myself up to Joan Little's struggle—as I let in women who fell, women who were abused by their husbands, women whom I saw every day—things immediately got softer for me and I could breathe with less clinched teeth. It might have saved my very life, this letting broken women into my world. It meant that Sweet Honey would not test women at the door as to what we were carrying. We assumed that if you were grown, Black, and female, you were carrying a load.

In 1977, I left the D.C. Black Repertory as vocal director, and I organized my own vocal workshop with the help of Rosie Lee Hooks and Elizabeth Whitfield. I called the workshop Motherdust. As we prepared for our first performance, I was sewing a dress for one of the singers when Amy Horowitz first came to my house. She was working with Holly Near, whose music my longtime friend Linn Shapiro introduced to me. Amy told me that she and Holly had recently heard my record *Give Your Hands to Struggle,* on the Paredon Record label, and they had decided that Amy should look me up when she came home for a visit. I told her that I was scheduled for a residency at the University of California at Santa Cruz during the spring of 1977. Initially Sweet Honey was invited out near the end of the residency and I wanted to use that opportunity to book a West Coast tour. However, I had just received word that funding had not come through and I was not sure what to do next. Amy said she would check with Holly and let me know what they might be

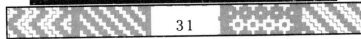

able to do. She called the next day to say that the tour was on. Amy booked the tour in less than two months. It was an Amazonian task.

As we prepared for the tour, we got a request from Holly Near to sing on a Meg Christian record she was producing. Amy told us that Meg Christian was a political lesbian and that the company, Olivia Records, was a collective of political lesbians. Pat Johnson asked what a political lesbian was. Amy defined a political lesbian as a woman who was probably involved with women sexually but, more importantly, chose women as the basis on which they did everything—performers, producers, and women committed to supporting women in every way, politically, socially, and financially. Having been nurtured and reborn through the rich sands of Black Nationalism, I understood this as a radical movement, and Sweet Honey decided that we could do this collaboration. In our only experience as a backup group, we sang harmonies on two songs for that project.

The 1977 tour to California was a cultural shock. We went from Washington, D.C., where we sang for Black people, churches, schools, theaters, folk festivals, and political rallies, to the radical, separatist, White-women-dominated, lesbian cultural network in California. Amy Horowitz was our bridge.

There were immediate and constant conflicts. A lot of the conflicts arose out of racism and cultural differences. Many of those conflicts came from our being "people-identified," which included men. We were working in a community that excluded men. The communities we moved among did a lot of checking, they wanted to be sure that they protected themselves and that they were dealing with women-identified women. I think we came up short, but they took us in anyway. In spite of reservations, the communities took an extraordinary risk in presenting us to the public that would come to events they sponsored. And Sweet Honey In The Rock—Bernice Johnson Reagon, Evelyn Maria Harris, Laura Sharp (who was substituting for Pat, who was having a baby—Makeda), and Yasmeen Williams—sang the songs of our people, our legacy, and created stunning concerts at a grueling pace that sometimes had us performing three times a day.

There was clearly a Movement energy that I understood and respected. People turned over their houses and cars to us, and they lugged around sound equipment. In two cases that I will never forget, Artemus in San Francisco and a bar in Albany, California—all-women establishments that never allowed men—suspended their "women only" policies when we performed because we insisted that some of our concerts had to be open to our entire community—and that meant men were included.

At the time of the tour, there was a boycott on orange juice in protest against the campaign led by Anita Bryant (who was the public spokesperson for the orange juice industry) to repeal a law that protected the rights of homosexuals in Dade County, Florida. At one of our performances, when we ordered drinks Yasmeen ordered orange juice. I thought I would go through the floor. She was told, "We don't serve orange juice here!" They let us in anyway . . .

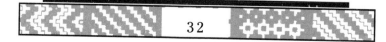

. . . and we stayed to do the work that we could do with these new audiences. I was keenly aware of the trauma that some of our early sponsors went through in organizing a platform we would accept. It was coalition work of the riskiest kind. The 1970s women's cultural network was doing some of the most radical work in changing the face of American culture by providing new forums for women to be heard; and Sweet Honey was a group of Black women singers who had something to say about the world we lived in.

Being women did not prepare us for being a voice within and beyond the women's cultural network. It was culturally a White, middle-class coalition. Sweet Honey was tested by fire. We had to learn on our feet how to be who we were, how to own ourselves, and how not to allow anyone else to define who we were. Being in a coalition was not a place to feel at home. Coalition work is hard and often threatening, but necessary to force change within a society such as ours. It is vital in advancing common issues and goals, and most effective if all parties operate from a solid base within their own communities.

Our early sponsors sometimes tried to make us them, and wanted to rename us. When we said that we were a group of Black women singers it was as if we had said nothing, that we were still in need of a title. I think the desire to name us was not malicious but came from a position of cultural privilege. When we insisted on our name, Sweet Honey In The Rock, an ensemble of Black women singers, we were asked what was wrong with being called feminist. I would answer, "What is wrong with being a Black radical woman and calling your organization an ensemble of Black women singers?" I explained that our radicalness was rooted in *our* history and models, and that the words and phrases we used were used by *our* mothers and our mothers' mothers, and we wanted to always name *that* connection. I also explained that in a struggle for justice in this society we would be on the same side, but we were not the same and Sweet Honey In The Rock had to name herself.

Out of Sweet Honey's experience, in the spring of 1977, with the radical women's movement, the phrases of a new chorus began to make itself known inside my head. I began to create a song about women loving women:

Every woman who ever loved a woman
You ought to stand up and call her name
Mama, sister, daughter, lover

This song scared me to death when it came out. I thought: Good God, what am I going to do with this? It was not an old song; it was *new* and running around in *my* head! When I sang it to Sweet Honey, Evie started to cry—we were all scared.

Would Sweet Honey survive in our base if we sang this song? Would Black people leave us before we got started? Would people think everybody in Sweet Honey was sleeping with women, or each other? With trembling, we decided to go

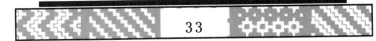

on. At that time and for all time since, we began to clarify for ourselves that we would not check Black singing women who came to Sweet Honey's door about their lives as sexually active adults. We would honor private spaces. We would sing richly about being lovers and loving, the songs and singing centered and coming from places of personal experience, but not offered as public entree into the personal details of our lives. We would sing about oppression of every kind, including the oppression experienced by the homosexual community. We would sing of the joy and the healing of love between two people. We would sing to celebrate and give comfort to women who were finding strength in spaces with other women. We would sing for freedom! Would we survive? Twenty years and . . .

THE VOICE AND THE SOUND

To sing a Sweet Honey concert, it is necessary to sing songs in the nineteenth-century congregational style, as well as the performance styles required for arranged concert spirituals, quartet singing, early and classical gospel, jazz, West African traditional, rhythm and blues, and rap—all in the same evening. Capacity and virtuosity differ from singer to singer, but everyone is challenged to move with intelligence from one sound palette to another, changing the places where the sound is produced in the body. The health and strength of the instrument are *crucial.*

One of the major attractions of the group for potential Sweet Honey members and our audiences was the primacy of the voice as instrument. New singers coming into the group who had had experiences as lead vocalists fronting bands or small combos talked about how refreshing it was to be in an ensemble where the singer, the voice, was the primary concern of a rehearsal and a performance. So many people in our audiences ask, "Why don't you use instruments?" And I respond, "We do use instruments—our voices."

When the voice is the central instrument, then the care of the instrument is *essential.* I urged the singers to consider the condition of their instrument their first and very personal responsibility. No one else could tell them what felt vocally comfortable for them. If while singing they felt a tickle or scratch, their instrument was signaling a discomfort that a thinking singer would never ignore. I could give them parts to sing in a song, I could ask them to try new areas, but they had to determine what was or was not possible for them to perform. A correct assessment of whether they could perform the part was important because not only were we a cappella singers, we also used no pitch pipe; the singer who started the song set the key. All of us had to learn to set the key not only for our individual comfort zone but so that when the song was raised, we would have an ensemble. Thus when you led a song you needed to know the parts—who sang the highest and lowest lines—and you had to have some sense of their range.

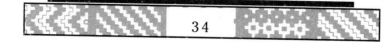

What is challenging about unaccompanied singing is that one's sense of key changes with each performance space and your sense of comfort changes with age. Ysaye, Maillard, and I like higher keys more now than when we started in the group, while Evie and Aisha Kahlil, who joined us in 1981, often favor lower ones. When I am in a larger room, I like a higher key, but I also have to try to consider whether the top lines in the arrangement I am leading can survive that key. For a singer in Sweet Honey, knowing the composition and the harmony system allows her flexibility—if the key of a song throws her line too low or too high, she can restructure her lines for comfort in delivery. This is possible only if you know the entire composition, a lot more than your part.

One foundational principle of the group was the importance of working with a voice teacher, forming a relationship with someone you trusted with your instrument. My voice teacher at the time was Frederick Wilkerson (Wilkie), and later his protégé, McLean Bosfield, who introduced me to my present teacher, Charles Williams. Wilkie taught me that every singer can learn something by standing in front of someone whose only purpose is to try to help them find vocal health. I constantly used the stance of concerned counselor, advising the singers not to take their instruments for granted and not to ignore changes in their vocal range. If they found that they were having trouble with their middle, upper, or lower registers, they needed to be working with a teacher who understood how to address vocal stress. I brought the group before Wilkie, McLean, and Charles as an ensemble, and told them that individually they had to do more. You can lead a horse to water . . .

SWEET HONEY'S VOICE IS NURTURED IN CHURCH

At some point in our concerts we sing to honor the contribution the Black church has made in our lives and in the survival and transformation of our people as a people in this land. The cultural anthropologist John Gwaltney told me once that people create religions to be more comfortable with themselves and their environment, and that oppressed people use religion to comfort themselves and to create an environment that resonates with their experience. When I study the works of David Walker, Gabriel Prosser, and Nat Turner, and witness the spiritually led lives of Septima Clark, Ella Baker, and Fannie Lou Hamer, I know that my people have many times made the church an instrument of their spiritual and physical transformation in a sea of racism.

Historically, Christianity has not always been a progressive force for Black people. One of the slave ships was called the *Good Ship Jesus,* and many slaver captains were "God-fearing men." In some cases, priests blessed slave ships before they left the shores of Africa, wishing them Godspeed and a safe journey . . . And the Klan burns the cross and prays to a God at their rallies. . . .

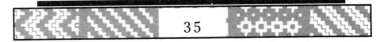

Yes, in every concert we acknowledge the power and presence of the historical transforming Black church in the survival of our people in this land. We sing songs that I learned growing up at Mt. Early Baptist Church in Worthy County, Georgia. . . .

> *Jesus, Jesus is my only friend*
> *Jesus, Jesus is my only friend*
> *Jesus, Jesus is my only friend*
> *Jesus is my only friend.*

The women of Sweet Honey learned to sing in the church, and there are elements of the African American church experience that we invite people into whenever we come to a stage. We try to invite people to come to a table and be fed, to learn, to rest, to laugh, to cry. Many tell us that this is a different musical experience than their usual concert fare. Many of our church songs come from my singing in church as a child; I have enjoyed sharing these songs with audiences all over the world.

To sing in a group which has come from many places within African America, to an audience from a wide spiritual background, and then to talk about finding contemporary solace in an old song like "Jesus Is My Only Friend" stretches many boundaries. The range and the tolerance of our audiences give me hope that there can be a world that accepts many cultures and belief systems. There is a way to practice through our living, being of oneself and among others at the same time. It happens in every Sweet Honey concert. In our performances we touch so much of the common human experience, we are given the room we need to be also different sometimes, even as we are embraced because we are the same.

Sweet Honey has always been a mixed group; we all come out of Christian backgrounds but have journeyed far and wide in search of a spiritual path: Unitarian, Baptist, no church, Muslim, African traditional spiritualism. And the search continues. In 1983, Sweet Honey performed a concert of gospel songs composed by the Reverend William Herbert Brewster, and two years later released an album of sacred songs, *Feel Something Drawing Me On*, with one of his songs as the title song. It was during this project that we worked out our concept of sacred as embracing the full range of spiritual journeys available to us. On that recording, there are gospel songs such as the title song by Brewster, "In the Upper Room" by Lucie E. Campbell, and "Try Jesus," a composition of gospel composer Roberta Martin; also "Meyango," a West African funeral song taught to us by Aisha, the Jamaican song "Waters of Babylon" of the Christian and Rastafarian traditions, and a lullaby I learned from my mother, "Hush Li'l Baby." All of these songs are sacred, all of them finding the air through the singing of Sweet Honey.

All of the energy of our living goes into our singing during our concerts. We

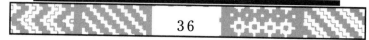

are sharing so much more than a concert of songs. We are calling our people together. As a singer and song leader, I draw upon the singing I sang in jail when singing was a bond. Singing gave us something to use as a weave and a connection. Even when we were becoming aware of specific ways in which we were not one, the songs helped us to find a oneness that was needed to continue to survive the place we were in. In our concerts I want a song and a singing experience that create community in our audiences right in the rooms we are in. I learned about creating a community of song growing up singing in church in Southwest Georgia.

It is important that when people come to our concerts they do not come to forget the day's troubles, to be taken out of themselves. We are not entertainers, although hopefully our singing entertains. I am not saying that entertainers do not do good work. People sometimes need to get away from everything and have fun and be in a different space. That is, though, not the purpose of a Sweet Honey concert. By going inside ourselves and singing specifically out of our lives, our community, and our world, we try to help those listening, in the sound of our singing, to create a celebration based on what they can embrace that is real to them at that time. And again, it is in church (where I first heard songs started by song leaders calling the congregation to help "raise" the song into its own life) that I learned how to create that space. Our audiences are often urged to help us out with the singing, to embrace all that makes up who they are. With those experiences and with that load, they can lift and celebrate being alive at this time with this opportunity to choose, to be clear, and to be heard.

SWEET HONEY'S REPERTOIRE

During the Civil Rights Movement, in Albany, Georgia, all of the songs sung in the rallies that took place in a local church were church-based songs. In the Movement office, in the streets, and sometimes in jail, we sang the freedom songs based on rhythm-and-blues tunes. The SNCC Freedom Singers, the group of singers I sang with during the early sixties, sang a range of songs that went further than the mass-meeting church-based repertoire. In our concerts, we would sing popular folk songs, traditional ballads, love songs, as well as those songs that distinguished our group, the freedom songs created as a Movement voice. When Sweet Honey In The Rock began, I had been singing a cappella for several years and had no intention of ever going to the stage with less than the full range of African American music forms.

The determination to be expansive in our repertoire evolved out of my experience with my first solo recording, *The Sound of Thunder,* produced in Atlanta in 1965 by a local Episcopal priest, Father Robert Hunter, and myself. On this album were church songs, hymns like "When I Take My Vacation in Heaven," spirituals like "Steal Away," and "Pastures of Plenty," by Woody Guthrie, a blues I wrote

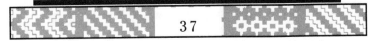

called "Black Woman's Blues," the work song "Sound Like Thunder" (the title song), two Langston Hughes poems that I set to music ("Out of Love" and "Southern Gentle Lady"), two songs I had learned from the Georgia mountain singer Hedy West ("Anger in the Land" and "Li'l Birdie"), Guy Carawan's "Ain' You Got a Right," as well as the gospel-styled "This Train Is Bound for Glory."

Most of the album was a cappella, but some songs were accompanied by flute, congas, and bass. When I sent the recording to an agent to review to help me get some concert performances, she wrote back that I needed to make up my mind about what kind of singer I was going to be—a gospel singer, a folk singer, or a blues singer, and she said some pieces could pass for jazz! I thought about it for a while, and concluded that everything on the album came out of me and from my experiences, all of which did not fall into one category. How could I choose to do music from one corner of my life?

Sweet Honey's existence as a professional ensemble would not limit our choice of categories or genres of music or singing styles. We would only be bound by our own ability to master the compositions we selected. This was a crucial decision because it meant that I was placing myself and Sweet Honey outside of conventional marketing categories. And we would challenge record stores, radio stations, and producers in finding our audiences because our performances and recordings covered a range of experiences, music genres, and topics. To this day, people ask, "Where can I find your records?" I say, "Look under folk, women, groups, gospel, world music; nag your record store owner."

I don't do music to scale Top 40 charts and neither does Sweet Honey, although there is no reason she, Sweet Honey, should not be there. It makes singing in Sweet Honey an ongoing experiment, a centering, expansive and unlimiting learning experience, and it makes a Sweet Honey concert a more affirming, echoing place for the human spirit moving through this widely varied world. So we sing church songs, and political songs, and children's songs, and songs about death, and songs about falling in and out of love.

During the first four or five years I was the dominant songwriter and bore primary responsibility for repertoire. I recognized early that all of the musicians I was working with had strong and widely varying compositional potential; I structured the group to stimulate the other singers to also assume responsibility for repertoire. I had seen groups that were one-writer or one-leader groups. But I was particularly drawn to the Roberta Martin Singers, the gospel group that helped to establish what became the classical choral sound of gospel. Each singer in that group was a soloist, and each (if she or he stayed in the group) began to write and record songs.

I found another model from my childhood in the games I had played, where everyone was both a leader and a follower. In Sweet Honey, I found that my leadership style came from the lessons I had learned as a child. I tried to create a structure that expected new ideas to come from all members, and thus I urged the

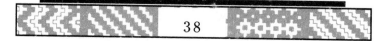

singers to bring in new songs and I set up sessions assigned to individual members to stimulate action. Sweet Honey's music palette changed as her singers became songwriters, composers, and arrangers.

I will never forget the feel of "Gift of Love," composed by Evie. She created a new experience of completing her compositions in the group. She would come in with the lyrics, the melody, and a general sense of the harmony and arrangement. And as we lent her our voices holding down parts she tried out, she completed the composition.

You are the gift of love to me
and I will love you as I love you
My door is open and you have the key
Come on in—spread your magic all around
Move my house to where you like it

Evie stretched us and our audiences with the intimacy and fire of her testimonies to love and loss.

Ysaye came into the group as an accomplished songwriter, composer, and choir director with a fine sense of choral singing. She was magical in creating musical settings for poems that moved her. Sweet Honey's repertoire received a different kind of air from her songs, such as "Breaths," "On Children," and "More Than a Paycheck." These are among our audiences' favorite compositions. In music and in text they soar across and within so many people's lives.

Yasmeen came into workshop one year with Grand Master Flash's "Beat Street," and Sweet Honey added the rap genre to her repertoire. This venture became more than a side diversion when Nitanju Bolade Casel used rap to define our hand-percussion gourd instruments.

I used to be a squash in Aminatta's field
Until the day she decided to collect her yield
I was so afraid she would come and choose me
But since I couldn't run away, I had to wait and see

She went back and forth and up and down every row
Then without choosing me, she decided to go
I was so relieved I began to shout
Which made her turn around and see me, so she picked me out

When she wrapped me in her sack and placed me on her head
And started walking toward her village I was filled with dread
Many of my friends and family had left the land
But never knowing where they went, I did not understand

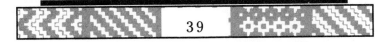

That a whole new life was just ahead for me
As a calabash, maracas, agbe, or axatse
I never knew a squash could be so many things
Full of colors and designs and beaded down with strings

When we reached the house they took me out of the sack
I wanted to go home! Somebody take me back!
As I looked around I just could not believe my eyes
I saw my friends and family, what a nice surprise!

They were happy to see me and they were looking good
And when they started to talk, that's when I understood
Even though each one was different in color and shape
When they all played together, the music was great!

My life was just beginning in the musical world
I'd be a shekere for these young boys and girls
A shekere!
A shekere!

Our rap repertoire was expanded again with Aisha and Nitanju's powerful statement, "Women! Should be a priority!!" The opening and closing lines of a brilliant rap song, "A Priority."

There have been times when things happened in my world that I felt strongly about and I had no song that would speak for me. I have found my voice within the songs of my sister composers. These women/singers/composers give me a range I could never have alone.

Some of our songs have come from collaborations with other artists. In December 1988, Ruby Dee, the actress, came to see us about a television special she was producing for PBS to be aired on the occasion of the first national holiday for Martin Luther King Jr. in January 1989. She sat at the Kennedy Street kitchen table with the script she had sent us to sing. Nitanju had composed melodies for the poems and she shared them. I had begun to work on a song chant system for a long, three-page, single-spaced creation by Sonia Sanchez.

We worked our way through Sonia's poem, "Letter to Martin," and Ruby responded at various points when we were on the right track. After we got a sense of what she wanted, we finished the work in rehearsals during the shoot for the show, entitled *The Dream and the Drum*. This composition has become a tradition; we perform it every year at our annual community concert with In Process . . . in tribute to Martin Luther King.

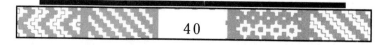

Dear Martin:

I want you to know that the sun is rolling in from faraway places; I watched it reaching out, circling these bare trees like some reverent lover. I been standing still listening to the morning and I hear your voice crouched near hills, rising from the mountaintops breaking the circle of dawn.

You would have been _____ this year. . . .

Then there is the composition in performance, the times when things happen that you have never heard before. Often, we, the three singers in the background, get caught between Nitanju and Ysaye when they start their double leads on the last chorus of "In the Upper Room" and I forget my part in the background. They are doing things I have never heard before and I cannot believe the weaves they are creating. My breath leaves and I come to myself and I am not singing . . . and I have to say, "Sing your part, Bernice, sing your part . . ." and I do the best I can in view of the circumstances. . . .

TAKING STANDS

It is an amazing time to be an artist and try to be a participant and commentator in the world. Sometimes there is so much happening on any given day you wonder how you can absorb everything and not shut down. Having a Sweet Honey concert means there is another opportunity to be clear about the things we care about in the world. One of the most important of those opportunities is that we celebrate our lives by taking a stand. If there is a major crisis in the country, a Sweet Honey concert or Sweet Honey music is a way to begin to affirm where one stands on the issue. Many people tell us they come to a concert to work things out, to get energy. I can personally testify to using Sweet Honey recordings to get through my day.

In 1986 I saw a television show on the violence in El Salvador, focusing on the assassination of priests known for their work with the people and against the military. It also focused on the training of men in our country who later showed up running death squads in El Salvador. This video documentary also looked at the U.S. support of the Contras in Nicaragua, as well as Jonas Savimbi, head of UNITA, who was fighting to destabilize independent Angola. He was being supported not only by the United States of America but also by the apartheid regime in South Africa. The show ended by showing how our tax money was used to try to direct and control the governments of small countries all over the globe. I composed "Ode to the International Debt."

There is money going overseas
To buy changes that will never come

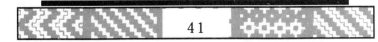

Dollar-backed Contras spill the blood of the people
In small nations we won't leave alone

Meanwhile in the corporate boardroom
They talk about the debt as if it could be paid
Money borrowed and loaned
For guns you can't eat
And buildings you can't live in
And trinkets you can't wear
It is a debt not owed by the people.

In 1990, the year of the Gulf War, we were doing the Black History Month tour while over 500,000 Americans were stationed in the Gulf. It seemed that every town we sang in during that tour had a military base, and the people who came to our concerts came to be treated.

Many of us in this country felt that the war was wrong, but singing in a community connected with the local military facility where some people in our audience had members of their families in the Gulf was an overpowering experience. Ysaye talked afterward about how exhausted she was, because she sensed that people came to Sweet Honey concerts in pain and in need due to the internal conflict they experienced over the Gulf War.

In my introduction to "Peace" or "Down by the Riverside," I talked about it being important to be able to be supportive of your people in a war zone, and to raise questions about why they are there in the same sentence. Responsible patriots, citizens, could ask hard questions out loud about the administration's decision to go to the Gulf, or for that matter to Panama or to Grenada. The audience always responded with amens and applauded this introduction. Then we sang "Down by the Riverside" or "Peace." About the second time during that tour when we did "Peace," Nitanju took off in the ad-lib section. The song as arranged by Nitanju has a repeated bass cadence sung by Ysaye, "I write your name," over and over throughout the composition. When we reached the instrumental, usually nontextual scat section, Nitanju got quite verbose. She wrote on people's hearts, on war guns, on the White House, on warships, on airplanes, on the bombs, on President Bush—we don't want no war. . . . On and on she went. The crowd was on their feet. . . . She was giving voice to what seemed stuck in our throats. . . . With her composition in performance, we, the women of Sweet Honey and the audience, could hear ourselves talking about the war.

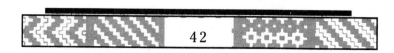

I WRITE YOUR NAME
  By the weight of one word
I WRITE YOUR NAME
  I start my love over again
I WRITE YOUR NAME
  I was born to know you
I WRITE YOUR NAME
  And call you by your name
PEACE

When the song was finished, the applause from us onstage and from the audience was overwhelming! This was one time I had no comment. It had been said. I called the next song.

Many of our songs began years before a particular song or an issue is addressed. For instance, Ysaye and I date our relationship with the struggle against apartheid in South Africa to Harry Belafonte and Miriam Makeba. In 1962 a friend gave me a recording of South African songs performed by Miriam Makeba with Harry Belafonte. It was the first time I had heard of South Africa from the Black perspective. It wasn't until I was living in Atlanta during the beginning of the Black Consciousness Movement and working in the Harambee Singers that I met the Reverend Nglabati Gladstone, a Methodist minister in exile from South Africa, who was trying to set up a support community for the work of the African National Congress. Gladstone taught us about South Africa, the freedom struggle, and my first South African freedom songs, "Tina Sizwe" and "Asikatali Nomaziabuswa."

When Sweet Honey In The Rock was first organized, songs about the South African freedom struggle were a part of our repertoire. At first they were the freedom songs I had learned from Gladstone or from the Bantu songbook edited by Pete Seeger. Then I began to write my own songs, such as "We Gonna Rumble Through the Streets of Soweto" after the June 16, 1976, riots:

We're gonna rumble, we're gonna rumble
We're gonna rumble through the streets of Soweto
We're gonna rumble, we're gonna rumble
We're gonna rumble through the streets of Soweto

In 1976, Nelson Mandela and Walter Sisulu and their colleagues were in jail with other leaders of the African National Congress. Mandela had already become the leader of the military wing, and a war was on, and in the United States, Sweet Honey In The Rock took sides. . . .

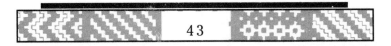

Somewhere there's a child a-crying
Somewhere there's a child a-crying
Somewhere there's a child a-crying
Crying for freedom in South Africa

They killed Stephen Biko this morning
Died for freedom in South Africa

Oh my mother mourning,
Child shot down dead in South Africa

There's a new day coming
I got freedom on my mind
Gonna take my freedom in the morning

Otis Williams, director of Nymburu, the University of Maryland's African American Cultural Center, sent me this poem entitled "The Azanian Freedom Song" (*Azania* was used by many of us in the United States as the name that South Africa would be called when she was free. By the time we recorded this song in 1983, it was clear that the term "Azania" was opposed by the African National Congress (ANC) because it meant "land of the blacks" and the ANC policies were directed toward a society that was not racially defined. The ANC believed that in a free South Africa all of her citizens could work and live together. Some organizations, like the Pan-African Congress (PAC), continued to use Azania.) The melody and arrangement came easily.

I was grateful that Azania was used only in the title of the song and not in the text. After talking to Otis, we began to call the song "Crying for Freedom in South Africa."

Yasmeen created the first lead in the song. She comes out of a strong gospel background and has a brilliant way of echoing the text laid out in a steady background by the chorus. When we got to the break, which had each line stated three times in an escalating chord, in a round fashion—Well! Yasmeen unleashed cries and calls over this section that made the piece take wings. By the time we got to the ending chorus chant—"Crying for freedom, crying for freedom!"—Yasmeen was preaching, ad-libbing the lines as she strode across the stage. We all could just "shout" in that song.

It was one of our most powerful statements on the freedom struggle in South Africa, and it became a way for our audiences to witness how strongly many of us in this country wanted to vote with our voices, our divestments, and our support in this important struggle against racism.

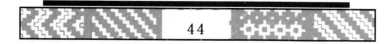

SWEET HONEY DRESS

When we walk onto a stage, we look good! Sweet Honey In The Rock upholds the legacy of the history of African American women; you can even see it in our clothes. From the first performance in 1973, our dress has been a cultural ensemble statement. We wore adapted bubas, a West African dress, made of a rectangle with openings for the neck and arms that drop to the floor. The side of the dress falls from the arm to the floor and drapes and flows as the arm is moved. A woman with a buba in her closet can dress her sister—any sister—beautifully. We decided that the women of Sweet Honey would always have bubas in our ensemble closets. We bought fabric of the same kind and had it designed in different patterns for each woman. It was clear that when we went to the stage we would have some outfits of similar fabric and patterns that created an ensemble look. Within this range individuals worked with designers to select different colors, necklines, sleeves, and head-pieces.

When we had performed at the Smithsonian Festival of Folklife (1974–76), we sometimes wore personal dress and found that our selections didn't work as an ensemble. We realized that some outfits that individual women wore as street or play or party dress were not Sweet Honey dress. This was the beginning of a group understanding that Sweet Honey existed in ensemble and that she had a style and a range that were not always the same as those of any individual woman in the group.

Coming to an ensemble statement in dress at different times with different singers has been hard for me. I kept feeling that I was going over and over the same discussions. Through the years, I have struggled personally with my sense that it was a waste of the people's time to talk so much about clothes. Put on the buba and let's go. But the women who struggle to bring life to Sweet Honey had ideas and needs, and we had to talk and experiment through trial and error until we determined that the Sweet Honey dress policy had to have a wider range of creativity. We looked for ways to achieve a balance between honoring our historical legacy in a visual statement and responding to changing ideas of the power and beauty of African American women.

African American women's bodies have been used as product and subject on stages that range from the auction block to the striptease floor. As Black women have moved within our community and larger society, we have sometimes been collaborators in marketing our bodies as well as our talents as entertainment, as performance, as art. I wanted to be sure that we understood what those cultural lines were and that as a group we found our visual statement standing on different ground.

Today, Sweet Honey's dress is varied—everyday and elegant during the same evening—or regular and flash. Our dresses are collaborations, which means that the Sweet Honey In The Rock statement in dress is also a presentation of art by African American designers like Sehar, Akiba, Januwa Moja, Kiko, and Lona Alias.

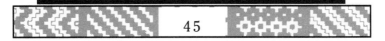

SWEET HONEY CONCERTS ARE CONVERSATIONS

Sweet Honey concerts are conversations with the audience. We come out and take a seat, since we are going to talk together. We many times walk into a conversation. Our audiences are so intense, everyone checking each other out, that sometimes we walk in and have to say "excuse me" to the air charged with nonverbal attitudinal exchange.

We do most of our concerts in local communities. In successful cases, there are people in our concerts who do not run with each other in their day-to-day lives. Our concert audience is a coalition. Sometimes people get to a concert and wonder how could they be there if those other people are there. The concert is an answer to that question. We come out and try, in the response, to answer why we have all come together in this place, using the songs and singing of the African American legacy as language.

When we come out and sit down on chairs, the opening song is usually gentle. In a conversation, it's better to say hello, no need to show off and try to find a showstopper in the first response. At first, I never knew what song I was going to call, it was all inside. By the time I walked on the stage, I was in a truly meditative state, I belonged to Sweet Honey. Often I started preparing for Sweet Honey concerts one or two weeks before. It was a seamless process where I felt myself headed for the stage. By the day of the concert things were still very much inside, but much more forward. I remember times when I would be dressing for the concert, not talking to anybody. Evie was the first to realize that I was not to be disturbed. I didn't know consciously that I was on my way somewhere else, so I couldn't tell anyone else. I first became aware of Evie's efforts to protect this pre-concert meditation space for me and then I could name it as a space I needed clearly enough so that the people working with and around us could understand.

As the programmer, I would be on the stage and would sit down and call a song or start a song and the conversation would continue. At a Sweet Honey concert the programmer is the person steering the discussions. Here the concert becomes a composition of the programmer. The singers turn themselves over to the programmer's composition and try to fulfill her efforts to communicate. We can shake off a song if we can't sing it, and the programmer is responsible for selecting another song, finding a way through songs to keep the conversation going. . . .

I like singing songs that come into my mind onstage that have never been performed by the group. This doesn't happen often, but it's important within the Black tradition. Many of the songs I know, I have learned in performance—during worship services and not in rehearsals. There are no rehearsals in the congregational tradition. Don't get me wrong, Sweet Honey rehearses, plans, arranges, prepares—it's one of the hardest-working groups I have ever had the opportunity to work with—but one vital area of preparation is being ready to compose in performance; being able to learn a song as you sing it. It is what we ask of our

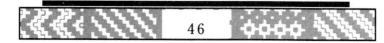

audiences every time I give you parts of a song to sing you have never heard, and I like keeping the group in touch with what you the audience face when asked to join in and lend your voices to the Sweet Honey chorus.

We use sound checks for trying out songs we were not certain about. To be a leader in Sweet Honey, one has to be a servant, one has to seek counsel from everyone and be willing to reformulate on the basis of the information given. If you want to sing a song and a singer says, "Not today," then as leader, programmer, you have to learn to accept with grace and support. And guiding that structure was and has been hard, challenging, sometimes scary, and a precious gift to me.

The first responsibility of the programmer is to her singers. She uses the sound check to become familiar with the group. If she has begun working on the concert before the sound check (and hopefully she has), there is a conceptual Sweet Honey that she brings to it. The session then becomes a reckoning between what she wants and the real Sweet Honey that is manifested that day on the stage. Sometimes there is a big gap between what a programmer has been conceptualizing and what the individual singers can conjure up as Sweet Honey.

Sweet Honey is a microphone group. Many people who hear our singing say, "Oh, you should not use a sound system, your beautiful voices can fill this room with no effort." Well, they don't know that our group has always been womaned by singers with voices of different timbres, strengths, and colors and that it is the visibility of these differences that makes the Sweet Honey sound distinctive. The sound system allows us to create a balance with each other. For us the sound system becomes an instrument that we play in concert with the sound engineer. And that brings up Arthur Steele.

In 1978, we were doing a concert tour booked by Amy, when one afternoon we showed up at the big concert hall at UMass at Amherst. Up until this concert, my experience with sound systems and engineers had been inconsistent. We had met good sound professionals and good equipment in some cities, but we also had encountered every possible worst scenario.

Most of our sound checks were frenzied and stressed. I dreaded them, and grew to like those sound people who seemed familiar with their equipment and those who had worked with vocal music. Art Steele was a new experience.

At the UMass concert hall, when I looked out from the wings of the stage, he was sitting in the center audience section. He was White and male. I asked when would he be ready to check the sound. He answered, "It's ready," and did not move, did not run to his board or come to the stage—he just sat there. I thought to myself: This is just like a White man, not taking women seriously as musicians. I called the group to the stage and we began to sing. For the hour sound check and during the two-hour concert, there was no feedback! It was impressive! It was sweet! It was the most relaxed sound check and concert I had ever performed. That day I began to revise my standards for sound engineers and what I needed from a sound system.

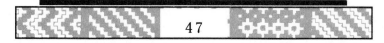

One year after Amy had booked the February tour, I said, "I do not want to do this tour without Art." Amy looked at me to see if I was crazy, assessing the extra work and the reaction of her partner producers if she really had to introduce this as a possibility. I explained that as I moved toward the two-week tour, with ten concerts in fourteen days, I needed the consistency that occurred every time we got near to Sunderland, Massachusetts, where Art was based. It was through working with Art Steele that I came to know a sound system as a musical instrument played from two points, the singers and the sound board.

Asking for Art Steele, a White male, was a major sticking point. This was the late seventies and early eighties; we were African American women building a cultural organization. The women in the women's movement were great supporters of Sweet Honey In The Rock and some of our strongest sound engineers were women who were a part of that network.

Amy, in total support of the survival of Sweet Honey and her growth, swallowed and went to work on the tour with the producers; she asked for concessions —time, and money from Art—and got them.

The rest is history.

A LUTA CONTINUA! (THE STRUGGLE CONTINUES!)

The premiere Sweet Honey experience is created *live* with and in our audiences, as well as within members of the group. We use the technologies of this century to extend that experience and to provide an expanded context. We have consciously decided to try to move this ensemble and her vision intact through this societal maze where art is product and integrity can be lost. We have chosen to utilize some of that system—touring, creating new songs, recordings, television, films—always looking for new, expanding collaborations with others traveling similar paths. We have worked to maintain an integrity with our goal to offer a different standard for our time. It has been a constant struggle.

This group is owned by the women in it. During the first two years, we sang to the community attending the D.C. Black Repertory Theater productions, we sang in schools in Washington, D.C., and slowly we began to branch out to sing at rallies organized for various issues. Our performances during the summer of 1974 at the Smithsonian Festival of American Folklife led to an invitation to the Toronto and Chicago folk festivals. Through those festivals we met Bruce Kaplan, founder of Flying Fish, a Chicago-based, nonprofit record company, who in 1976 released our first record, *Sweet Honey In The Rock.* The experience with Bruce and Flying Fish was significant because we were allowed to explore commercial audio recordings as a stage and found a different performance and forum there without the usual pressures that would have come from a profit-driven organization. Our recordings

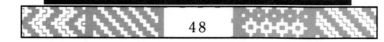

were never the same as a live performance, but they serve as scores, a way for our audiences to find songs and lyrics they have heard us sing.

In August 1977, I attended an international Peace Conference in Hiroshima, Japan, as part of a delegation of four women, the others being Holly Near, Amy Horowitz, and Sally Savitz. One of my most important songs, "B'lieve I'll Run On, See What the End's Gonna Be," was begun in Hiroshima's Peace Park on August 6 —on the anniversary of the dropping of the atom bomb in the place where it hit the hottest. During the anniversary morning, I saw thousands of people coming into the park carrying necklaces of paper cranes in memory of those killed by the bomb. When I entered a building in the park with a memorial exhibit, I walked around looking at the pictures. One picture ingrained in my memory was of a woman walking down the street holding her skin. Not only were people killed, but the people who survived were not protected and the rescue workers were contaminated. I walked around feeling strangely American, a member of this country that could do such an inhuman thing.

Walking out of that building and into the sun, I saw people still suffering physically and emotionally from the impact yet very much alive. I was staying in a city that had been decimated and rebuilt—and I wondered in awe at the regenerative nature of the human spirit. I decided then that I would go on with my life and my fight and this old chorus started circling in my head:

B'lieve I'll run on, see what the end's gonna be . . .

The verses came on a plane ride with Sweet Honey that fall. Beginning with the biblical story of the Flood and Noah's Ark, I wrote my own poem because I never learned the Golden Gate Quartet version I grew up hearing sung by Sister Mary Floyd and the Trumpet Sisters, a gospel group from Albany. I wrote out the story as I had remembered it from sermons and from the Bible:

Sin and corruption all over the place
My God decided to end this wicked race
Decided to destroy the world by flood
'Cause sin-filled men would not hear His word
Called on Noah to build the Ark
Load all the animals before the rain start
Noah built the Ark and he loaded it down
Water fell from heaven, everything else was drown
Forty long days and forty long nights
Water kept a-falling to set the score right
Then the rain stopped and the sun came out
Dried up all the water, Noah let the creatures out

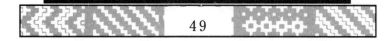

God gave Noah the rainbow sign
Said no more water there'll be fire next time

Then I wrote about the flood of fire in the U.S. bombing of Hiroshima and Naga-saki in 1945:

Now it seems like, we're about to see the other side
There's a black rain that falls just like burning fire
The U.S.A. built a bomb in 1945
Hundreds and thousands were burned alive
Fell on Hiroshima on August the sixth
Three days later, Nagasaki was in the same fix
The terrible thing that I have to share
Is that my chronicle does not end there
To this day, you know, we still pay the cost
Over six hundred thousand lives have been lost
There's nuclear testing all over the world
Little boys playing with buttons
Child, it makes my hair curl
We've got the A-bomb and the hydrogen too
And one would think that, that would really do
We've got a man in Washington, who's leading the fight
To protect human beings and to give equal rights
Carter made a statement just the other day
Concerned with the danger of nuclear display
When the bombs fall the buildings do too
And that is not the object, the victim is me and you
We've got a new toy called the neutron bomb
Kills only people, bringing property no harm

After Carter and the neutron bomb came Ronald Reagan with his Star Wars de-fense, and the nuclear-power-plant disasters on Three Mile Island, Pennsylvania, and in Chernobyl, Soviet Union. Evie and I fashioned an update to keep the song working in our repertoire and in our lives:

We've got men in Washington always itching for a fight
Building new weapons, it just don't seem right.
We've got a new system called the Star Wars defense
Aimed at world domination and it just don't make good sense

This song became the title song of our second album, *B'lieve I'll Run On, See What the End's Gonna Be,* released by Redwood Records in early 1978.

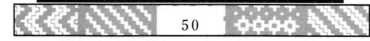

We started that year with the decision to perform full-time. Ernestine Potter, an African American friend and colleague who had administrative experience in cultural organizing, agreed to coordinate our bookings for us.

During the late spring, Amy, then a member of Redwood Records, organized our second tour to California. We performed at La Pena in Berkeley, and I had an experience that clarified a lot for me as an artist in the world. It was after the sound check, the room was almost empty, and I looked at a photo exhibit that documented the violence and oppression in Chile as the Allende government was overthrown.

I stood a long time near the photos of the ballpark where so many had been arrested. Among them were photos of Victor Jara, a Chilean singer and songwriter, who sang his songs and played his guitar until he was killed. As I looked at this particular panel, into my head came a clear message: "In this country, you/Sweet Honey are Victor Jara." It came to me like a touch of words, if you can imagine such a thing, like standing in and feeling a text as soft falling light or like feeling the visual moment as touch when the photographer brings the subject into clear focus. I remember being sobered and having to walk quietly through the next few days.

We traveled on to Los Angeles and the revelations continued. In L.A., we did two concerts at the Inner City Cultural Center with the actress Beah Richards. It was the second time we had worked with her; the first time was when Val Gray Ward presented us in joint concert at the Kuumba Theater in Chicago. I can still see her performing her long poem "Black Woman Speaks" with tears running down her face.

First, on Sunday morning we went to church. We had asked our sponsoring organization, Women on Wheels, to find a Black church for us. We wanted to sing in church Sunday morning. On the morning in question we piled into two cars and drove through Los Angeles, going past Black church after Black church, and I wondered where they were taking us. They said that they had looked a long time and found a minister who seemed to be open and progressive. We finally pulled up outside an Episcopal church. My heart fell, not Baptist or Methodist! Why were we here? But as soon as the exasperated question formed in my mind, I got the message, also inside my head: "There, there, you are where you are supposed to be."

We went inside and met the minister and his wife. He said he didn't know why we were there but we were welcome. It was a small congregation, mixed, Black and Spanish, and they would welcome our songs. We went in and sat in the second row. When the service started, there were maybe twenty-five people with us. The opening prayer was congregational style, started by one person, and it built, moving through the room. I heard the opening line behind me, then the prayer grew line by line as people added their meditations. Then I heard Yasmeen's voice, and my own, then Evie's, and I knew this was not going to be a regular service.

We sang the sermon and after the service there was communion. The entire

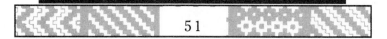

51

congregation filed up to the pulpit, including Sweet Honey. There was a chalice of real wine and a loaf of bread. The minister started at the end of the C-shaped line, offering bread and wine. When it came to me, I broke a piece off the loaf of bread and dipped it in the chalice. As the red wine colored the bread a deep rose, I felt the voice saying, "This is Victor Jara's body," and I knew with a certainty who I was in this land as an artist. I knew that, no matter what, I had to always maintain an integrity with the history and experience of my people. From that moment in 1978 it has never changed.

During this period our effort to go full-time failed. By the end of July 1978 it was clear that if the group was to go on, we had to find another way. There simply was not enough work, not enough money, and what work and money there was demanded too much time away from home. Our being away from home for long stretches created such a strain that it almost resulted in the end of the group. The effort was abandoned. Sweet Honey In The Rock would be a professional group, but not full-time.

I had observed another performance model other than full-time as I grew up, and that was the way quartet singers organized their lives to create music. These were basically weekend groups, comprised mostly of men who held down regular jobs, rehearsed one or two evenings a week, and sang almost every weekend. For these singers, their music was a primary stabilizing presence in their lives and everything was organized around their commitment to this activity. These groups owned themselves, performed mostly regionally, and went on tours during vacation times. I liked the quartet model. It allowed me as a performer to remain connected with family and community and gave me time to develop my own ideas and needs about songs, their message, and the sound I strove to create with my colleagues.

Outside of this most committed group of artists I have ever worked with, Amy Horowitz shares major credit for the success of Sweet Honey's testing this new model. She had moved from Redwood Records to found Roadwork, Inc., which became Sweet Honey's artist representative. She listened to us talk about wanting to be at home, and wanting to work two weekends a month, and wanting to manage ourselves, and wanting to get good wages, and wanting to go anywhere once, and wanting to sing to Black people, and wanting to sing to White people, and wanting to find radical, courageous local sponsors who would bring us in before we could sell out a house. She listened and did not say we were crazy, she acted as if it might work—she would try. And what a try. The road to Sweet Honey's national and international audience is also paved with the vision, sweat, and tenaciousness of Amy Horowitz and Roadwork, Inc.

It was during this period of questioning and wondering how to go on—if we were to go on—that collaborations were key. We moved from the live concert to recording and then to our first experience with film. I met the Ethiopian filmmaker Haile Gerima. After I had finished giving a lecture at Howard University in 1978,

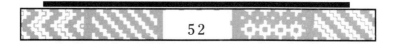

Gerima introduced himself and said that he wanted us to work together on music for a film he was making on the Wilmington Ten case.

In 1970, the city of Wilmington, North Carolina, was ordered to desegregate its schools. The Black high school was turned into a junior high school and the Black students were bused to the formerly White high school. The ensuing incidents of racism were so intense that the students and their parents created after-school support sessions at a local church for the students. There they would try to process or survive the day. They began to wear armbands to school to connect with each other as a community of support. The hostility and assault continued and the Black community asked for help. The United Church of Christ (UCC) Commission on Racial Justice, headed by the Reverend Charlie Cobb, sent in the Reverend Ben Chavis to assist the students and the community. Soon after they arrived, eight male high school students (Wayne Moore, William Vereen, Joe Wright, Reginald Epps, Connie Tyndall, James McKoy, Marvin Patrick, and Jerry Jacobs), a White female VISTA worker (Ann Turner), and the Reverend Chavis were jailed for acts of arson and conspiracy to assault emergency personnel (police and firefighters). They all protested and declared their innocence. After a mistrial that resulted in the dismissal of a jury consisting of ten Blacks and two Whites, a second trial (in the fall of 1972) with a jury of ten Whites and two Blacks brought in a guilty verdict. Except for Ann Turner, who received a sentence of ten years, the rest of the Wilmington Ten were given harsh sentences that averaged twenty-seven years.

The Black parents and the UCC Commission on Racial Justice began to organize a campaign to win the freedom of the Wilmington Ten, and in spite of appeals, on February 2, 1976, nine members of the Wilmington Ten began to serve their sentences. (Ann Turner was released on parole after serving her statutory minimum.) Sweet Honey, now established in the community as a group that would respond to struggle in song, had already sung at a rally for the Wilmington Ten at which the mother of Ben Chavis spoke.

I had a number of song ideas when I finished the session with Haile. His film linked the current case with the 1898 Wilmington Massacre, during which Whites threw out the elected Reconstruction government in Wilmington and killed Black and Republican leaders or ran them out of town. The film also linked other struggles for freedom—the Biko story from South Africa and that of Assata Shakur, a native of Wilmington, who was a political activist, organizer, and poet, in jail in New Jersey. Haile said he wanted the film to show that the hand of oppression in Wilmington was the hand of oppression in South Africa, was the hand in Chile that brought down the Allende government—they are all the same hands. And I wrote "Chile Your Waters Run Red Thru Soweto."

The hands that turned the key in ten Wilmington jail cells
Put young Steve Mitchell in a dusty hill grave

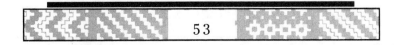

The hands of oppression are the hands of hunger
The waters of Chile fill the banks of Cape Fear

Chile your waters run red thru Soweto
The same hands, same waters . . .

Working on the film that August was the most productive thing I did with the group. Sweet Honey In The Rock was Bernice Johnson Reagon, Evelyn Maria Harris, and Yasmeen Williams. Pat Johnson had left the group. Because of their other commitments, I could not get Evie and Yasmeen into the studio at the same time. Each session I was working with one singer. Thank goodness for multitrack recording. Evie and Yasmeen learned the songs in the studio as I wrote them. Near the completion of the film, Haile asked for two more songs. One was "If You Had Lived," and the other was "Echo." I wrote "Echo" in response to a poem that Assata Shakur reads in the film. I wrote it without seeing the film footage, so Haile paraphrased it. The poem said that we had seen it all before, all that is happening now is like an echo of the past—the killings, the jailings, the rape, the starvation— these are echoes of a system put in place long ago.

Another song that came straight out of the film footage is "As Long As I Have Breath in My Body," a statement by the mother of one of the Wilmington Ten, Joe Wright. When asked if she was tired, she responded, "Tired? I am not tired. I have just begun to fight. As long as I have breath in my body, I'll see this battle over. I'll see it through."

Then there was the film testimony of Ben Chavis. In an interview from his cell he declared, "I will not obey racism, I will not bow down to injustice, I can't stand oppression." And I wrote "I'm Gon' Stand."

In one of the film's scenes Haile had pictures of marches against apartheid in South Africa juxtaposed with an image of a baby being pushed into the air, like the promise that the struggle would continue. From that hope and promise, I wrote "You can break one human body, I see ten thousand Bikos."

Biko, Biko, Biko
Here come Stephen Biko walking down the waters
Hey, hey, what you gon' do with Biko, Biko, Biko!

Waters of fear and hatred, waters of starving babies
Hey, hey, what you gon' do with Biko, Biko, Biko!

Come all the way from Capetown to Wilmington, N.C.
Hey, hey, what you gon' do with Biko, Biko, Biko!

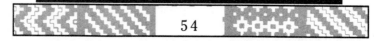

"Let Your Light Shine"—Historical Notes

You can break one human body, I see ten thousand Bikos!
Hey, hey, what you gon' do with Biko, Biko, Biko!

One day in the studio as I worked, Haile told me that he was reorganizing the film to use all the songs. It was the greatest compliment I could have received. My songs that came out of his vision and the story he was weaving were being used to reweave the story. It felt like an extension into territory I could not enter alone because I did not speak the language of film. This was one of the most significant collaborations for me as a songwriter and singer. I found in the conviction of Haile Gerima a warrior spirit, a struggle to harness film as an instrument of freedom—it was good company.

For Sweet Honey, it was the rarest of testing grounds, where I learned that sometimes when you feel that all is gone, and that there is nothing left, and that the end is near—you don't know everything.

When September came, Amy Horowitz asked about an anniversary concert. I thought: Anniversary concert! With whom? But it was a nudge, right? So I tried to see if it was possible and it was. Pat Johnson agreed to sing as a substitute, and in November 1978 we performed our first anniversary concert, celebrating our fifth year, at All Souls' Unitarian Church, produced by Amy Horowitz and Michelle Parkerson. Tulani Jordan walked into the concert on the last song, I auditioned her a few days later, and she moved to Washington to join Sweet Honey In The Rock the following week.

Tulani's presence was crucial to Sweet Honey's having a sixth anniversary concert. I will always believe that she was sent by the ancestors to keep the singing woman Sweet Honey In The Rock in front for us when we could not see her ourselves. I remember Evie and I—burnt out—stumbling over each other with various dates for leaving the group. Tulani was the only one of us who could consistently see the group. She kept saying, "No! This cannot end! This cannot stop here!"

The next year somehow we were still together. I could not believe that I was still in the group that next anniversary in 1979. To this day, I cannot explain how I got through the year. Ivy? Tulani? Amy? Sweet Honey? The ancestors? It must have been also, in part, my habit of looking at a goal in the future but paying more attention to where to place my feet for the next step. In cases where you cannot see the goal, or even around the next bend, sometimes you can see how to make the next move and that keeps you moving.

During September 1979, we performed at Chapel Hill, North Carolina. Before the concert, into our dressing room walked Ben Chavis, who had received clearance while in prison to attend the concert. We sang the songs that were now a part of the film *The Wilmington U.S.A. 10,000,* and we sang the songs that were based on words I had heard him and the mothers of the students say in their struggle against racism and oppression.

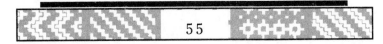

We will not bow down to racism
We will not obey injustice
I just can't tolerate exploitation
I'm gon' stand, I'm gon' stand

As the ancestors seemed to send Tulani, they also seemed to send so many people to come to us during that period and say that Sweet Honey was a part of their daily bread, a part of what they put together to support their ability to move through their lives with strength.

And then Tulani was gone. After working with us for a little more than a year, Tulani developed vocal problems and decided to take total vocal rest.

Our next film experience was another testing ground for the group. In 1982, Michelle Parkerson, who had made the production of the record *B'lieve I'll Run On* possible as our production coordinator, came to us as a filmmaker with a proposal to make a movie with Sweet Honey In The Rock as subject.

We were impressed with the sensitivity with which she articulated our need to be in charge of any statement created to represent who we were. Thus, in the proposal we were collaborating producers with her. We developed a contract agreeing to participate, and laid out a calendar that allowed us to review her work at three distinct stages of production, which would give her spaces as filmmaker/artist without us looking over her shoulder. We asked people to participate, and Alice Walker, Angela Davis, Pete Seeger, and In Process . . . took time to talk about who we were. Each member of Sweet Honey worked to design individual spaces in which to be interviewed, and plans were laid to record the ninth anniversary concert at Gallaudet College. Amy Horowitz and D.C. photographer Sharon Farmer, representing Roadwork, were a part of Michelle's production team, covering every event.

We went over the first preview, and felt good about how our feedback had been received. This was August 1983. When Michelle came to us later with a completed film, cutting out several stages of collaboration, we were devastated! Michelle had finished the film!

We were blessed in that when we developed the contractual agreement we had put in an arbitration resolution remedy in case of disagreement. Thank goodness for community. We, Sweet Honey, and Michelle were able to turn to our community, the same community, for legal advice and members who agreed to hear and resolve our grievances. A compromise was reached to make the deadline and not hurt Michelle's career. The film would run as it was in the first showing, then it would be revised, to eliminate two songs that did not meet our standards (we wanted three changed). Another song was chosen because it had more of Shirley Childress Johnson, our Sign language interpreter, who was almost nonexistent in the first version—the changes were made and we all went on—bruised and battered.

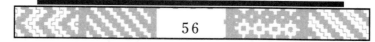

It took several years for me to be able to send Michelle a card saying to her that, traveling through the country, I had met many people who were introduced to Sweet Honey In The Rock through her film *Gotta Make This Journey* and decided that they had to have that group for their community, or they had to attend a concert of this group, or their children had to be exposed to these women. I was finally one day able to tell her that with her talent and through the struggle, including the arbitration, the film had made a statement that held within it an important tribute to what we as a group of artists try to do. I began to understand that success was hard and fraught with challenges and that some of the most intense struggles would be internal.

SIGN LANGUAGE INTERPRETATION

Through the prodding of some of our concert sponsors we began to find a new audience in the Deaf community. Today, Sweet Honey travels with a Sign language interpreter. That was not always the case. It began with Holly Near, who had performed concerts that were interpreted for the Deaf community. When the same women who produced Holly Near contacted us to perform for their local production companies, they introduced us to a new kind of cultural event.

For the first time, I experienced a policy of wheelchair accessibility that worked even when there were no elevators. I saw teams organized to carry people in wheelchairs up stairs to ensure that they could attend a Sweet Honey concert. Women who were parents with very young children had the option of attending a concert because child care was available. These producers explained to us that they also wanted to serve their local Deaf communities and asked whether we, Sweet Honey, would work with a Sign language interpreter. Well, I understood and appreciated the availability of child care at our concerts and I loved the fact that these concerts were wheelchair-accessible, and even though I could not see how a cappella music could be accessible to the Deaf community, I agreed to cooperate. When I was asked to send in the list of songs and the lyrics, I couldn't; I never programmed a concert except on the stage and I never wanted to know six weeks in advance what Sweet Honey would sing. Reluctantly, I began to work with local interpreters who would show up at our sound check and begin to sign for our songs. During one rehearsal, when we sang a song that had the word "Africa" in the text, the interpreter put her fingers through her nose to make a ring. I asked her to repeat the sign to be sure she had used it. I then asked her to find another sign, to which she responded by spelling the word out.

When I tried to have discussions with some of our local producers about using Black Sign language interpreters, they seemed to feel that I was bringing the race issue into a situation where race did not apply, although to that date all of the interpreters were White and women, a decision that ignored the multiracial

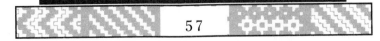

makeup of local Deaf communities. I was muddling through and in need of some help, and help was on the way.

One Sunday in August something touched me and woke me up at 10:45 A.M. and said go to All Souls' Unitarian Church; I am an obedient child, so by 11:05 A.M. I sat in a pew in the front of All Souls'. The Reverend David Eaton, the senior minister, was on vacation and they were using lay ministers. As I was wondering what I was doing there, a Black woman came up front and began to sign everything the speaker said. Not only did she sign, but she looked Colored when she did it. Then she sang "He Ain't Heavy, He's My Brother," and signed while she sang, and I who was lost was found and fed at the same time.

I rushed up to her afterward and introduced myself.

Our help had arrived. Here was Dr. Ysaye Maria Barnwell, speech pathologist, singer, choral director, and Sign language interpreter. When she came to the workshop she began to sing with us, revealing an astonishing instrument. She had one of the warmest bottoms (vocal range) I had ever heard in a woman singer, unused except in teaching choral work. She was to also find, in Sweet Honey, her upper range, which was also spectacular.

As Ysaye began to discover her vocal instrument, she began to talk to us about what it would take, if we were committed, to make our music accessible to the Deaf community. She taught us that the lyrics of our songs were poetry, and that they needed to be translated into another language, American Sign Language (ASL) or English Sign Language (ESL) or a combination of both; and in some cases a kind of pidgin Sign would best accommodate the spirit of our lyrics. To do a good job, an interpreter needed time with the lyrics and also time in rehearsal.

Ysaye suggested that we find an interpreter to work with us. I was stubborn. It meant another person and I didn't want to hear it. It meant expanded resources, working and traveling with six people instead of five, and it meant an unknown. But she was firm. By the end of the workshop, she had made it clear that although she could and often did sign and sing at the same time, she could not interpret and sing simultaneously; the two were not the same. She told us that when she sang and signed she tended to sign what she was singing, and if she was not carrying the lead text, it would not work. We asked her to choose whether she wanted to join Sweet Honey as a Sign language interpreter or as a singer and she chose to join us as a singer. She agreed to do our anniversary concert as interpreter and to help us find a Sign language interpreter after that.

When our anniversary concert opened that year, November 1979, at Crampton Auditorium, Howard University, Dr. B. (Ysaye) stood alone at center stage, and from the wings I lined the hymn:

Amazing Grace, how sweet the sound
That saved a wretch like me

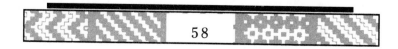

As I lined the text, Ysaye's body went into flight. I could see by her arms and hands and spirit that the grace was quite amazing. I was committed.

In 1980, Dr. B. introduced Sweet Honey to Shirley Childress Johnson, who began to work with us in 1980 as our Sign language interpreter. Shirley agreed to work as a translator, and thus she traveled with the group when requested by a local producer or producers who would pay her way, her fee, and advertise in the Deaf community. These were the producers who had asked us to help them reach their local Deaf communities. And now we were working out our own way of responding to the call. We decided that it was important that our interpreter be African American, and in response the Black Deaf community that has come to our concerts has thanked us many times for addressing what they often experience as racism within the Deaf community.

So in 1985, after several years of interpreted concerts under Ysaye's leadership, we began to talk about how important providing Sign language interpretation was to us. We had begun to include Shirley's picture on our albums and in our publicity photo shots and people were beginning to expect us to have her as a part of our entourage, even when we didn't. This was brought home at a concert on an Ohio college campus, where the sponsors said they had no Deaf students and we would not need our interpreter, so Shirley did not come. When we came out onstage there was a group of Deaf people who had driven some distance because *they* knew that at a Sweet Honey concert Shirley would be there. Ysaye had a challenging evening trying to deal with the situation and we had a policy discussion when we met again.

Sweet Honey decided that we would do everything in our power to bring along our own interpreter whenever we performed in a community where the sign language was ASL. Equally important, we would assume the cost of paying the interpreter. We asked sponsors to pay for travel, room and board, and advertise within their local Deaf networks. This seemed to work. The act of providing multi-avenues for communicating to those who could not hear, who were often not included in public events, increased the emotional power of the singing experience.

TWENTY WOMEN: NEW SINGERS, NEW EXPERIENCES

Tulani left the group in 1981 and we were again looking for a new singer. When Aisha Kahlil walked into a Sweet Honey workshop in August 1981, after one session I knew, without knowing why, that she was to be a part of the Sweet Honey journey. Aisha happened to Sweet Honey as much as or more than Sweet Honey happened to her. She was more like an invasion, and not always a comfortable one. She was different from anyone I had ever worked with, feeling best when she pulled from within, with little attention to what was going on around her. Over the more

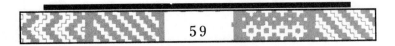

than twelve years she had been with the group, she has always been a vision, ever changing. Why was she sent to Sweet Honey? I kept asking myself. Where is the lesson? What am I supposed to learn here with this powerful creative woman?

Well, Aisha, a dancer, actress, singer, percussionist, came into a group that asked for a part of her range as an artist. She talks about entering the group and finding it strange that the singers moved so little while singing; it seemed incompatible with the group's vocal, emotional, and spiritual power. It was as if we were not in tune with our physical bodies.

Sometimes when I lead songs in concert, especially Otis Williams' "Crying for Freedom in South Africa," I move out in front of the group and turn to face them, and I can feel Aisha walking the air. She has a move onstage where she is stepping high in place, her arms are pulling freedom from space, and the energy of her physical being is in "the shout," and the sound of her voice electrifies the response —she has taught me more about singing with my body than anyone I have ever worked with.

It was after Aisha came into the group that I took my first vocal leap as a soloist. There was something about the additional fire and fervor in her sound that allowed me to turn to my singing and find new ways to extend my voice. Aisha had immense experience with improvisation. That first summer in 1981, she started to work with us on how to open up to the infinite possibilities available. Using the songs in our repertoire as a foundation, we began to leave text and structure and move out on the winds of sound that came to us after we vocally took flight in the performance of a song. Aisha has clearly been trying to get us to fly; we are still trying. . . .

In early 1983, Amy Horowitz and Ivy Young (who was then working with Roadwork) reminded us that in November we would be ten years old. I said that I wanted to celebrate with a reunion concert. By the summer, Bruce Kaplan at Flying Fish said, "It would be a shame for you to reach your tenth anniversary without a new recording," and Evelyn Harris began working as producer on *We All . . . Everyone of Us*, which was completed in six weeks.

The tenth anniversary concert was special for me since fifteen out of eighteen women came back to sing. We could not locate Laura Sharp who had substituted for Pat Johnson on our first California tour in 1977. Ingrid Ellis was dead, a victim of domestic violence. Ingrid had been a member of the group in 1974–75 with Evie, when we performed as a trio. Pat Johnson was too near delivery of her baby to travel, but the rest of us were there.

Louise and Maillard came in early to perform several concerts with us in the local D.C. prisons for women and men. What always affected me at the prison concerts was how Evie, Louise, and Yasmeen would see their classmates in jail and Yasmeen would always leave crying. It is so hard facing in any way how many of our children are locked up behind those walls.

Rosie Lee Hooks, who had helped us get through an impossible time in the

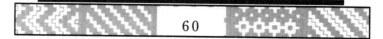

fall and winter of 1974, came from California, and Ayodele Harrington, who had worked with us in the fall of 1974, came as well. Dianaruthe Wharton, who also had worked with us from the spring of 1974 until she graduated from Howard, and who had contributed the major works we did with piano in our repertoire, reminded us of "Shine on Me," "We Are a People," and "Dream Variations" with piano accompaniment.

Geraldine Hardin was there; she had traveled to Japan with us as a substitute in 1980 when Tulani left. Tia Juana Starks was there; her brilliant soprano soared as we reconstructed "No More Auction Block for Me" and "Sitting on Top of the World." Tulani Jordan came down from New York, where she was establishing herself as a master braider. She and Aisha worked out a cross jazz improv lead on a song written by Pat Johnson called "All Praise Is Due to Love." Helena Coleman was there, with her full family in the audience, which included two sets of twins; she led "A Woman." The current members were Aisha Kahlil, Ysaye Maria Barnwell, Evelyn Maria Harris, Yasmeen Williams, Sign language interpreter Shirley Childress Johnson, and me.

We sold out three concerts at the University of the District of Columbia's new auditorium, singing a different concert each night. Some of our audience members came to all three concerts—Henri Norris sticks out in my mind as one who held a front-row seat each time. Our workshop, "In Process . . . ," was then twenty women strong; all were present and in support. They stood along the sides of the auditorium throughout the concert, coming to the stage at the end to perform "Crying for Freedom in South Africa" with us. I was finally sure inside myself that there was a Sweet Honey In The Rock and that she was going to be around for a while.

Sweet Honey is who you see onstage; on the other hand, she is always more. Over the years, twenty women have walked on her stage to create her and we have depth in the wings. These women are a wonder to me. I would not want to think about my life without them. Sweet Honey would not be but for them.

March 1985 found us discussing an invitation to participate as a group at the Women's Conference to End the Decade scheduled for July 1985 in Nairobi. We decided to go even though I had been ill since February and surgery was strongly recommended by my doctor.

Working with Lucy DeBardelaben as Roadwork's representative and the singers from my hospital bed, we began to build Sweet Honey sans Bernice. Aisha called Yasmeen, who had left the group for Atlanta, who said she would go. When Ysaye finally agreed to go, it was settled, Sweet Honey was going to be in Nairobi.

The summer and fall of 1985 were such big seasons for me. It was the first time I experienced the existence of the group when I was not in it. It felt at first like a part of myself was somewhere else. Then the challenge of major surgery and the care from my mother, daughter, and friends made me know that I was in Washington, D.C., healing and resting. My son Kwan became a father that same summer; I

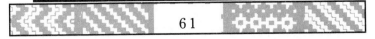

was a grandmother. Early August, my sister Mae Frances called my mother to come to her side. She was in what was her last health crisis before she moved on to the other side. She died in early September.

During that time, McLean Bosfield, my voice teacher, who had kept more than my voice going after Wilkie moved to New York, left for a new home in Mexico. She sent me to study with Charles Williams, who was then head of the Voice Department at the Levine School of Music.

I had produced, with the assistance of my daughter Toshi, two Sweet Honey recordings that summer—*Feel Something Drawing Me On* and *The Other Side*. I finished mixing the records just before the surgery, and Toshi supervised the creation of the masters after I got home from the hospital. It was a stretching time for me, and Sweet Honey was singing and producing a major festival in Nairobi, Kenya.

Evie said that as they flew over to Kenya, it was announced that a state of emergency had been declared in South Africa. When they got to Kenya, she found Kenya was itself involved in taking away the freedom of those who dared to oppose the government. While the conference was being held, several people were executed, although the news did not make the papers. Desperate women tried to get the conference to take up the issue of the government's repression. Evie talks about wanting to scream . . . and the result was "State of Emergency." We used this song to close out our *Live at Carnegie Hall* album, released in 1988, and it was nominated for a Grammy.

AAAAAAAAAAAANNNNNNNNNNNNNNNNNNNNNNNNNN
Working in the mines from dawn to dusk
Getting no money, getting nowhere
Diamonds and gold, they filter thru my hands
Just like the Krugerrand, the coin of death

Thousands laying on the funeral pyre
My sisters, my brothers, and never afraid
They keep on marching and they keep on singing
With yesterday's coffins on their heads

Well I'm looking up to heaven for some clear sign
For who to kill now and who to let be
You know you got no freedom when your family is gone
Everybody is your enemy
Apartheid's in a State of Emergency . . .

When Sweet Honey returned from Kenya, I knew that there was a Sweet Honey without me and that we needed to begin to explore the ways in which the

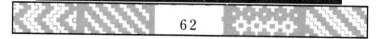

other women could share in the survival of her underpinnings. When we gathered in August 1985, I had programmed Sweet Honey for twelve years and for several of those years I had felt that others had also been programming her on the stage under their breaths. Everyone agreed that they felt they were ready to program a Sweet Honey concert. We set up a rhythm, and that September I sang my first Sweet Honey concert as a singer and not as concert composer.

In the fall of 1985, I was scared about how I would feel—singing a Sweet Honey concert I did not program. I found, to my surprise, in the midst of all sorts of opinions about the conversations that began to be expressed from Sweet Honey stages, that it was a release, a weight lifted. Trying to be ready for Ysaye, Aisha, and Evie as they unfolded a concert experience, going on a two-concert weekend where I did not have to program, was a gift, a carefree light feeling. I was still the leader of the group, however, and I was still responsible for the overall integrity of the ensemble's work. I had to work at being a master teacher to a teacher, a leader to a leader.

During our anniversary concert in November 1985, we introduced a new singer. There must have been guardian angels who convinced Nitanju Bolade Casel to travel some of her life journey with us. She had a quiet and caring spirit about her that changed the air in the ensemble's space. When she came into the group, the quality of my personal life in Sweet Honey immediately improved. First, when she smiles, and she smiles easily and often, a soft glow warms the space around her. She came to Sweet Honey with the experience of being an innovative leader of two cultural organizations and with a rare and important understanding about leaders. Bolade Casel knew that leaders are human, flawed, often too tired to stand or keep going. For the first time since the group started in 1973, I moved through my work with someone watching me. I could feel her wanting me to have some ease. She helped with my bags (often loaded with my clothes and those of other singers) and instruments (shekere case). I was taken aback, surprised, and had to learn to accept an offered hand. My load lightened appreciably.

The support Nitanju gave seemed to radiate throughout the group. We opened up new areas and different women took on new responsibilities. We began to talk about what it took to keep Sweet Honey going and how that work could be spread around. My role as founder of the group and artistic director was acknowledged publicly. It was as if Nitanju understood that to support me as a leader, it was important sometimes to respond to those parts of me that were vulnerable, weak, and leaning—and it never meant that I was less because I was supported and propped up in places. I began to experience the phenomenon of the group improving the leader by making it possible for the leader to be less. Sweet Honey was coming of age.

"ON CHILDREN"

We have always had children in our audiences. When we would sing Ysaye's arrangement of "On Children" by Kahlil Gibran, usually a child would sound clearly in the audience. Many parents brought their newborn to her or his first concert as the mother's first outing. They let us know that Sweet Honey's music was an important part of the pregnancy and that our songs had been played in the birthing room. One sister told me that she was in labor before a Sweet Honey concert in Los Angeles, but she had her ticket and came anyway, giving birth to a son later that evening!

Our entry into children's recordings was not planned. Through participation in an anthology recording, co-sponsored by Ben and Jerry's, we received a catalogue of the recording company releasing the anthology, *Music for Little People*, located in Redway, California. As I looked through the catalogue, I was impressed with the range of titles and their efforts to represent many cultures. I asked if they would be interested in Sweet Honey developing a recording for younger audiences. They agreed and *All for Freedom* was the result.

Our goal was to present a Sweet Honey In The Rock concert so that it would be accessible to families and especially to small children. We sent out a tape of our music to the recording company. They played it for some children and sent it back saying that the songs were generally too long and that the children walked out of the room on this song or that one. We ended up with a mixture of traditional material, some songs Aisha, Nitanju, and Ysaye remembered from summer camp days that were for fun, and songs that sang of friendship and play. Our most extensive work was on the songs that carried the message of freedom, and particularly the struggle of African Americans to be free in this land. We recorded "Calypso Freedom" and "If You're All for Freedom" from the Civil Rights Movement and "Juba" and "Amen" from our spiritual repertoire.

In December 1989 we performed our first concert for younger audiences since 1975, when we had performed a series of concerts produced by the Rep for Black History Month. It was produced by Toshi Reagon, who came up with the brilliant idea of putting "no adults allowed without children" on the posters. I began to get calls from my friends saying, "I'm coming to your concert, and I am borrowing my neighbor's child." We sang that concert with a group of children who had performed on the recording and others who were members of our extended family, having grown up with Sweet Honey from the womb.

There was a lot of activity in the concert and we used volunteers from the audience for the "Red Caboose" train. I thought it was going to circle in front of the stage, but the young woman who was the engine turned and headed for the back of the room. I was not going to be in charge of this train, I could only sing the song and pray inside: Hold on, children, hold on. The train arrived back at the station on time and intact.

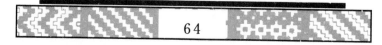

SOUTHERN AFRICA

In 1990, our efforts to be a continuing voice of struggle without our country brought us the experience of traveling to countries in Southern Africa, themselves still battling the impact of colonialism and the oppressive presence of South Africa. For three weeks we traveled and performed on a USIA-sponsored tour in the countries of Uganda, Zimbabwe, Mozambique, Swaziland, and Namibia.

In our concerts we tried to do two things. First, we were sponsored by the U.S. government. However, our repertoire celebrated the legacy of a people who were constantly at odds with the government regarding racism. People who lived in countries with a one-party government, where opposition might mean death or at least imprisonment, asked how it could be that we were supported by our government and against it and alive at the same time. The importance of the African American presence representing a struggle against systems of injustice became more real to me as we moved through those communities where people still searched for ways to have open dialogue about their government.

Second, I told our audiences that we were the children of those taken from this place long ago. In singing our concerts, we were reporting back to our people how and what we had to do to try to make our way in a strange land, the land of our birth, our country, the United States of America.

Slavery happened not only to those of us who survived it in this hemisphere; it also happened to Africa. The organized commercial trade in human life across centuries had ripped the heart out of so many and was still a sensitive subject in some places. There was not much discussion, but I could feel them listening to us in new ways after I talked about how we in our hearts and our sound continued to be so much of our original homeland.

At the end of our concerts, we sang "Nkosi Sikelel' l-Afrika" ("God Bless Our Mother Africa"), and on the opening line everyone in the audience rose and sang with us. They knew this song and sang it in relationship to their struggle to build independent nations, free from colonial powers. We learned the song as a way of expressing our support for an Africa free from subordination by any forces, and the singing was joined in a mighty way. They stood and sent their fists upward at an angle that I loved. And they had a way of taking what was a hymn structure and dragging the end of the line in a soft swoop, connecting the sound with the next line of text without a break. These were front-line countries and these people had personal experiences with South Africa, personal experiences supporting the struggles against apartheid. And the song "Nkosi Sikelel' l-Afrika" itself was important; it was the national anthem in Tanzania and Mozambique and the equivalent of it in Namibia.

"How do African Americans get so much out of being Black?" we were asked. Our host during one session told how it seemed that in his country the leaders were

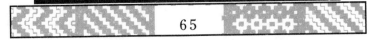

rushing to bring in as much of the West as they could get to address problems of development for their people. The indigenous culture was taken for granted and did not seem to be viewed by some as a source of contemporary strength. On the other hand, African Americans seemed to be saying, with our lives and our culture, that if you take Western civilization and give up your culture and traditions you will not know how not to be enslaved by that civilization. We agreed that there is much that Western technology can offer human society today, but we in the United States have learned that the foundation for applying that knowledge must come from a cultural perspective that is not driven by greed, or all will be lost and prostituted and the problems will not be addressed. Consciously pulling from a deep Black American cultural base was crucial to our ability to survive and develop.

When we returned to the United States, we had a call from Harry Belafonte: "Could Sweet Honey sing at some of the rallies for Mandela when he traveled to the United States?" "Yes." We sang at Yankee Stadium and the Brooklyn Academy of Music (BAM) in New York, and we sang at the Convention Center in Washington, D.C., and at Oakland Stadium in Oakland, California.

At BAM, Winnie Mandela sat on the stage while we sang "Crying for Freedom in South Africa." I will always hold dear the memory of witnessing this woman up close as she listened to us sing the songs we had sung all over America for more than a decade, teaching and building a culture in support of South African freedom. Winnie Mandela has been crucial to the development of that culture. It is her voice, her pain, her defiance, her loneliness, which we heard across a quarter of a century, that helped to make the struggle against apartheid our struggle. It was often through her story that we truly understood the power Mandela continued to build even while he was locked up in jail. It was a miracle to have them walk this land together for a short time.

Participating in the rallies was important because sometimes Sweet Honey fights because she believes, and every once in a while you do see that your voice can make a difference. I have seen Angela Davis and Ben Chavis . . . out of jail. I have seen Mandela and Walter Sisulu . . . out of jail. I have also seen and felt the cost. Winnie Mandela, whose spirit and fire reached us in the deepest ways in this country, is now in trouble in her land and in her community. I remember hearing her talk about the twenty-five years of struggle, of life under house arrest. Now we are told about charges and rumors about the brutality of guards while under her supervision. My heart is in pain at what must be a bitter pill and a bitter cost to have strong lives twisted by struggle. We do not go through battle without cost and scars; we do not all come out standing together. But Winnie, I want her to somehow walk in the sun through it all.

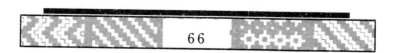

SWEET HONEY IN THE ROCK IS A COMMUNITY ORGANIZATION

From our beginning we took ourselves seriously as a community organization. We do come and serve when we are called.

One evening in 1975, Steve Henderson from Howard University called me to tell me that Mick McQuire, also a faculty member at Howard, had been killed in a car accident in South Carolina and that his wife wanted me to sing at his funeral. Mick had heard me sing at a conference held in Atlanta at the Institute of the Black World during the summer of 1968. After he got home from the conference he told his wife, "When I die, I want Bernice Reagon to sing at my funeral."

When I went over to the McQuire home, I found that Mick McQuire had been Catholic and that they wanted a service that celebrated both his Catholic and cultural heritages. She wanted the recessional to be the African American national anthem, "Lift Every Voice and Sing." I told her I wanted to use Sweet Honey In The Rock.

The service was my first Catholic funeral. The priests were White and the congregation was Black. Candles were burning, and the priests came up the aisle and into the altar area swinging black pots with smoke piling out of them. I thought: This sure does feel like an African ritual. We sang "Balm in Gilead" as a part of the service and then at the end "Lift Every Voice and Sing." It was good to be of healing service.

The day came, though, when I felt that it was not enough to call yourself a community organization and only come if you were called. We must participate in building something, supporting something. I also wondered what we as individuals in the group were learning from our experience as singers. These questions also led to the start of a new workshop that offered to other Black women the experience of singing. This was 1980. We conducted a workshop every Thursday evening for women who found the time to come in to sing. The only requirement of the group was that they share what they had found with the community. At the end of each season we went into an intense rehearsal period and produced a concert.

Beyond teaching women to sing, Sweet Honey as a group gained a source of support that has only grown with the years. For myself, I made a few lifelong friends. I found other women going through tremendous struggle to get through the day and the week with their families. I saw the workshop become a source of strength and comfort for those who stayed.

After four years, members of In Process . . . , as the group had come to be known, were well on their way toward developing their own independent directions. With difficulty Sweet Honey discussed among ourselves whether we should go on or end the workshop. Ending the workshop would not necessarily mean ending the relationship—we would be there if they called—but they would have to find a way to be if they were to continue to have music in their lives.

Initially, they were not pleased. Some were upset. However, today in Washing-

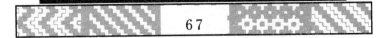

ton, D.C., there is an ensemble of seven women singers, In Process . . . , making her own distinctive presence known in the community. The lesson—you do have to let your children go or they will never be able to help you when you really need their support.

Another opportunity to work with our community in a new way came in 1985 when I began to study voice with Charles Williams of the Levine School of Music. After our first session, I asked if he would work with Sweet Honey. His response was to take me to the director's office and suggested to Joanne Hoover that Sweet Honey In The Rock become artists-in-residence at the Levine School of Music, and so it was.

Sweet Honey has come with her songs, when she was called, to family reunions, jails, rallies, tributes to those who have helped to build our community . . . and celebrations . . . Kwanzaa, Black History Month, weddings. . . . We have participated in several weddings, but it was particularly special to be a part of the bonding service of one of our own—the wedding of Nitanju and Tayari in the fall of 1987.

I don't remember when I first connected our survival as a group to our audiences. Slowly over the years, I became aware that Sweet Honey was a vocal point of a community that had few geographical boundaries. Our audiences will travel miles to be in our concerts. If they cannot attend, they'll push and insist that their parents, sisters, and brothers go any distance to have the experience. I realized that *I* felt at home in a Sweet Honey concert because I knew the audience and they knew us.

Sweet Honey In The Rock is a part of a community in which priority is given to expressing one's own vision in a way that is not destructive, exploitative, and oppressive to others sharing the same universe. We are a fragile community. It has been important that when we, in our songs and singing, embrace and celebrate our heritage as African American women, we nurture this community.

For our tenth anniversary album, *We All . . . Everyone of Us,* I wrote a poem that bowed in salute to this community that has made it possible for these singing women to be so many places with so many songs and in such good company:

> *We come to you*
> *You in every color of the rainbow*
> *With your freedom and struggle stances*
> *In every position of the moon and sun*
>
> *We come to you*
> *Offering our songs and the sounds of our Mothers'*
> *Mothers*

In libation
To everyone of us

There really is a community
We have seen and felt and been held by you
These ten years

There is this community we belong to without
geographical boundaries
D.C., Atlanta, Berea, Chicago, East St. Louis, L.A., Toronto, Chiba, the Bay
Area, Newark, Seattle, Chapel Hill, Boston, Frankfurt, London, Richmond,
Little Rock, N.Y.C., Denver, Albuquerque, Nashville, Brixton, New Orleans,
Vancouver, Portland, Berlin, Albany, Durham, Tokyo, St. Louis, Detroit, St.
Paul, Dallas, Peoria, Jamaica. . . .
There really is a community
Lovers
Searchers
Movers into life
Fighters and builders
of a place where
Military machines, hatred of women, abuse of children,
homophobia, societal male suicide, racial bigotry,
starvation, work that kills and cripples, social orders
driven by greed, the U.S.A. invading whoever . . . this
week. Where the dying and acting out of fear, anger,
and terror
Will find no feeding ground.
I wanna be there!

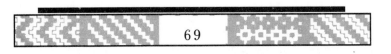

4

SWEET HONEY
STREAMS OF CONSCIOUSNESS

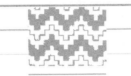

NIANI KILKENNY

Who makes me sing when my voice is silent
Songs have left me for places unheard
Who bids me sing when all singing seems
useless

—Bernice Johnson Reagon, "Mae Frances"

For the past twenty years, Sweet Honey In The Rock has shared in my own definition of who I was, who I am, who I want to become. Her collective power, beauty, and spirit have enabled me to name and express my joys, sorrows, hopes, and visions. She has offered me her gifts and created a space for me to clap my hands, stomp my feet, sit and cry, stand and scream, levitate and rejoice as she sings her songs that tell my stories.

Sweet Honey's essence—her song literature, voice, energy, and aesthetic provide my "way out of no way" that years and layers of political, economic, and cultural oppression have blocked. She fine-tunes the radar that locates my center, nurtures my spirit, and repairs my heart.

Knowing and loving Sweet Honey has allowed me to reclaim my SELF, mold

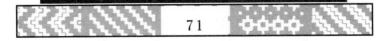

a new woman, circle my being with love, and form a concentricity of awareness for my husband, children, grandchildren, family, and friends to honor.

As Sweet Honey In The Rock streams through my consciousness, I visualize:

Women
Muse Women
Drawing us into harmonies, melodies
Vocalizing/lyricizing lessons from the past
Realities of the present
Hopes for the future
Echoing griots whose truths mirrored in songs are
propelled into the cosmic record for all time

Healers
Women ministering to the human tribe
Nurturing people with a laying on of songs
Transforming lives in the process
Connecting circles pushed to another place
Earth's daughters whose remedies soothe the heart, mind, and
Soul

Activists
Women using voices as weapons
Revealing the human condition
Reminding us of trouble spots, danger zones
Challenging us to take a stand against racism, oppression
Exploitation, discrimination in all of its forms
In all of its places
Warning the enemy to get back because
We will not bow down

Sisters, mothers, lovers, friends
Raising children
Negotiating romances
Affirming passion
Loving, giving, clinging, and letting go
A living testament to a universal wholeness that only
real self-respect can know

Sweet muse/healer/activist/sister/mother/lover/Honey
In this hard cold unyielding planetary rock
Clasp my hand

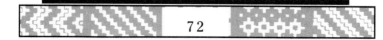

Sweet Honey Streams of Consciousness

Take me back down the road to yesterday
Hold me
Teach me
Sing me
All the way to tomorrow

Sweet Honey In The Rock
You make me sing when my voice was silent
When Songs have left me for places unheard
You bid me sing when all singing seems useless
Thank you for holding my hand
Thank you for holding my hand

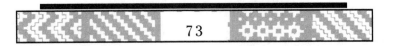

LEFT: YASMEEN WILLIAMS WITH DAUGHTER SUMMER ASI WILLIAMS, NOVEMBER 1983. (PHOTOGRAPHER, ROY LEWIS)

TOP RIGHT: YASMEEN, 1977. (PHOTOGRAPHER, ROLAND FREEMAN)

BOTTOM RIGHT: YASMEEN, 1992. (PHOTOGRAPHER, EDGAR THOMPSON)

5

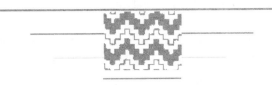

TIMELESS

YASMEEN

I met Sweet Honey (they hadn't met me) in 1975 on the Smithsonian Institutional Mall, where they were performing for the Festival of American Folklife. The outdoor concert space had a stage that was set like a front porch but they clearly had control of the entire yard. Walking by, as if observing artifacts in a gallery, my body gradually stopped moving. As they sang, I heard my great-grandmother, Big Mama, moan. I stopped, making sure that what I'd heard was really what I thought I'd heard, my mother's father calling out from the pulpit the common meter: "A Charge to Keep I Have, a God to Glorify." I stood there listening; eyes fixed on their stage but for a while seeing no one. Hearing foot stomps from the stage took me to the old country church my father pastored in Elizabeth City, in North Carolina—church windows wide open, moaners on the front bench, church women fanning flies, dust flying outside the windows from children playing in the church driveway, and not to mention the smell of chicken frying from somewhere.

As I heard Sweet Honey, my heart beat faster and my chest felt full with memories/imagination (my daughter Summer says they are synonymous). I felt at home—as if my sisters and I were sitting at the dining-room table singing or at Aunt Vera's piano on New Year's morning. I felt the ancestors that I'd known—mostly gospel singers and preachers, my father, his brothers and sisters. All these sounds were being dispersed from this one spot into their entire outdoor area. I knew that something had been missing in my life because of the space filling up in

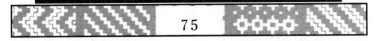

my spirit. I felt I needed to go back and hug a part of me that somehow I'd left unattended, and becoming this music once again would be the way back.

When I finally looked up and paid attention to the singers onstage I saw five Black women—Bernice Johnson Reagon, Evelyn Maria Harris, Carol Maillard, Patricia Johnson, and Louise Robinson—twisting and turning melodies in the same styles as their bodies. Evie's eyes were closed. Her slender body leaned back with an "I'm bad and I know I'm bad" expression on her face—her mouth slightly curved. And indeed she was! Bernice was like: "All I have to do is open my mouth and you will understand regardless of what your perception is of me or anything else." Carol was a walking song; with every step she made or note she sang I could imagine a whole 'nother song. Pat was light and jazzy, standing mostly still, but enjoying the movements around her. Louise was a theater company within herself, the words to the songs she sang came from her hands, feet, facial expression, neck, everywhere.

I watched until they'd finished and when they had I said to myself, "My God —I belong in that group."

I had just left Spelman College in Atlanta, Georgia. One of my teachers was Christine Farris, sister of the Reverend Dr. Martin Luther King, Jr.; to be in her class was almost like being in the same room with him because they looked so much alike. The smoke from the Civil Rights Movement was still in the air in Atlanta, so, although the Movement only touched my consciousness as a child, those that the Movement had directly affected were teaching me. Their spirits were steeped in freedom fighting.

When I moved back to Washington, D.C., I joined the D.C. Black Repertory Company and auditioned for the vocal workshop with the song "Got the Blues from My Baby Down by the San Francisco Bay" by Phoebe Snow. I accepted Bernice's invitation to come into her workshop, aware that her reputation at the Rep was as a "tough disciplinarian." I thought to myself: I'm gonna like her; she demands much. Shortly after joining the workshop she asked me to audition for Sweet Honey and I began singing the songs of the Civil Rights Movement.

I spent more time on the road with Sweet Honey than in the classroom, but I did earn my B.A. degree in English from Bowie State College. Singing and being a student wasn't all hard times. I thought it was great, but it took huge amounts of determination and I had to want both badly. I live my life by challenging myself to fill life with drama; by the grace of God I manage to survive.

The music that helped raise me had now found me again through Sweet Honey, and my spirit was compatible with it. However, I simply have a love for music—period. raised in a Black Baptist environment, I was not allowed to listen to secular music at home. I learned to like classical music by traveling to and from preaching engagements with my father. Year after year we'd travel, driving to New York or Georgia to either churches, vacations, or occasional shopping sprees to Philadelphia. On the road, classical music was always on the radio, to which I

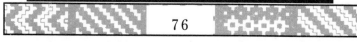

would (lying in the back seat of the car) be writing lyrics—love songs, game songs, or poems. Sometimes the classical tunes would be background music from some contemporary song like "Alfie" or "My Guy." I eventually took up violin lessons, returning some of the musical training and favors afforded me in our travels by practicing some long hours at home. My favorite practice song was "Mercy, Mercy." It gave excruciating pain to the family, though.

There was another side to this music appreciation process in my home, however. The underground—our side! When my father left for work (he was a barber and a minister then), my sisters and brother and I would turn the stations to R&B. Yes, we'd sneak, but I could have sworn my mother was tapping her feet in the kitchen and I don't remember her ever telling us to turn it off. My brother Edgar Jr. (Eddie), now a minister, had his favorites, "Up on the Roof" by the Drifters, and Eddie Holman singing "What Becomes of a Broken Heart." I used to watch him run up and down the steps and hear him in the shower singing. I learned all the lyrics from his singing of these songs. Now he's singing songs like "A Charge to Keep I Have, a God to Glorify" and "Lay Your Hands on Me Jesus." What has been wonderful to me is the pride I learned in this music through Sweet Honey.

My sisters and brothers are all very close. But sing! My sisters were something else! At home—you could not have told them that they were not the Supremes or Martha and the Vandellas. My oldest sister, Elisabeth (Jerrie), was more into keeping house while the rest were clowning. She used to sing "Ave Maria" and boy could she sing "Oh Holy Night"—I mean with force. She's not changed her music much. She still sticks pretty much to the sacred, loves to sing, and, like me, is in her own world when she does.

Next to her is my sister Ernestine (Stine). She was the real live wire in the family. Stine *knew* she was Mary Wells. She dressed like her, wore her hair like her, and had home-based talent shows and became her. She kept us laughing all the time. But at church this girl got serious when she sang and that's when the real fire came out. She was sincere about what singing meant to her and her relationship with something on the inside. She was one of the most supportive members of my family regarding Sweet Honey In The Rock.

The sister next to her is Ossie. Ossie is the quiet, sweet one in the family with a mean alto. She carries the name of my father's mother, a name passed down through many generations in our family. Ossie, the prettiest woman I've ever seen, was Stine's sidekick; they were a duet. When Stine was Diana Ross, Ossie was Mary. Ossie taught me to read by singing songs to me from nursery rhyme books and by urging me to interpret the pictures. She used to make up songs—short and playful ones to make people laugh. But in church she became very serious. The songs of the ages began to surface, a thoughtfulness and a certainty came over her face, and that smooth, rich, deep alto would start to heal wounds.

The brother next to me is Alphonso (Alley). Although Alley suffered brain damage from a high fever as a baby, he grew up singing anything he heard us sing.

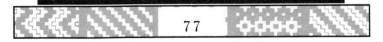

We played together and learned our ABCs together. From him, I learned humility and compassion, love and respect for someone differently abled. He's forty now and has his own immeasurable kind of intelligence. He knows almost every hymn in the Baptist hymnal, and is the loudest one in the church when it comes to saying Amen. The love and attention given him, especially from my mother, have moved him into the "miracle" category in our family.

My mother, a woman of deep faith, to this day begins her day on her knees. Afterward she begins her chores for the day and she'll be singing. As a child I remember her humming around the house, and it comforted me. And some songs I could tell she'd sing to comfort herself. Her voice was high and soft—it rippled with a velvet soulfulness. She held the family together with sweetness, tenderness, consistency, and gentleness, and firmness when it was absolutely necessary. We knew when Mama got firm that we had gone too far, because she has patience I will never have. She has always been supportive in everything I've ever done, and calls me the "go-getter" in the family. I like that.

So when I started singing nationally with Sweet Honey, I knew I was considering everything and every person I was a part of. Into this group I could bring these parts, and the richness from each that nurtured me would surely nurture others.

The beginning of my professional singing career was with a gospel group called the Spiritualettes, directed by my cousin Shirley Ables. One of my father's sisters, Vera, founder of the gospel group called the Service Gospel Singers, had connections with all the radio stations in the area that would play Black gospel music and she and Shirley Ables had us traveling up and down the East Coast singing everywhere. I even remember the little burgundy robes Shirley made for us to sing in. Mine had a big bow in the front because I was only four years old.

We—the Spiritualettes—were seven Black females: Shirley Ables, pianist, my sisters Jerrie, Stine, and Ossie, and my two cousins Sandra Allen (Coosie) and Brenda Sharp, and me. Our *hot* spot in D.C. was the Union Hall, which used to sit across the street from where the Georgetown University Law School Library is now. Gospel shows were held at the Union Hall almost every Sunday. These shows were orchestrated by local gospel DJ masters like Cosby Zellers (now deceased) and Lucille Banks Miller Robinson. We had a chance to perform alongside such gospel giants as the famous Caravans with Shirley Caesar, Inez Andrews, Albertina Walker, the Five Blind Boys of Alabama, the Southern Gospel Singers, and many others. We grew up singing with the now renowned gospel singer, songwriter, and pianist Richard Smallwood. (I remember being asked to audition for the Richard Smallwood Singers at the same time I was asked to audition with Sweet Honey.)

The late 1950s and early 1960s were a great time for gospel music. We would get together, and all those who understood the music would sing and shout wherever we were at the time—in the car, on the road, in church, in the living room, much like the way Sweet Honey stops to sing, meet, and/or discuss. I was young

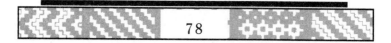

and did not know many of the early influential pioneers of gospel music like Willie Mae Ford Smith or the Barrett Sisters, but we did know a little Sally Martin and Thomas Dorsey because every church I know sang "Precious Lord." Besides, he and Sally would sing at the National Baptist Conventions with the convention choir. It was at one of these conventions that I had a chance to sing under the direction of the Reverend C. Derricks, author of the hymn "Have a Little Talk with Jesus." Sweet Honey made these gospel pioneers real and tangible to me. Bernice, a cultural historian, researched the historical content of the music, and through her research Sweet Honey not only performed the music, and learned of the musicians, but were introduced to them. We performed on Oprah Winfrey's show with Sally Martin, Albertina Walker, and the Barrett Sisters the year before Oprah's show was nationally syndicated.

Shirley Ables could hit the highest to the lowest of the lowest notes with her voice. My sister Stine could never finish "The Rough Side of the Mountain" without shouting. Sandra (Coosie) had this vibrant and sharp soprano that could cause the listener to sweat. She can still be heard today on recordings with Donald Vail and the Salvation Corporation Singers. Brenda was contralto, cool, calm, collected. Ossie's voice was smooth hot chocolate. The harmony was incredible considering how young we were. At four years old I sang with no fear or inhibitions—pointing my finger up to heaven like Aunt Vera told me to—with a gospel growl and struttin' at the same time, resounding "My God Is Almighty, My God Is Righteous!" We would have the Union Hall standing and shoutin' every time. So you see, even now with Sweet Honey, if the congregation or audience (Black or White) is not standing, clapping, and shouting when I lead "Ol' Landmark," I will not have done my duty. So far so good after twenty years.

When my sisters grew older, moved away, married, I was often the only child in the congregation singing and listening to the elders while the other children were outside playing. I was learning common meter, dissonance, hymns, spirituals, and early gospel—and when we moved from a church where music was a cappella to a church with piano accompaniment, I learned more contemporary styles of these forms. The a cappella will always be my favorite, though.

After working with Sweet Honey for a while, I realized how precious the people and places were to me that I may have taken for granted during those early years. That music was a part of my soul as well as training. I learned to be proud and grateful for all that I am, all that my people are, the ground we stand on, the roads we've walked, the ways we've come. I was proud that I could be instrumental in maintaining that richness. Throughout my youth, I surrendered myself to this music without really understanding how powerful that surrender was.

My teenage years were fun, fun, fun, and music became third on my list. First were boys, second were extracurricular activities at school, third was music. I had a good, solid, dependable family and I took freedom and change for granted. I went

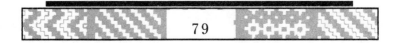

through rebellious periods, but I had other directions in which to channel my rebellion—the Civil Rights Movement, the dress code in the schools, cultural awareness, all of this was happening in the late 1960s and 1970s.

Santana and Funkadelic were hot groups then and I remember just letting music carry me. But the songs with messages seem to be the ones to stick with me, such as "Harvest for the World" by the Isley Brothers or "I'll Take You There" by the Staples Singers or the soulful messages of Donny Hathaway and the early songs of Earth, Wind and Fire. I was always holding on to the music that gave hope and life to all people even if it had to free a small group to do it. For example, though the Civil Rights Movement was initiated by Black people, the Movement changed the face of the entire world. This is the power of music that speaks to the heart, soul, and consciousness of people—music as a life source.

My first real love was Curtis Pearson (now deceased), and it was during this relationship that I received the name Yasmeen. After Curtis, however, boys didn't turn out to be as good as my brothers or dear ol' Dad. My father raised me to question authority with respect. He taught me that girls were intelligent and sometimes much more so than men. He taught me that I could do anything I wanted to do and have whatever I wanted to have in life. "This world belongs to you," he used to say, and as a result, I learned to be sort of feisty and independent.

These deeply ingrained thoughts and feelings about independence were just more things that attracted me to Sweet Honey. They are women who "bow to no man's word" (a line from "Ella's Song," written by Bernice).

By my second year at Spelman College, a couple of years before Sweet Honey, I began to recognize sexism, racism, bigotry, and many others isms. So I joined the Nation of Islam under the Sunni Muslim sect. The Imam, the head of this particular temple, instructed me about the respect for women in Islamic culture. One reason I attended Spelman (an all-women's college) was to limit distractions from brothers. Well, I began to wear the garb—the long dresses, the veil, everything to cover my body and face. I began to practice the religion and lost lots of my old friends who had no idea of why I had turned to Islam. The feelings I had I felt no one else was having. I needed to be my own thinking self. When I talked this over with my parents, they told me that there were many paths to take and not one would be the only way I'd find at this stage in my life, so I should go ahead and keep trying to find myself.

While practicing Islam I found exploitation and a basic smothering suppression of women. My spirit felt freed by the lessons Islam teaches on prayer, submission to one God, lessons on cleanliness, ancestral respect, and healing through certain foods, but my spirit felt caged by the laws, rules, regulations, and trappings. Among this particular group of practicing Muslims, physical and mental abuse toward women was rampant. When they told me that according to the Koran a woman's husband could beat her as long as the object was no thicker than his thumb, a fire began to stir inside me. One day the Imam sent some brothers to me

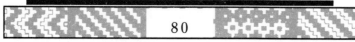

to tell me that I was not allowed to sing in public—only for my child and husband in the privacy of my own home. Since I had neither then, this meant I could sing only to myself. Another fire raged. These practices were life-threatening to me then and cause war inside me now. When I thought about this attempt to quiet what gives me life, I imagined a world filled with birds that could not sing, violins being strummed with no strings, I thought of the wind blowing and not being able to feel it, and said to myself, "My God! These people are feeling-impaired!"

Some years later I learned that the practice of physical and mental abuse toward women is rampant in almost every country I've traveled in with Sweet Honey. Women are fighting misogyny everywhere. I have personally been a victim too. I have been pregnant and abandoned; I have been physically abused by a husband—from broken bones to nearly a broken spirit. I was saved because I had the love I'd grown up with and the love of people around me to hold on to until I could get back to the love for myself. Music was still my lifeline, so I wrote and recorded the song, "Walking in the Way of Love":

He's out of my life
He's out of my way
He's out of my path
He's out of my days
And I'm still walking
Walking in the way of love

He's out of my Summer sun
He's out of my pretty
He's out of my shining
Out of my witty
And I'm still walking
Walking in the way of love

He's out of my seasons
Winter, summer, spring, and fall
He's out of my reasons
For any reason at all
And I'm still walking
Walking in the way of love

In Sweet Honey, I have consciously tried to understand how to use love as a way to get through all times—good and difficult—by being focused on our common ground. I've heard all my life that women cannot get along with each other. I never knew what that meant. I had three sisters, and a mother, and we got along. In Sweet Honey, I traveled with five sisters and we got along and settled our differ-

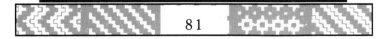

ences with respect. Sweet Honey introduced me to songs that talked about women, honored women, and gave a Black woman's point of view. I no longer had to feel these things about women in the privacy of my own thoughts but I could sing them out loud. And sometimes to get help to say these things out loud I will call on some ancestors through prayer.

One cold, rainy night in 1989 in the backstage dressing room of a Washington State theater auditorium just before the Sweet Honey concert, I lit a candle, poured a libation in a small glass bowl, and closed the door to my dressing room. I surrounded the glass bowl with semiprecious stones like amethyst, clear quartz crystal, rose quartz, jasper—the stones they say heaven is made of—healing stones. I began to pray. I said to myself that if we can pray to our ancestors like Jesus, Moses, Lydia, and Ruth and pray to be like them in church, surely I can ask God to send down some help to me tonight that will enable me to sing as I've never sung before and touch somebody's heart. So I asked for the knowledge of my father's father, Granddaddy Arthur, a music teacher, whom I've never known. I asked for my Aunts Aurelia and Carrie, both my father's sisters, who used to sing with the Service Gospel Singers. I asked for the presence of Sarah Vaughan so she could remind me of how to breathe in a song, then I asked for some biblical ancestors.

After the prayer I left the candle burning, checked to see if it would be safe, and answered the five-minute call to concert time. I always know when the ancestors come; I can feel the presence. They did not come during this concert. After the concert I did my usual routine by going straight back to the hotel room and got in bed. Near daybreak I heard this consistent thumping in my head, pulsating. The pulsations were saying womb, womb, womb. The words were moving in and out of the song but I could not make them out or understand them at first. As I listened, I knew they had come and were trying to deliver a message. The words came through the womb lines as silhouettes of three women's lives: one woman was the victim of rape, one woman the victim of abandonment, and the other a victim of incest. Thus the song "Colours":

 Womb—womb—womb—womb—womb . . .
Working hard all of my days for finer things in life
A happy life—then one peaceful night
When I went out for a walk—a hand around my mouth
An intruder to the colours of my womb.
 Womb—womb—womb—womb—womb . . .
I was young and did not understand the facts of life
Broken home, love was rare and life a fight
Till I came across a young boy who would hold me tight
And leave me lonely with the colours from my womb.
 Womb—womb—womb—womb—womb . . .
Sometimes he could not tell the difference between night and day—

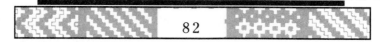

Intoxicated days had rearranged his ways
When my father—my own father took a turn one day
From my mother to the colours of my womb.
    Womb—womb—womb—womb—womb . . .
Now the president and all his men dare try to say
When I might or when I may
Make the decisions that they set me up for anyway
Insult my mind—my rights—the issues of my womb.

Each member of Sweet Honey is a role model. Ysaye for her multifaceted intellect, Bernice for her brilliant common sense, Aisha for her stunning creativity and the way she makes me feel when she sings "See See Rider," Nitanju for her heartwarming and thought-provoking genuineness, and Evie for her ethereal imagination as a songwriter and her good ol' country humor. Bernice taught me to study the music, the music business, ways to negotiate, and how to deal with integrity and honesty.

We don't waste much time in Sweet Honey. It seems every minute of a concert day is used to focus on what we are doing and the purpose of our being where we are. That focused approach also applies to Sweet Honey's meetings. Each Sweet Honey meeting, usually held once or twice a week, is like a classroom where new issues are discussed and worked through. Meetings usually take place around Bernice's dining-room table on Mondays. Bernice sits on one end and Ysaye at the other. I don't know if this was done consciously or not but I always see them as "the two heads." I'd usually sit next to Bernice, but with Evie on the other side, so that when sitting next to Bernice got heavy I could reach over to Evie and crack a joke. Evie was my favorite when it came to talking country and laughing (much like me and my sister Ossie). Many nights we'd meet late to clear our minds on the issues before us. Discussions could become so intense that we sometimes had to find additional ways to rehearse.

I experienced the group expanding its supportive capacity when they encouraged me to continue to sing throughout my pregnancy. In 1983, I traveled big and pregnant. Often the members had to help me in and out of the vans. This was a time in the group when I needed support, so I really learned some lessons in humility. After the birth of my daughter, I toured Scotland with the group and with another little piece of baggage named Summer. I was responsible for making all babysitting arrangements with the sponsors. So all I went on was the assurance (of the other voice on the phone) that my baby would be taken care of by a complete stranger.

My rules were that the sitter stay with me until the sound check. At the sound check the babysitter was required to hold her where I could see her; the sitter would then give my baby back to me until it was time to go onstage. During the concert my baby and the babysitter had to be in the front row where I could see

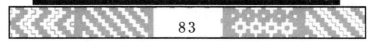

both of them and Summer could see me. She had to know I was still there. During intermissions Summer was brought to me immediately for changing, feeding, and hugging, until I was ready to change into my clothes for the second set. After intermission my baby was to be right back in the front row where I could see her and immediately following the concert she was to be back in my arms. This went on for two years, even on tours out of the country. Talk about functioning through humility. It must have been a tremendous strain on the group but they were wonderful with us. Even so, there were times when I ached when I had to travel without her.

By Summer's third year, taking her sometimes and leaving her other times became too much for me, so I decided to leave the group full-time and make raising my daughter a priority—with no regrets to this day. The relationship I was blessed to have with the group and the music has transcended every aspect of my life, even adding to the close relationship my daughter and I now share.

Singing this music now, with the group or solo, for me is the same as it was then. The music heals me. When I sing, certain sounds flow through my body and I literally feel my blood purifying itself, like channels opening up and a renewal taking place.

Singing is always giving and taking and giving and taking. The lyrics supply the focus. They determine how the song is sung each time it's sung, and those same lyrics may have a different meaning from one day to the next. Five women are onstage and each of us is different. We each have our own interpretation of how we hear a song and what we mean personally regarding the words of the song. We even live the words to the songs differently from one another. But you can believe we have discussed most of these differences and each of us knows our perspective on the topic and that perspective will reveal itself to the audience in five different ways from a Sweet Honey stage. The listener has at least one of us she or he can relate to, which is powerful for me, and yes, we do talk to the audience while we sing, and yes, the requirement at a Sweet Honey concert (and now also at my solo performances) is that the audience responds during the singing, not only afterward. I told you—give-and-take.

Relating to myself and others around me through the music of Sweet Honey and singing of issues that affect me in my daily social and political life allow me to think about where I stand on these issues. I take the time to address them, discuss them with five other women, and form opinions about them. As a result of this process, I can relay this message from the stage or I can now do the same in a workshop at a school or at choir rehearsal at church. I can now accept that we may not all come to agreement from the same place and might not actually share the exact position; however, we must all share the commitment to present the issue in a particular way to our audiences before going to the stage.

Sometimes coming together on certain issues requires discussions and search-

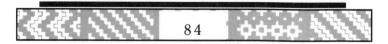

ing for common ground that can take years. It is a growth process. Sweet Honey stays in touch with the issues and finds time to revisit where each person is on it. For example, one rule I proposed was that the group become alcohol- and drug-free, not because we had a problem but because prevention's worth megabucks for a cure. This rule took some time to be implemented. People saw nothing wrong with an occasional glass of wine with dinner. However, the rule was suggested during a time when substance abuse was killing many people, and artists were dying left and right from overdoses. I wanted the rule because alcohol abuse among women is rampant. I want this group to live. Like an overprotective mother, I never want this group to experience the slightest risk of being hurt or disrespected. I felt this would make the group stand out as the focused, directed, and committed group it is. If this group folds for any reason at all, I pray that it will never be under the slavery of drugs or alcohol.

After I proposed the rule, the group refined it to cover work, travel, and social environments when members moved under the auspices of Sweet Honey In The Rock, from airport departure to airport or station return. It was adopted, and that was just the beginning. Through the years this rule has been an area of review, experience, and discussion as we try to share understanding with each other and new members about the benefits of trying to maintain an alcohol/drug/smoke-free zone.

My being a member of Sweet Honey allowed me to experience working with familiar and unfamiliar personalities. Each woman is a powerful universe within herself. For these universes not to collide, lessons about territory, respect for boundaries, specific talents, and characteristics had to be learned. I worked through much of this with prayer.

It was Bernice who told me I was a solo singer. I didn't want to believe her. All my life had been spent—up to that point—singing with groups. I thought she was trying to get rid of me. I sulked inside, but I listened. Now I am working as a solo vocalist. I left Sweet Honey as a full-time member in 1985 and have since remained a substitute Honey—me and Tulani Kinard, a powerful sister, singer, and friend. The rewards are innumerable, and I remember my teacher(s). I humble myself when Bernice speaks in public on my abilities as a singer and I'm honored to receive her praise. Maybe I've not been so bad a student. But then I wanted only to sing with her. I still do, but I'm fronting my own band now, recording and producing my own music, writing my own songs, exploring genres outside the Sweet Honey repertoire, establishing my own publishing company, and recording on my own label.

My parents gave me special blessings to go ahead and sing as many love songs as I like. Luther Vandross, watch out. As a Baptist minister's child who had to sneak listening to popular music growing up, their blessing meant freedom and innocence. I started writing like crazy. A dam of music burst inside me. Though

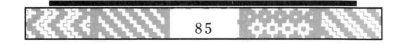

gospel is my music of choice, there is still some Marvin Gaye, Curtis Mayfield, Mavis Staples, Randy Crawford, and Phoebe Snow I've been dying to arrange and perform.

My band has three pieces—bass, percussionist (drum), and piano. I sing R&B, and inspirational, like "Knockin' on Heaven's Door" by Bob Dylan, John Lennon's "Imagine," Oscar Brown Jr.'s "Afro-Blue," and Cassandra Wilson's version of "Angel." I scat and bebop as much as possible; and my daughter, Summer Ossie Lydia (eight years old), writes jazz that I perform in all my performances.

I'm grateful to allow myself to be used as a vessel that will set good things in motion. My praise still goes back to my Creator. If I don't sing, I get physically sick. If I don't sing, I'm afraid I'll ball up in a knot and die. It is healing for me. Humility keeps me in touch with purpose, goals, and responsibilities. It keeps me in touch with a physical and a spiritual reality.

Sweet Honey has shown me how to put a singing career in perspective concerning my personal life. Whatever I practice in my personal life, my business life practice is not far behind. It's practicing what I preach—like the words from that classic gospel song: "I'm going to live the life I sing about in my song."

It is important to me that I maintain a balance in my life. It is important to me that I am the person I am offstage that I am onstage. I don't believe in putting on a costume and becoming someone else in an enhanced state. As a member of Sweet Honey I learned to relate honestly to an audience.

Shakespeare said, to paraphrase, that the whole world is a stage and that everybody plays a part, but one of my goals is to strive to *be* my part. I want to be a sort of a spiritual revolution. I want to continue and pass on some of the power and love passed down, through the ages, to me through my culture, my people. Martin Luther King Jr. said, "Power is the ability to achieve purpose. It is the strength required to bring about social, political, or economic changes." For me music is that power moving unbroken from my ancestors, through my family, through Sweet Honey—me—instruments to carry and continue timeless power and timeless messages.

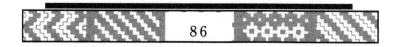

TOP: LOUISE ROBINSON, SMITHSONIAN FESTIVAL OF FOLKLIFE, 1976. (PHOTOGRAPHER, ROSIE LEE HOOKS)

BOTTOM RIGHT: LOUISE ROBINSON WITH BASS FIDDLE, HIGH SCHOOL FOR MUSIC AND ART, NEW YORK CITY. (PHOTO COURTESY OF LOUISE ROBINSON PERSONAL COLLECTION)

BOTTOM LEFT: STREET SOUNDS, 1992. TOP: RONDA CRAINE, MICHELE JACQUES. BOTTOM: JOEY BLAKE, LOUISE ROBINSON, L. STEVEN THOMAS. (PHOTOGRAPHER, JAMES DENNIS, PHOTO COURTESY OF LOUISE ROBINSON PERSONAL COLLECTION)

6

TAKING IT
TO THE STREETS

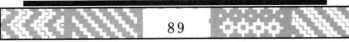

LOUISE ROBINSON

It was one of those hot "New York" summer nights. The rhythm of conga drums rising from the playground of the Foster Projects could be heard in the distance. Record stores were blasting their jams over loudspeakers that poured onto the street. There's a certain smell about a New York summer night—when you breathe in the air you are filled immediately with the excitement and the energy of the city. Cruising down 125th (that's the only way to drive through Harlem), I inhaled the colors and the movements of this rich community.

As we pulled up to the Apollo, my focus was snatched back by my father's command: "Y'all get out here while I park the car." The marquee seemed to consist of a thousand lights that lit up the entire block, and as we stepped onto the pavement I secretly pretended it was all just for me. As we entered the lobby, we were greeted by a bouncer-type gentleman in a neatly fitted uniform asking, "May I help you, ladies?" "Yes," I answered coolly. "We're here to perform on Amateur Night!" I strolled through the lobby, my head moving slowly up and down and left to right trying to take in the entire wall covered with pictures of "Black Stars" who had appeared at the Apollo before me. Every one of them so beautiful and classy. Ella Fitzgerald, Duke Ellington, Lena Horne, Ray Charles, James Brown, Smokey Robinson and the Miracles, Billie Holiday, Pearl Bailey, Little Richard, Stevie Wonder, the Temptations, Marvin Gaye and Tammi Terrell, Sammy Davis Jr., Sarah Vaughan, and "Moms" Mabley were just a few of the many faces that smiled on me that night. I took their stellar smiles as well-wishes and hurried to catch up to my singing buddies. . . .

Backstage was very busy. As we made our way through the confusion, the glamour of it all quickly left me. People were moving about everywhere, yelling to one another to take care of this or that. All of our questions were answered abruptly as though they had been asked a million times before. When things finally slowed down, warmth and laughter began to fill the atmosphere, and that felt good. But then there was still the matter of facing one of the toughest audiences in the country, the Amateur Night crowd. What was so unnerving about the Amateur Night audience was it would vote you in or out by loud cheering or booing. If they booed, it would be the Clown's cue to come onstage, interrupt your act, and find some embarrassing way of telling you to get off the stage. That alone could stop you from ever going onstage again. But part of the decision to appear at the Apollo on a Wednesday night had to include the desire to feel like a winner just for walking out there!

I stood in the wings rubbing my wet palms together and looking anxiously back at "T," who was plastered against the wall talking to our could-be executioner, the Clown. Fran was standing a few feet away from me, calm as usual. A surge of hot energy rushed to my head as I heard the announcer proclaim, "Ladies and gentlemen: The Velvetones." Moving quickly to center stage, we jumped into our routine. As we approached the last vamp of the song, with our gold accordion dresses slightly swaying to the movement of our arms, the crowd began to cheer. I could feel the energy of every great performer who had graced that stage moving through my limbs, encouraging me to stand in my light!

The performance stage was an early intense love for me. I guess it had to do with growing up in New York. If I could compare growing up in New York City to music, I would liken it to bebop. The complexities, the quick pace, the mixture of smells, sounds, movements, and colors, all contributed to this tasty melting pot.

The first place that I remember living was on Charlotte Street in the South Bronx. We moved there when I was about two years old. I loved the excitement of that neighborhood. Merchants and store owners crowded the busy sidewalks, wooing the pedestrians to their doorways to take a closer look at their goods. The sound of haggling voices was second only to screaming fire engines racing to the scene of a fire.

One of my favorite rituals on Charlotte Street was visiting Jake the Pickle Man. Jake was a short, round man who always wore an Applejack cap and a friendly smile. Jake didn't own a store, just a four-foot-high wooden pickle barrel on the corner of Charlotte and Jennings streets. He would search around in the pickle juice until he came up with the biggest, crunchiest, juiciest pickle he could find, slip it into a brown paper bag, and hold out his hand to collect one penny. Every time I took a bite I'd hold up the remainder, to measure just how much pickle was left to enjoy. This busy street scene went on from early morning to early

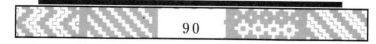

evening, when only the sunset, seduced by the rhythms of the Puerto Rican brothers drumming in the park, could quiet the drama of Charlotte Street. I lay in bed many nights and let the drums lull me to sleep.

Sunday was a strange day on Charlotte Street. It was so quiet and deserted, as if something bad had happened. I felt kind of sad and lonely. We attended Tried Stone Baptist Church on Boston Road. It was a small stone building on the corner of a large street, with steep stone steps to climb. Sunday school was held in the basement of the church and it was there that we received both the love and the discipline of Sister Campbell, our Sunday-school teacher. If anyone got out of line, Sister Campbell, dressed in a white uniform with white shoes, stockings, and a nurse's cap to match, would slowly come and stand by you, and without saying a word, would reach out her arm and cluck you upside your head! If you weren't the recipient of her punishment, you could enjoy the moment . . . silently.

The sound of footsteps above our heads meant that Sunday service would start soon. After Sister Campbell dismissed us, we'd race upstairs just in time to see the congregation strolling in, decked out in their finest clothes, exchanging compliments and greetings. No matter how much thought went into the outfits, no one ever topped Sister E. Kennedy, who always rushed quickly down the aisle (after most of the congregation had been seated), wearing some outrageous hat, to take her seat (but not before she gave the Reverend the eye) right down front.

I loved the opening procession. The opening and the closing were the two scheduled times that the whole church sang together. The choirs marched in singing an up-tempo song of praise and thanks. The ushers and nurses, with their air of authority and support, followed behind with their right arms folded across their lower back and their heads held high and proud. Once they were in place, the service began.

The music, of course, was the highlight of Sunday service for me. We had four choirs. The Number One Choir for the children was cute, the Young Adult Choir had a lot of energy, the Adult Choir was made up everyone who ever wanted to sing, and the Senior Choir never sang in pitch or in time. But no matter what the level of musicianship, the spirit was always sure to take over and move through the music.

I remember listening to my father sing "Cheer Up My Brother" in church and my heart would get so heavy. I guess I was feeling compassion but I don't really know. Then there was "Come Ye Disconsolate." That song would touch something so deep inside me that tears would start streaming down my face. I did not understand all the words, but that song let me know there was a place where I could go to release all of my sorrows. I couldn't wait until I'd be able to sing something that would bring such emotion to another.

When I started school, I was finally old enough to join the Tried Stone Baptist Church Number One Choir. Membership was open to kindergarten through third-grade students only! The two songs I got to sing lead on were "Satisfied with Jesus"

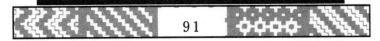

and "Soldiers in the Army." When it was time for my solo, I stepped away from the rest of the group toward my audience:

I looked at my hands and my hands looked new
I looked at my feet and they did too
And ever since that wonderful day, my soul's been satisfied!

As I sang about my hands, I held up my hands. As I sang about my feet, I pointed to my feet. The energy of the music moved my body. It felt so natural for me to be there. Although I had succeeded in moving my audience, I could tell that they were also amused by my flamboyant delivery as they shouted, "Go, little Robinson, go ahead!"

We moved to the Eastchester Projects, in the East Bronx, when I was in the second grade. Then Eastchester was a landscaped community of sixteen seven-story buildings, spread out over eight city blocks. The supervised playground, or "park" as we called it, was the meeting place for many hot summer days and intense summer nights. I grew up in these projects. I went from hanging on the monkey bars to hanging out on the park benches at night listening to music, singing, and just being loud! Playing 45 rpm records and using a banana to simulate a microphone with my closest friends was the daily routine. We sang everything from rhythm and blues with Sam Cooke to gospel with the Harmonizing Four. The only place my sister and I (she was six years older) would hang out together was around the record player, because I could strike up harmony with her and she loved to harmonize!

Nothing was like the city in the summer. It had to be the most diverse, stimulating, spacious, fastest place in the world. We were so proud of our city that we used to walk around saying, "New York, New York, so nice they named it twice." Sometimes we'd walk all the way from the Northeast Bronx to the South Bronx, taking a path through the Bronx Botanical Gardens. The gardens were a maze of greenery so lush that we'd automatically get quiet to hear the sounds created by the breeze and the birds in the bush.

Traveling to the Brooklyn Fox
I remember now
Traveling to the Brooklyn Fox
To see Patti LaBelle and the Blue Belles
In awe of Frankie Lymon and the Teenagers
Screaming my lungs out for Little Anthony and the Imperials

I remember now
Concerts down at Central Park
Hanging out at the Museum of Modern Art

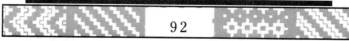

Taking It to the Streets

Taking a Staten Island Ferry ride
All night all right salsa dancing

I remember now
Ice skating in Central Park
Roller skating at Fordham rink
Going to the cabaret with my parents . . .

I Love Lucy, Amos 'n' Andy, The Little Rascals, Rocky and Bullwinkle,
American Bandstand, Soul Train, "Say It Loud, I'm Black and I'm
Proud," John F. Kennedy, Lee Harvey Oswald, Robert Kennedy,
Malcolm X, and Martin Luther King Jr./Assassinations!!! The World's
Fair, Coney Island, Rye Beach, and Pelham Bay Park/Amusements!!!
I remember, I remember, I remember . . .

I remember when they first built Freedom Land, a theme/amusement park built on top of swampland in the upper Bronx. The theme was the U.S.A. in the nineteenth century. Various cities and towns were represented by life-size model structures, sometimes depicting events of that period. But the entertainment stage was the place to be. All the major stars like Mary Wells, the tempting Temptations, Smokey and the Miracles, and Little Stevie Wonder were within arm's reach. There were no mobs to fight or heads to look over, no security guards ready to rip your head off for getting too close. Just you, the star, and the stars above. Maybe that's why they called it Freedom Land. It was great to get so close to the entertainers. They'd come off the stage and talk to us all the time. I say all the time because we'd sneak into Freedom Land almost every night. One night the Temptations even took us on some rides. The week Stevie Wonder appeared was one of the best of all. I thought we had an instant bond because we were both twelve years old and could sing. Stevie came off the stage one night and we called him over to the gate. He came and we introduced ourselves. I remember that when I told him my name, he said, "Hi, Louise baby." I guess my friends and I got a little too excited, because his mother came over to lead him away, but not before he gave me his tie. My friend Deborah was so upset over this gesture that she whined all night until I cut the tie and gave her half.

The first time I felt like a musician, I was thirteen years old and in junior high school. A monitor came into my classroom one day and announced that there were a few vacancies in the music program and asked if there were any brave souls who wanted to try out. My hand immediately went up. I followed the monitor through the hallway until we reached the band room. I didn't even know what instrument I wanted to play, so I tried all the strings from the violin to the bass. Never having played a string instrument before, I just went by how the instrument sounded to me and how it felt in my hands! Settling on the bass, I played it for the remainder of

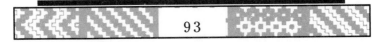

my junior high school years. I liked the bass because it was tall and brown like me. I could make full body contact with it and that felt good.

Playing in the orchestra was my introduction to classical music. I loved the dynamics of the music. It could be so aggressive one minute and then sweet and angelic the next. I was intrigued by all the different types of sounds and rhythms going on simultaneously. I really began to experience myself as part of a whole. That's when I took being a musician seriously. (The first instrument I ever played was the accordion. I received a toy accordion for Christmas when I was in the second grade. By the third grade I was taking accordion lessons, but after three years, we were clearly totally incompatible. I never felt in touch with that instrument. Besides, it always drove a wedge between me and my friends. Every time I started to play the accordion, the space would quickly empty out!)

In my senior year of junior high school, I auditioned for the High School of Music and Art. When I got to my audition room, I was greeted by a woman and a man. I felt comfortable with them. Good! They asked me what I was going to play and I said, "Beethoven's Fifth Symphony." They nodded to one another and then to me. I took a deep breath, fingered my starting position on my bass, and began to play. As I approached the most difficult passage, I felt them come to attention. My fingers moved quickly over the strings, engaging my body, and then settled perfectly into the slow passage. We all took a breath. The expression on their faces let me know that I had made a good impression. Auditions usually leave me sweaty, and anxious, and uncertain, but this time I felt like I had been flying and I was!

I attended the High School of Music and Art that fall and it was the first time I'd been exposed to such a large community of aspiring artists. These students came from all over the city, from every kind of cultural background. The downtown kids met the uptown kids; the Brooklyn kids met the Bronx kids; the East Side kids met the West Side kids; the Harlem kids met the Park Avenue kids, and the poor kids and the rich kids met all those in-between kids. I loved it!

Monica was one of my best friends in high school. We were more like soul sisters. We used to sing together, eat together, laugh together, and just plain enjoy each other.

I remember we came home from school one day after receiving reports cards that were not so good. My father, who was an even-tempered man, began to pace around us breathing heavily. It seemed as though his anger was caught in his throat and he could not speak. The tension was building up and Monica and I dared not even glance at each other. His deep sigh let us know he was about to say something. "Do you know why you got grades like this?" Before we could answer, he asked again loudly, "Do you!? Do you!!!?" I knew he was mad, because he could not find the words to express himself. So he continued: "Because of this!" And he struck a dance pose. "And because of this!" And he struck another pose. As his rage continued to build, so did his gestures, until he was literally dancing in front of us. By now the fear was replaced by our poor efforts to hold back our laughter.

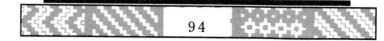

My father was not laughing. When he finished his dance, I guess he has shaken the words loose from his throat. He doesn't yell a lot. He spoke calmly and slowly. It was his wise and loving manner that evoked discipline, by our sheer desire to want to please him. Friends and family members alike are drawn to my father. He calmly let us know that our purpose in school was to learn as much as we could so that we might integrate the knowledge into our daily lives. My father strongly believed that the "real" school was outside the classroom, but that we should be equipped with as much as possible.

One day Monica and I were riding the A train to school. We were standing in the aisle holding on to the pole and singing when this slender man with a thin black mustache and a marcel hairdo interrupted us with "Excuse me, ladies, but I couldn't help overhearing your singing. My name is Gordy." He handed us a card. After he got off the train we laughed and mocked him but called him a couple of days later.

We went to his office on Forty-seventh Street between Broadway and Sixth Avenue. It was a small, somewhat dingy place. Typical small-time New York producer's office. When we arrived he introduced us to his partner, Joe. Joe was a sight for sore eyes because Joe was the down-to-earth type. He had a natural hairdo, took his time when he spoke, looked you straight in the eye, and had the warmest smile and disposition. Joe was also the piano player and composer—the artistic one. Within a few weeks (without consulting anyone) we had signed a contract and were learning tunes. We did background vocals for several male artists.

It was a lot of fun hanging out in the studio until the wee hours of the morning. But the strain of singing all night and going to school all day was starting to take its toll. Besides, our mothers were getting a little tired of being chaperones. The decision to end our association with the studio and cut things loose came at a party where we heard a very famous singer singing a song that we had done in the studio using the background vocals we had developed. We had been ripped off!!

The spring of 1968 rolled around and those who had applied to college were beginning to receive acceptance letters. I had not applied to college and only began to think about it when I realized some of my close high school buddies would be leaving town. I applied quite late to Howard University, since that's where one of my friends was going, hoping to be considered, and I was.

Once I got to Washington, I entered as a music major but I changed my major to drama before registration was complete. I knew in my gut that the theater was the platform for my soul expression. I felt much more confident as an actor than as a musician. I could immediately tap into places within me—without hearing Louise thinking—to deliver the characters I needed. It felt so natural to use my body demonstratively.

During my freshman year, a notice went up in the Drama Department announcing that the Arena Stage's Living Stage children's theater company was looking for actresses. I panicked when I found out that everyone and their mother were

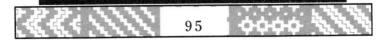

going to that audition! They were auditioning in New York City and Los Angeles as well as D.C.! Thank God for my boyfriend Will, who was more than encouraging. He just about took me to that audition himself. I survived the first round and received a call from the company manager saying that the director, Robert Alexander, wanted me to return to do another monologue. Although this was good news, it really brought the pressure on because I now knew I had a chance of getting the job.

Before my next scheduled audition, I ran into a friend of mine who had performed with the company the previous year. She informed me that the director liked way-out stuff. "Great," I replied, "right up my alley!"

I decided to deliver my monologue as though I was trapped in a box with the four sides closing in on me. It gave me great motivation on which to build tension. I don't know who got the biggest high, me finding out how far I could go or him waiting to see how far I would go. Anyway it earned me a third callback. Let me tell you something. When you get to a third callback, even if you didn't care about getting the job in the beginning . . . you damn sure want it then!

Arriving at the last audition, I thought this would be my final shot. I was not asked to bring anything to this audition, just to show up and be prepared to stay a while.

Robert Alexander (a slight man, on the short side, with curly hair, thick mustache, vulnerable smile, and intense, passionate eyes) was pacing the room looking a little nervous. His facial expression was going back and forth between a forced smile and a serious glare. I stood quietly watching him but not too closely. Thank goodness there was someone else in the room. He finally introduced me to the pianist. He began to give me direction. He wanted me to pretend that I was a soldier in Vietnam. As I played out what I thought it would be like to be in the middle of a war in that jungle, a chair flew across the room and crashed to the floor. But just as I was about to question his action, another chair flew across the room. While all this was going on, he started shouting out descriptions of what the weather would be like, what the heat and bodies would smell like, what the destruction would look like. Just when I thought I had a handle on how he worked, he yelled to me at the top of his voice to sing "On a Clear Day." I sang it as I continued to dodge chairs. More scenes and songs followed, but nothing topped that "opening number." To this day, that was my most unusual audition.

I worked with Living Stage for two seasons. The company consisted of five actors (three women and two men), a company manager (who handled bookings), a stage manager (who took care of our technical needs), a musical director (piano player), and the director. We were an improvisational children's touring company. This is where I began to understand my power onstage. We took turns leading the performances. The leader was responsible for direct communication with the audience and then back to the actors. Our improvisation was based on audience suggestion. I never wanted to lead. It made me very uncomfortable and I was going to

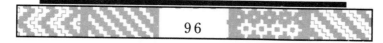

have to face this company's concept called "the leader." I know now that a good leader is present always; however, I was still wondering if I was all right onstage. I know now that I *was* ready then.

I'd completed one year in Howard's Drama Department by the time I joined the Living Stage company and up until then I thought I knew what improvisational theater was. By the time I'd finished training five days a week, eight hours a day, for eight weeks, I had gained great respect for the process. My whole perspective about it changed. I used to think it was an accepted way of loosely presenting an acting scene. But I soon found out that good improvisational theater could appear to have been directed and rehearsed. I see why jazz musicians love that form so much. It's built on improvisation, and everything is fresh and exciting, even the mistakes.

I met Robert Hooks, the founder and executive producer of the D.C. Black Repertory Company, in 1970. He attended a play that I was in at Howard University and I met him backstage after the show. He told me that he was starting an acting company and would like me to audition for it. I auditioned and was asked to be a member of the resident company. It took almost two years and several variations of workshops before the company was finally underway.

The artistic director was a man by the name of Motojicho. Moto (as we called him) was big in stature, with dark smooth skin and a very strong presence. He loved the theater and loved his stable of young actors that he could teach and mold. I use the word "teach" instead of "direct" because Moto was interested in training us for a life in the theater, not just to act in a play. Moto's personality was more like that of a parent. He was stern and disciplined. The more we were together, the more he'd laugh with us, but he always had that "I'm the boss" attitude. Everybody loved Moto, even when he made them mad.

Robert Hooks was definitely *the* personality. He was warm and very easy to approach. He too had a tremendous love for the theater and the desire to give us young black actors as many opportunities as possible to perform in this arena.

The D.C. Black Repertory Company (or the Rep) was the fertile ground out of which grew a family of creative journeywomen and -men. The acting company consisted of twelve members. All other actors were in training in the hope of joining the company (and many of them eventually did). There were several classes that all members were required to take. Dance was taught by Mike Malone and Charles Auggins, scene study by Moto, voice by Bernice Reagon (assisted by Carol Maillard), and I taught improvisational acting.

When I first met Bernice, I watched her very closely. When I first meet another strong personality, I am usually very quiet and I watch them closely. She was a slow-talking, no-nonsense type of woman, but there was something different about her no nonsense. Well . . . it wasn't just that she didn't tolerate distracting behavior; she didn't tolerate insecurity. It was okay to feel insecure; you just couldn't sound like it! If Bernice gave you a vocal phrase to do and you were busy explaining why you couldn't do it, she'd cut you off in the middle of your sentence

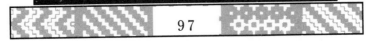

with a calm "Uh-huh, cum mon, sang." Bernice would be halfway through the song and you'd still be sitting over in the corner trying to get yourself ready. Bernice could sing a line differently than I had ever heard anyone sing a line. It wasn't that it was so high or so low or so intricate; it was that her delivery was to the point and meaningful.

Bernice's vocal classes were fun. Everybody had a voice as far as Bernice was concerned. Some voices were prettier than others and some people knew their voices better than others, but everybody had one. They just needed something to sing about.

A company member by the name of LeTari suggested that we get together as a smaller ensemble of singers, and we went to Bernice with the idea. So on one of those summer evenings we all met in that little room next door to the main theater to rehearse. Bernice named us Sweet Honey In The Rock. She sang it for us and we immediately took it on as our own. The name was perfect for us.

At one evening rehearsal there were only four of us. That became the original group: Carol Maillard, Bernice Reagon, Mie, and I. Carol and I were just out of college, Mie was just out of high school, and Bernice was a mother of two and had already begun her journey in the world. That was the seed of what we now know as Sweet Honey In The Rock. It's funny how this particular quartet became the solid group. I think that this was the group all along and sometimes the excess has to be chiseled away before you get to the form that was meant to be in the first place. It's like a marriage; when the right people come together, you know you got it. You just know!

It was a privilege to carry the word to so many people in our music. The music was strong and powerful and so were the women who sang it. Our first full Sweet Honey concert was held right there in the theater. Carol in white, Bernice in purple, Mie in blue, and me in red. We looked beautiful. Everybody was excited to see what we were going to do and I couldn't wait to show them either. We walked onstage. We stood silent. I looked across at the other women. Mie was standing like the "queen of everything," Bernice stood as though she was where she belonged, and Carol and I looked like we were about to fly. We broke into the first song. We sang about love coming, love going, going to get love, we sang about Joe Willie, we sang about our lives in struggle, we sang about our sisters and brothers and mothers and fathers. We sang our hearts out. Everyone was moved by the evening, and when it was over, I knew that I was a part of something that was going to have a great impact on the human community.

It did not take long, however, before we started to experience internal conflicts related to schedules and other career interests. Mie left the group in the very early stages of Sweet Honey. I can't say why for certain—but Mie was a very independent young woman and had very strong ideas about the way her life should go. We held auditions at the Rep to replace her. Many people came to sing.

I remember when Evelyn Harris walked into the theater. I knew her from

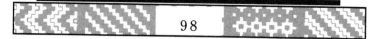

school, since we'd entered the College of Fine Arts at Howard the same year. I encouraged the group to take a special listen, and Evie clearly held her own. We all decided that she should be the person to replace Mie.

Carol and I were also actresses and we had opportunities to perform in plays. Once, Carol was in a play and could not take a trip with us to Philadelphia. We had to find a substitute. We took two, Rosie Lee Hooks and Ayodele Harrington. We decided to have five people so that if one person had to be out, the sound of the group could remain intact with the remaining four to perform. We traveled up on the Amtrak train. I'll always remember that trip. My daughter Asha was born that same month. Very tired and somewhat blue, I sat in the seat by the window holding this five-pound person in my arms, on my way to perform a concert. I cried quietly in that corner. I was tired. I tried to recall Bernice's words to me when I was carrying Asha. She told me not to stop, to keep going, to put my child on my back and keep stepping. She told me about how she went into the studio with her little babies in her arms. I tried to hear her words, but I felt so tired . . . and confused.

When we got to Philly, I had a crib sent up to my hotel room. I had already left that bout with self-pity on the train and was in motion trying to get what I needed for myself and my baby so that I could sing my concert. Although the women in Sweet Honey were very supportive, you still had to take care of yourself, because everyone else was doing whatever they had to do to get themselves ready. I hurried about gathering everything I needed to take to the theater for Asha and me. When we got there I asked an usher if she would be willing to hold my child while I performed. She agreed and I went onstage to join the others for the sound check. When the concert was over, I thanked the usher, got my baby, and returned to the hotel.

Sweet Honey's stage extended far beyond what the human eye could see. It did not begin with the introduction and end with the audience's applause. We were living people trying to pursue our music and maintain families, maintain love relationships, maintain contact with family members, and maintain clarity regarding their (and our) personal paths—maintain clarity regarding who we were. Some of us were even maintaining careers in the theater simultaneously.

To be in Sweet Honey you had to constantly look at your life, because the music was all those parts of your life that the DJs did not play on the radio stations and the TV did not flash across the screen. It was not what you call popular music. But it was food for the soul. Sweet Honey's stage was where I got to test out my ability to "be present" with my audience. I had done a lot of work with that during my time with Living Stage. Bernice was also a great teacher in that area. She had a way of talking to the audience like she was in her living room. It was always a natural inclination for me to move toward the audience when I felt like I was really cookin', but I was still learning to take my time with them, to feel comfortable taking a moment to think about something and letting them see me do it. I was learning to ask for their participation and getting it even if they initially thought

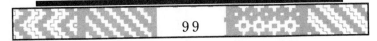

they didn't want to participate. Sweet Honey's stage is a big stage and I think that's the reason it has a worldwide audience. There is enough room to accommodate them as a part of that stage.

I remember walking onstage at an outdoor festival concert. The crowd was enormous. When we walked out, the sound of so many people seemed like a continuous sigh until we sat and then there was a hush. I really had a sense of myself as this vessel that could expand larger than I could imagine.

One of the best stages I ever sang on was at Wolf Trap in 1976. I cannot forget that sound system. We came for the sound check, sat down, and when the sound man asked us to sing something, we went into our usual thing. I heard myself think about taking a breath. That is how good this system was. You could hum in the tiniest voice and that mike would pick up the sweetness of that hum and place it all the way on the ear of a person sitting in the last row. It felt so good singing and not feeling like I had to project my voice a certain distance to be heard. It really gave me the opportunity to invite the audience into my world. I got to play more and find more places in my voice.

The summer of 1975, we performed at the Mariposa Festival in Toronto, Canada. We shared the stage with the singer and guitarist Taj Mahal and I was too happy. It was a beautiful place, on an island. The sun was shining, the breeze blew easy, and we began our concert under blue skies. I guess we were halfway through the set in the middle of one of Carol's leads when a few drops of rain hit the stage. The sky quickly darkened and the rain just broke through the clouds. Before I knew it we were running from the stage for cover. A tent on the site was provided for the entertainers and we found shelter there, but when the water started rising *inside* the tent . . . ! Announcements were being made for people to calmly leave the island and for women and children to be taken across first. I started to feel a little funny. Everyone hurried to the ferry, but the crowd was too much. Somehow the group became separated, but Bernice and I were still together. We started to look for another route off the island. I remember climbing a fence, walking forever, taking a city bus after a ferry ride, until we found our way back to the hotel, soaking wet of course, but so glad to be there!

Later that same year, we performed at a festival at the University of Chicago. We landed in Chicago one night in the middle of a snowstorm. I was in awe all the way from the airport to the university because Chicago looked so much like New York. We were tired from the trip but needed to make it on to the concert hall for a sound check and the show. When we arrived at the school, we were shown to our dressing area and told that we would be sharing it with the other group that was performing that evening. That was not what we wanted to hear, but that sort of thing came with the territory. As the first member of the other group walked through the doorway, Evie asked (as if to claim territory), "And who are you?" "George Benson," he answered. Evie started screaming and carrying on, and

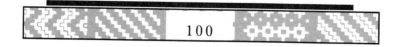

George Benson, the Grammy Award-winning guitarist, just quietly laughed it off. It was very funny.

It was at this concert that we met Bruce Kaplan, founder of Flying Fish Records, who released our first album, *Sweet Honey In The Rock,* during the summer of 1976.

There are so many stages and experiences that I could write about but that would take as much time as I actually spent with the group. Some things that stick out in my mind are:

♦ Burning up the stage at the Smithsonian's Festival of American Folklife, 1974–76, especially in 1976, when they celebrated the bicentennial of the country with a twelve-week festival. We sang in the pulpit area of the church stage, a structure that resembled a small country church with no side, but with a pulpit and roof and small tower. We also sang on the porch of the house-and-yard stage. I sang "Traveling Shoes." I would actually take a journey when I did that song. The group's voices, rising and falling behind me, filled every space with music.

> *. . . Well—death come riding by the sinner's door*
> *He said, "Come on, sinner, are you ready to go?"*
> *Well, that sinner stooped down*
> *But he didn't have no shoes*
> *And he counted up his cost and he began to move*
> *He move on down to the Jordan stream*
> *And he cried, "Oh Lord, I ain' been redeemed . . ."*
> *Buckled up his shoes . . .*

♦ Getting stuck in the mud on some back road in Peoria, Illinois, with my brand-new expensive pumps on, trying to push the car.

♦ The first time I sang "Joan Little" I felt like I was doing the most important thing in the world. It was not only my privilege to share my voice as a singer but my responsibility to share my voice as a human being!

♦ Going to see Odetta perform in a club after a concert in Chicago. The group went onstage and sang "Amazing Grace" with her.

♦ Recording our first album. The studio is such a different medium. The challenge of bringing the urgency of the sound to the record was a big one. I think it takes more than one album to do it.

♦ Leaving the group in 1976 and moving to the Virgin Islands to spend time raising my daughter and myself and finding out that I didn't have to go anywhere to do that.

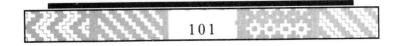

♦ Moving back to New York in 1977 and forming a group with Carol Maillard (who had since left Sweet Honey) and Dianaruthe Wharton (who wrote one of the songs on our first album). We were hot! It was the Sweet Honey school of counterpoint and multiple leads, singing conscientious R&B accompanied by a smokin' band!

♦ Going to see Sweet Honey in concert and being called onstage to do a number with the group. Feels good. Feels strange sometimes but always feels like home.

♦ Being in Sweet Honey's Tenth Anniversary Concert in 1983. All the women who had ever sung with Sweet Honey were invited to perform. Fifteen women came. The week prior to the concert was spent organizing the program and rehearsing. The original group met the present group. The in-betweeners were lost in the drama. The rise and the surrender of egos took place. The result? One, two, three amazing concerts performed for full houses in Washington, D.C., in November 1983.

After more than a decade of following the theater, I moved to San Francisco, in search of the rest of me. In 1988 I walked up Seventeenth Street to the glass door marked "Festival at the Lake" to interview for a job. Festival at the Lake is an annual three-day urban fair held in downtown Oakland, California, on the shores of Lake Merritt, highlighting the diverse cultural community of the Bay Area.

On the way to the interview I had decided that I did not want to work for the festival after all, because then I would not be available to audition for acting jobs. But by the end of the interview I had made clear my interest in coordinating the festival's *six hundred volunteers.*

It was not long before the intense detailed work of coordinating six hundred people was working my nerves. I needed some creative outlet desperately. One day I came into the office and with the publicity director, Gillie Haynes Joseph, began to write a song about this great Oakland community event. When the song was completed, I gathered everyone in the office to hear what I had done. I had already taught it to a few of my friends, so I could present the song in harmony. It was sweet. The festival director asked if we could perform the song at our open house. I said yes.

My first year at the Festival at the Lake was in a brand-new office space and we were having an open house to inaugurate our new home. Our office was perfect for the debut of the song.

We sang from the second-level balcony which overlooked the offices below. Everyone who was anyone on the Oakland business and political scene came by. When we finished singing they were amazed. The Festival at the Lake had just presented to them a live musical press release about an event that highlighted their city. Before the party ended I had received several requests to have the group come and sing "Festival Song" at various organizations and places of business.

By the time I had my exit interview I had put together an idea for a program

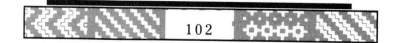

that would solicit volunteer singers from the Bay Area community and have them sing a musical press release (written by me) for various community organizations and businesses. The festival director was right there with me. We agreed that would be my program for the following year. I named that program "Street Sounds." We were bringing the word about this annual Oakland event to the streets for all the people to hear. I wrote a bluesy shuffle:

Ba doom dee dop— Ba doom dee dop— Ba doom de dop
Gather Round Everybody
And let me tell you what's going down
Oakland's throwing a party
we're gonna light up this whole town
we got rhyme and rhythm to rock you steady
a weekend of pure delight—get ready!!

In November 1989, I formed a professional singing group of six singers: Darlene Spears, Michelle Jacques, Bobby Williams, Naomi True, Steven Thomas, and myself. I kept the name Street Sounds because people had begun to identify the name with the faces. The response was overwhelming and there we were trying to prepare enough material to perform at holiday celebrations. Word spread quickly about the group and about me writing jingles for special occasions. We spent the first year and half trying to catch up to the requests. It was good but it seemed like there was another way to do it.

At the beginning of our second year, I decided that the group should be in concert more. By May 1990, we had performed in concert four times and one was with Pete Seeger, in a benefit concert for the Middle East Children's Alliance. I was told that Sweet Honey had performed with him in New York just a week before us.

The first Sweet Honey song we did was "Seven Principles." We were doing a lot of Christmas parties and I thought it would be great to throw in a really empowering song. At the same time the group was searching to find its own legs. As we moved along, a few more Sweet Honey songs crept into the repertoire, and if they were not Sweet Honey songs, they were traditional African American work songs, or African chants, but something other than our R&B and jazz.

At first not everyone was comfortable singing this music. It wasn't slick enough and it wasn't popular. But the music started to reveal itself to us in such a way that we all just stepped onto the path. One member read an article in a book that inspired them to know more about the old music. One day someone came into rehearsal and could not wait to jump into "Down by the Riverside" because he had seen Bernice Reagon on TV the night before and her interview opened up a new space for him.

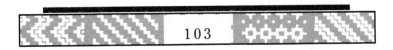

There was an energy that was emerging in the group when we sang these old songs, not to mention the healing that seems to take place in the audiences that we sang them to. We were doing a concert in Santa Rosa in the spring of 1992 and we were performing "Juba." I went into the audience to different people to sing along with me. When the concert was over, I was in the parking lot getting in my car when this woman pulls up and gets out and comes over to me. She asked if I remembered a man sitting in a wheelchair in the aisle. I said, "Yes, I do." She pointed to the same man, who was in her car. She told me that he was her husband and was in a wheelchair because he had had a stroke. She said that she was somewhat anxious when I came to her husband and placed the microphone in front of him to sing. She then informed me that her husband had not uttered a word since his stroke until that moment when he sang his part in "Juba." I got chills, thinking about the power of singing. . . .

We still sing contemporary music, but now the music is sewn with the thread of our African roots. The textures are three-dimensional now and we are surrendering to our calling. We are discovering ourselves as songwriters, singers, and musicians and as family members.

It is 1992 and I am constantly looking at the people whom I have met on my journey, some of them there for just a short time and others there for a lifetime. Looking back, I see that everything that I've done has contributed in a big way to what I am doing now. It's been a full circle but all the better.

May 1992, it is evening, and I am sitting in a hotel restaurant in Berkeley, California, talking to Bernice Reagon. "I have a group, Bernice." She is very excited to hear that. She asked me the name of the group; I told her, "Street Sounds." You couldn't have told me fifteen years ago when I left Sweet Honey that I would return to the music, to the sound, return home. Two years ago when it was clear that I was starting a vocal group, I had no clue that the old music and chants would find their way into this group. I should have known, because spirit will always find its way into a space held open for it.

I am discovering myself as a leader. Twenty-one years after Living Stage and I am still growing into that role. There are so many times that I look back on my days in Sweet Honey working with Bernice because so many of her actions have become clearer to me since I've been wearing the same shoes. I am happy to know that my teacher and friend is also happy about my California family. It is an extension of the Sweet Honey family, which is an extension of the D.C. Black Repertory Company family, which is an extension of the families we grew up in. I don't know where we're going, but I do know that we're in good hands and traveling the "high road" and I got on my "Traveling Shoes."

Sweet Honey is my rock
It is the reputation that precedes me

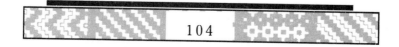

Taking It to the Streets

It is the light that guides me
It is the shadow that grounds me
  and it is the earth that holds my flower.

Bernice, Carol, Mie, Evie, Pat, Yasmeen, Tulani, Aisha, Ysaye, Shirley, Nitanju, Rosie Lee, Ayodele, you are all of me and I am all of you and I love you!!

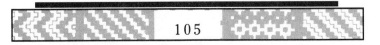

7

"HI, I'M AN ORIGINAL SWEET HONEY IN THE ROCK"

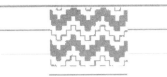

MICHAEL HODGE

One of my favorite ways to introduce myself to a Sweet Honey In The Rock fan is to say, "Hi, I'm an original Sweet Honey . . ." There's always a perplexed look and a stuttered "I thought they were always all women." I then explain that I never sang publicly with the group but worked with Bernice and a couple of other guys and three or four women while Bernice designed the group.

If memory serves, we went through several different configurations—two men and four women, three men and three women, three men and four women. And all of a sudden, as far as I knew, there were no more rehearsals.

I spoke to Louise about it last year and she said, "And one day we went to rehearsals and none of the men showed up."

"No, sweetie, that's not the way it happened," I laughed. "We weren't asked to show up."

When I spoke to Carol, her memory of that rehearsal when the men didn't show up was the same as Louise's. So maybe it was serendipity, fate, or whatever—the way it's supposed to be.

I didn't really know what had happened with the group until that first night they performed at the Last Colony Theater on Georgia Avenue in Washington, D.C.

It still counts as one of my most exhilarating, beautiful memories.

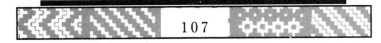

As the audience filed into the theater before the show, I saw Carol Maillard in the lobby, just kind of hanging out.

"What are you doing out here? Shouldn't you be backstage?" I asked.

"No, I'm all right. Just wait," she responded.

The lights began to flash, indicating that the concert was about to start. When I made my way to my seat the house lights went down. I was suddenly engulfed, totally surrounded by the lush full sound of these four women who were my friends but at that moment could have been angels. At first, I didn't know where the sound was coming from. Then I realized that it truly was coming from all around me as the women made their way to the stage, each from a different corner of the room. It was a moment that truly filled my heart. I listened with tears in my eyes. Bernice, Louise, Carol, and Mie made me know what pure song is all about. Beautiful. Bernice, I love you.

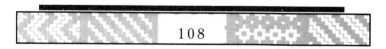

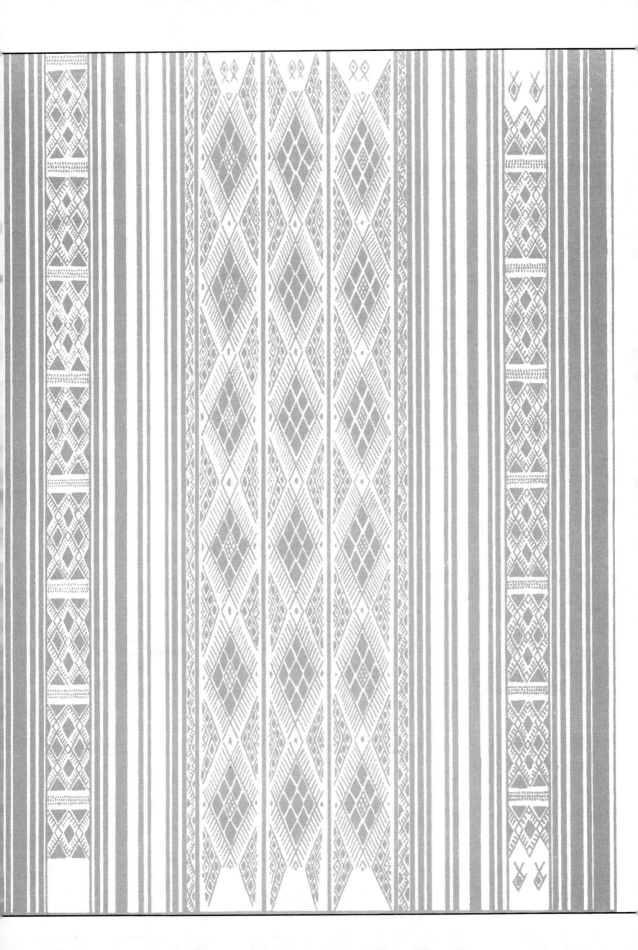

LEFT: WORKS-IN-PROGRESS: CAROL MAILLARD, DIANARUTHE WHARTON, LOUISE ROBINSON, NEW YORK, 1979.

TOP RIGHT: CAROL MAILLARD-WARE WITH SON, JORDAN MAILLARD-WARE.

RIGHT: CAROL MAILLARD'S MOTHER, SHIRLEY ELIZABETH PARKER MAILLARD.

BOTTOM RIGHT: CAROL MAILLARD IN SONG, NEW YORK, 1984.

(ALL PHOTOS COURTESY OF CAROL MAILLARD PERSONAL COLLECTION)

8

I ALWAYS KNEW
I COULD SING

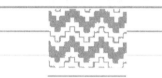

CAROL MAILLARD

They must have done something to me in the womb. My parents loved to sing.
Thomas and Elizabeth, Bo Bo and Liz, sang jazz every day. They loved music;
and in some way, they seriously passed it on to me. That must be where I got the
idea early on that I could sing.

The first song I remember singing is "Hey There," composed by Richard
Adler for the Broadway show *Pajama Game.* They would have me stand up in the
doorway, like it was a stage, and I would sing to them. It made them so happy, and
we clapped, and laughed, and sang together some more. It's one of the few memories I have of the three of us together, as a family. Although I was about two at the
time, whenever I hear that tune I am back in that moment. The sounds and the joy
are alive for me again.

So I sang . . . all the time. I acted with my best friend Deborah Hackey and
made up all kinds of songs and shows. She always played Olivia de Havilland and I
played Marilyn Monroe. And I played the piano with great passion, although before
the age of seven I'd never had a lesson. I played whatever came into my mind, and I
played by ear. My grandmother used to have a lot of tolerance then. I was really in a
world all my own. The idea that I could be on the stage one day, or in a movie, was
not a foreign concept. It was a natural place for me to be. Where that came from, I
cannot say. And anytime there was a movie musical on television, I sang and danced

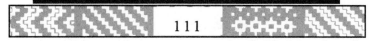

with abandon. My destiny was clear to me and at no time did I ever doubt that I'd be the best at it! I was obsessed!

My grandparents, Lawrence Parker and Ada Powell Parker, moved from Baltimore to Philadelphia in the 1940s, I think around 1945, when my Mom turned thirteen. I was born in Philly and my early memories are quite vivid and rich of 1234 North Fifteenth Street. In that household, a three-story red brick row house, lived my grandparents, whom I called Mamma and Daddy, my Aunt Lucille's son Michael Parker (I was crazy about my cousin), me (my nickname was Lynnie), and occasional tenants to whom Mamma rented the third floor. This home was a wonderland to me. Before coming to 1234, I lived with my parents, Mommy and Daddy Bo Bo, a block away in an apartment. But in my grandparents' house, I had room to grow, places to hide out, a stage, a backyard, and a big picture window . . . and quite an imagination. . . .

> *Playin' games and fantasizin'*
> *Alone,*
> *My only-child self*
> *Lovin' the light streaming*
> > *down over my bed in the morning,*
> *Where's Michael?*
> *I follow his big ol' self,*
> *anywhere I can, everywhere*
> *I can*
> *I make daily music*
> > *on my mommy's upright piano*
> *So much music pours*
> > *from tiny hands*
> *And I cry*
> > *from some deep pool*
> > *of liquid love inside*
> *The smell of Gran'daddy's pipe*
> > *is like cherry smoke*
> *He sings me to sleep each night*
> *And teaches me how he*
> > *skins possum.*
> *Only child*
> *Games, playin' dress-up.*
> > *and my daddy Bo Bo*
> > *told me I was so full of love,*
> *I ran all over*
> > *sayin' to everyone*
> *"I love you"*

Ah-men
And Ada,
My mommy and Auntie Cille's mamma,
Braidin' and brushin' and greasin'
My already too long and thick hair
Bathin' me in a big tub in
  the middle of the livin' room floor
  then combin' my hair, her passion.
Sometimes,
  she'd take white cord
  and
  wrap, wrap, wrap each section
  so tiiight—and stiffff . . .
Just hoping it'd
  grow some more . . .
Music flowin', words crashin',
  as time moves on, life changes from light to dim . . .
Where's my mommy and daddy?
There are
    tears,
But no longer from
Music pouring from a child's heart.

By the time I was three, my parents both had to leave Philadelphia and I stayed at Fifteenth Street. Soon after, my grandparents started having a hard time together. They were battling it out after forty years of marriage and everything was in turmoil. Because I could pretend that I was somebody else, I could remove my real pain from the surface by changing my voice or my clothes.

In 1959, my grandparents finally broke up. Mamma and I had to move from our three-story house to a small apartment, a room on the top floor of a Holy Sanctified Church owned by the Reverend Hinton and his wife, Miss Daisy. By the time we moved there, we had joined about five different churches and Mamma had settled on the Catholic church because they had a good educational system. If we became Catholic, she wouldn't have to pay for me to go to school. It was a good deal as far as she could see.

The Catholic church was perfect for me at the time. It was quiet and ordered. Everything was clean and reverent. For some reason, when I heard the chants and hymns, I would want to cry. Not out of sadness, because I didn't have a name for the feeling, but I knew it had something to do with my heart and my perception of God. The same thing would happen to me at night as I fell asleep listening to Sister Lawrence thumping that piano and the Reverend Hinton preaching in the church on the first floor. Sometimes I just couldn't keep my body still. I knew that as a

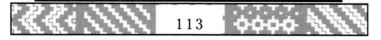

Catholic girl I wasn't supposed to be enjoying this holiness experience so much, but I kept "This Little Light of Mine" and "I'm a Soldier" right up there with Kyrie Eleison and Agnus Dei. My soul was enchanted and stimulated by them all.

My Aunt Lucille took me to a rock-and-roll show at the Uptown Theater in Philadelphia when I was about six. She tells me now that she took me to concerts and shows because she knew I wanted to be an actress. How blessed I was to have had those early influences and her support. I heard Baby Washington (a popular rock-and-roll singer in 1958) sing that evening. I remember thinking intensely: I can do that.

The sixties . . .
1617 Poplar Street,
two rooms with private bath
a new neighborhood
Mamma's getting older and really impatient with me
Too loud, too quiet, too womanish, too mannish,
I dance, I sing,
I dream of escape
into
The Shirelles, Patti LaBelle and the Blue Belles (I
could hit that high note at the end of "Down the
Aisle")
The Duke of Earl, the Marvelous Marvelettes, Martha and
the Vandellas
Thank God for the Uptown and Motown Revue
Me and Robert, first Saturday of the month, third in
line, waiting for a ticket, rain or shine (Robert
Stephens was my best friend of all times)
Then practicing in the hallway till Mamma says, "Y'all
stop all that noise! Robert, go home."
So much music going on in me as I fall asleep still
Sister Perpetua and my piano lessons,
glee club,
"The Name Game,"
writing poems,
Smokey Robinson,
Odetta and Peter, Paul and Mary
and Nina Simone and Louis Armstrong
A grand time,
time of growth and struggle,
my own search for a safe place to be,
to be loved and appreciated and understood.

Daddy Bo Bo is back home and
all is well on many levels,
he still sings all the time.
"I'm gonna be an actress and a singer,
and if I can't do that,
I'll be a hairdresser."
Daddy says, "What a talented child you are.
I'm proud of you."
Can heaven be any better than this?

Here come the Beatles, Dusty Springfield, Lulu,
and the British Invasion.
A bit of Coltrane's sax train is in there too,
and Stevie Wonder, Ahmad Jamal, Sammy Davis Jr.,
Barbra Streisand and
yes, the Supremes and
yessss Marvin Gaye and Tammi Terrell,
and how could I do without gospel Aretha, jazz Aretha, and
Aretha, Aretha . . . Aretha.

When I started attending John W. Hallahan Catholic Girls' High School in 1965, I decided that my extracurricular activity would be the glee club. Maybe I'd get a solo, maybe I'd get to be president of the glee club, maybe . . . As I sat in the rehearsal classroom, I looked around at all the other freshmen. I didn't know one of them. There was no one from my parish or my neighborhood. And that wasn't so good, because my grandmother, Mamma, was not going to allow me to come home after a rehearsal alone, especially if the sun was about to set.

Suddenly I heard my name being whispered at the door. "Carol, come on and join the orchestra." It was my friend Gale Dingle. The nun wasn't there at the moment, so she ran into the class excitedly. "If you join the orchestra you won't have to take gym. And you won't have to do detention if you get in trouble with the discipline office, *and* Renee, Pat, Alene, Donita, and Dorothy are all joining. We can have a good time. Come on." How could I resist? I dashed down to the other end of the hall and asked if I could sign up. Gale passed me a note. "Tell Sister Giovanni that you want to play the violin. That's what I'm doing." Okay, violin. And before I could even open my mouth Sister Giovanni was checking out my full African American lips and saying, "Oh, how about the horn?" "No," I said, "I want to play the violin." She looked at me, and smiled, and signed me up. Mamma would not complain now since Gale was coming home with me.

During my four years at Hallahan, the orchestra became the focal point of my life. I loved it. I loved the music, the rehearsals, the people, and most of all, I loved my teachers. Sister Giovanni had plans for me from the beginning. At the end of

my second year, she had placed me in the first violin section and let me study and sit with the seniors, which definitely added spice to the mix. The Black orchestra members were proud and excited but some of the White girls did not like it. I could play better than any one in my section, so their grumbles didn't phase me at all.

Since Mamma's health was fragile—she had had two strokes and suffered from diabetes and high blood pressure, and her nerves were a wreck—she kept a tight rein on me once we moved to Poplar Street. Her daughter, my mommy, Liz, had strayed and Mamma believed that "fruit don't fall far from the tree." I was, no doubt, headed for a life on the streets just like Liz, so she did everything she could to keep me on the straight and narrow, by any means necessary.

In 1966, Mamma had a stroke when our apartment was painted with some of the worst, cheapest paint imaginable. I couldn't see, my eyes were so swollen. We both had headaches. Suddenly her speech was slurred, her face was distorted, and her movements were pained. Aunt Lucille came, and the ambulance arrived, and we went to the hospital. Father Jordan gave her the last rites. I told her she would be all right. I hugged her the best I could, since we never hugged each other. That was January 25. She stayed in a coma for exactly one month. She died on February 25.

Mamma passed away during my freshman winter and I went to live with Aunt Lucille. My life was to open up in a way that it never could have with Mamma, because she was so terrifyingly strict with me. Aunt Lucille enjoyed fun and shows, and music was a very big part of all that I did and thought about. But still, my singing was personal, I sang to myself, around the house, but never, ever sang publicly in front of a soul. I'd practice playing my violin anywhere, anytime, but my voice, my singing, that aspect of myself was private and well hidden. Besides, Gale made fun of me every time she heard me. But when I picked up my instrument, no one could make a joke.

By my junior year music was clearly going to get me to college. I took private violin lessons and joined chamber groups. When senior year arrived I was concert-master, student conductor, and had a little after rehearsal quintet that I conducted. It was really unheard of for a Black girl to be involved in an aspect of Hallahan life that was usually dominated by Whites. I did not care what others might say or think. I was determined.

Catholic University of America accepted me into their violin performance program. My family was elated, but couldn't figure out how I could earn a living playing the violin. *I* knew I could sing and play the violin. So if I got a job playing in a recording studio, maybe someone would hear me singing on a break and would hire me as a singer too. Hey! I could dream, couldn't I? They all thought I was nuts, but went along with the program. Onward to Washington, D.C.

How mysterious the ways of fate. Violin was much more fun at Hallahan. At Catholic University, it was downright boring. I wanted to play jazz and show music.

I Always Knew I Could Sing

The Music Department was so stiff. But I *was* in college and I was in Chocolate City, U.S.A. I did my work and went back to singing and playing the piano in my dorm late at night. When I'd sit down to the piano in the social room, my hands would move effortlessly across the keys. I'd hum along, maybe adding a few lyrics. I'd burn incense and turn the lights down low. Peace, stillness, and sweetness.

I couldn't quite figure out how I was going to incorporate my musical preferences into the rigid structure of the Music Department, but in my sophomore year I received the opportunity to do just that.

One evening as I sat playing, composing, and singing my little heart out, Paula Acoin, a student in the Drama Department, said, "I love what you're playing. Can you write music?" I told her that I could make a melody out of just about any words I heard, and I played her a few of my melodies.

The next day, Paula asked me to compose the music to the Annual Soph Show, which was a showcase for the up-and-coming shining stars of the Drama Department. It was just what I was looking for, and I said yes. They put me in the show. I sang, solo, for the first time in public my own original music and lyrics.

The head of the department, Father Hartke, fell in love with my voice and declared me a part of the Drama Department. This acknowledgment marked the beginning of my life as a singer. That Christmas, 1970, I went on my first tour with the Drama Department as a featured performer in a USO tour to Germany, Belgium, and Holland. When we returned we were invited for tea at the Nixon White House with his daughter Julie.

At the end of my sophomore year, it was evident a change had to come. I decided to change my major to voice since I was traveling and singing regularly and my violin studies were falling behind quite a bit. My pianist, John Franceschina, and I picked out three songs to show my vocal range: a classical German Dieder Keider lied, a jazz tune, and a song from the Broadway musical *Purlie.* I set up an audition to switch my scholarship from violin to voice. We didn't have time to do the classical piece, so we did "Since I Fell for You" and the song from *Purlie,* "I Got Love." I sang with all my being, using as many textures in my voice as I could. The dean told me quite coldly, "The way you want to sing, you don't need any lessons for that." I was really taken aback by that remark. What do I need this for? They don't know what's going on. I'll just leave the school, since there's nothing here for me. I'll go to Howard and do it all. Father Hartke heard about my situation and my decision and offered me a full scholarship in the Drama Department. I could sing, act, compose, play violin if I so chose . . . and travel with the touring company too? Shoot, could it be any better? Now, let me rewind a little. . . .

Wintertime 1970. I auditioned for a Black professional acting company (the D.C. Black Repertory Company) being formed by the star of the TV show *NYPD,* Robert Hooks. This is what I should be doing. I go; I am seen; I get a callback and I am accepted. Black theater, what does it all mean? Will this make me a star? When do we start? . . . Summer 1970. I will be there. It is my first summer away from

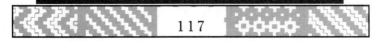

home and I gotta make this journey. I want to act and perform. I work hard and meet some people who will remain in my life for always. When the summer ends, I get involved with school, my Soph. Show, and I get a call saying that the D.C. Black Rep workshop is being restructured. A whole year and a half passes, I've changed my major, and I am traveling all over the place with the Drama Department. During the summer of 1972 I hear that Bobby Hooks has started the D.C. Black Repertory Company again and that he will try to get me involved.

That's when I met Bernice Reagon.

I remember the first time I sang for her. Being a veteran of auditioning and singing, I felt that I could really make an impression. I sang "Sometimes I Feel Like a Motherless Child" and she kind of went, "Oh, UH-HUH," and told me to sing with the altos.

The D.C. Black Repertory Company was filled with some of the most unusual characters I'd ever met in my life. Some of them were just weird, but what was stabilizing and comforting about the place was that I met and worked with people who were involved in the theater with a single purpose, the Glory of the Black Race through dance, drama, and song. We learned from one another on every conceivable level. We learned how to give, how to protect, how to trust, and how to love. We were all alive and vital, eager, and we often functioned like a family. We fought and made up, cried, partied, and shared some of the sweetest memories of our lives together. It was an incredible, precious, and special time in the universe.

Back to Bernice.

She was *so* doggoned tough. She was sometimes rigid, but generally always on the mark with her manner. We had vocal class at 6:30 P.M. every Monday. If you were one minute late and the door was closed, stay out there, 'cause Bernice would not admit latecomers to class. We worked a cappella in almost every show, so that was the way she taught us. She taught two hours of vocalizing, harmonizing, and learning to solo. Everyone was treated with total respect and with the expectation that everyone could make some contribution to the structure of the song being sung. She also taught us the value of understanding *and* believing in what we were singing about. This was invaluable to us as actors, since Motojicho, our "acting/ improvisation guru," worked for a natural, believable quality in our work.

In the beginning of our first season together, I got up to do a solo for Bernice. Since this was "theater," I chose to do a song from a Black show (again *Purlie)* and I sang Melba Moore's version of "Purlie." She stopped my choreography and my staging and my singing and said, "What are you doing?" I told her the name of the song and said that it was from a Broadway show. I was told we weren't doing Broadway here, so pick a song I understood that meant something. Crushed, I took myself back to my seat. What does she want from me? I did *not* get back up that day to sing.

Just what was "real" for me in 1973 was very complex. How could I even begin to sing about losing my father through a mysterious gunshot the year before

and living in my marriage that was dying a slow death? What songs could I sing to express my rage about those things, not to mention not knowing where in the world my mother was? Where did I fit in? There has to be more to life than "screamin' at 'whitey,'" because inside me somebody was screaming to be let out. I had no idea how to approach that somebody to get rid of all the pain that was ticking away inside me like a time bomb. I started writing poetry and meditating.

It was 1973; Louise Robinson and LeTari wanted Bernice to form a singing group out of some of the more experienced voices at the Rep. I remember being asked along with Mike Hodge, Mie, Robert McFadden, and of course Louise Robinson and LeTari. Bernice brought in a song entitled "Sweet Honey in the Rock." It was sounding so sweet. We kept it for the name of the ensemble.

We had several rehearsals with the entire ensemble. There came a point when the summer season at the Rep separated us all. When we got together again in the fall, Bernice put up a notice for a Sweet Honey In The Rock rehearsal. When we finally started our rehearsal, there sat Maillard (me), Mie, Louise, and Bernice. We waited a little while, and Bernice started up a song. I wish I could remember which one. I think it was "The Sun Will Never Go Down," and the sound was perfectly balanced and electric. We stopped and looked at each other. That was that. Next thing I knew, we had a gig! It was the W. C. Handy Blues Festival at Howard University, November 23, 1973. We tore it up.

The next three years in D.C. were full. Full of changes, shows, concerts—full of life. During this period, my emotions were often in upheaval and I felt very unstable. There were times when it was difficult, literally, to put one foot in front of another, but my relationships with Sweet Honey, with the Rep and all my friends there, helped to keep me going. And one special relationship, with Lyn Dyson, gave me the courage to face my problems and continue to make the journey.

We lost Mie in 1974 and by the spring of 1975 (after several configurations of singers) we gained Evelyn Harris and Pat Johnson. What a combination. The play among the five of us (Louise had gone and come back after the birth of her daughter Asha) was like a comet zipping through a midnight sky. Passionate, full, expressive, and sweet. Our voices were very distinct, as were our styles of singing, but when it all came together, it was ecstasy.

There were many opportunities to assist and learn from Bernice. I was always surprised and pleased when she offered various jobs and responsibilities. I don't ever recall her saying, "Maillard" (no one called me Carol), "you'd be great at this," or "That was *bad!*" (good). Her trust in me was revealed by her actions, and I didn't want to disappoint her.

When I listen to tapes of our early classes, I'm tickled, I really am. Bernice would sing a line (this was after vocalizing) and we'd repeat it until we had every nuance. Then she'd go down the line. Each person would do it aloud. And everyone would move that sound around without reserve, feeling good when it was accomplished. Many songs were used to get across certain lessons. For example,

Bernice taught "Abiyoyo" and "Bayeza" to work breath control and simple harmony. "Lord Make Me More Holy" worked the diaphragm/abdominal strengths and vocal projection. "Red Cross Store" gave us subtlety and color because the song was a plaintive whisper about the hardships of the Depression era in the United States. "Down the Road" put us in the solo spotlight, and there were many African songs/chants, spirituals, blues songs, and hollers that stretched us and educated us.

In addition to the vocal training at the Rep, Bernice allowed me to teach a beginner class and to help her direct a production of *Upon This Rock*. During 1974, she hired me as a field researcher within the D.C. Caribbean community for the Smithsonian and to work with her in the African Diaspora Program during the Festival of American Folklife. During the next three summers (1974, 1975, 1976) I did field research, sang with Sweet Honey on the African Diaspora Program stages, and served as tour manager for each performing troupe visiting the festival from Trinidad (1974) Jamaica (1975), and Surinam (1976).

Memories abound . . . of the W. C. Handy Blues Festival; singing LaBelle's "Moonshadow"; our first concert at the D.C. Black Repertory Theater in May 1974 (four chairs on an empty stage, no microphones); and daily offering song at the Festival of American Folklife, African Diaspora Program, 1974, 1975, 1976, "A Day, Life, People." At the Mariposa Folk Festival in Toronto, Canada, I sang "God Come to Me in a Vision" and they say I made the thunder roll and it *rained*. More memories include making our first album together (while Bernice worked on her doctorate), sharing outfits (mostly mine) to get that early Sweet Honey look, "Spread a Little Sunshine," Berea, Kentucky, the Chicago Folk Festival, the Philadelphia Folk Festival, the Michigan Women's Folk Festival, the John Henry Folk Festival, Black Liberation Day in Malcolm X Park, Washington, D.C., and being Bernice's assistant and a workshop leader, teaching the beginners at the D.C. Black Rep., and deciding to move to New York, saying goodbye to my dear sister Bernice.

By 1976, D.C. was drying up for me. I was feeling restless, even with Sweet Honey. I wanted to hurry up and be a star! The theater had always been my first love. The D.C. Black Repertory Company was slowing down, and many of my Rep friends were going to New York and were doing quite well. Maybe I could do it too. But I didn't yet have a taste for the Big Apple.

Dianaruthe Wharton was a piano player and composer Bernice had met at Howard University. Dianaruthe had moved to New York, so I'd visit her from time to time to get a feel for the place. It wasn't so tough. No tougher than North Philly!

I started auditioning in New York and began working a bit and would join Sweet Honey whenever there was a gig I could make from my new home. I wanted to hear music behind me, drums, guitar, bass, and piano. I wanted to arrange all kinds of music. Dianaruthe and I were working on songs together, making demos, and we became very good friends. So one day we got on the phone and called

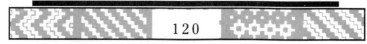

Lovely Lou (Louise), who was then living with Asha in St. Croix. We'd been the best of friends, like sisters, and I loved singing with her. "Come home, Louise. There's lots of work here in New York. I miss you! Let's sing together with Dianaruthe." She thought about it, and it didn't take long for her to pack up and come to New York.

Louise, Dianaruthe Wharton, and I started a band in New York in 1977 called Works-in-Progress. We tried (and often succeeded) to bring the style and passion of our a cappella days to the band. We'd take standards and contemporary songs and rearrange them with new rhythms and lots of improvisation. Dianaruthe's originals were also a strong part of our sound. And of course, there was always a section of the show that was pure a cappella music. Every time we sang, we paid honor to Sweet Honey, and many people would remark, "It's like Sweet Honey In The Rock with a band. It's fierce."

Works-in-Progress did well in terms of critical response, but because Louise and I were also actresses, sometimes our trio would be missing one part. The first time I left was in 1978 with an Australia-bound tour of Ntozake Shange's *For Colored Girls Who Have Considered Suicide When the Rainbow Isn't Enough*. I still felt very much a part of Sweet Honey, and Dianaruthe Wharton had written the songs and music for the original New York production of *For Colored Girls*. So, with great enthusiasm and pride, I packed about a dozen copies of Sweet Honey's first album (which also features Dianaruthe's music) and gave them away while touring Australia. Eleven years later, in 1989, I joined Sweet Honey on their first tour to Australia. We rocked it out!

After Australia, my buddy Aku Kadogo and I did not want to go right back home since we were so close to many interesting places. We traveled to Bali and China for three weeks and then spent four months in Los Angeles doing *For Colored Girls* again. So by the time I got back to New York City, I did not want to be bound by a *thing*. I wanted to work, work, work, and party, party, party. I recommitted to Works-in-Progress, but then so many other wonderful things started to happen. Broadway called and I got on the train with three shows—*Eubie, Comin' Uptown,* and *It's So Nice to Be Civilized*. I also worked at the Negro Ensemble Company, the Actor's Studio, and the New York Shakespeare Festival. Then commercials started coming in. I was moving fast and was considered hot by my agents. Horace Silver featured my voice on his album *Music of the Spheres. For Colored Girls* was taped for *American Playhouse*'s premiere season on PBS, and I was doing demos and voice-overs. Works-in-Progress could not command my full attention. We did our last big concert in 1980. To this day, fans still ask if we'll ever get together again.

In the midst of all this show-biz heat, I was still restless, still searching. There was just enough money to make ends meet because work was erratic. My journals, dreams, and poems started to reflect a deep inner longing. Work started to feel like

drudgery. "Why am I doing this?" "To what end?" "Who even cares?" I was bored, sad, and lonely . . . and searching for light. I prayed and prayed for direction.

In September 1980, I received a card in the mail about a meditation retreat entitled "Creativity and Meditation." What did I need a guru for? I mean, I'd learned to meditate back in 1973. . . .

Then I thought: Maybe this will help . . . maybe this is what I'm looking for. I made my way to the retreat center (Ashram). Everything about the place had a sense of familiarity. Nothing I could put my finger on, but it was like home, very comfortable. We meditated a short while, and during the talks that ensued over the course of that afternoon I heard many things that made me know I was really home. I was deeply moved by the idea that we are all actors in God's Great Play of Life. God is the director; and like acting in a play, we can assume many roles, changing interpretation and nuance according to the scene. But inside we *are* who we are. Not the costume or the voice or affectations. We are the Inner Self, and God's love and light exist in everything created. And, when you sing, sing for God. I wondered: How do I sing for God? What do I sing? Where?

"WE ALL . . . EVERYONE OF US, HAVE TO COME HOME AGAIN"

It is the fall of 1983. I'm finished doing *I'm Getting My Act Together and Taking It on the Road* in Rochester, New York. I am a bit restless, but very excited. It is Sweet Honey's tenth anniversary and we are all coming home. Ten years—it went by not-so-quickly.

It also had been about six years since I had packed up and moved to New York. I remember vividly the anticipation of our first rehearsal at Bernice's home. Oh! Louise and I just couldn't wait to put that good ol' Sweet Honey sound back on the map. We burst in with a fierce energy, ready to assume our "ancestral" places. It was exhilarating to see all those women who followed us assembled, ready to join in song. We sang, rehearsed, tugged at our memories. The quintessential heavenly choir.

On the morning of October 11, 1985, Elliott Ware and I became parents to a boy-child we named Jordan Maillard Ware. He was born at home with Auntie Cille, Auntie Louise, Auntie Joy, and our midwife, Sandy Fields. Elliott sang to me most of the night, we sang to Jordan after Elliott cut the cord. He is a very beautiful child with a "head fulla hair."

Several days after the birth, I got a call from Toni Morrison about an audition for a new play she was doing. I brought Jordan, but was nervous out with him so soon. I remember the bright lights in the waiting room. I read the script while I nursed him. Then Toni came out, scooped him up, cooing to him, "No Nicaragua,

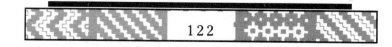

no Vietnam, no Grenada, no South Africa, no Chile . . ." and she continued calling on the ancestors to bless and protect him.

It's the first Friday in December 1985. Sweet Honey is performing at Carnegie Hall for their Twelfth Anniversary Concert. Louise is sitting next to me; we are very visible in the first row. In my arms, I am holding my sweet eight-week-young son, Jordan Maillard Ware. He nurses and sleeps during the concert. I sing along with almost every song. He doesn't stir; he doesn't cry.

Toward the end of the concert, Bernice acknowledges the presence of former Sweet Honey members who are in the audience. She invites each to come onstage. Suddenly I'm terrified! I'm nursing Jordan, there are no steps . . . maybe I can just stand up and wave. Ayodele's onstage, Lovely Lou is onstage, and when Bernice leans over the edge of the stage, gestures for me to come up, I quickly unhitch my baby and hand him over to her. The audience gives a great sigh. I'm hoisted up by two fine gentlemen, I take Jordan, and we are introduced. A splendid moment . . . He makes his debut cooing while Mommy sings at Carnegie Hall. Life is so dear.

My mommy died on October 20, 1985. The only way I can describe her sudden departure is that it was devastating. I was newly married to Elliott Ware, Jordan's father, and was a new mom. Through all the years of my life, when Mom wasn't around, my love and need for her was strong. We loved each other dearly, but managed to distance ourselves although we lived in the same city. She and my dad shared the same problem through most of their adult lives. My mom died of pneumonia, chronic intravenous narcotism, and cocaine abuse. I knew she was slipping when she visited us at home the night Jordan was born. She was in bad shape, underweight, and a bit delirious, but when she saw Jordan, I saw the woman who brought me into the world, gave me songs and a sense of humor, the one who nursed me and told me stories no one else could remember. She came to my shows, bragged about me, and could talk about Daddy Bo Bo and jazz for hours. And that night, October 11, 1985, she sang to Jordan and told him things I couldn't hear, but from the look on both of their faces, I knew why he was smiling. It was the last time we saw or spoke to her. Thank you, Shirley Elizabeth, with all my heart.

Time truly marches on and the Lord does move in mysterious ways.

Elliott and I had an extremely difficult time maintaining a life together. I managed to keep working after Jordan's birth. Whatever I did would require my bringing a nursing babe along. One day, I got a call about an audition for a 1960s musical, *Beehive,* and I got the lead! It was a huge success, putting our pictures in *Time* and *People* magazines and "us" on the Phil Donahue show. It was a tough year. It was exhausting. But God really took care of me. I made it to the theater, sometimes with Jordan and Margaret (his babysitter), nursed him between acts, sent them home, finished the performance, and made it home by 11 P.M. I learned how to be consistent yet be creative and open each night. My character was thirteen

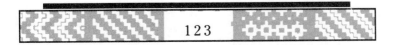

years old (I was not) and there was no room to say, "I'm too tired." I left *Beehive* exactly one year after I began, May 1, 1987.

After *Beehive,* Elliott and I devoted ourselves to creating an a cappella musical together called *Redlights & Blues.* It was tough going and much hard work was required to present it in concert form to the public. But a group of talented singers and actors formed an inspired ensemble so that Elliott's words and my music could come to life in front of a packed house in August 1987.

Fall 1987. Broadway again. Thank you, Lord, for *Don't Get God Started* with the Winans and Vanessa Bell Armstrong. When the show closed in New York in January 1988, I am asked to go on the tour. Not much decision making needed here. It's time to get away. I'm very unhappy with the way everything is going. A Gospel tour, good money, I can take Jordan; we're gone.

When the tour ends in August 1988, I know I cannot resume living with my husband. It is all too painful. I don't even have any songs to sing except the beautiful chants and hymns from the Ashram. "When you sing, sing for God." I start singing at the Ashram . . . much comfort and peace are in this work.

Many folks try to tell me I am often a difficult person to find. (Okay, so I didn't have a home phone at the time either.) One day mid- or late May 1989, I was at Mike Hodge's apartment while he was out of town, checking his mail, watering plants, when I heard a message from Bernice. I called her the next day and she said, "Mai, where are you in the universe these days?" "Oh, I'm here in New York, Bernice."

Bernice was gentle as she continued the conversation, telling me that Sweet Honey was going to Japan and Australia for a few weeks. Great, I thought.

"Can you join us?" My jaw dropped and I don't even remember if I said more than "Huh?" She said she'd allow me some time to think about it, but to "hur' up."

I had so much to contend with. Jordan was three and a half years young, and my child-care resources were minimal. But Japan? Australia? A job? Sweet Honey? Could I handle learning at least twenty-five new songs in about two weeks? Well, betcha by golly yes!

I was shaky at first. I did not really know these ladies. Would they be patient with me? Bernice had the utmost confidence that my vibe would be just right for all concerned. I made the journey. I substituted for Evie from the end of May 1989 until the middle of June. Jordan went to Philadelphia to be with my Aunt Lucille and Uncle Stanley and his cousins in West Philly. He had a ball! And so did I.

But I have to say I was a bit reserved. I was used to really singing out, trying new lines and altering a chord whenever I was so inspired, or even jazzing up an existing rhythm. I love to improvise. With Ysaye, Nitanju, and Aisha, I felt as though we were really just meeting one another, somewhat like the first date. I didn't want to let it all hang out.

Traveling with this Sweet Honey was an eye-opener . . . the handling of baggage, the sound-check routine, not eating in vans while traveling, protocol with

sponsors, rehearsals, meetings, crossing borders, schedules, and doing "duty" (greeting the audience after the concert) were all new to me. Sweet Honey was so patient with me. It was a lot to digest, so I didn't try to, I just let it wash all over me and I rode the wave.

So many tears and emotions in Japan—from the audience, from us—hearts opening like seeds sprouting at springtime. By the end of Japan, I felt very much at home in the group.

Australia is one of my favorite places in the world. I really love the spirit of the land. We played in two places I'd been before and some of my friends came to the concerts in Melbourne and Sydney.

My favorite story from this tour is about a gentleman who heard us sing for the very first time in Sydney. He came up to us after the concert and said in pure Aussie dialect, "Oy jus' loved the song y' sang about 'Stralia!" We were puzzled.

"Which one was that?"

"Ahm 'Stralian, 'Stralian here, ahm 'Stralian everywheah." We collapsed with laughter. And sang, as best we could, the blues lyrics:

I'm a stranger here, I'm a stranger everywhere
Lord I would go home but I'm a stranger there . . .

I didn't sing with Sweet Honey again until January 1990, when my longest stretch as a substitute would begin. Yasmeen would replace Evie in the fall, I'd do winter and spring, Tulani would do the month of March. Not only did we all survive the changes, I think the growth process was fantastic, giving me more lessons in surrender and support. And I'm telling you, we laughed about almost anything, especially after a long travel day—sound check—concert experience. Great camaraderie, great sisterhood. The highlight of this season was a five-week tour from the end of April through the end of May. We spent two weeks touring Belgium and Holland with the Voices Festival. After that the United States Information Service sponsored a tour of Southern Africa: Uganda (where we were greeted by Ramona Harper, the cultural liaison for the United States and the only Black female in my high school first violin section when I joined; I hadn't seen her since 1967); Zimbabwe (where we learned the Zimbabwean way of singing a freedom song Bernice had taught us during the D.C. Black Repertory days called "Tschotsholoza"); Mozambique (here our show just barely got on because of a brownout, an interruption of electrical power right before our concert); and Swaziland (beware shopping in a great store with Sweet Honey; these ladies are, as Oprah Winfrey calls it, "Black Belt shoppers"). In the newly independent Namibia, the capital, Windhoek, was the most different of all the African cities we visited; it felt very White. Oh, and an overnight in Addis Ababa, Ethiopia.

It was my first trip to Africa. Each country had a unique and tangible beauty, not just in the land but in the faces, the ways and the strength of all the people. I'd

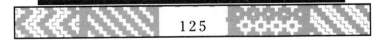

seen them all somewhere in New York, in St. Croix, in Belgium, in Sydney. We are everywhere on this globe. There was no difference between them and me. I bathed in the beauty of my own Self, reflected all over the world. I Love Africa.

As exciting as the trip was, when it was time to go home, we were all ready. Each suitcase was stuffed. I mean *stuffed* to capacity. Our magnificent tour manager, Arlene Jackson, managed to get all of our baggage through customs each time; she really took good care of us. I was pleased to see Bernice relaxing, not having to worry about the travel details she was used to attending to. Sweet Honey's road manager, Madeleine Remez, and Arlene made a great team and did all they could to make our journey a little smoother.

My fondest, I mean *fondest* memory of Africa is singing "Nkosi Sikelel' 1-Africa"—"God Bless Our Mother Africa." I cried every time we did it as an encore. Just about everyone stood up and raised their fist as they shouted "A Luta Continua!"—"The Struggle Continues!"

And making it back to the States wasn't the end of it. When we returned, we were asked to participate in many of the rallies being planned for the arrival of Winnie and Nelson Mandela. My heart was just about to burst! Yankee Stadium, the Brooklyn Academy of Music, and finally Oakland Stadium. I felt so much love and power emanating from the two of them. And a sense of determination and inner peace. When we finished singing "Crying for Freedom" at the Brooklyn Academy of Music, Winnie, who seemed to be being rushed out to keep on schedule, jumped out of her seat and ran to hug each of us as the audience roared with approval and enthusiasm. I send many blessings to them both, that their lives will be richer and full of the fruits of their commitment to ending apartheid in South Africa. Amandla!

". . . PASSING ON TO OTHERS THAT WHICH WAS PASSED ON TO ME . . ."

Over the years, I've had the good fortune to study with many fine teachers. Wilkie and Bernice were my anchors, the shapers of my technique and my sound. Many people used to ask me to teach them how to sing. After years of asking myself "What do I even know enough of to teach?" and wondering if I should even sing or act in public anymore, I am now vocal coaching and offering master classes. Helping others to experience their own inner music has transformed student *and* teacher. I teach them to breathe more freely with proper support. I show how sound has a healing and rejuvenating effect on the physical, spiritual, and emotional self. We play theater games and vocalize and always end the session with either a Sweet Honey song or a vocal improvisation (which they create). I have to reach out to them, and simultaneously I have to reach inside myself for truth and clarity.

Through my spiritual journey I began to shed limiting concepts about "work."

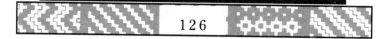

Seva, or selfless service, where the giving of one's time, energy, and talents without expecting to experience the "fruit of labor," transforms and liberates. Within this practice, Seva, I've finally been able to allow my inner voice to soar past my insecurities. God's grace has blessed me immensely through my spiritual practice. When I "work" singing, teaching, acting, I surrender every bit of myself to God's power. It is an offering of my love through sound so that each person gets what she or he truly needs. I am not in charge of the exchange. I am only a vessel. It took several years for me to understand that kind of surrender. Music has touched the center of all that I am. Today, I live in service to God through this gift He has given. When I now sing, I experience an offering of love, through sound. It belongs to the universe; it belongs to the Lord.

I am writing songs again, guiding an inspirational choir, and I am once again a full-time member of Sweet Honey, almost twenty short years after its inception. I sometimes have felt left out in the past. I've sometimes had a longing to recapture and relive the early days of Pat, Evie, Lovely Lou, Bernice, and Mai.

I am a part of the full circle that is Sweet Honey In The Rock; past, present, . . . to come. It touches the heart and soul yet it's extremely tangible. It's a rhythm, a new riff, a mad dance, swirling melodies, history remembered and reborn, a baby's cry, the elders in prayer, the first mother, it's all colors, all textures of skin and hair, it's Africa adorned all over the world . . . It's life. I feel all of it profoundly when I am in song, and when I'm teaching.

The basis for how I express myself musically is Sweet Honey, a fantastic support system and fertile ground for ideas that help us as members grow within the group structure. I am ever making the journey, and glad to be in the number.

Sadgurunall Maharaj Ki Jai!
(Praise the Lord!)

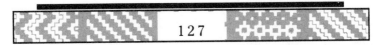

9

SWEET HONEY IN THE ROCK:
A FEW MEMORIES

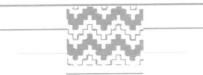

IVY YOUNG

It's the D.C. Black Rep. An old, battered former movie house on Georgia Avenue, transformed into a performance theater. Tonight is a workshop performance with song and skit. The actors sing. The singers act. In the aisles, on the stage, sitting amid the audience, performers flow through the darkened theater, brightening the space with music. They are good, these performing Black folks. And the music is different; the sound is old. The actor-singers converge on the old dusty, wooden stage, the lights go out and they disappear. A beat or two and the lights are up. The actor-singers have been replaced by four women singing this ancestral sound. But the words are not old. The words are as current as tomorrow's headlines: nuclearpower—southafrica—politicalprisoners—lovegonebadgonegood —freedom. Who are they? Who? Sweet what? They make you think. They make you shout. They make you cry. Captivated. Captured. Hooked like a big fish. They're not even done yet and already you're trying to find out where they'll be performing after this. Next time, I'm bringing my momma. I mean, these Sweet Honey In The Rock girls can saang.

2. Multipurpose rooms at community centers, smoky, crowded little dance clubs all over town, church sanctuaries with brick-hard wooden pews, that's where you could find Sweet Honey performing in the early years. "Sweet Honey In The Rock in a performance to benefit . . ." Fill in the name of just about any grassroots organization. Sweet Honey, always there, giving her time and talent to the

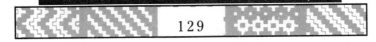

community. And at countless political rallies, Sweet Honey was there too, singing for free: "Free Angela, free the Wilmington Ten, free Zimbabwe . . ." Always introduced as the "musical break" at political rallies, Sweet Honey's two or three songs inspired and mobilized as many of the endless, long-winded speeches could not. (Sweet Honey taught a lot of activists about popular culture as politics.)

3. "Thank goodness, it's Thursday. Been waiting all week for this day." I'll be spending this and four more years of Thursday evenings with other Black women from D.C. We will move our chairs into a circle in a little room at a local church; and we will sit in that circle and learn songs and history from the women of Sweet Honey In The Rock. We will laugh together, and cry together, and share moments of pain and power. We will stretch ourselves and challenge each other. We will argue and forgive, trust and grow. We will bring to the circle tales of that day and weariness from that day. We will sing the songs Sweet Honey brings us, breathe deeply and release the burdens of that day. Sweet Honey created a space where we could be and become. I will be forever indebted, forever grateful.

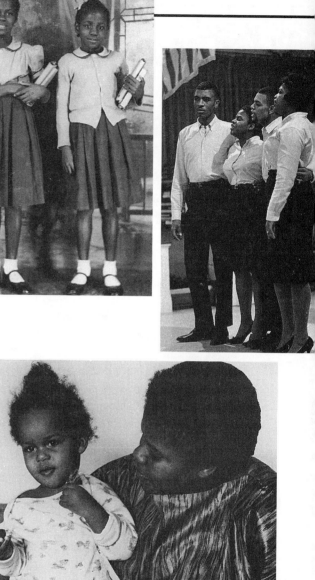

LEFT: BERNICE JOHNSON REAGON WITH SON KWAN TAUNA REAGON, 1966. (PHOTOGRAPHER, DIANA DAVIES)

CENTER: BERNICE AND MAE FRANCES JOHNSON, SISTERS, CIRCA 1950. (PHOTO COURTESY OF BEATRICE JOHNSON)

TOP RIGHT: FREEDOM SINGERS SINGING "WE SHALL OVERCOME," JUDSON MEMORIAL CHURCH, NEW YORK, 1963. L TO R: CHARLES NEBLETT, BERNICE JOHNSON, CORDELL HULL REAGON, RUTHA HARRIS. (PHOTOGRAPHER, JOE ALPER)

BOTTOM RIGHT: BERNICE JOHNSON REAGON WITH DAUGHTER TOSHI, 1965, NEW YORK. (PHOTOGRAPHER, JOE ALPER)

10

SINGING FOR MY LIFE

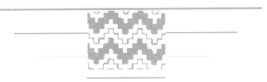

BERNICE JOHNSON REAGON

When I look back over the short span of my fifty years, when I wonder how it is that I have been blessed to walk this path through the music of Sweet Honey In The Rock—there are songs that spring into my mind like stairsteps, marking the way I have traveled with the constant sound of singing in my life.

> *I wonder do you, love the Lord like I do?*
> *He gave his life for me and for you*
> *I wonder do you, love the Lord like I do?*
> *What He gave for me given to you*
>
> *Oh He died on the cross*
> *Yeah He died for the lost*
> *I love Him this I know*
> *Yeah I tell it, tell it wherever I go*
> *(falsetto)*
> *I wonder do you . . .*

My favorite singers as a young child were Sister Rosie Daniels and Archie Brownlee. Sister Daniels was a member of the Usher Board at the Mt. Early Baptist Church, where my father was pastoring when I came to myself enough to know that

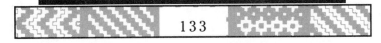

he was a minister; and Archie Brownlee was the virtuoso tenor lead of the Five Blind Boys of Jackson, Mississippi. Even as a child of five and six, I could sing his songs in his key. I don't really know if "I Wonder Do You, Love the Lord Like I Do?" was my first song; but when people ask about the first song I sang it comes to mind. I heard it over the radio in my house sung by Archie Brownlee. I loved everything he did. His voice touched me deeply, and the minute I heard the opening lines, "I wonder do you, love the Lord like I do?" I stopped to listen. I knew I could sing that song; and Mae Frances, my sister, and I learned it after hearing it twice.

My father was the Reverend J. J. Johnson, the pastor of Mt. Early Baptist Church in Worth County, Georgia, the husband of Beatrice Wise Johnson, and at that time, when I was five or six, the father of Fannie, Jordan, me, Mae Frances, and Aaron, whom we called "Bubba." On the first Sunday of every month we would all pile into the car and go to Mt. Early. I loved to hear Sisters Daniels and Doll Baby sing "Swing Low Chariot." Doll Baby was on the Usher Board too. Mrs. Rosa Daniels always stood by the door nearest the pulpit, and Doll Baby stood in the center aisle near where Mae Frances and I would be sitting. Sister Daniels would always start the song with the call "Oh swing low chariot," and the church would thunder back, "Swing low," and she would call, "Oh lower and lower," we would respond, "Swing low!"

> *Oh swing low chariot*
>   *Swing low*
> *Oh lower and lower*
>   *Swing low*
> *I got my ticket,*
>   *Swing low, swing low chariot, swing low.*

After two or three cycles the song would be really going strong. Then, without any signal that I could see or sense, Sister Doll Baby, who had a slightly darker voice, would take it up.

> *I know I got religion*
>   *Swing low*
> *I got it one Wednesday*
>   *Swing low*
> *One Wednesday morning*
>   *Swing low, swing low chariot, swing low.*

The church would be rocking. I was not a member of the church, so I could not add my voice to the singing. You had to be a member to help make a meeting in the congregation I grew up in. Services were created by Christians, those who had been

saved. After services, you could sing a song if you asked my father; it was the only time we were allowed to sing in church before we got religion, except on the Easter program.

Anyway, Mae Frances and I learned "I Wonder Do You . . ." and then asked my father if we could sing it the next first Sunday.

The next Sunday meeting, after the sermon was preached, the doors of the church were opened to those who would come and be counted among the saved, the collection was taken up, and the benediction had been said, my father called us up to sing. The entire church stayed after service to hear a song sung by children.

I remember being called up to the front of the church, getting up there and looking out at the congregation, feeling small in a very big place with big people. I felt sort of out of place, singing to people who were saved even though I was not and thus could not sing with them during regular service.

As we started to sing, things felt a little shaky, but I recall feeling my voice calm down. It was a slow song, but the church found the beat and began to pat their feet to it. It was reassuring, singing and feeling the time of the song reinforced under my feet as I sang. At the refrain of this song, you have to lean back and pull with your voice to get the right sound the way the Five Blind Boys did it. So we went, "Ohhhhhhhhh He died, on the cross, yesssss he died . . ." As we went into the "Ohhhhh" the church started up—not shouting, but gently, with conviction and support and satisfaction and smiles, talking us up: "All right now!" "Come on up now!" "Sing, children!" The energy from the pushing congregation seemed to become a part of the sound of the voice coming out of my throat. At the first surge in feelings, my voice quivered, but then it smoothed out and got stronger as I sang down the line, "Yes He died, for the lost, I love Him this I know, for . . . He made me whole . . ." It was the first time I had experienced allowing the energy and support coming from the congregation to come into my voice and it changed my voice. I was five years old.

"WON'T IT BE GRAND," "THAT AWFUL DAY . . . ," AND "OH PO' SINNER"

Daddy always ended his sermons with "Won't It Be Grand" and he always opened the doors of the church with the common-meter hymn "That Awful Day Will Surely Come." We sang hymns using traditional tunes set to different meters. The most popular meters I grew up with were: long, short, and common. Each meter could be done in several tunes that were familiar to that particular region. For example, I know three common-meter tunes and every hymn in the hymnbook marked CM can be sung to any of those tunes. The tune my father used to sing "That Awful Day . . ." was mournful. I loved to hear him line out the powerful second part of the stanza. The first two lines of the hymn text would be lined in

chant form in almost the same regular voice he used coming out of "Won't It Be Grand." He would intone: "That awful day would surely come. The appointed hour make haste." He would raise his hands and we would all stand and sing the line in the common-meter tune. At the end of the congregation's singing of this line, which ended in an up note, he would lean back and call the second line: "Ohhhhhhhhhhhh . . ." If the meeting was high he might call two or three times with the church answering back, "Yeah!" "Ohhhhhhhhhhhh when I must stand before my judge and pass the solemn test. When I . . ." We would move through the line, singing and shouting.

I loved his songs and I loved his singing. The song that got engraved in my heart was his revival song. Mt. Early always held a revival meeting the week coming up to the first Sunday in September. We usually went every night during preaching week.

The meeting, like all meetings at Mt. Early, was opened by women. I grew up thinking all church meetings in the world were begun by women because of Mt. Early, and did not learn better until I began to do field research several decades later and found that in the same region most church meetings were opened by the deacons. Anyway, Sister Florilla Jackson would be up front with another sister and they would open the service. To this day, I am grateful to Mt. Early for this practice, it was an important thing for a girl, me, to see women being the first voice in the most important institution in my world. And church *was* important. School was also crucial, and my mother was determined to see to it that we went to school, but church was more important because it took care of the condition of your soul, and without a well-developed soul all the education in the world would not do you any good.

On revival meeting night, as soon as Mae Frances and I entered the church, we would go up to the first bench and sit down. If you had not joined the church, you had to sit on the mourner's bench in the front of the church. Being preacher's children, Mae Frances and I started sitting there at a very young age.

The women's part of the devotional service usually followed the pattern of: church song, hymn, prayer, church song, hymn, prayer. Whenever anyone prayed, those of us on the Mourner's Bench would get on our knees; they were praying for our souls and we were expected to pray for our own souls. After the second prayer, a deacon would begin the next church song from their amen side of the church, and the women would go to their amen corner. Two deacons, usually Deacon Durns and Deacon Laster, would take the two seats next to the communion table under the pulpit and the pattern would be repeated. The amen corner of the church was traditionally reserved for the elders, with the women to the left of the pulpit and the men to the right. In most of the churches I saw growing up, this section was usually two or three rows of benches turned so that they faced each other across the room, with the general congregational benches lined in rows facing the pulpit. During my childhood, these devotional services led by members of the

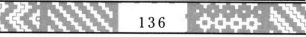

amen corner lasted forty minutes to an hour and then the service was turned over to the pulpit.

The pastor, my father, or someone he designated, would line and raise a hymn (lining is chanting the text, raising is leading the congregation in the singing of the chanted text), read the scripture, and then the evangelist for the week would come forward. The evangelist would usually be a regional preacher who was known for his preaching skill. He would rise, sometimes singing, then he would read the scripture from which he would take his sermon theme, and begin his sermon. These evangelists always came out of their sermons with a signature song that they were known by. They would always be men. This was the late forties, they were Southwest Georgia Black Baptists, and they believed that the pulpit belonged to men, and most of them still do.

The preacher would move out of the pulpit (if he hadn't already come down to the congregational level during the highest point of his preaching) and bring the church into singing with his song. After the song, the doors of the church would be opened and everyone would stand and sing a hymn, and the ushers would put two chairs facing the pulpit for those who would come. "Opening the doors of the church" does not mean literally opening the doors of the building; it is the invitation and the place within the service where people are asked to join the Christian family. If someone came up and sat in one of the chairs it meant that there were new soldiers in Christ and the entire congregation would throw up "thank you's" and "hallelujahs" for the increase in numbers. If the doors of the church were opened and nobody came, my father would sing "Oh Po' Sinner."

Daddy was a stocky man and he would sing the song with his head back walking back and forth in front of the mourner's bench, where we would be still sitting.

Oh po' sinner
Sinner, now is your time
Oh po' sinner
What you gon' do when the lamp burn down?

Lamp burn down and it's too late to pray
    What you gon' do when the lamp burn down
When the lamp burn down and it's too late to pray
    What you gon' do when the lamp burn down

Oh po' sinner
Sinner, now is your time
Oh po' sinner
What you gon' do when the lamp burn down?

As he walked the floor, the kerosene lamps (Mt. Early then had no electricity) hanging from the ceiling would swing and their flames would flicker, and I thought they might go out before I joined the church.

I love the song to this day, and can always feel the tension it caused in me. I was caught between wanting to be among those who were saved from sin, wanting to join the church, and understanding that being saved was not a simple phenomenon. I knew then at the age of seven and eight that something had to happen inside, that it was important that one went through a strong personal experience before coming forward.

A sinner was supposed to go through a seeking period. I knew of older cousins and my oldest sister who began praying to be saved. They did not eat; they also separated themselves from everyone else. We never saw them during the day. They went into the woods to their own praying ground. At the end of the day they would come to the house looking drawn and not talking to anybody. We talked in whispers around them: "Fannie is praying." They would go to revival meeting and go straight to the mourner's bench. The church members would sometimes comment, "She is really serious." And when they found the Lord, the whole neighborhood would know it. They would come running back shouting, "I found Him!" or "I got it!" Sometimes they came through singing a song, but they always came through with a sign.

I knew from watching people who had "come through" that I had not been touched in that way. So I could not accept the invitation to join just to please my parents or because I wanted to be saved. I had to really be saved and come forth with a story that told of the transition. Although the invitation was being extended with pressure, accepting the invitation required a searching and finding I had not yet experienced.

In late August 1953, I went to my praying ground. I got up in the middle of the night and went into "the bottom." This was a wooded area near our house that I never went to alone during the day. I positioned myself under a tree and began to pray that my sins be forgiven. I was struck with a great fear, and I prayed that as a sign of forgiveness, my fears be removed. I don't know how long I stayed there shaking in fear and praying, but then I felt a great change. I was swept throughout with a quiet and deep calm. I felt quiet inside, the fear was gone, the shakes were gone, and all the sounds of the woods were gone, there was no sound anywhere. Within me was a peace I had never felt before. I got up from my praying place and don't remember the walk back to the house. When I got inside, I woke up my mother and told her what had happened to me and that I felt I had it. She said, "Keep praying, baby."

I was in conflict; I was clear that I had been heard, my prayers had been answered, but my mother did not share my clarity. Were the sign, the stillness and calm, the absence of fear not big enough? Or did it come too fast? I went to church that evening and sat on the mourner's bench, crying when the doors of the church

were opened. The next thing I knew, I had walked out and fallen at my father's feet. I know now that it was an important step in me moving forward based on what I knew, even when I was not certain that my parents saw things the same way. Mae Frances came the next night on belief.

By the time I actually joined the church at eleven years of age the times were changing and I joined under a minister who would quote from Mark 16:16: "He that believeth and is baptized shall be saved. . . ." This was a break with the tradition. This minister stressed that the Bible did not require a sign, the scriptures said that one could come to God based on belief.

The minister, the Reverend Jones, was staying at our house, and during the day he talked about the scriptures. He said that the old tradition of sending people back who did not have a strong enough conviction story to pass muster with the elders was not consistent with the scripture. He would say that the Bible stated, "Whosoever will let him come, and forbid him not, for such is the Kingdom of Heaven . . ."

I overheard someone asking my mother if she was going to let us be baptized and she said yes, she was going to let us go ahead, and we went. I was baptized by my father in the Mercer Mill Creek.

CLIMBING JACOB'S LADDER

We are climbing Jacob's ladder
We are climbing Jacob's ladder
We are climbing Jacob's ladder
Soldiers of the cross

I guess I never really heard that song sung until I heard Miss Nanna lead it. She sang it at Mt. Olive No. Two in East Albany, a section of Albany, Georgia, which was the county seat of my home county, Dougherty. My father was called to become pastor of that church while I was in high school; it was his first and only Albany city congregation. Most of his ministry was in churches in small cities or in counties throughout the Southwest Georgia region. Mt. Olive No. Two was a large church that my father successfully rebuilt while he pastored there.

Mt. Olive had some strong services, especially the revival meetings, which were always unaccompanied. Although the church had a strong choir and great gospel singing with piano accompaniment, these services were always a cappella. Miss Nanna used to raise two songs that I remember; one was "Jacob's Ladder" and the other was "Time Is Winding Up." In both cases she would start the song and soon be up moving and weaving across the floor as the song grew in the congregation. With "Jacob's Ladder," she would start the lead:

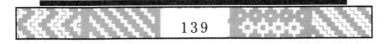

We are

and we would join in:

climbing Jacob's Ladder

and all together:

We are climbing Jacob's ladder

Then she would seem to hand us the song, and shift her position so that the song moved to a "call and response" pattern by sounding a call, "Whoahuuuuuuuu," just before the next line would be triggered.

> *Whoahuuuuuuuu*
> *We are*
> *Whoahuuuuuuuu*
> *climbing*
> *Whoahuuuuuuuu*
> *Jacob's ladder*
> *Ohhhhhhhhhh*
> *Soldiers of the cross*

And then she would start us on the next cycle:

> *Every round goes higher and higher*
> *Every round goes higher and higher*

and then shift to the call and response:

> *Whoahuuuuuuuu*
> *Every*
> *Whoahuuuuuuuu*
> *round goes*
> *Whoahuuuuuuuu*
> *higher and higher*
> *Ohhhhhhhhhh*
> *Soldiers of the cross*

And then she would go to the next:

Rise shine give God your glory . . .

She pushed us higher and higher and the church would rise to the occasion. The congregation would be leaning every ounce of strength into the singing of the song, leaning back, standing up, holding on to the bench in front for traction for the next line. The power of congregational singing has made tracks in my soul—I am who I am because I was raised in the shadows between the lines of my people living their lives out in a song. It really is a way to come to yourself.

"I'M BOUND FOR THE PROMISED LAND" MT. EARLY BAPTIST CHURCH CHOIR

I don't think I had a first awareness of God. I don't think I had a first awareness of breathing. God is like that for me, like the air that I have never been without.

When I joined the church, Daddy baptized me and Mae Frances along with Roger and Mary Drakes. The next year, Daddy left Mt. Early as pastor but we stayed, and the new minister, Rev. Richard Jordan, organized a choir. My sister Fannie was the pianist; we were a three-family choir, the Johnsons, the Drakes, and Deacon and Mrs. Laster. We were country but we could sing.

The very first song I led for the choir was "I'm Bound for the Promised Land." That was the first time I was able to sing a song and pull a feeling from inside myself for the express purpose of creating the right spiritual feel for the song. Describing Black singing is not easy to put in words. In singing songs in a Black style, you have to be able to change the notes with feelings before the sound comes out of your body. It's like the feelings have to be inside the sound. So you are not singing notes and tones, you are giving out pieces of yourself, coming from places inside that you can only yourself visit in a singing. It is having what is inside yourself ride the air in the song you are singing.

With mature Black singing, you can't sound like a feeling, you can't act like you're feeling, you have to feel, be in the feeling, and have the feeling establish the quality of your sound. Growls, broken notes to convey release, cries in the middle of a word, are characteristics of the African American vocal style. If it is right, those sitting in the sound of your voice will not only hear you singing, they will feel you singing in a deeper part of themselves. The emotion that has shaped and changed your tones as you move through the song will be experienced by the listener.

I was just beginning to develop the power in my singing, and in this case the song was "I'm Bound for the Promised Land." We all sang the verse together:

On Jordan stormy bank I stand, to cast a wishful eye
To Canaan fair, a happy land, where my possessions lie.

Then I led into the chorus section with a call that began before we finished the final phrase of the last verse line:

Ohhhhhhhhhh good Lord I'm bound

The choir thundered:

> *I'm bound for the promised land*
> *For the promised land*
> *I'm bound for the promised land*
> *Oh yes I'm bound*
> *I'm bound for the promised land*
> *For the promised land*
> *I'm bound for the promised land*
> *Oh—tell me who*
> *Who gonna come and go with me*
> *Oh who*
> *Who gonna come and go with me*

Everybody:

I'm bound, bound, bound, bound,
I'm bound for the promised land

It was on this last line of this first chorus that my singing was different. I laid the call across the last phrase, signaling that I was going to do another chorus; like we did in rehearsal, but this time, as I started my "Ohhhhhhhhhhhhhhhhhhhh," it was unlike anything I had done before. It was hot! And the church responded; and I got warmer and my voice sounded more fervent and my body changed, and the energy in the whole choir changed. . . . I pushed everything in me I could get to into the line and the choir and the piano leaped in response, the air in the church went electric, it was like there was fire dancing in the air that was carrying the song —I was learning to sing a Black song.

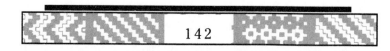

"WHAT ARE THEY DOING THERE NOW?"
MRS. MAMIE LEE DANIELS AND THE BLUE SPRINGS SCHOOL

We lived about seven miles outside Albany and I went to the Blue Springs Elementary School in Dougherty County, which was a county school. These schools were usually named for the local Black church; this one was named for Blue Springs Baptist Church. Every church in the county seemed to have a school next door to it. At first, the schools were located in the church until the congregation could build a separate building for the school on the same property. During the early part of the century, the county began to pay a salary to a teacher to teach in these rural schools.

Mrs. Mamie Lee Daniels was my teacher, and I still think she is the best teacher in the world. Mamie Lee Daniels was born in Charles County, Georgia. After she married, her new husband, Will Daniels, went into the Army and sent back support (fifty dollars a month) to his wife. Mrs. Daniels took that fifty dollars and went to Albany State College. She said that she did not receive much encouragement for her decision since it was unusual in her community for a married woman to go off to school. She went because she wanted something different. Her first job after college was at our school, the Blue Springs Elementary School.

When she came to teach at Blue Springs she took on the entire community. It seemed to me that she transformed the vision of our community. She was a skillful organizer and never stopped working to move us forward and expand what and how we experienced life. She wanted us to experience everything. Her work with the PTA was phenomenal. First, she made the school the center of the community, where there were several family enclaves, and second, she pulled us all together in the interest of the children.

I still do not know how she did the things she did, except she managed to make the parents feel they were important and that their children were the best children in the world. She had my father (who was a carpenter as well as a minister) and some other fathers build a stage in our one-room standard red schoolhouse so we could use it for our school programs. They also built a playhouse big enough for us to walk in and play in. They bought playground equipment.

It was Mrs. Daniels who worked with my father and my uncle, Mr. Elijah Williams, on what to say when they went to the superintendent of Dougherty County schools to ask for a school bus to take children to junior and senior high school from the rural areas of the county. Until that request, if you were a student who finished the seventh grade in our county, the only way you could get to junior and senior high school was if your parents drove you or if you could board in town. Most students could not make it to school until we got that bus. Busing was a given for White students in the county; they did not want us to have it. Our parents and my uncle, with Mrs. Daniels as unseen backup (as a teacher she would not have

survived if it was known that she was involved), took up the challenge to change that and thus changed the possibilities for all students who finished at the Blue Springs Elementary School.

Mrs. Daniels went beyond the walls of our classroom to find things for us to learn about. When she found out we had never been on a train ride, she took us on the thirty-mile train trip to Americus, Georgia, and back. She tried to schedule a plane ride, but the parents drew the line; most of them thought if the Lord wanted us to fly, we would have been born with wings. Mrs. Daniels told those of us who had no toothbrushes that we could still clean our teeth with softened sticks from the branches of a pine tree. She found out that even though most of us lived on farms, we were not getting milk every day. So Mrs. Mamie Lee Daniels had the milkman (who stopped at a small store about two miles from school) come to the school to deliver milk. My sister Mae Frances would not drink white milk, so one carton of milk was chocolate. I still do not know how we let her get away with that. Mrs. Daniels also got the PTA to pay for a pipe to run from the farm a distance from the school (about a city block) to the yard behind the school, and we had running water for the first time. She believed in pulling us into the twentieth century, but she respected the wisdom of the folk, and when she forgot her watch (the school had no clock), Mrs. Daniels would send Booker T. Sayler outside to tell the time by the sun.

Oh yes, she also taught us to read, write, and do math. She told the parents to send the children to school as soon as they stopped wetting in their clothes. I started when I was three and passed from first to second grade at the age of four.

When I was seven and Mae Frances was five, Mrs. Mamie Daniels taught us the first funeral song I ever sang. One set of parents who lived in the community had a water-headed baby; when the baby was four years old, she died. Mrs. Daniels helped to plan the funeral and she asked my mother if we could sing. Mrs. Daniels taught us "What Are They Doing in Heaven Today?" It was a composition of the gospel hymn composer Charles Albert Tindley. More than thirty years later, as a scholar at the Smithsonian Museum, I would organize a research project that would document his works and his role as a pioneering figure in gospel music history. When I learned this song at the age of seven, I did not learn the name of the composer; this song came as so many songs that were Black came, passed from someone else. I learned it as I learned all music—orally and by rote.

My mother has a picture of Mae Frances and me standing in front of the opened coffin, and I remember singing with Mae Frances:

I am thinking of friends that I used to know
Who lived and suffered in this world below
They've gone on to glory and I want to know
What are they doing there now?

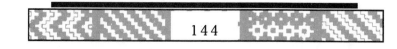

SWEET HONEY IN THE ROCK, JUNE 1992. WEARABLE ART: JANUWA MOJA. (PHOTOGRAPHER, RICHARD GREEN)

LEFT: SWEET HONEY IN THE ROCK, FIRST FULL CONCERT, D.C. BLACK REPERTORY COMPANY, LAST COLONY THEATER, WASHINGTON, D.C., APRIL 1974. L TO R, BERNICE JOHNSON REAGON, LOUISE ROBINSON, CAROL MAILLARD, MIE. (PHOTOGRAPHER, ROY LEWIS)

RIGHT: L TO R: BERNICE JOHNSON REAGON, CAROL MAILLARD, MIE. (PHOTOGRAPHER, ROY LEWIS)

TOP LEFT: SMITHSONIAN FESTIVAL OF AMERICAN FOLKLIFE, AFRICAN DIASPORA PROGRAM, 1975. L TO R: LOUISE ROBINSON, BERNICE JOHNSON REAGON, EVELYN MARIA HARRIS, PATRICIA JOHNSON. (PHOTOGRAPHER, ROSIE LEE HOOKS)

TOP RIGHT: SMITHSONIAN FESTIVAL OF AMERICAN FOLKLIFE, AFRICAN DIASPORA PROGRAM, 1974. FRONT TO BACK: BERNICE JOHNSON REAGON, LOUISE ROBINSON, MIE. (PHOTOGRAPHER, ROSIE LEE HOOKS)

BOTTOM RIGHT: SMITHSONIAN FESTIVAL OF AMERICAN FOLKLIFE, AFRICAN DIASPORA PROGRAM, 1975. L TO R: CAROL MAILLARD, PATRICIA JOHNSON, BERNICE JOHNSON REAGON, LOUISE ROBINSON. (PHOTOGRAPHER, ROSIE LEE HOOKS)

BOTTOM LEFT: SMITHSONIAN FESTIVAL OF AMERICAN FOLKLIFE, 1974. L TO R: MIE, LOUISE ROBINSON, BERNICE JOHNSON REAGON, CAROL MAILLARD. (PHOTOGRAPHER, ROSIE LEE HOOKS)

LEFT: IN AFRICAN WRAPS, MARCH 1976. L TO R: EVELYN HARRIS, PATRICIA JOHNSON, BERNICE JOHNSON REAGON, CAROL MAILLARD. FRONT: LOUISE ROBINSON. (PHOTOGRAPHER, RUDY JACKSON. PHOTO COURTESY OF SWEET HONEY IN THE ROCK ARCHIVES)

TOP RIGHT: FALL 1977. L TO R: BERNICE JOHNSON REAGON, YASMEEN WILLIAMS, EVELYN MARIA HARRIS, PATRICIA JOHNSON. (PHOTO COURTESY OF SWEET HONEY IN THE ROCK ARCHIVES)

BOTTOM RIGHT: WASHINGTON, D.C., FEBRUARY 1975. L TO R: ROSIE LEE HOOKS, LOUISE ROBINSON, CAROL MAILLARD, TIA JUANA STARKS, BERNICE JOHNSON REAGON. ON PIANO: DIANARUTHE WHARTON. (PHOTOGRAPHER, ROY LEWIS)

TOP LEFT: L. TO R: YASMEEN WILLIAMS, BERNICE JOHNSON REAGON, PATRICIA JOHNSON, EVELYN MARIA HARRIS. PHOTO FOR BACK COVER OF REDWOOD RECORDS RELEASE, *B'LIEVE I'LL RUN ON, SEE WHAT THE END'S GONNA BE*, 1977. (PHOTOGRAPHER, ROY LEWIS)

BOTTOM LEFT: 1977. L TO R: EVELYN MARIA HARRIS, PATRICIA JOHNSON, CAROL MAILLARD, YASMEEN WILLIAMS, BERNICE JOHNSON REAGON. (PHOTOGRAPHER, ROY LEWIS)

TOP RIGHT: FIRST TOUR TO CALIFORNIA, WOMEN'S CENTER, UC AT BERKELEY. L TO R: BERNICE JOHNSON REAGON, EVELYN HARRIS, LAURA SHARP, YASMEEN WILLIAMS. (PHOTOGRAPHER, CATHY CADE. PHOTO COURTESY OF SWEET HONEY IN THE ROCK ARCHIVES)

BOTTOM RIGHT: ROCK CREEK PARK, WASHINGTON, D.C., SUMMER 1977. L TO R: EVELYN MARIA HARRIS, YASMEEN WILLIAMS, BERNICE JOHNSON REAGON, PATRICIA JOHNSON. (PHOTOGRAPHER, ROLAND FREEMAN)

LEFT: WINTER 1977. L TO R: BERNICE JOHNSON REAGON, YASMEEN WILLIAMS, PATRICIA JOHNSON, EVELYN MARIA HARRIS. (PHOTOGRAPHER, SHARON FARMER)

RIGHT: 1979. L TO R: YSAYE MARIA BARNWELL, EVELYN MARIA HARRIS, BERNICE JOHNSON REAGON, YASMEEN WILLIAMS, TULANI JORDAN. COSTUME DESIGN CONCEPT BY AFI SAUNDERS. (PHOTOGRAPHER, OLIVER NAPHLIN. PHOTO COURTESY OF SWEET HONEY IN THE ROCK ARCHIVES)

TOP LEFT: JUNE 1980, L TO R: EVELYN MARIA HARRIS, YSAYE MARIA BARNWELL, HELENA COLEMAN, BERNICE JOHNSON REAGON. (PHOTOGRAPHER, MARGERY TABANE. PHOTO COURTESY OF SWEET HONEY IN THE ROCK ARCHIVES)

BOTTOM LEFT: VOICES OF THE CIVIL RIGHTS MOVEMENT CONFERENCE, SMITHSONIAN INSTITUTION, 1980. L TO R: EVELYN MARIA HARRIS, TOSHI REAGON (ON GUITAR), YSAYE MARIA BARNWELL. (PHOTOGRAPHER, ROLAND FREEMAN)

RIGHT: VOICES OF THE CIVIL RIGHTS MOVEMENT CONFERENCE, SMITHSONIAN INSTITUTION, FEBRUARY 1980. L TO R: E. D. NIXON, LEADER OF MONTGOMERY BUS BOYCOTT, BERNICE JOHNSON REAGON, ELLA BAKER. (PHOTOGRAPHER, ROLAND FREEMAN)

暖かくやさしく強く岩にひびく

スウィート・ハニー・イン・ザ・ロック

蜜のように

5人の黒人女性ボーカルグループ
愛と平和をうたう

12月11日（木） PM 6:30　姫路市市民会館
会費　一般2,800円（各割引有）入会金100円
後援／姫路市教育委員会・姫路市民文化協会

1/27　桂米朝独演会　　PM6:30
　　　　　　　　　　　姫路市市民会館

お問合せ　姫路労音　姫路市本町46−2
　　　　　　　　　　　福永ビル3F

BOTTOM RIGHT: 1980. L TO R: HELENA COLEMAN, TULANI JORDAN, YASMEEN WILLIAMS, BERNICE JOHNSON REAGON. (PHOTO COURTESY OF SWEET HONEY IN THE ROCK ARCHIVES)

BOTTOM LEFT: SWEET HONEY IN JAPAN, POSTER, DECEMBER 11, 1980. (PHOTOGRAPHER, DIEM JONES. POSTER COURTESY OF SWEET HONEY IN THE ROCK ARCHIVES. TRANSLATION: SWEET HONEY IN THE ROCK, AFRICAN AMERICAN FEMALE VOCAL GROUP SINGING LOVE AND PEACE, DECEMBER 11, THURSDAY, 6:30 P.M., HIMEJI CITY MUNICIPAL HALL, GEN. ADM.: 2800 YEN, DISCOUNTS AVAILABLE, MEMBERSHIP FEE, 100 YEN. SPONSORED BY HIMEJI CITY BOARD OF EDUCATION, AND HIMEJI CITIZENS CULTURAL ASSOCIATION. LIGHTER BACKGROUND WRITING ACROSS THE PHOTO: "WARM, GENTLE, STRONG, THEY ARE HIDING IN THE ROCK—JUST LIKE HONEY. AT BOTTOM: A LISTING OF FUTURE ENGAGEMENTS)

TOP: IN CONCERT IN JAPAN. L TO R: EVELYN MARIA HARRIS, YSAYE MARIA BARNWELL, GERALDINE HARDIN, BERNICE JOHNSON REAGON. (PHOTOGRAPHER, MUNESUKE YAMAMOTO. PHOTO COURTESY OF SWEET HONEY IN THE ROCK ARCHIVES)

1981. L TO R: BERNICE JOHNSON REAGON, YSAYE MARIA BARNWELL, YASMEEN WILLIAMS. SEATED: EVELYN MARIA HARRIS. (PHOTOGRAPHER, OLIVER NAPHLIN. PHOTO COURTESY OF SWEET HONEY IN THE ROCK ARCHIVES)

Mrs. Daniels always asked an older student to lead Devotion. It was where I learned one of my largest repertoires of songs. I remember "Wade in the Water" mostly because of a story Mrs. Daniels told about Harriet Tubman, a story that was echoed by older people in the community through the years as I grew up. We were told that this was a song used by Harriet Tubman, who was a conductor on the Underground Railroad. I had never heard the term before going to school, so I thought there was a tunnel under the ground with tracks on it for the train driven by a woman conductor named Harriet Tubman. This story was not in any book I read during those years and I read them all. This story was out of the stories that my teachers, first Mrs. Daniels and then Miss Darnell Lee, taught us in the spaces between the curriculum pulled from the books.

The Harriet story is in my blood, flesh of my flesh. I learned it in the air I breathed. I learned it as I learned who I was. Stories like this taught me that for my people songs were more than singing to feel good, they were also instruments, offerings that we created to help us fight and survive and sometimes leave slavery.

Wade in the water, wade in the water children
Wade in the water, God gonna trouble the water

See those children dressed in white
The leader looks like that Israelite

Miss Lee told us that her grandmother had been a slave and used to show her the marks on her body from being whipped. She said her grandmother told her also that the slaves would go out and have meetings against the wishes of the master. They would take one of the slave cabins and put a big black iron wash pot in the middle of the floor so the sound of the singing would go in the pot and not out the door. I thought about my mother's wash pot; it was the biggest I had ever seen. We used it every week to boil clothes in potash water, before we brought them to the washtub to be scrubbed on the washboard with Octagon soap or homemade soap we made every year when we killed a hog. I wondered if that pot was big enough to catch the songs of a meeting in a slave cabin.

It was Mrs. Daniels who said I was a contralto. I didn't know what it meant. She explained it by saying I had a low voice. I sang all the songs an octave lower than the rest of the students; they thought I sounded funny. Mrs. Daniels brought out Nurse Jolly, also a contralto. Mrs. Daniels said that she had a beautiful voice. Nurse Jolly sang "Talk About a Child Love Jesus, Here Is One," she sang in an operatic style, which sounded strange and not so beautiful. We could see that Mrs. Daniels was holding her up as model for good singing. We also began to realize that what we thought was beauty and what someone else thought was beauty might be

different. We were being introduced to another system of sound that had different standards. For me it took some work to get used to, then to learn to perform, and then, out of the doing, to learn to love more than one way of singing beautifully.

We did not sing gospel or blues there. If in school we sang songs that were spirituals which we also sang in church, we sang them differently. You could not get happy off the singing we did in school. The whole point of singing in church was to transform, to feed the soul. In school we sang to learn, we sang to know ourselves, but the part of our tradition that was emotionally charged, close to the ground, stayed outside.

No, we did not sing gospel in school. And during Negro History Week we did not put Mahalia Jackson in our scrapbooks. We put in Marian Anderson and Roland Hayes, who were trained in the European classical vocal tradition, along with Booker T. Washington, who after slavery founded Tuskegee Institute in Alabama, and Jackie Robinson, who broke the racial barrier in baseball when he played with the Brooklyn Dodgers, and Joe Louis, "the Brown Bomber," who was the heavyweight champion of the world, and George Washington Carver, the scientist who revolutionized Southern agriculture by developing multiple uses for the sweet potato and the peanut, and we put in Harriet Tubman, our "Moses" conductor on the Underground Railroad. We did not put in Paul Robeson, singer, actor, world fighter for justice, or W. E. B. Du Bois, one of the greatest intellectual minds of the twentieth century, scholar, educator, fighter for justice. Du Bois and Robeson were considered leftist radicals sympathetic to socialism and communism—too hot to handle for that Southern Black school in a Southern White-run school district.

Mrs. Daniels introduced me during elementary school to what would later be called oral history. One Negro History Week, she took some of us to Albany State College to interview the teachers. I interviewed Mamie Reese, a national leader of the Colored Women's Club organization as well as a college professor, and Mr. Samuel Elkins, who had been director of the Wings Over Jordan Choir. Then we went back to school, wrote up the interviews, and put them in our scrapbooks next to George Washington Carver and Marian Anderson. I began to consider that people I could talk to in my life, people I saw walking around and working in my community, could be considered leaders, if only someone took the time to talk to them about their lives and their work.

"CRIED AND I CRIED UNTIL I FOUND THE LORD"
THE RADIO

We got a radio when I was four years old, during the first Christmas in our new house that my father had built. I heard the Wings Over Jordan Choir broadcasts, with the Reverend Glenn Settles narrating on that radio, under an opening

hum that moved into their theme song, an uplifting rendition of the spiritual "Cried and I Cried."

Cried and I cried
Cried all night long
Cried and I cried
Until I found the Lord

After that broadcast, *Sweet and Swing* featuring big-band music would come on. The music was always jumping, it was jazz, and at this point my mother would always cut the radio off. One day when she let it linger, my brother J.W. started popping his fingers. Momma told him, "The devil will get you if you pop your fingers." He stopped popping his fingers and started patting his feet and asked, "Will he get you if you pat your feet?" The radio went off.

Every Sunday morning our home was filled with the smells of breakfast cooking—chicken, or country-fried steak, biscuits, grits, gravy—and the sounds of the radio featuring local quartets from Albany and surrounding counties, and the latest gospel records. It was here that I first heard Mahalia Jackson singing "Move On Up a Little Higher." (In 1963, as a member of the Student Nonviolent Coordinating Committee (SNCC) Freedom Singers, I sang standing right next to her to close a benefit concert at Carnegie Hall for the Civil Rights Movement.)

I heard Brother Joe Mays, the "thunderbolt of the Midwest," singing "Search Me Lord." My mother and I listened to Rosetta Tharpe sing "Strange Things Happening in This World," and I remember Momma talking about how she sometimes sounded like she was singing "reals." "Reals" are secular songs, usually about love relationships, sometimes called blues, rhythm and blues, soul—they are all called "reals."

Through radio gospel programs, I was introduced to the sound that set the mold for what is today known as the classic gospel choral style. This was the music of the Roberta Martin Singers. Gloria Griffin was the contralto lead and I tried to sing like her; I loved the way she sang "God Specializes."

The radio brought the sounds of the Davis Sisters from Philadelphia; I loved Ruth Davis leading "Twelve Gates to the City" and "Tree on Each Side of the River." My Aunt Fannie would die to hear Clara Ward and the Ward Singers singing anything and she especially loved Marion Williams leading the Ward Singers' "Surely God Is Able," a composition of the Reverend William Herbert Brewster, whose work and legacy were the subjects of a research project and major conference at the Smithsonian in 1983, with the Reverend Brewster in attendance.

Every gospel choir in Southwest Georgia was singing Lucie E. Campbell's "Touch Me Lord Jesus" recorded by the Angelic Gospel Singers. The Caravans singing "Oh Mary Don't You Weep," led by Inez Andrews, and the Gospel Harmonettes, led by the great voice of Dorothy Love Coates singing "Get Away

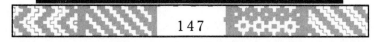

Jordan" and "He's Calling Me," Alex Bradford and the Bradford Specials singing "Too Close to Heaven," all of these people coming through the radio (we did not have a record player) became an integral part of who I was as a young Black girl growing up in Dougherty County.

The quartets that sang in our local churches, and those that became national names, provided me one of my strongest, most consistent harmony lessons. I learned to sing quartet, listening to the Spirit of Memphis, the Five Blind Boys of Jackson, Mississippi, the Soul Stirrers, the Fairfield Four, the Skylarks, the Swan Silvertones, and the Swanee Quintet.

My father took us to two gospel concerts at the Albany City Auditorium. The first one featured the Five Blind Boys of Jackson, Mississippi, and the Sensational Nightingales. The concert was sold out and they didn't want to let us in, but my father pushed his way in, saying he was a minister and that was that. I remember the stance and force he used and was not familiar with it. I had seen him work hard, or use his physical strength to move a heavy object or to lift something, but this was different; while it was not a physical motion he made, it was the stance he took. There was no way we were not going to be inside that hall. They put us on the stage and I could see Archie Brownlee up close. I think I fell in love with the Sensational Nightingales; they all had processed hair, and one member played this shiny big guitar.

The next concert was also the Five Blind Boys, accompanied this time by the Soul Stirrers. My mother came back talking about how that Sam Cook could sing. For myself, I was thrilled with Archie Brownlee and the Five Blind Boys. No one was sadder than I when he died; I was shocked to hear my father say he drank a lot. I thought that if he sang like that, he had to be a good Christian and live a righteous life—I was young.

"THE HEAVENS ARE TELLING"
MONROE HIGH SCHOOL

In September 1955, I started high school at the age of twelve and immediately tried out for the glee club and the chorus so I would be able to wear stockings. I also hoped making the audition would accelerate the time when I would be allowed to wear makeup. When I auditioned, Miss Anne Elizabeth Wright, the choir director, had me sing songs, and she tested me to see if I could harmonize. I had been doing a little in the gospel choir at Mt. Early, but this music was different and I was unsure how to transfer skills I had learned in gospel and congregational singing over to this audition where you had to sing more "polished, cultured, and refined," words used then to describe the European vocal concert tradition. Almost by accident, as Miss Wright sang a spiritual, I slipped into the alto line, and I was in the

chorus. By May of my freshman year (1956), when the chorus sang for commencement, I had on stockings and lipstick for the first time; I was thirteen.

Rehearsals were wonderful. Miss Wright would hit that piano with the opening chord and we would explode into:

The heavens are telling the glory of God
The wonder of his word, proclaim its firmament
The wonder of his word, proclaim its firmament

We would be so excited! I would feel as if I was flying in the song. And she would say, "Now, now, choir, you don't have to scream it out," but we weren't screaming, we were flying in the singing.

I became the contralto soloist. My solo selections were "Stan' Still Jordan," which moved me deeply, and "Through the Years," which I could not feel. I also sang "September," and the sextet sang "Old Cape Cod."

If you're fond of sand dunes and salty air
Quaint little villages, here and there
You're sure to fall in love with old Cape Cod

I did not know what a sand dune was, had never tasted salty air, neither did I know anything about farms that had wheat fields waving, oats and sheep. There were no stories in my schoolbooks about farms that grew sweet potatoes, corn for grits and eating on the cob and making into meal, turnip and collard greens. That's another story, but I did love the feel of songs even when they told stories that were far beyond anything I could imagine.

We learned to make our sound round and covered. It was the same way Nurse Jolly sang in elementary school. I *learned* to really like this style of singing and this repertoire of songs. It was an integral part of the educational culture created in the Black community and an indicator of an African American strategy of advancing with the larger society by becoming fluent in the ways of that culture.

Six of us girls in our homeroom formed a doo-wop group called the Anglets. Barbara Gilyard led the title original song, called "I Wanta Be Your Angel," and I led "Been So Long" and my boyfriend almost jumped over his seat.

Mrs. Chadwell heard me sing "Stan' Still Jordan" and arranged for me to audition at Albany State College for her husband, John H. Chadwell, who was the head of the Music Department. She was insistent that I take myself seriously as a singer. He told me that he would have a place for me in the choir when I came to Albany State College. I began to feel like a singer.

"ALLELUIA"
ALBANY STATE COLLEGE

At Albany I started out as a music major, but had real trouble feeling music in the theory and harmony classes, so I thought I could not be a real musician. I could sing, but it was clear that that was not enough to be considered a musician. The Music Department of Albany State College, like most college and university Music Departments, was organized to make you feel that if you could not read music and if you conveyed music only orally you could not succeed as a musician. It took me decades to come to understand that music that is written down is not superior music. The music score is only one way of transmitting music. Music that is conveyed literally makes up the smallest portion of communicated music in the universe. Most of the music of the world is transmitted orally. To be a master at learning and teaching music orally is to be at the center of music making in the world. However, this was 1959, and "musician" and "music literacy" were synonyms. I could be in the choir, I could sing solo, but the music majors were required to be literate and fluent in reading music. Paper was the mode of transmission, and though I had had sight-singing throughout high school, I felt more centered when I learned music through my native oral transmission process.

I had changed my major to biology. I made the decision to change in response to my frustrations with the Music Department and the fact that I was making straight A's in all my first-year science and math courses: biology, geometry, and trig. This turned out to be an error—I was destroyed by physics and chemistry—I couldn't feel anything there either.

Although I had changed my major, I kept singing, and studying with Mr. Chadwell. I did my first improvisation on "Summertime," while the Reverend Brown played the organ. I still don't know how it happened. He did a soulful introduction on that organ, and when I started to sing, I skirted the melody and regrouped the phrasing—it was a monumental step in my development as a singer.

I attended Albany State College with two scholarships, one from Delta Sigma Theta and one from Alpha Kappa Alpha, my sorority. At the end of the first year, I was the highest-ranking freshman. I was in every organization I could be in and was having a great time!

"OVER MY HEAD I SEE FREEDOM IN THE AIR"
THE ALBANY MOVEMENT

I found my voice and my stance as a fighter, and earned the right to change traditional songs to new freedom songs in the Movement, as a member of the first Youth Chapter of the NAACP in Albany. I was the secretary. This was spring 1959, and I was a senior in high school.

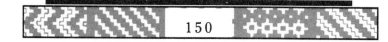

Singing for My Life

My consciousness about Black people struggling for freedom went back further. I had felt the change in the air in my home when in 1954 Emmet Till and Charles Mack Parker were lynched in Mississippi; the Supreme Court had handed down the *Brown* v. *Topeka Board of Education* decision, and our teachers were telling us we had better get ready because integration was coming.

As a junior high school student in 1954–55 I had lived daily with Autherine Lucy, who through a suit launched by the NAACP integrated the University of Alabama. I fantasized going to school with her every day.

In December 1955, the Montgomery Bus Boycott was born when Rosa Parks refused to get out of her seat on a Montgomery, Alabama, bus and was arrested. She, with E. D. Nixon, Ralph David Abernathy, Martin Luther King Jr., Mary Ethel Jones, and all the Black people of Montgomery, made us believe that we could stand because they walked for a year to draw a new line in the dirt in their hometown of Montgomery.

The Little Rock, Arkansas, school desegregation case, in which nine Black students attended the formerly White Central High School, took place in 1957 and I learned my first military division unit. President Dwight David Eisenhower sent in the 101st Airborne Division to ensure the admission and protection of the Little Rock nine attending Central High School. It was forced integration.

An initial action of the first NAACP Youth Chapter in Albany in 1959 was to send a delegation to the White owner of the Harlem Drugstore (located in the Black community with Black clientele) to request that a Black clerk be hired—he refused. Early in 1960, during my second quarter as a college student at Albany State College, the Sit-In Movement erupted. All over the South, beginning with the February 1 Greensboro, North Carolina, Sit-Ins, Black students (sometimes joined by White students) sat in lunch counters, movies, restaurants, churches, and racially segregated establishments that served the public. There were supportive demonstrations all over the nation; there was even a bus boycott in Johannesburg, South Africa. The country was in an uproar and Black students were moving out of the classrooms into the streets in growing numbers.

Julian Bond, then a student at Morehouse College and a member of the Atlanta Student Movement, called the student government office at Albany State and asked for sympathy demonstrations on Black campuses across the South. I was in the small group of students that got together to demand that our president, William H. Dennis, take a stand. He did take a stand; he suspended student government for the rest of the year and forced the dean of students to resign for supporting us. Understanding a little more about taking stands, we went into the summer waiting for the next opportunity.

In the fall of 1961, I met the Reverend Charles Sherrod from Virginia and Cordell Hull Reagon, from Nashville, field secretaries for the Student Nonviolent Coordinating Committee. SNCC had come to town and it would change my life. This was an organization formed by students who had been involved in their local

sit-ins; many of them had been sent to jail during the Freedom Rides. The organization was led by Charles McDew, Diane Nash, and James Bevel out of Nashville and Marion Barry, James Farmer, Charles Sherrod, and Bob Moses. Ella Baker and Howard Zinn served as advisors. The group decided to move out using two strategies, direct action, in which local people would be mobilized to move in demonstrations against local segregated institutions, and voter registration drives that would be launched in key Black Belt areas of the South where Blacks outnumbered Whites.

Sherrod and Cordell had been sent into Southwest Georgia to start a voter registration drive because in most of the counties, although Blacks outnumbered Whites, they were not registered voters because of terrorism and fear for their lives and the lives of their families. The threat was there every day. It was the local police, it was the employee who refused to serve you, it was every White person a Black person had to face in trying to survive. Voting was not one of the things you did in Terrell, Mitchell, Baker, and Sumter counties if you were a Black American citizen. A voter registration drive in the late forties and early fifties, however, put a large number of Blacks on the rolls in Dougherty County, where I lived. SNCC decided that they would set up an office in Albany and work from there into the surrounding target counties.

Sherrod was accompanied by Cordell Hull Reagon, a veteran at seventeen of the Nashville Sit-Ins, the Freedom Rides, six weeks in Parchman State Penitentiary, the McComb, Mississippi, voter registration drive, and the Cairo, Illinois, campaign. He had a singular energy about him when he was trying to get people involved in Movement activity, whether for joining a demonstration, registering to vote, or attending a workshop on nonviolence. He was a beautiful singer with a warm high tenor voice, and was passionate about the struggle for freedom. We fell in love, working and singing together in the Albany Movement. We were married two years later, and have two children, Toshi and Kwan Tauna.

SNCC set up their office in the beginning of the fall quarter of 1961. In my first discussions with Cordell and Sherrod, I often asked about the name of the organization, the Student Nonviolent Coordinating Committee. I had no cultural reference for the term "nonviolent." It did not compute for me as word, or as a concept. I could not figure out why anyone would name their organization that. "Coordinating" wasn't much better. The only part of the name that made sense to me as part of an organization's name was "student." These men who were my age were already moving in the world in new ways that I knew nothing about. The thing I understood was that I wanted to be a part of the Movement developing throughout the South. I wanted to participate in changing Albany, Georgia. I wanted to find a way to stand with my life.

By Christmas 1961, I had participated in nonviolent workshops (I had settled for a functional definition: if someone hit me I was not to hit them back), argued with the NAACP about whether SNCC was a responsible group and whether

NAACP members should work with SNCC, gone to jail, been suspended from school, sung freedom songs, and found a new voice.

Sherrod and Cordell organized workshops in nonviolence. They talked about nonviolence as love, turning the other cheek. They made it clear that if I wanted to participate in the Movement, I could not fight. It wasn't a major problem for me since I did not have a history of getting into physical fights.

One evening in the fall of 1961, state representatives from the NAACP came to town to tell us of the Youth Chapter in Albany that we could not be in SNCC and in the NAACP simultaneously. They said that following SNCC would land us in jail, and that the NAACP, which was testing court cases and had the financial resources, would have to get us out. They told us to choose between the two organizations. Mr. Thomas Chatmon, our advisor, spoke to us quietly, saying that he would be with us no matter what, so we took a vote. Blanton Hall and Bertha Gober voted to go with SNCC, and I think I voted to stay with the NAACP or did not vote at all. The process was so painful, I only remember sitting there feeling that someone was telling me there was a choice for me to make that I could not see or feel. Why couldn't we work together? We were all working for freedom, weren't we? I didn't have the courage to vote with SNCC and against the NAACP, because they were one in my soul; their existence as two groups meant nothing to me. I was so angry with Rubye Hurley for putting the question to us and asking me to choose that I stopped attending NAACP meetings altogether. It would be another twenty-five years before I would become a life member of the NAACP.

In November 1961, I learned the name of my first agency of the federal government. The Interstate Commerce Commission (ICC) ruled that any commerce that involved transportation across state lines was in its bailiwick and could not operate or use segregated facilities. It was during Thanksgiving break when student members of the NAACP Youth Chapter went to the Trailways bus station to test the ruling. They were arrested when they tried to buy tickets from the White waiting room window and were bailed out by the NAACP as planned.

However, it was different with Bertha Gober and Blanton Hall, who went as SNCC representatives to buy tickets. They were arrested, refused to pay bail, and stayed in jail. I think I was still mad at being split between the NAACP and SNCC, but the arrest of Bertha and Blanton settled it for me. Clearly, the action in Albany was going to be led by SNCC and I was going to be involved. I learned an important lesson. Groups who should be partners will often jeopardize the overall struggle over issues of control and power. The divisiveness between these two organizations with the same goal of increased freedom for our people was painful, and their blunt way of demanding that we choose between them was a scarring process.

That winter in 1961, I decided to work where the key battle was going to take place, the one I wanted to be in, the one that was attacking racism in my community. When Sherrod and Cordell, who had been joined by a third SNCC field worker, Charlie Jones, called for a support demonstration on Albany State's cam-

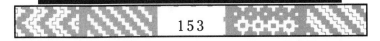

pus for Blanton and Bertha, I joined in. We were marching to protest their arrest and to give them support while they were in jail.

There was no singing as we walked through the halls of the campus buildings trying to get students to join us in support of Bertha and Blanton. We were quiet as we walked the blocks up the hill to the Flint River bridge. I walked with my best friend, Annette Jones. I felt like we had failed because there were so few, so I just kept my head in front and kept walking. When we got almost to the bridge, Annette said, "Bernice, look back!" But I wouldn't and I kept walking. Then she said, "Bernice, just look back!" I turned around and almost shouted out loud, because from the bridge to the campus there was nothing but students. It was the same feeling I felt when I would watch TV reports during the Montgomery Bus Boycott, when every day the buses would still be empty as my people held it together and kept walking; only this time it was me, it was Annette Jones, Janie Culbreth, Bobby Burch, Cordell Reagon, Charlie Jones. It was Albany's time now.

We walked silently, two by two, twice around the courthouse and then headed back to the campus. When we got to the corner, Charlie Jones asked the Reverend William Boyd if we could meet at Union Baptist, because it was obvious we could not go to the campus. The administration had shown its hostility to all efforts related to the growing activism of Black students the year before, when it suspended the student government. Inside the church, Charlie Jones said, "Bernice, sing a song," and I began to sing "Over my head I see . . ." Usually in the opening line I always sang "trouble in the air"; however, since Albany had just had its first march that wasn't a homecoming or thanksgiving parade, I did not see any "trouble." I saw "freedom," so I switched the words as I sang and everyone followed, raising up the song.

Over my head I see Freedom in the air
Over my head I see Freedom in the air
Over my head I see Freedom in the air
There must be a God somewhere

Over my head I see glory in the air . . .
Over my head I see music in the air . . .

It was the first time my living had changed a song even as it came out of my body. Freedom!

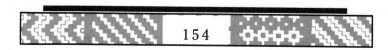

"IF I DO LIKE MY LORD SAY DO, EVERYTHING WILL BE ALL RIGHT"

If I do like my Lord say do, everything will be all right
He will make my yoke wear easy, and my burden will be light

If I sing like my Lord say sing, everything will be all right
He will make my yoke wear easy, and my burden will be light.

Glory Glory Hallelujah, since I laid my burden down
Glory Glory Hallelujah, since I laid my burden down

That was my jail song. We sang the new freedom songs that Cordell and Sherrod had taught us, but the ones that I sang the most in jail were the old ones that I had learned growing up in the Mt. Early Baptist Church. We sang the spirituals that we learned in my high school and college choirs, changing words to make them speak for us. And we sang the songs we were making up every day.

The day after the first march for Blanton and Bertha, another support march was called, and Annette Jones went on this second march and everyone was arrested. However, I had gone to school to take a test, and I was in the student center when a student came in to announce the marchers' arrest. I thought I would die; I had not been there and was not in jail. I made sure I made the third march, and when Sheriff Laurie Pritchett said, "I will count to three and I want you to disperse," we didn't and we were all arrested. I was in jail! Freedom!

The marches continued and people were getting arrested every day. By the end of the first week of demonstrations there were over seven hundred of us in jail. It was an American record for mass incarceration of its citizens! We were a historic first!

I learned again in that cell that everything in the Movement did not go smoothly or in one accord. It was an important lesson. People knew why they were there, but there were a variety of sub-reasons underlying the main reason they had decided to march and risk going to jail. One woman was a minister's wife and said she represented her husband. She asked me if I was representing my father, and I said that he would have to go for himself, I was in jail for me!

We were high school and college students, wives, mothers, workers, educated and uneducated, churched and unchurched, sober and non, and grandmothers—our elders. It was not reasonable to think that there would be constant harmony, but with effort, we did stay together, and songs and singing were indispensable ingredients.

One woman in jail with us had been drinking with her husband in Harlem when she decided to join the march. Albany had a two-block district we called Harlem; it was where the juke joints were and some of the Black businesses. It was

a place where things could get rough and people could get cut, shot, or even killed, except during the Civil Rights Movement, when the violence level almost disappeared within the Black community. There is a lesson here somewhere. Maybe when we oppressed people rise up and challenge the real source of our rage, then the members of our families and communities are safer. Maybe a lot of the domestic and inner community violence that ravages our homes and communities is misdirected.

Anyway, this sister was having a good time with her husband when our line of marchers turned the corner to go through Harlem to get downtown to City Hall. She said that her husband could not stop her from going to be with her people. She ran into the line and was with us when we were arrested and was with us the next morning, a little hung over and a bit upset to be in jail. She did not express herself in Christian-approved language, and this was not comforting to the older women who believed that God was with us and we must keep to a certain amount of respect and decorum. When things would rub between people of different persuasions, someone would say, "Sing a song, Bernice," and I would. People were not necessarily changed, but singing collectively created more space to be together in a cell with no space.

Conditions in jail were grim. It was a little early in the game, and even though most of us had consciously prepared to march and go to jail if necessary, we had not yet learned to bring our toothbrush, wear three pairs of panties, two pairs of jeans, three shirts, and bring deodorant. The more experienced women had us damping soap for deodorant and there was a bit more breathing space.

The marches continued and so did the jailings. One day we were loaded on buses and driven to the Lee County Stockade, where about sixty women were put in one large room lined with cots. This jail provided more space, but it was the first time we could not hear the men. In the city jail, the men's cells were right next to ours and we could talk and sing together. There were several of us who continued to do a lot of the song leading. I was very clear about why I had marched and why I was going to be in the Movement. As we talked, I found that I was listened to by others in spite of my age. I also found that it was good to be in a space with a lot of women who were of different ages. My clarity was helpful sometimes when others got down or depressed; the singing seemed to connect people, and I was perceived as one of the leaders. To be perceived as such was unusual for me in a multi-age group, and in a group where there were already many leaders.

In jail I found out that I had already been trained to lead songs, to choose songs, and to teach songs. It was easy to know what song would be good to sing. Things that I had learned by growing up in church, where you had to select from the inside, on a spiritual and intuitive level, were being tested and I was ready. Freedom!

In jail, I practiced a kind of singing that has stuck with me. It is the kind of singing where the song and singing are used to say who you are and what you think,

and to confront and be an instrument for getting through the world. It was not a kind of singing that had "profession" written on it. It was the kind that was seamless with your existence. This singing took place on a different level than the singing that I had done in the glee clubs and choruses of my life. It was more related to the singing of the elders in church, but different because it was me and now I knew what I was singing about and how it carried me through. Without a lot of conscious work I was beginning to become a singing fighter.

There is a difference between choosing a profession and becoming your adult self. Growing up, it seemed like every adult I met asked me what was I going to be when I grew up. In my early years, it felt like I changed it every time I was asked: a teacher, a lawyer, a doctor, a nurse. Whatever it was, they nodded and said, "Well, that's good. Study hard."

One night, when my sister Ruth asked me what I was going to be, I looked at the Singer sewing machine and said, "I am going to be a singer!"

There was a great distance between that game and what was happening to me in jail. I was conscious of being centered, feeling safe, being at ease with myself, and knowing that I was where I was supposed to be.

When I got out of jail, I was hoarse from around-the-clock singing. At the next mass meeting, I was asked to lead a song. I started to sing "Over my head I see freedom in the air." My voice! It was bigger! It had grown! It was as if my living through the jail experience had also been a voice lesson. I still think that to do Black singing, you not only need to do some struggle and living, you also have to sing your way through. You can actually feel and hear the changes in your instrument and the way in which you handle a song as you sing your life.

Later, I would talk about being born again during the Civil Rights Movement, and I was. I got a new walk! I got a new talk! I got a new song! I got a new taste in my mouth, which I still use to know if I am walking the path of freedom. The taste has taken me many places. I was against the United States' involvement in the war in Vietnam; I understand and support the struggles of the indigenous people of our country; I believe in the United Farm Workers of America and the right of the workers who harvest the crops to lead humane lives; I support the struggle of women to organize and change our condition within our specific communities and the larger society, it is with me at all times; I have sung and marched for peace, against U.S. military aggression and nuclear proliferation; I am a part of the struggle for dignity and justice led by lesbian and gay communities; and I have created songs that sing of the sanity of ecological balance that include the acknowledgment of poor and indigenous populations. . . . It is a treasured journey I make and the path I walk is worn clear by those souls who have gone before me and those who keep me company. We are a mighty chorus!

"GO ELIJAH!"
WILLIS LAURENCE JAMES

After being suspended from Albany State College in January 1962 because of our participation in the protest demonstrations (my suspension letter stated that I could not return because of behavior unbecoming a student of Albany State College), efforts were made to get us into schools in Atlanta. Morehouse College, Spelman College, and Morris Brown College all agreed to accept us as students after interviews. Marian and Slater King drove us down to Atlanta. Mrs. King had gone to Spelman and she wanted me to sing for Dr. Willis Laurence James, the head of the Music Department. She called him and he said that he would see me the next day. When I auditioned for Dr. James, he did not ask me to sing anything, he only allowed me to sing scales, and I was impressed. I felt as if he was trying to determine what there was in my instrument to work with.

This was the second time I had met Dr. Willis Laurence James. During my senior year in high school I had performed in a regional high school soloist contest at Atlanta University. Dr. James was the judge for the contest and I placed second. He offered me a scholarship that paid half the tuition cost to go to Spelman, but that still left too much money for our family to come up with, so I went to Albany State College.

At the close of the audition, Dr. James told me I could come to Spelman as a student in voice and that he could make me another Marian Anderson. I must have looked funny, because he asked me what was wrong; I said that there was already a Marian Anderson, I wanted to be Bernice Johnson. My elementary school teacher had told me the same thing, and it was not something I wanted. While I understood these comments were meant as compliments, they ran up against a deep feeling inside me that did not need to be anybody else. I could learn from Mahalia Jackson or Marian Anderson, be inspired by them, but being like them would be an automatic second-class position. How could I possibly beat these divas at being them? I could only join them and sit in their company if I brought myself along with my own offering that was me.

I loved Dr. James, though, and I loved that glee club, with those wonderful songs: "Lord Thou Hast Been a Dwelling Place," and "Go Elijah," and "Lord Everywhere." I was in the second alto section, where we would just rumble in the bottom. It was the fullest and richest sound I had ever experienced in a female ensemble and for the rest of my life I would always be reaching for that sound.

"WE'LL NEVER TURN BACK"
THE FREEDOM SINGERS

The SNCC Freedom Singers were organized by Cordell and Jim Forman during the fall of 1962. I was a student at Spelman when Cordell asked if I could go to Chicago to sing in a Gospel Sing for Freedom, a benefit concert to be held at McCormick Place. Dr. James refused to grant me permission to go, saying that I had done a great thing in the Movement but that I needed to turn my attention to finishing school. I obeyed by not going, but I knew then that I still had to be free to be in the Movement whenever it called.

On November 11, 1962, there was a Pete Seeger and Freedom Singer Benefit Concert for SNCC held in the Morehouse gym, and I asked Dr. James to announce it in chapel. He talked about meeting Peter Seeger and seeing and hearing him work. He said that here was a man who did not have a great voice but he had seen him get an audience of thousands to sing "Balm in Gilead" in four-part harmony in a matter of five minutes. I sang with the Freedom Singers that Sunday, November 11, and left Spelman on November 12, 1962, and started to travel with the group in December 1962.

When I left Spelman, however, I did not go directly to SNCC. I needed to go to myself, I needed a neutral place. Leaving school was wrenching, I was on full scholarship at one of the best schools in the country and I needed to not be there. I needed to be in the Movement, but I also needed to go to a place where I could have time to make the transition and be clear about my next move. I needed a space that was not school, not family, not Movement, a space that would give me the time to get a new grounding. Anna Jo Weaver, an exchange student from Washington State, gave me eighty dollars and I bought a bus ticket to Saratoga Springs to stay with Lena Spencer at the Cafe Lena, a folk music coffeehouse. I sang in the coffeehouse, helped to run it, and spent hours talking to Lena about everything. I met some people who became lifelong friends through the Friends of SNCC organization they formed in that area.

One day, I got a call from Toshi Seeger, who invited me to spend my first Christmas away from home with them. Toshi Seeger is one of the most amazing women I have ever met. She has brilliant organizing skills; it seemed to me that she could do and did everything. She cooked, cleaned, took care of the place, took care of children, took care of me, and handled the administrative end of Pete's career. I was fascinated and learned all I could. If, today, I am a decent producer of cultural events, it is because of what I learned watching and working with Toshi Seeger. Our connection was personal; when she thought about beauty, it was not conventional. She helped me to make a dress, and said that since I had big shoulders we weren't going to cover them up; or said, "Let's change the A-line in this pattern to give you a little more room for your hips." We talked about everything. When my first child was born, a daughter, I named her Toshi.

I left the Seegers a few days after Christmas and traveled to Dorchester, Georgia, for a SNCC staff meeting. On December 30, the Freedom Singers Cordell Hull Reagon, Rutha Mae Harris, Charles Neblett, Chico Neblett, and I left Dorchester in a six-cylinder Buick station wagon donated by Len Dressler, a singer Cordell had met in Chicago, with a thousand dollars donated by SNCC worker Bobbie Yancy, and headed for our first date, the national convention of the YWCA and the YMCA being held in Carbondale, Illinois.

During my year with this group, I traveled this land of my birth, the United States of America. The Freedom Singers met and performed with the Georgia Sea Island Singers, Dock Reese, the Moving Star Hall Singers, Odetta, Bob Dylan, Pete Seeger, Joan Baez, Theo Bikel, Peter, Paul and Mary, the Chad Mitchell Trio, and Len Chandler. We met thousands through our concerts who as citizens of this country and human beings wanted to be a part of the struggle against racism in this land.

On tour with the Freedom Singers, I was the contact with Toshi Seeger, who had volunteered to book us. At the convention, we received many requests from the Y student representatives to visit campuses around the country. Working with Toshi Seeger by phone and mail, I developed coordination and administrative skills that I continue to use today.

We've been 'buked and we've been scorned
We've been talked about sure you born
But we'll never turn back
No we'll never turn back
Until we've all been freed
And we have equality
We have hung our heads and cried
Cried for those like Lee who died . . .

We opened many a concert with that song written by Bertha Gober, and for a short period Bertha was actually onstage with us as a member of the group. Cordell would tell the story of the Reverend Herbert Lee of Amite County, Mississippi, who, although he could not read or write, gave support to the organizers who came in to try to get a voter registration campaign going. The Reverend Lee was shot and killed by E. H. Hurst, a member of the Mississippi state legislature, but Hurst was never arrested or tried for the murder.

With the death of the Reverend Lee, the Civil Rights Movement organizers knew that their presence as activists in Mississippi would exact a mighty cost. This song by Bertha Gober expressed the struggle to stay in touch with that reality and to keep up the determination to go on through all threats and costs for freedom. In Mississippi, this song was sung sometimes more than "We Shall Overcome," be-

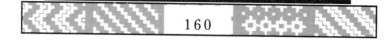

cause it expressed the constant threat surrounding those involved in the struggle for freedom in that place.

On the road and in concert with the Freedom Singers, I was a part of a developing network that gave support, financial and otherwise, to my organization (I was now a SNCC field secretary, earning ten dollars a week). We told stories in song (sometimes we called ourselves a singing newspaper) that let our audiences know firsthand about racism in the United States and that helped them find ways for themselves to witness for freedom. Many people who went South were introduced to the possibility of becoming Movement organizers as a result of contact with the Freedom Singers or other speakers who covered the country telling the story that seemed to never make the paper or the six o'clock news.

"FANNIE LOU HAMER"

Fannie Lou Hamer, Fannie Lou Hamer
Fannie Lou Hamer, Fannie Lou Hamer

This little light of mine
Her song would fill the air
She rocked the state of Mississippi,
Now a few more Black people stand there

For twenty years she weighed cotton
Down on a White man's farm
She received threats on her life
Was fired from her job, scorned and kicked off the farm

We're sick and tired of being sick and tired
That's what the lady would yell
Her body was beaten and she walked crippled
Trying to vote she was thrown in jail

In the land of the free and the home of the slave
She criticized the law of the land
And for hundreds of years, Blacks had lived in fear
Now we marched, took our lives in our hands

She came by here and she didn't stay long
Helped to turn a few things around
Cancer took her body, her struggle got her soul
Now we laid her body in the ground.

As a member of the Movement, a field secretary for SNCC, and a Freedom Singer, I was a part of a unique community of people who felt that what we were doing in fighting racism was important enough to die for. There were special people I met and worked with that changed the way I looked at myself and the world I lived in. One such person was Fannie Lou Hamer. Such was the impact her struggle had on me that I wrote a song for her when she died and the following statement:

> Every once in a now and then somebody moves in such a way that makes us jerk up and take note. Fannie Lou Hamer made some decisions during the early part of the sixties that made us stand up and follow, feeling a little stronger and going a little farther because of the price she had paid for the stances she took. Mississippi will never be the same; I will never be the same. Black song was wedded with struggle in her hands.

I had heard about Mrs. Hamer long before I met her. When I listened to her speak, as I did many times between 1962 and when she died in 1977, she often told the story of being born in Ruleville, Mississippi, and being jailed in Itta Bena, Mississippi, after she and a busload of Black people from her county decided to try to register to vote.

As the bus of mostly Black Mississippians approached the courthouse, they were stopped and arrested. However, with them was Annelle Ponder, a student from Atlanta, who was working on voter registration with SCLC. Mrs. Hamer would tell of Annelle being taken from her cell and of hearing her scream when she was beaten. And then it was her turn. Fannie Lou Hamer was taken into a room and made to lie on a bench and was beaten by two Black male trusties. They beat her while two White guards held guns on them to make sure they beat her. As they beat her around the thighs, she tried to keep her dress down. Her dress was hiked up over her head by one of the White guards, and the beating continued. Fannie Lou Hamer was beaten; she lost her job and her house; she was shot at—all because she tried to vote in Mississippi. That was just the beginning.

I saw, heard, and sang with Mrs. Hamer many times at SNCC staff meetings, in mass meetings, in Mississippi, in Georgia, and on the boardwalk in Atlantic City at the 1964 Democratic convention. . . . When she led a song, she always raised one arm, elbow bent in a strong fist to about the top of her head. She called us to sing by the sound of a powerful, ringing voice and the swinging of that fisted arm. "This Little Light of Mine" was her signature song: "This little light of mine, I'm gonna let it shine."

Speaking or singing, Mrs. Hamer was always sweating; sweat poured from her face. She was one of the fiercest women I ever had the grace to alto.

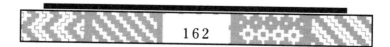

"WE'VE COME A LONG WAY TO BE TOGETHER YOU AND ME"
MOTHER, SINGER, CULTURAL WORKER

When I had my first child, Toshi, in January 1964, the Freedom Singers reorganized and I no longer traveled with them. I began to look for ways to continue to be who I was. My life over the next seven years was full of a personal inner searching for balance with all of my loves and wants, with a real practical experimentation to see if I could be a wife, mother, singer, and worker sharing the cultural history of my people.

This period was turbulent because it marked a major transition for Black people. From the period of nonviolent demonstrations and "We shall overcome someday," to rebellions in the major cities of this nation, the transition was immersed in demands for acknowledgment of African Americans as a people with a culture and history worthy of being taught to all Americans. It was a time when I and many of our people went inside ourselves and our communities and reconsidered our sense of what was good and what was beautiful about us. The cry of "Black Power," which was first heard on the Meredith March in Mississippi in 1966, became a new breath of life as we struggled to become the people so many of us almost never got a chance to know.

I sang occasionally, but mostly spent time being a mother. I joined the Unitarian Church; they had child care and a class for young mothers. I read Eric Fromm and other books and talked adult two hours a week. Sometimes on Sunday I sang at a church. In November 1965, my son, Kwan Tauna, was born and I continued to look for the rhythm that would allow me to be a mother, and all the rest that I needed to be to be all right with myself.

I moved into this turbulent period searching for real survival for me and my family. Which increasingly was me and my children, since Cordell was more gone than present. Kwan was three weeks old when Toshi Seeger called to see if I would do a television special with Pete Seeger on Woody Guthrie for Camera Three Television Productions. I knew she wanted me to know that I could still sing and be a mother. She is a woman who speaks through her actions. In so many ways, as an organizer I am her protégée, and I always felt that she was watching me out of the side of her eyes.

During this changing time I and many others like me survived because we were looked after and over by those in our community who knew how hard the change was from full-time organizer in the Movement to finding a way to continue the struggle when the organizational and broader support was no longer there for you. I needed the support and the opportunity to work. In this period, as I scurried from one job to another for most of the year, I got steady work during the summers at Camp Webatuck in New York State. At one point, my mother asked me if I wanted her to keep the children. I told her no, that I wanted to try to keep and raise them myself. I kept Toshi and Kwan and kept looking for the rest of me.

I was able to keep singing because those around me helped create the opportunities. One day Ruth Howard and Lloyd McNeil came to my house; Ruth had started a club called the Loving Spoonful and she asked me to come and sing. I had known Ruth in SNCC. I had met Lloyd, artist and jazz flutist, at Spelman, where he was artist-in-residence. I went to the Loving Spoonful and sang almost every week. Sometimes Ruth paid me money, but what she really gave me was space and a place to know inside myself that what I had to do was sing. I did not need to be famous; I did not need to be rich; I was a singer and I needed to assume responsibility for that need because it was mine.

From 1964 to 1966, from my home in Atlanta, I worked with Guy Carawan (whom I first met at the SCLC Citizenship Education Classes) to organize several conferences to bring together the new song leaders coming out of local Movement struggles. They were traditional singers like the Georgia Sea Island Singers and the Reverend Dock Reed, and topical singers out of New York like Pete Seeger, Theo Bikel, Phil Ochs, Len Chandler, and Tom Paxton. In these sessions we met our prototypes from an earlier generation. They knew the old songs and knew the stories from slavery that revealed them as documents of a historical record created from the perspective of our people struggling against bondage.

Meeting and listening to the Georgia Sea Island Singers was like going to a holistic university. Bessie Jones, who sang with the group, had been born in the same region as me—Dawson, Georgia, in Terrell County, twenty miles from Albany. We shared the same repertoire, only she knew so many more of the old songs and games than I did. When I first heard her she was singing and playing tambourine with the Georgia Sea Island Singers. They introduced me to the repertoire of the Sea Island music, which was so old and missing in my life.

Just as important as the depth of the repertoire was the way Bessie Jones and John and Peter Davis talked to us about what the old songs meant. Finally I was beginning to find a way to really know what I knew. Bessie Jones and others in the Georgia Sea Island Singers, and Janie Hunter of the Moving Star Hall Singers, took time with those of us who were song leaders of the Civil Rights Movement. Through the stories of Bessie Jones and John and Peter Davis we were able to reconstruct the line that connected the music of the slaves fighting against slavery to the songs we were singing in the Movement. These great singers taught us their songs and told us stories so that we would know what they meant:

> *Way down on the old Tar River*
> *Oooh uhooo uweeeee*
> *Way down on the old Tar River*
> *Oooh weeeee talking 'bout the river*

They told us this was an Underground Railroad song and that Big Willie and Major Bailey worked to help Black people escape to freedom.

Singing for My Life

Big Willie and Major Bailey
They say the old Tar River gonna run tomorrow

Got a letter from Major Bailey
Say the old Tar River run black and dirty

Got a letter from Major Bailey
Say the old Tar River a-running North

They wanted us to know that the Black singing, Black songs, and the work we were doing as singers in the Movement had been going on a long time. It was like being personally connected to a part of yourself that you had only known through stories and now you met great singers who still sang the songs in the old ways and still remembered why—you could stretch out and touch your history.

My involvement in the Movement triggered an insatiable thirst for looking back into my background to understand who I was and why we as a people were so strong. I began to question the negativity that some young people and some educated Blacks carried about the use of "old-time" music that held the memory of slavery in its sound. I had been to jail and it was the only music that worked for us there.

Through my work with Dr. James, Guy Carawan, and Bessie Jones, I caught sight of a history I'd never seen before and I liked it. I then thought: Why not make this available to more of our young who are having problems being who they are.

Early in 1966, I answered a knock on my door. When I opened it, standing in front of me was a White woman with strawberry-blond hair, and she said she wanted to talk to me about producing a festival of Southern Black and White progressive culture. She too had attended a conference that had had a great impact on her. There, SNCC leaders had met with Southern White students organizing to work in White communities for change. Her name was Anne Romaine and she was from Gastonia, North Carolina, and we had work to do together. At this conference, it had been suggested to Anne that she might be able to organize a tour of Southern culture and to come to me.

By March 1966, Anne and I booked our first tour; we took the Southern Folk Festival of Song on a Southern journey. We traveled with Black and White singers —Len Chandler, Hedy West, the Georgia Sea Island Singers, the Reverend Pearlie Brown, Hazel Dickens—doing traditional and contemporary songs from Southern culture with the message that Black and White people had always shared music, so on with it. I traveled with my children. We sang in churches, in schools, and in both hostile and friendly territory in the South. We were followed and bumped in our cars, we were scared and we traveled all over the South singing for freedom. During that first tour, we presented twenty concerts in three and a half weeks in Southern states.

SOUND OF THUNDER
I WILL ALWAYS BE A FREEDOM SINGER!

It was during the mid-sixties that I began to buy my first Black books. I began to try to work out a way to practice Kwanzaa. I say "work out a way" because when I got a copy of the structure of the holiday (which we were passing around in Atlanta), I was dismayed to find that there was no symbol for the mother.

There were the candles that represented the seven principles: Umoja (unity), Kuujichagalia (self-determination), Ujima (collective work), Ujamaa (cooperative economics), Nia (purpose), Kuumba (creativity), Imani (faith). These were principles identified by Julius Nyerere for the philosophical structure for rebuilding the East African country of Tanzania.

There was a cornstalk that represented the father and an ear of corn for each child. There was a mat. I was a Black woman; I was a mother; I had two children, Toshi and Kwan; there was no father in our home. What was I to do?

I took the principles and the candles, I took the idea of harvest and made a harvest offering table. I wrote a song:

Umoja, unity that brings us together
Kuujichagalia, we know the purpose of our lives
Ujima, working and building our union
Ujamaa, we'll spend our money wisely
Nia, we know the purpose of our lives
Kuumba, all that we touch is more beauty
Imani, we believe that we can, we know that we can, we will—any way that we can!

Back in Atlanta after a rough summer in 1966, and a definite clear message that I was no longer in a marriage, I had to get a "real" job. I mean a nine-to-five. Piecing together income from variously spaced projects was not enough for the family, and the support I had been receiving from Cordell stopped after he left. I found work in a Black bookstore for seventy-five dollars a week and loved it. Sometimes Vincent and Rose Harding, activists and organizers with the Mennonite Church, had me over for dinner at the Mennonite House and I went to the SNCC office, but I was not consistently active in singing or in the Movement. That year I had clothes because Alice Bond let me come over to her house and gave me some fabric, which I sewed up so that I would have dresses to wear to work.

In Atlanta in 1967, I joined a group of parents who started a preschool. For our first fund-raiser we organized a Penny Festival. We went around asking people to donate money so that we could charge a penny at the door.

Father Robert Hunter, a local Episcopal priest, called me after the production

and asked me to sing at his church service and then worked with me to produce a recording. The album, *The Sound of Thunder,* was released in the spring of 1968.

When the festival was over, and the school had raised money, I answered the door one night and there was Mary Ethel Jones and Mattie Casey saying let's sing. I said okay and organized an a cappella female sextet and we called ourselves the Harambee Singers.

This was when I began to find my way as a songwriter and arranger. The Harambee Singers was my first effort at leading a group. I found myself challenged and sometimes coming up short. It was the first time I was able to try with a group to develop an organization that made sense to the members. The first thing I put in place was that we would try not to be an additional financial burden on our families. It was the time of Black Consciousness, and the Harambee Singers sang at many of the conventions and rallies held on the East Coast. We would charge a fee, and try to give each singer fifty dollars every time she sang so that babysitter and transportation costs would be covered. We would also try to get fifty dollars for the group, which would go into a bank account for organizational purposes. We named this pot "Joe Willie," after a song we sang.

I worked with the Harambee Singers until it was time to move on. During the summer of 1970, I had to stop singing because of throat problems, and when I was on the other side of that crisis, I elected not to go back to the group. Based in Atlanta, the Harambee Singers continue today, singing songs of freedom and justice. It is a proud legacy, and I am glad that I was there at the beginning to help get it started.

In 1969 Steve Henderson asked me to work with him in organizing the Soul Roots Festival. This was the first festival of traditional music presented at a Negro college since the early forties, when Dr. James had presented Ham and Egg Festivals at Fort Valley State College under the administration of Horace Mann Bond. The Soul Roots concerts tried to establish the continuity that exists in our music from slavery through today, whether sacred or secular. I went back to Spelman to finish my undergraduate degree in 1968. Vincent Harding was head of the History Department, so I went into history. By then even though music was my life, I had worked out that it was not the music that was taught in Music Departments. Vincent also asked me to work out a budget after my first semester, because he was in touch with people who might be interested in helping me through school financially. I asked if I could include babysitting costs, and he told me to put it in. I did and I received money from someone who did not give permission to have their name known to me. This generous gift allowed me to finish school with a great stress removed. I have never done anything of worth without support.

"UPON THIS ROCK, I'M GONNA BUILD MY NATION!"
HOWARD UNIVERSITY AND WASHINGTON, D.C., AND THE REP

In August 1971 I moved to Washington with my children to attend graduate school at Howard University. This was a major step, the furthest I had moved for the longest time away from my mother. She was my leaning post—always there. She was the reason I thought I could finish school, since I had seen her so many times step out on faith and come through with what she went after. She is the strongest woman I have ever known. And she had been in my corner with my children, with my travels, always backing me up. Now I was going to Washington, D.C. Was I finally leaving home?

Shortly after arriving in D.C. and finding a place to stay, getting the children in school, and getting started with my classes, I got in touch with Vantile Whitfield, whom I had met in Atlanta and who was director of Expansion Arts at the National Endowment for the Arts. Also known as Motojicho, Vantile was the artistic director of a new theater being organized by Robert Hooks. He asked me if I would become the vocal director of the D.C. Black Repertory Company. I replied that I was not in a position to create something myself, but if he was clear about what he needed, I would try to deliver. He said that he wanted the voices trained as singers for any kinds of sounds they might have to produce onstage.

In my vocal workshop, I was the first student. I actually learned what I knew about singing and voice by teaching others who had in some cases never tried to sing some of the sounds and harmonies. It was a powerful stretching period for me and I worked with some of the most talented people on the face of the earth: Rosie Lee Hooks, Carol Lynn Maillard, Louise Robinson, Smokey, Moon, LeTari, Mike Hodge, Carol Ann North, Charlie Brown, Carlton Poles, Lynnjicho, Lyn Dyson, Chester. They were all pioneering members of a wonderful experiment in Black theater.

I grew up a bit working with them and their vocal instruments, and forming the creative team for the theater with Motojicho, Mike Malone, and Louis Johnson in dance, and Kenneth Daugherty in dance and theater arts. I taught, created, or programmed the music for many of the shows developed at the Rep. I created two original musical pieces, *Upon This Rock* and *A Day, A Life, A People,* a work I called a songtalk. Then, in 1973, after pushing from two of the strongest singers and actors in the theater, Louise Robinson and LeTari, I called the first rehearsal for the group that was to become Sweet Honey In The Rock.

11

A TASTE OF HONEY

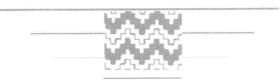

E. ETHELBERT MILLER

I

When I think of Sweet Honey In The Rock, my first impression of the group is not shaped by their singing; the memories I cherish are those in which they can be seen entering a room or walking across a stage. Sometimes they take their individual seats or stand behind separate microphones. There is always that brief meditative pause, a moment of silence before they begin singing.

I guess I've always been attracted to how women walk, how they move and communicate with you across a distance. The women of Sweet Honey In The Rock sing when they walk. They are usually dressed in robes which not only enhance their beauty but elevate it. Their clothing links them to royalty. They could be oracles. We are a people in need of oracles.

The jazz musician Sun Ra was often escorted by sun goddesses when he took to a stage to perform. His female associates always appeared to be from the future or representative of a higher form of intelligence from another planet outside our solar system. Sweet Honey at times seems too good to be from Washington, D.C. Where did they come from? Why do they always take my breath away? How can I survive without air? What makes me believe I could live on simply their music?

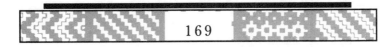

II

I think Bernice Reagon is the only genius I have ever met. I have told people that I am happy to be living in the same historical room with this woman. I like how she thinks and writes. She must be placed among the best topical songwriters of our generation. Her own compositions are only surpassed by her creative adaptations and interpretations of the poems and words of others. Her ability to keep a group together for such a long time places her next to Ellington. Why has Bernice Reagon not been given one of those titles of royalty like Queen, Princess, or even Lady? Why has no one proclaimed this woman a priestess or guardian of our traditions and values? At every performance of Sweet Honey that I've attended she has been wiser than Du Bois or Robeson. Can I get a witness! How often did her comments and introductions to a song make you laugh, reflect, or clap your hands?

III

My favorite Sweet Honey In The Rock album is still *Good News*. This recording was an outgrowth of the group's Seventh Anniversary Concert, November 7, 1980. "Chile Your Waters Run Red Through Soweto" and such compositions as "Oughta Be a Woman" are extremely moving. The political and the personal, the connection and the tie, the relationship between the two spheres is what the true artist must balance. Seldom will you find a group that has such a musical and political range as Sweet Honey. This can also be seen by just looking at the people who attend a performance by the group. Here is the Rainbow Coalition celebrating its existence with song. The music of Sweet Honey opens our hearts and releases a moral force which has the potential to change the world. Listen . . .

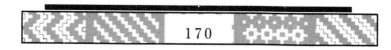

12

ONE MOMENT, ONE MELODY, ONE SONG

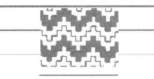

EVELYN MARIA HARRIS

*everywoman
who is sweet honey in the rock
is testimony
to a new world coming.*

*everywoman
oughta be a woman
oughta stand up
and call her name*

*everywoman
oughta run on for a long time
'til time no longer runs*

*listen! listen to the rhythm
of their lives
marching across times and battles to us
listen, and see in the sound of the singing . . .*

harriet tubman with her life boldly waded in the water
sojourner truth shouted run, mourner, run
joe hill trumpeted a song of the exiled
nat turner mightily gave his life in battle
paul robeson affirmed here I stand
I shall not be moved!
marcus garvey asserted i believe i'll go back home
to the land of my fathers and mothers
fannie lou hamer, crying for freedom
sick and tired of being sick and tired
steven biko valiantly rumbled through the streets of Soweto
ella baker's song called the children to lead us
let her life and love be a light for them
malcolm's living propelled changes through generation
calling us to lay down the usual

we are their children
sweet honey in the rock
to live with this chosen lot
to truly hear their breaths
is to sing their song
our song
together weaving a patchwork quilt
of justice, truth, and love
Now . . .
Listen to the rhythm of their march
our march
the steps of everywoman
sweet honey in the rock
walking to the freedom drums
of our ancestors in this circle

I am a singer and I've known that from as early as I can remember. I always loved it when the Christmas season came around. Unlike other youngsters who wait with anticipation for Santa Claus, I could hardly wait to start singing the seasonal songs and carols. One day when I was six, while dusting the living-room furniture, and singing "Oh Holy Night," my grandfather came in the room. Without my knowing he was there, I continued. After a while he asked, "Girl, where'd you get that voice from?" For the first time I realized my gift was not only for me but also for others.

Our home church in Richmond, Virginia, Ebenezer Baptist, was right across the street from my grandparents' home and I joined the Cherubim Choir at age six.

That was a year younger than the required age the director wanted to work with. I got all the solos and now the whole congregation was admiring my gift. I don't know how I learned to harmonize except maybe from listening to records at home. Living with my grandparents, Evelyn and Clarence Clay, and my Aunt Sallie, and my mother, Gwendolyn Harris, and brother Byron Everette (his middle name came from my parents' decision to name him after me), the music played around the house was jazz. The rhythm-and-blues era came right on the heels of my development as a constant songbird at home, at church, and at school, and I began buying every 45 I could handle with my allowance. Saturday meant going to the record store and the movies . . . religiously. And I learned all the words, all the harmonies, all the stops, and every little quirk in every little tune. In fact, those lyrics have never escaped me and I can recall them verbatim today when I hear one of my favorite oldies but goodies.

I went on to join the junior choir at church and got to sing, learn, and read music written for chorus. In junior high school I also got all the solos in the choir and began to say out loud that I wanted to be a singer. That was quite a variation from my grandparents' theme for my future, and even after realizing how serious I was, they encouraged me to go to college and take education courses so that I'd have "something to fall back on." Being the rebel I was, I never took one education course in college. I didn't want to fall back on anything. I wanted to make a living at performing.

Armstrong High School was great for me. Instead of following all my friends to Maggie Walker High School down the street, I decided to go across town to Armstrong. Built in 1865 and named for rebel soldier, General Samuel Chapman Armstrong, this was the first colored high school in town. When my mother and her mother were there, all the instructors were white. By the time I got to Armstrong, like Maggie Walker High since its beginning, it was an all-Black school. I went to Armstrong because I wanted to make new friends and have new experiences with those new friends, and I also felt I was doing something special and something my family would cheer about as it was their alma mater. I was an honors student there, in the choir and the drama club. Upon graduation, I was voted Best Actress and Best Singer of my 1968 class. I decided to major in music and minor in drama at Howard University (I got a full scholarship and at the time—1968—it cost $1,900 for *everything*). But Howard was not going for that. All voice majors had to minor in piano and I could take drama courses as electives after my second year. After three years, Howard was no longer serving me—so I thought—and I left.

I had come to Howard in the fall of 1968 amid student protests begun the previous semester. All across the nation, colleges and universities were in an uproar as the student movement challenged the educational status quo and Howard led the field among Black colleges. We wanted a seat on all administrative boards making decisions for the student body. We wanted African studies to be a part of the credit curriculum, and one of the offshoots of our demands was to allow the

gospel choir to use Howard's name. I was immediately involved in the politics of student demands in my freshman year and grew to understand that my opinions about the world's issues would be crucial to my growth as a human being. What I decided to stand for would also be my name.

I had one of the largest Afros on campus and I made a statement with it. My mother had insisted I get a permanent before coming to college because I had to take swimming classes, but as soon as I got the word that someone in my dorm was stripping perms for women who wanted Afros, I got in line. My grandmother was color-struck and I had always felt that was wrong. My high school boyfriend was very dark and she would warn me never to bring any Black babies in her house. But I always wanted my children to be darker than myself so they would hopefully be able to escape the ridicule I endured as a light-skinned, curly-haired kid. As I fought in the student rights battle, I wanted to look as African and natural as possible.

The Howard students closed the school down that fall of 1968, took over the "A" Building, and would let no one outside of our school family onto campus. My station was the Home Economics Building, and with no weapon but my voice and a purpose, I held off unsympathetic students and teachers, inquiring press and strangers. I felt like somebody special. Those upperclassmen and -women who were the leaders of our movement didn't know me personally but they felt my dedication and strength. During the student movement, I learned the difference between riot and protest, rebellion and demonstration, militant and activist.

After the demonstrating students had won everything they wanted, Howard returned to some semblance of normalcy. Rather, let's say, classes resumed. I was not a good student at Howard because I let drugs into my life. It cost me a lot, as years gone by have taught me. I left Howard so that I could start singing for real. I worked in all the jazz clubs around D.C. but I was not going anywhere. The musicians I worked with were mostly ten to twenty years older than me and never wanted to rehearse with me. They only did music on the side. A singer would come into the club that night, call her key, and do all the standards. Well, I did that too, but I wanted so much more. Having been influenced by Nina Simone, Sarah Vaughan, Nancy Wilson, Gloria Lynne, and Dakota Staton, I knew there really was more. But I got so frustrated with those men who were so comfortable playing the same songs the same way every weekend that I stopped singing in 1972.

One day in October 1974, while riding around with a couple of friends near Howard, I ran into Camilla Parker. She was a home girl and a violin major at Howard. She told me about a sign in the Fine Arts Building elevator announcing auditions for a singing group called Sweet Honey In The Rock at the D.C. Black Repertory Theater further up Georgia Avenue. Well, I went there and I was late according to the time on the flyer but they were still sitting there. I sang my two favorite songs of the day: "Trying Times" as recorded by Roberta Flack and "Impossible" as recorded by Gloria Lynne. Then I went down to sit with the four

women (one of whom, Louise Robinson, I knew from Howard's Fine Arts Department), and they checked out my harmonizing skills. Then they said they'd give me a call . . . and they did that following Saturday. My first rehearsal was the next day at Bernice's home.

I had wanted that job as soon as I walked into the audition. I never wanted to stop singing, I'd just wanted my singing to be the best it could be and have it say something positive. I could tell these women were on the ball and their work was not something they took lightly.

Initially, I think they talked to me about how varied the repertoire was and how the social and political commentary was an integral component of that repertoire. I loved it! Sweet Honey's vast repertoire is one of the many things that set her apart for me. The full richness of our culture is communicated through a staggering body of music. We are required to be vocally proficient in a wide mixture of African and African American song forms.

I loved it! I loved singing all those traditional songs we never sang in my highbrow church and all those original compositions penned mostly by Bernice. What a genius she is and I sure wanted to be like her in that respect. I was a member of a group whose activist stance in this ever-changing world dictated her ever-changing repertoire. While holding fast to a solid base in traditional material passed down from our ancestors, Sweet Honey also became a group of composers and arrangers reaching out in contemporary modes and trying out nontraditional works.

Bernice knew exactly what to do and say to get me to search for my composer self. She then had to stay on my case to get me to trust my creation. In 1982 I wrote "Battle for My Life" and brought it to the group.

"Leave it alone," she'd insisted. "Don't keep messing with it." I'll be forever grateful to her for that. In fact, I love her so very much for all the ways she has moved me, pushed me, held me, and let me go.

I always wondered how in the world one person could write so many songs! I always wanted to lead the ones that she led (smile!) but I was such a baby in my vocal development. It was an absolute thrill to learn these original compositions and breathe life into them. I never stopped listening to pop music, rhythm and blues, jazz and rock, and I was developing a new level of appreciation for folk music and all its cousins. In Sweet Honey I felt a bit disadvantaged because in my home church I had never heard the traditional music my African ancestors had created in this country to save their lives. But I got over that each time I led the group in the opening refrain of "Wade in the Water." In Ebenezer, I was never taught to line out a hymn. This is the process in singing a hymn that has the person raising the hymn line out the text line by line in a chant form, then the congregation sings the lined text using tunes familiar to that region's repertoire. I got over feeling disadvantaged because I learned these old song ways in Sweet Honey. Bernice would line the Charles Wesley hymn, "Father I stretch my hands to thee no other

help I know," and I actually raise the Joseph Scriven hymn "What a Friend We Have in Jesus." Thank God! Sweet Honey's music helped me come to know me and consequently work on saving my own life.

I am a drug addict and an alcoholic. My recovery time is still short because I went back out and/or transferred addictions. But I have now learned that any drug will lead you back to your drug of choice. I lost Sweet Honey because of alcohol. You see, I'd used for all the years I'd been in the group, off and on. As I look back, I could still have my job and still be using something or another. Only after getting the boot for drinking did I surrender to a residential drug rehabilitation program. Now, recovery in its infancy, I am going on with my life . . . for real.

> *One moment in my life*
> *One melody stirred my soul*
>   *and*
> *One song*
>   *was born of many*

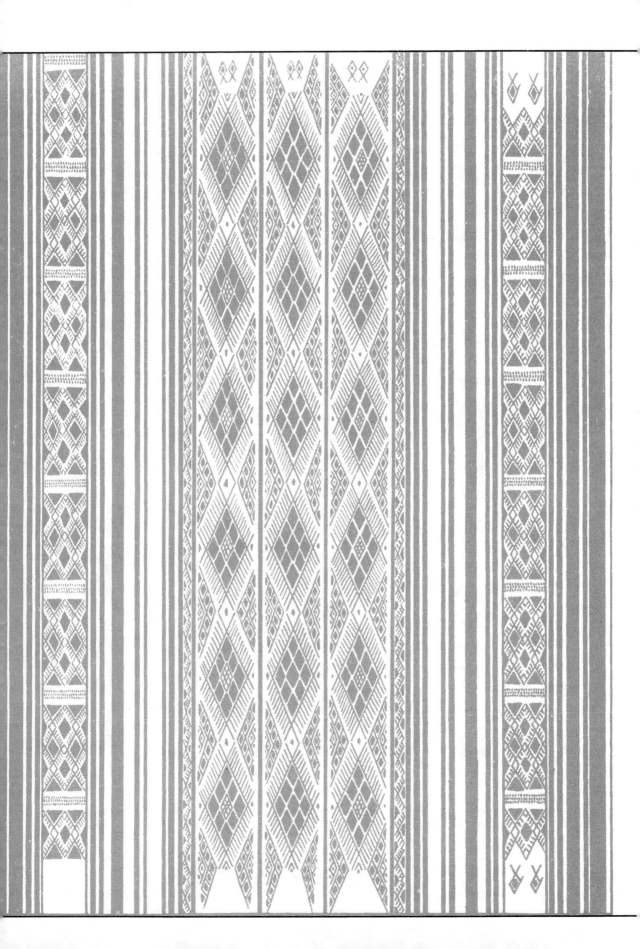

FREE SOUTH AFRICA: AMY HOROWITZ DEMONSTRATING AGAINST APARTHEID IN FRONT OF THE SOUTH AFRICAN EMBASSY. L TO R: EVELYN MARIA HARRIS, AMY HOROWITZ, KIM JORDAN, 1985. (PHOTOGRAPHER, SHARON FARMER)

13

SOME FACTORS IN THE EQUATION

AMY HOROWITZ

They leave the stage like a multicolored wind blowing through the waning light of late afternoon . . . the stage still reverberates with the last chord left hanging in the midst of half-filled water glasses . . .

Backstage Sweet Honey stands catching her breath. The stage manager and lighting director wait to see if the group will gather the energy to go back to the audience, whose thunder has not subsided. The group listens for a lull in which to turn the house lights up. Sometimes this pause will not come . . . then they go back out like a lullaby and sing "Sweet Honey In The Rock" . . . or they might raise the lights to full.

Some nights even after the third encore there is no disengaging. People are up on their feet, in the aisles, down by the front of the stage, and they are singing "Down by the Riverside." The applause is more than a call for one more song. People choose to stay because it is hard to break the moment. They applaud for the feeling that is flowing in the room, in their bodies, in hidden valleys of the spirit now mapped out after so many years. They applaud the sound of their own voices filling the hall. They applaud this fragile ecosystem, the variety of colors and lifestyles, ages and reasons for coming, and they wonder if it will survive once the lights are turned up to full.

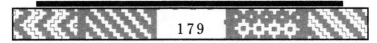

IN THE BEGINNING THERE WAS EXPLAINING THE LIGHT

I didn't grasp the centrality of Sweet Honey's lighting approach until I disregarded it on the road. One night, faced with a choice between the lights all the way on or off, I chose off. The intimacy of the interaction between the group and audience was greatly diminished. The group could not read the faces and watch the body language in the audience, and the audience became invisible to itself.

When I explained Sweet Honey's policy of keeping the house partially lit throughout the concert, producers responded with apprehension or dissension. The nature of the problem varied. For some, there were close working relations with lighting designers who saw themselves as artists in their own right. Elaborate lighting designs were part of the signature of a producer's concert series. For others, older halls did not contain house dimmers, so the lights were either all the way up or all the way off. Sometimes the problem was resolved if the stage light spilling into the house allowed for reciprocal visibility. Other times the house was swallowed up in a darkness that dropped like a curtain between Sweet Honey and the audience.

"Do you have the set list?" asked the lighting designer.

"There is no set list," I answered.

Pause. "Oh, I see. Let me know when the set list is ready."

"There won't be a set list. They work according to the principles and aesthetics of orally based tradition. That is, they often have an idea of what the songs will be but that may change as they begin to develop their relationship with the audience. The concert is a composition in an improvisational form and sometimes Bernice will feel a song that some group members don't know, and they'll learn it as they sing it. And there aren't any lighting changes either."

I notice her eyes darting around. I am lecturing instead of communicating. . . . The producer has not grasped this concept and thus has not explained it to the lighting designer. And now, fifteen minutes before the show, I face the panic of someone who has always relied on a predefined set of instructions.

I explain that the job is only to re-create the ambient hues of dawn . . . and then not alter the lighting. She is not to change colors and levels according to the song and she is not to define the mood. The definition process will come from the interaction between the singers and the audience as they build the evening together.

The stage plot calls for four upright chairs without armrests, four vocal mikes on boom stands. Four glasses of spring water are placed carefully at the base of each mike stand so that no one will trip. Three shekeres (beaded gourd drums) are laid out on top of African cloth. The chairs are set in a semicircle which curves around toward the edge of the stage to meet the chairs in the theater. The chairs' arch formation blurs the sharpness of the stage edge.

Often technology in theaters is used to render an audience invisible to itself

and to the performer. This theory proposes that a curtain of darkness facilitates intimacy. Since people won't be self-conscious, they can let go secretly and merge with the energy onstage. In contrast, Sweet Honey's design seeks to bridge distances by asking the audience to see itself not as a passive observer but as a vital factor in an equation.

A Sweet Honey concert calls technology into play to create a self-conscious audience to nurture reciprocity between audience and performer. It draws on the African American church aesthetic in which the congregation sits one minute and is up on its feet the next. Some parts of the concert are congregational and other sections are given over to the ensemble as leader and soloist. . . . Sweet Honey leads the service and the congregation cannot maintain a static position, they move around through horizontal and vertical space.

New audience members tell me that right before the show starts there is a sense to expect the unexpected. An orange glow warms up the shadows. If the lighting designer is good, it's hard to pinpoint the moment when day breaks out of dawn. This is how I explain the lighting to producers. The lights are raised slowly to a warm glow between dawn and day. They remain this way throughout the show . . . never arriving into the bluer and harsher light of midday, never being the focus, only helping to create a focus. Two hours later we arrive at dusk.

Before the show, stage lights are at half intensity so that the empty chairs are encircled by the moment before sunrise. There is a dawning sense as the audience settles in hushed tones. Backstage, group members are gathering on stage left.

For audience members who have been here before, this is a moment brimming full of possibilities. Audience members are visible to one another; they are visible to the singers. . . . They are seated inside the equation. None of this is conscious.

One woman wrote that as a new audience member she did not know in advance that the house lights would stay lit, a rush of colorful fabrics and footprints filled her senses as Sweet Honey entered, adjusting the chairs to allow for eye contact, moving the water glasses closer to the mike stands, taking a sip, and touching the mikes to gauge proximity. Her heart pounded as if she was responsible for the mistake. Someone forgot to turn off the lights! She shifted in her seat along with the singers, cleared her throat as if to get ready to apologize for this oversight. Around her a human waterfall applauded in cascades of sound that washed over her discomfort.

Bernice begins: "You all look really beautiful tonight. Give yourselves a hand!!!"

The woman forgets the lights and enters the equation.

There are spontaneous reactions and interactions between the group members. This interplay is out in the open and ever-changing, such that their internal conversation is never the same in Scotland as it is in Albany, Georgia, or New York. The conversation includes the audience. Sweet Honey teaches "Run, Run, Mourner

Run" in Brixton, England. You watch as the audience stretches to let their bodies fill with sound. Then those sounds meet the other sounds in the space and then that combined sound fills a hall; in that moment you feel the power of congregational song. Bernice says, "This song comes out of slavery. And a mourner in the church is someone who is not saved and a slave on a plantation is someone who certainly is not saved. There were times when the most radical thing you could do about your situation was just to get out of there. This song says that the only reason I am running is because I don't have wings to fly."

She beats on the shekere to accent the point, then continues: "I know you all think you don't have a reason to sing this song but you never can tell!!! And I ain't seen no human beings with wings yet. . . ."

She starts to sing the line "Run, run, mourner run," then pauses.

"You have to open your mouth and just rock down deep . . . Oooh run— you not supposed to look at anyone else!!!!

Oh run, run, mourner run . . .

You're missing a note there. You have to drop down on 'run' at the end of that line! 'Run' is not up there where 'mourner' is, 'run' is saved and 'mourner' is trying to get there . . ."

Now all of Sweet Honey begins to join in.

"You notice that there are more people than me up here. We need help . . . in harmony. We can't have plain singin' or it won't be a Sweet Honey concert. Do you know your part, Evie?"

Evie answers, "Yeah."

Bernice shouts back, "Sing it! Somebody help her out!!!"

"Yasmeen," she calls, asking Yasmeen to teach her part to the audience. "Help her out . . . now wait!!!! The same people that helped Evie can't help Yasmeen!! You gon' have to do some choosing here tonight!!! Help her out; she needs more help than that!!"

The chord is growing.

"Ysaye . . . help her out!" Ysaye moves in with her line and is joined by members of the audience who choose her.

And Bernice calls for Aisha to teach.

"Aisha . . ." Gasps are heard as Aisha weaves a surging blues line through the underbelly of the swelling chord. Bernice turns to the audience after Aisha wails. "For those of you who have courage!" She commends the harmony building in the room. "All right!" Harmony singing fills the hall. Purses fall from laps; feet stamp; hands clap, and voices unfurl.

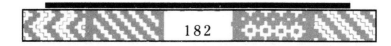

PERSONAL SNAPSHOTS:
I WAS SUPPOSED TO DO SOMETHING WITH MUSIC

When I was little my head barely reached up high enough to see the black and white colors on the piano keyboard. My grandmother's fingers looked like a whole family of little angel feet dancing up and down the keys. The sound was huge and her body swayed on the bench toward the edges. She was always tipping and I wondered if the angel feet kept her from falling off. She and her eight brothers and sisters grew up playing Yiddish and gypsy music and later my grandmother played jazz piano in the 1920s in New York. . . . I grew up on these sounds; the mysteries of jazz and the minor keys of Yiddish and gypsy intonation redefine the distance between sadness and joy.

Yiddish and jazz music were not on the sound track when my father took the family to live in a working-class Irish Catholic community in southern Illinois while he went to graduate school. I was nine, and the little girls in the neighborhood had informed me that if I really was Jewish, then I had killed their God, and if I was Jewish I should have horns and a tail. I thought it was a joke until they told me I couldn't spend the night at their homes. I realized I was Jewish.

When we moved back to Washington, D.C., I joined the Montgomery County Little Singers. We learned songs from different countries in foreign languages and sang at embassies for special occasions, at the New York World's Fair, and at the White House when Kennedy was President.

At the age of eleven I fought for a Bat Mitzvah. My parents said girls didn't have to have them but in the end they agreed. I told the Rabbi that I wanted to chant the Torah portion. He said no girl in the congregation had chanted, so that made me want to do it more. I worked with the cantor and he showed me how to sing the ancient melodies that accompany the biblical verses. When he chanted, I felt the power of his voice in my head and I could see his vocal cords vibrate and it made me laugh.

By the time I entered high school, Vietnam was all around us. We tried to take the flag down when a neighborhood girl named Allyson was killed at Kent State University in the antiwar student protests. I was singing in the Northwood High School madrigal ensemble and traveling around the world as the International Youth President of B'nai B'rith Girls. My experience in B'nai B'rith trained me as a leader, the war in Vietnam trained me as an activist, and music was deeply in my blood. I wanted a profession that combined social commitment and music.

After I graduated from high school, I hitchhiked to Oregon and ended up in a small mountain community called Ashland. I produced local festivals and learned how to build a cabin. In 1973, the local college hired me to travel overseas, and I was on the last plane into Tel Aviv before the Yom Kippur War started. I sang for wounded soldiers and I met war resisters who were living with Bedouins in the

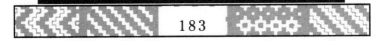

Sinai. I learned the names of the places on the roads behind metal fences—Palestinian refugee camps. This hadn't been a part of my official tour when I traveled to Israel as International Youth President of B'nai B'rith Girls. I wondered where they were refugees from. It would take the next ten years for me to transform this question into a proactive commitment to the policy of self-determination and coexistence for both Palestinian and Israeli peoples.

GENESIS ON KENNEDY STREET

Seven springs after high school I started working with Sweet Honey In The Rock. I have worked with Sweet Honey longer than I have done anything in my life besides being a sister, a daughter, a granddaughter, and an aunt. These cherished positions came by way of inheritance. My work with Sweet Honey came by way of conscious choice.

The winter of 1975, I moved to Los Angeles from the mountains of Oregon to work with the singer and political activist Holly Near. In the evenings after the phones stopped ringing, Holly and I brainstormed. We envisioned a cultural resource center that could provide services for women performers and began to test the idea by booking tours for Lucha, a group who sang Latin American music, Wallflower Order Dance Collective, and Iris Films.

In the midst of this new activity, the seasons changed and Passover was a few weeks away. I planned to travel back home to Washington, D.C., to spend the holiday with my infant nephew Daniel and other family members.

A few days before the trip I came across an album with these words printed on the cover: "Give Your Hands to Struggle: The Evolution of a Freedom Fighter/ Songs by Bernice Reagon." The package included a booklet with song lyrics and history. I read Bernice's biographical introduction and stared in amazement at the picture of this woman who had not only written the songs on the album (a gift large enough in its own right) but had also spent the past fourteen years working as a community organizer and scholar. The biographical treatise unfolded a depth of credits befitting a major national organization. My eyes rested on these words: "As leader and singer in the female vocal quintet called Sweet Honey In The Rock, I continue to seek new ways to make my music respond to the social and political needs of the Washington, D.C., community."

It was not the phrase Sweet Honey In The Rock that struck me. In fact, by the time I sat face to face with Bernice, I had forgotten the name of the quintet altogether. My desire was to find this woman who had already spent years realizing dreams that I was only beginning to grasp. I wanted to talk to her about the resource center. I was determined to find her when I traveled back home to Washington the following week.

As I approached Bernice Reagon's house, a young boy, her son Kwan, ran out

the front door calling back over his shoulder. A gray cat was perched in the window. The porch swing was swaying from side to side. From somewhere inside the house, the rhythm of a sewing machine underlined the soundscape. Above the whirl a voice invited me in.

I met Bernice for the first time as she basted costumes at a Singer sewing machine. She never missed a stitch, even when she looked up at me.

I have never felt so strongly the intersection of metaphor and materiality as I did sitting in this first meeting with Bernice, her sewing machine humming along to the untested rhythms of our initial dialogue. We fit our words around the pauses in the costume design, conscious that other deadlines, projects, and priorities were simultaneously in the making. I told her about my work with Redwood Records and Holly Near. We talked about coalition work. Bernice told me about Sweet Honey In The Rock. She told me that Sweet Honey's first California concerts, planned around Bernice's scholar-in-residency at Santa Cruz, had just been canceled.

This was 1976, and you didn't mention political work and astrology in one breath. However, I knew at that moment, with the sun in Aries and the full moon in Libra, that I was going to stop everything else I was doing and book a Sweet Honey tour, though I had never heard of them before the previous week. This is not what I said to Bernice, however. What I said to her was: "I might be able to pull together a two-week tour. Most of the producers will probably be either women's groups or university organizations. I might be able to do it." She nodded her head as she finished sewing the third hem and we set out on our first joint project. I ran around the corner to a drugstore and called Holly back in Los Angeles. Her excitement about the new project echoed across the phone wire. A few days later, armed with a few albums, two reviews, two pictures, and notes from my meeting with Bernice, I arrived in Los Angeles. As Holly drove back from the airport, we were already thinking of potential producers for the tour.

I don't know why the fear never set in. Maybe it was the Passover season filled with legends of wondrous acts and unexpected journeys. Although this tour would take place only six weeks from the moment I was sitting in Bernice's living room, I didn't wonder about the lack of promotional materials or biographical information. I simply got off the plane at the L.A. airport and proceeded to work twenty-hour seven-day weeks until I succeeded in organizing a break-even tour.

After three weeks of relentless motion up and down the West Coast, the tour was partially booked. Our major supporters were women in the growing radical women's cultural network. Bernice arrived in Santa Cruz to begin a residency at the university. Our second meeting took place on the Santa Cruz University campus. As I walked over to the classroom where she was leading a vocal master class, streams of harmony lines spilled out into the redwood forest.

Bernice nodded for me to enter. She was explaining that her vocal classes were only for participants and everyone had to sing. I cleared the tour notes off my lap

and tried to locate my voice. It had been a few years since my madrigal singing and my mind was filled up with budgets and dates, but when Bernice started explaining the subtext of "Oh Lord Hold My Hand," I forgot that I had come to meet with her about a tour and unleashed my alto line into the equation.

"The Lord was there to offer support but Black people had to do the work to get to freedom." Bernice unveiled the lyrics as an encoded call between slaves who would meet at night to try to make a run North. Though the first three lines held the same lyric each time she sang it, she "upped the ante" and improvised on the accent marks. Bernice explained the thin boundary between asking for a supporting hand to hold and expecting someone else to run your race. This repertoire was deeply radical and profoundly spiritual. The categories of my understanding were undergoing a revolution. Three weeks later I met the members of Sweet Honey In The Rock for the first time.

JOURNAL ENTRY: MAY 4, 1977

On tour with Sweet Honey in California I witness racism. I can smell it. It's not a theoretical term and it's not just out there. It's in the women's movement loud and strong and it's in me despite good intentions, despite what I know about anti-Semitism. . . . This is not a guilt trip. It is a coming to terms with how oppression is woven in language.

We were sitting in the living room of Russell Avenue. Holly was cooking a turkey and the smell filled the house like a holiday. Evelyn was sitting on the sofa and Laura was walking to the piano. Bernice was sitting on the big chair and Yasmeen and I were sitting on the floor. We were talking about getting stuck up in trees when we were children. Yasmeen's eyes grew wider than they already were when she told about realizing she was stuck up there. I told how I climbed after a kitten and went too far, so that a firefighter had to coax me down. I turned to Yasmeen and said, "I was shivering with fear. You know how it is when even your knuckles turn white with fear?" She looked at me, her eyes growing even wider, and said, "No, I don't know about white knuckles." And we all laughed till we cried. . . .

My travels with Sweet Honey, on this first tour, brought into focus the extent of the work to be done to build a progressive cultural movement in the wake of racism, classism, sexism, and homophobia. These had been rhetorical slogans on picket signs. Now they were actual menaces with real-life incidents.

I was still working with Holly's record company, Redwood, and that fall we embarked on a collaborative project to record Sweet Honey's second album. Bernice and I wrote the coalition statement over the phone. This was the first time I thought that coalition building would become my life's work. I moved back to my hometown, Washington, to work with Sweet Honey.

LIVING IN COALITION

The women of Sweet Honey In The Rock and Redwood Records consider our coming together for this recording project to be a major effort in coalition politics. In our development of the project we have tried to form a political/ conceptual base that offers respect for the concerns of Redwood and Sweet Honey, as well as some guidelines of how we work out areas where there may be conflict in our identities and responsibilities to ourselves and our communities. It is with much hope that we all approach this project. We see that the project may in fact serve as a model for ways in which women working in coalition can grow and broaden our boundaries as we identify points of unity while still maintaining our individual political priorities.

For us, the idea of joining together in a coalition project means that we share from our political base enough common ground to warrant the union. At the same time, being in coalition means that there may be aspects of our political bases that are not identical. It has been important to articulate our personal and political needs and priorities to each other. One of the primary responsibilities we share in building the coalition is constantly articulating and reviewing as we develop. It is only from this communication that we will keep close sense of what ground we mutually share, what ground is mutually supported but not necessarily shared, and what ground may present conflicts in identity and focus.

We believe that to be in a coalition means to come to the union with all that we have, to come to the union open and with full awareness that working together will result both in a concrete product and in the process that brings about the product. The issues that bring Sweet Honey In The Rock and Redwood Records together center on all of us sharing a responsibility to be articulate around social, political and economic struggles. We are all committed to cultural work as a means of speaking to these struggles. We see this process as one of growth for all of us.

—From Redwood Records album booklet, 1977

I live on the borderland. My identities crisscross ethnic and cultural boundaries. My passport is stamped with internal landscapes that struggle to coexist. I refuse to establish a hierarchy of importance out of the plurality that is me.

We are not socialized to communicate easily across the fault lines of difference. Acquiring such skills requires uprooting deeply entrenched notions of trust and suspicion that are transmitted across generations. Determining "otherness" is the mechanism that consolidates a group. Closer scrutiny quickly reveals the problems of trying to create pure categories of inclusion or exclusion.

I am sure that my desire to develop skill as a communicator in coalition zones was in part an act of retribution against growing up in the shadow of *Father Knows Best, Leave It to Beaver,* and *Amos 'n' Andy.* For there were other dimensions to

the sound track of my youth that constantly undermined the Wonder Bread illusion.

I come from a culture of outsiders, from an ancient tradition of mediators and wordsmiths. As a Jewish child from a family with fresh wounds from the Nazi Holocaust, I grew up hearing my grandmother cry out in nightmares of loss. I could not easily melt into the American pot. It seemed to me that this melting pot was an attempt to submerge difference into boiling water so it would evaporate in a white Anglo-Saxon milieu.

I did not consciously think of such issues when I came to work with Sweet Honey. I chose to work with them because they articulated with clarity and musical excellence issues central to human survival. I wanted to help build an international audience that would support this artistry and social intelligence.

Sweet Honey and I don't know everything about each other's histories and we will never stand inside each other's skins, but we have carved out shared territory and mutual respect. I came to my work with the group as a Jewish radical and woman activist, and in working with Sweet Honey my pride and self-knowledge have blossomed. Their rich vibrant sense of self-respect is contagious.

In 1978, the first year that I produced Sweet Honey's anniversary show in Washington, my parents asked if they could help out. I suggested that they provide backstage catering. For my mother, it was natural to cook matzo ball soup. After all, the concert was in November, Sweet Honey would be cold, they'd be working hard, what more would they want but chicken soup? It was her way of contributing to the cross-cultural dialogue, and matzo balls have grown into the annual anniversary concert tradition.

> . . . My godson Mario, nephews Dan, Jonathan, and Micah, and niece Sandra were brought up on Sweet Honey's songs. Their earliest memories include crawling around at concerts.
>
> . . . One Passover, my niece Sandra informed me that it was "the king" who led the Hebrew tribe from slavery. When I questioned her, she got impatient. "The king," she said. "The king?" I asked again, still not understanding. "It was the king," she said defiantly. "Like Bernice said in the concert, it was the Martin Luther King that did it."
>
> . . . Yasmeen's daughter Summer is my goddaughter. One year, Jonathan and Summer were playing backstage, and when he told her he was my nephew, Summer responded that she was my goddaughter. They came to ask me if that meant they were godcousins.

Coalition work takes different forms and can be simply sharing music. I met Yiddish actor Herschel Bernardi in Los Angeles in 1975. A few years later he came through Washington starring as Tevye in *Fiddler on the Roof* at the Warner Theater. When I told him about my work with Sweet Honey, he wanted to meet them.

Over dinner at Kennedy Street, with Bernice at one end of the table, Herschel

at the other, Sweet Honey sang a song. When they finished, he quietly said, "That reminds me of an old Yiddish song that my mother used to sing." He sang the song, and when he finished singing, it was followed by another from Sweet Honey, and the evening unfolded in a continuum of memory. . . . One song led to another across cultures, continents, languages, and religions; it could have been a key, a theme, a vocal style. A Black spiritual against slavery triggered a song about anti-Semitic Cossacks raiding a Russian Jewish village; they sang love songs, lullabies that were sung in the sweatshop, lullabies sung by Black women nursing white babies while theirs lay unattended. . . .

Coalition building is a fragile art. It is multivocal ground between sameness and separatism. It is coexistence of disparate priorities and incongruous/discrete memories. From the coalition between Sweet Honey and myself, I hold a position of middle ground as I communicate Sweet Honey's goals, technical requirements, fee structures, and media strategies to producers in different communities.

The position takes on different dimensions depending on the nature of the sponsoring organization or person. Sometimes an African American church group, a woman's production company, and an antinuclear group join into a coalition production. The concert becomes a combination of groups learning about coalition building and logistical details. As the groups work to find enough common ground on which to stand together, there is a fixed and unmovable goal looming in the near future and that is a concert. Coalition members strive for a balance between exploring internal dynamics and issues and focusing on the goal of concert production.

INTERPRETING THE INTERPRETER: TRANSLATING "IN THE UPPER ROOM" INTO JAPANESE

In non-English-speaking contexts, audiences are accustomed to receiving American performers who are more interested in maintaining the sanctity of the aesthetic of their performance than in providing a translator onstage.

In 1989, we worked with Borderstep, Inc., an extraordinary team of producers founded by an African American woman, who had been introduced to Sweet Honey in her native Ohio, and her Japanese male partner. Borderstep agreed to honor Sweet Honey's request for onstage translation. In fact, they upped the ante by asking that the event also be accessible to their Deaf constituency. We were a month into the planning process before I remembered that American Sign Language is a national language and is not universally understood by Deaf communities outside the United States. We soon discovered that finding a Japanese Sign Language interpreter with theater experience was difficult enough, finding one fluent in spoken English or ASL was impossible.

It became clear that coordinating the interpretative component of this series of

concerts might need a choreographer to situate the two Japanese translators required to carry out the full cycle of interpretation.

Problem One: Translation of Sweet Honey's stories and intersong raps equals one English-to-Japanese translator.

Problem Two: Translation of Sweet Honey lyrics and stories and intersong raps from Japanese into Japanese Sign Language equals one Japanese Sign Language interpreter.

Problem Three: This requires space for Sweet Honey singers plus three: Sweet Honey's American Sign Language interpreter, an English-to-Japanese interpreter (White American), and one Japanese Sign Language interpreter (Japanese); we needed a stage big enough to accommodate eight women.

This show redrew the lines between the performers; eight women rehearsed their newly established performance alliance onstage in front of the audience.

The interpreters, accustomed to the more reserved Japanese performance aesthetic, began the first set standing stiffly amid Sweet Honey's lively stage motions. Then Aisha unlocked the floodgates by coaxing them into joining the onstage dancing. By the second night their pastel outfits had been discarded and replaced by bold colors and designs, including headbands and head garb.

When Bernice introduced "In the Upper Room," she noticed an electric buzz that came not from the sound system but from the audience itself. So she stopped the song and asked the people if they had understood the translation of "In the Upper Room." One confused audience member responded yes but wanted to know what the composer was doing sitting up in the attic with Jesus.

As a result, the viewers felt included within the unfolding design of the event. As the concert progressed, the audience freely communicated with the various interpreters, giving reactions to word choices and verifying whether the message was getting through.

ROADWORK

The Sweet Honey legacy serves as an inspiration. Two young Ysayes bear the name of Ysaye Barnwell. Numerous African American and European American women's a cappella singing groups throughout the world began as variations on Sweet Honey's theme. Bobby McFerrin started singing after hearing a Sweet Honey concert. Alice Walker claims they—collectively—should be President.

In 1978, I founded Roadwork as a result of my work with Sweet Honey. It may have been more logical to create a profit-making business for my booking work. Instead, I envisioned a nonprofit organization based on coalition principles as both a booking home for Sweet Honey and a vehicle to initiate other cross-cultural projects.

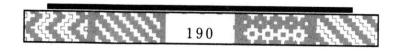

Some Factors in the Equation

The story of Roadwork is a testimony to a multiracial, multicultural community as well as staff, volunteers, board members, and supporters dedicated to creating public forums for the presentation of women artists to their communities and to wider audiences. We produced dozens of concerts in Washington, booked thirty artists on 150 national and international tours, and provided a booking home for Sweet Honey. Roadwork's first intern was a fourteen-year-old aspiring African American singer, drummer, and guitarist named Toshi Reagon.

As a multiracial women's cultural organization, Roadwork sees no contradiction between working with women's communities and people's networks, between being a viable business and part of a global radical movement devoted to fighting exploitation. We know that an antiracist, antisexist posture must begin inside ourselves and our own organization.

"TEST, TEST, TEST"

> Sisterfire was conceived as celebration . . . an acknowledgment of women as vital carriers of culture. This festival is a demonstration of commitment to social change and hope. . . . We acknowledge the hard work all of us, women and men, have contributed to this festival. We are building bridges between the women's movement and other movements for progressive social change. We are playing with fire, and we want nothing less from this event than to set loose the creative, fierce and awesome energies in all of us.
> —From the Sisterfire Statement of Purpose

The Old City of Jerusalem is a fitting landscape in which to write about the Sisterfire festival. From my window, I see ancient stones baking in afternoon summer light. I can hear the cry of the Muezzin calling Muslims to prayer and soon a horn will sound heralding the Jewish Sabbath. Like Sisterfire, this is a site of contradictions and intense passions. The scales and the time depth may be unequal, Jerusalem existing for millennia as an uneasy mix of legend, myth, and history. Sisterfire is by comparison a brilliant flash of beloved and conflicting herstory. Yet these two locations draw from the same age-old well.

Roadwork had just celebrated her third year and Sweet Honey's audiences were growing when board and staff members sat around Bernice's dining-room table together in the winter of 1981. The time seemed right to produce a "women's cultural day." We would invite our communities to celebrate together. This "cultural fair" would be a public articulation of the multiracial coalition goals we had struggled to realize over the past three years. As Sarna Marcus, Bernice Reagon, Susan Allee, and Evelyn Harris bounced ideas back and forth, the name Sisterfire was born.

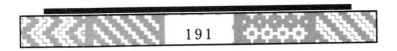

The idea was born out of bold hopes and a special mix of naïveté and chutzpah. We knew we were taking a risk in producing a festival consisting solely of women performers to which the public (all genders and orientations) would be welcomed. We were conscious of a lack of role models and a fundamental lack of skills in building multiracial institutions. Yet the years had also taught us the value of hard-won progress in this direction. We moved forward with the Sisterfire idea immediately.

We hardly slept. We were propelled by a sense of purpose and the task loomed enormous for a small crew of staff and volunteers high on hope and low on budget. I built a loft over my desk. Others brought sleeping bags. We camped out day and night. Sometimes someone would remember about eating.

Then we stood in the Takoma Park field. The stage had gone up and the sound equipment and the electricity were plugged in and we heard the voice of Boden (the sound engineer): "Test, test, test." All work ceased for a breathless minute as we stood together in a sleep-deprived reverie.

From this beginning in 1982, the festival grew into a two-day four-stage program with overnight camping and a marketplace of over two hundred craftswomen. Ten thousand participants shared in the sounds and sensations of a stunningly unique celebration.

By late Sunday afternoon, nature's own cycle provided a better lighting design than I had ever been able to communicate to Sweet Honey producers. We gathered in the brilliant golden sun to close Sisterfire for another year. It was traditional for Sweet Honey to perform the final set, and after their last song they called all the performers and workers to the stage to join in singing the finale, usually "Down by the Riverside."

It was a moment filled with pride and hope and harmonies pouring from thousands of open throats. Thunderous applause exploded as people celebrated their success in standing together across so many differences for two solid days. Yet, in this fleeting moment of unity, time did not stop, and without warning dusk settled onto the field and thousands of people returned to their daily routines.

Sisterfire illustrated that multiracial coalition through hard-won and complex negotiation could produce brilliant cross-cultural programming. The festival was at the cutting edge of introducing a special mix of underrepresented performance genres.

Elizabeth Cotten was ninety-two years old when she took out her left-hand guitar and played "Freight Train" and "I'm So Glad I'm Here in Jesus' Name" and talked about being a Black woman guitar player. Flora Molten, a visually impaired Black woman street singer, added her blues lines to the festival before she also passed on. Alicia Portnoy, an Argentinian political prisoner, took to the stage in English for the first time at Sisterfire and dedicated her "Song of the Exile" to our efforts. Tracy Chapman played on the small stage before anyone outside Boston had

heard her name, and I still have a handwritten letter from Whoopi Goldberg describing her comedy act and asking to be considered for the 1984 festival. The children had their own stage area called the Hearth. Ella Mae Jenks was the first Deaf performer at Sisterfire and a few festivals later we produced an entire Deaf performance stage.

Toshi Reagon did some of her early performing at Sisterfire festivals. Alice Walker sang with Sweet Honey In The Rock. June Jordan wove her bold words in rhythm to Adrienne Torf's jazz piano. Ethel Raim brought us Yiddish and Balkan tunes. The Moving Star Hall Singers brought us the Sea Island sounds. Sisterfire stages have held: Holly Near, Meg Christian, Cris Williamson, Margie Adam, Ferron, Buffy St. Marie, Asian American Dance Theater, Lillian Allen's Caribbean beat, and Sistren's Jamaican Theater. Hala Jabour and Shelly Elkayam offered Palestinian and Israeli poetry; In Process . . . presented their first public performance; Yolanda King and Atalla Shabazz (daughters of Martin Luther King and Malcolm X) brought Nucleus Theater; Kate Clinton brought humor; Alexis DeVeaux brought rich words and endless encouragement, and Safyia Henderson Holmes brought more rich words. And these are only a handful of the performers who created the Sisterfire legacy.

For six years we were able to carry on the experiment. Like all festivals, Sisterfire was suspended reality.

There were always problems among the wonder and the magic. As Sisterfire grew bigger, we were not able to meet the challenges created by the mix and, yes, clash of cultures that occasionally emerged. There were among our supporters women who wished that no men would be allowed and came grudgingly to the festival because it was a rare chance to witness so many women performers in one space. There were White women who thought there was not enough women's music (read White) and Black women who thought there were too many White women. There were straight people who wondered why there were so many gay and lesbian people around, and there were political people who thought the festival was not addressing substantive issues, and there were festivalgoers who thought the performers were too politically oriented. There were women of color who claimed we were a racist institution and White women who denied the existence of racism within their circle. And there were those of us by the thousands who celebrated this new woman-child.

As sometimes happens from the accumulation of culturally based hurt, the festival was a tempting ground on which to unleash unexpressed disappointment and expectation. In 1987 a series of cultural/racial/sexual clashes on the grounds proved too heavy a load for the delicate suspension of the Sisterfire experiment. A national boycott, fueled by some of the women's music press, kept attendance down the following year and we stumbled, we did not survive the resultant withdrawal of support.

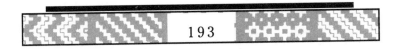

I like to think that Sisterfire is sleeping, in hibernation, gathering new strength and insights from the efforts of the first years. I like to think that she will wake up renewed again . . . soon.

THE PERFORMANCE OF BUSINESS AND THE BUSINESS OF PERFORMANCE

The business of performance occupies more hours than the performance itself, yet if done artfully it remains invisible. Audience members do not think about how many connecting flights it took for Sweet Honey to arrive at their local airport or how early they got up and packed to make their flight. They do not wonder if the vegetarian meals were delivered or if aisle seats were available. They do not know that the local producer had to write a long letter to Sweet Honey explaining political, fiscal, and technical components of their concert plan before Sweet Honey agreed to enter a contract with them and that the producer first balked at the idea of writing such a letter that no other performer had asked for.

They do not know that seven phone calls were necessary to discuss the specifics of sound equipment and outreach to the Deaf community and that the venue changed twice and that two of the hotel rooms didn't have bathtubs or double beds. . . .

But the performance of business truly starts back in Washington, D.C., on Kennedy Street. Clap your hands together and the echoes of twenty years fill the room. Bernice's dining room on Kennedy Street has been the main stage for the Sweet Honey Monday-night business meeting. Never mind that in the past few years the meetings have been on Tuesday and that they don't take place every week. The Monday-night meeting has grown into an institution, and like all institutions, it is allowed its inconsistencies and innovations.

The room is warm yet sparse beyond the essentials, like the Sweet Honey stage. A long teak table sits up against the wall. There are eight sturdy and simple upright chairs with no arms. An upright piano rests in the far corner. A cabinet sits up against the other wall. There are a few framed posters and photos of Kwan and Toshi standing at the Kwanzaa table, and another photo of Bernice's brother Tosu. Lately flowers are on the table and there is always a big pot of Bernice's special Sweet Honey tea in the center.

As she does onstage, Sweet Honey sits in a semicircle. I sit slightly outside the semicircle, stage right of Bernice, who always sits in the same seat at one end. For a few years, Lucy DeBardelaben (who booked Sweet Honey during 1984–86) sat with me, and for the past four years Madeleine Remez (who now shares my role as artist representative) more often sits in what was my place.

Here in the Monday-night meeting in the semicircle around the teak table with piles of agendas, letters, and performance requests, here in Bernice's dining room

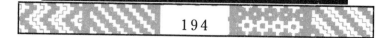

194

with the sweet smells of honey tea, Sweet Honey constantly grows itself by letting each voice speak. Ideas surface and submerged aspects of issues are exposed as they wind around the semicircle. As in an improvisation, there are new tones when each voice expresses its fullness. Here Sweet Honey attends to the business of performance.

I anticipate these meetings with a sweet urgency. It is the forum where I perform the business of transmitting the details of performance. After sitting for long days on the phone without face-to-face interaction, I share the small glitches and victories of the week, funny stories and not so funny stories.

Preparation and presentation of the agenda require sorting critical issues that need full exposition from tangential footnotes and subjective comments. The process is not always easy, especially if I am the bearer of disappointment or overlooked details. It took years to learn not to dart around straight answers; I learned to present the facts unveiled.

Monday nights are a listening ground as Sweet Honey debates decisions, explores details, and grapples with central concepts and policies. For Sweet Honey the overarching context is African American identity and tradition. Yet there are many variations within this theme. Over the years there have been three, four, five, six, or sixteen women speaking at any given time. Each learned about listening to many voices. As the person representing Sweet Honey's ideas to producers and technicians, I witness their interactions so that I can internalize the root of a decision.

At the Monday-night meeting new language is tested, positions are adjusted, and policies are transformed. Road experiences become canonized into oral lore, collective memory, and artful humor through the individualized storytelling techniques which each group member has mastered.

The Monday-night meeting process works because it gives voice and air to everything and anything that needs work. Sometimes changes and developments emerge unexpectedly and the Sweet Honey process evolves. We add things to the contract and change wording that is not clear.

Sometimes my role in these meetings requires a new understanding of achievement and the internalization of the time-tested Sweet Honey doctrine: if it is not broke, don't fix it, and even if it is broke, check out the human cost of fixing it.

My weakness for attempting the impossible is held in check by this seemingly simple doctrine. Yet it is hard to differentiate between what is and what is not broken, let alone to remedy a deficiency or assess the cost of repair. Not everything that falls apart is broken, sometimes it is merely a fortunate indication that wholeness was unrealistic; the problem is a blessing.

It was 1983, before international travel was a regular fixture in Sweet Honey's annual schedule. I arrived at Dulles Airport with plenty of time to check on flight details, had a cup of coffee, and awaited the members of Sweet Honey. Bernice walked in accompanied by daughter Toshi, who was smiling from ear to ear after

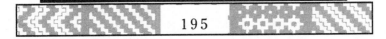

navigating the highways out to Virginia from D.C. with her newly attained driver's license. Bernice walked up to the counter to check in and I could tell by the way she searched through every inch of her bag that something was missing.

There was no way to get Bernice to Berlin from Washington without her passport. One hour remained until takeoff and Toshi, still grinning from her earlier victory, hopped back in the car to retrieve the forgotten document.

At fifteen minutes till takeoff Toshi was nowhere in sight. I noticed a commotion at the ticket counter and discovered the flight was overbooked. Even those at the airport who had passports might not get on the plane. With a pending gig in Berlin, I now realized that if Toshi did get back in time, I had to convince someone to let Bernice use my boarding pass. This would be tricky amid the angry shouts of passengers indignant at the overbooked conditions.

Five minutes and counting.

I pulled an attendant aside. He agreed to let Bernice wait inside security with my boarding pass in case the passport showed up within the next five minutes. I must have run ten miles between the unloading zone and the check-in counter. Finally, in the last thirty seconds, Toshi pulled up visibly shaken from her encounter with a huge truck that had pushed her off the road. With no time for comforting words I ran like a relay racer to the counter. Speechless, breathless, and looking half crazy, I dragged the attendant to the gate. Everyone had boarded except Bernice. As the attendant whisked Bernice onto the transit bus and they sped to the plane, I realized that none of the Sweet Honeys knew where they were going or who was meeting them. I yelled to the air, "Their names are Tom and Ozay, they'll meet you at the Berlin airport. Oh, and the work papers!!!" I saw no visible chance of getting myself on the plane. When I got back to the counter, attendants were consoling angry passengers with free hotel rooms, drinks, and first-class flights in the morning. People calmed down and the crowd thinned out. Finally, I saw my opportunity to plead my way onto the plane . . . if it hadn't taken off.

In an ironic and yet pleading voice, I explained that I couldn't believe I was begging to fly to Germany since I had vowed that I would never set foot on German soil. However, I was tour manager for a singing group who were sitting on a plane without knowing a single detail about where they were headed. I asked if the attendant could check and see if there was possibly someone on the plane who wanted to trade places. The attendant looked uneasily at his colleague. I saw a crack in the previously unyielding exterior and took a shot in the dark, hoping to enlarge the fissure: "Like maybe there is a flight attendant flying on holiday who wouldn't mind waiting so a passenger could fly." Unknowingly I had touched the heart of the reason for the overbooking! Suddenly, the head attendant turned and whisked me away toward the gate.

The plane had now been sitting on the runway for fifty minutes and edgy passengers were offered drinks and explanations. Bernice had turned to Ysaye and whispered, "Amy's getting on this flight!!"

I took the seat of a flight attendant who was asked to deplane and tried to avoid eye contact with Sweet Honey members so I wouldn't start laughing or crying. (Now I didn't say that every time I weighed the human cost of fixing a problem I decided to honor the expenditure!)

Monday-night meetings, surviving road travel, walking through day-of-concert details with local producers who have told me that producing a Sweet Honey concert is not just another gig in their annual calendar. For producers like Virginia Giordano in New York and Jeanne Rizzo in Berkeley, like the Roadwork crew that produces the anniversary in Washington, like Wanda Montgomery and Liz Karlin and Philip Thomas, it represents an annual cycle of renewal and recommitment to community organizing. One might expect this response from longtime producers, but the same sentiment echoes from people who take on a Sweet Honey concert for the first time. Balancing the specialness of each concert to the local producer with the need to provide Sweet Honey with adequate rest and downtime on the road is one of the most difficult negotiations.

A voice cannot be packed in an instrument case. It is difficult to convey how swiftly Sweet Honey's collective mood plummets in the face of a prop plane (which will send their vocal instruments lurching), often after flying through turbulent skies, to confront a full schedule of interviews, sound check, and meetings and then to start singing at 8 P.M. This has always been a difficult notion to explain to producers who are understandably focused on the concert they are producing. It is common to try to pack the most into the limited time that exists. Sometimes saying no to activities that will tax the vocal instrument ensures the success of the event.

STRUCTURE, FLOW, AND SURVIVAL

"Just as a river needs a bed and banks to flow so do people need framing and structuring rules to their kind of flowing."

—Roger Abrahams

Roberta Flack and Patti Austin approached in a determined rhythm. It was backstage at Wolf Trap's ASCAP celebration and Ysaye and I stood talking with Bobby McFerrin. Patti glanced at the names on the dressing rooms and remarked, "See, it says Sweet Honey."

"Yeah, I see," answered Roberta, "but I wanna *see* the Rock."

Bernice is the bedrock. She carved out the canyon through which the waters of Sweet Honey have coursed, inch by inch—issue by issue—for twenty years. The Sweet Honey discourse flows through intentional design.

A solid structure empowers musical improvisation. Vocal lines playfully test the boundaries . . . stretch the fabric . . . reweave tradition into new forms . . . voices dance at the edge . . . the interplay of harmony and dissonance in-

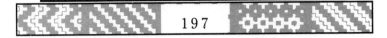

vites the ear to open into an unexplored soundscape. The air spills over with delight, surprise, and hope.

Yasmeen floods the banks in "Ol' Landmark."

Nitanju soars to the outer limits, then Ysaye plunges to unfathomable depths "In the Upper Room."

Aisha's body lurches backward, catching you off guard. Her blue tones migrate back into painful visions as she asserts that "your worries ain't like mine."

Evie infuses the dawn with sensuality by asking, "What does it do for you?"

Shirley takes a solo in American Sign Language and the room vibrates like wind through swaying branches.

People have not caught their breath when Bernice arrives at the last line of the next song. She holds the note beyond human capacity, then lifts her mike away from her mouth, straight in the air . . . throws back her head . . . her voice soars above the shouts of disbelief. Effortlessly . . . she holds on to the note foooooor-eeeeevvvveeeerrr.

It is the structure that allows for the flow of the concert. It looks so easy, almost unconscious; abandon is the heir of forethought.

Bernice fashioned banks and bedrock that anticipated shifting social tides and political crosscurrents. It is not only the drought from unexpected failure that threatens survival but also the flood of unexpected success. Sweet Honey adapts to a half-filled hall in Atlanta or a packed house at Madison Square Garden. She survives sudden changes in personnel, canceled gigs, criticism and adoration, illness, acts of God, being fogged in in Fresno, lost luggage, lost sleep, long journeys across time zone changes, mountain ranges . . .

This notion that adaptability and survival are the by-products of a solid foundation extends to the dynamics between Sweet Honey members and to how they regard the Sweet Honey institution.

I am talking about more than the wisdom of having individual hotel rooms, sitting apart in different rows on airplane flights, or the per diems that allow each member to eat where and what she wants. I am talking about a structure that encourages each woman to give her all to Sweet Honey and simultaneously develop an independent creative and personal identity. It is a philosophy of interdependence rather than dependence. It is an ideology that encourages a multiplicity of expressive possibilities. It is one that sees no contradiction between dancing, acting, teaching, scholarship, motherhood, loverhood, family life, community participation, computer networks, technological literacy, ancient ritual, vacation, science fiction, mystery novels, and Sweet Honey membership.

Producers often ask why Sweet Honey can't perform on a Tuesday and why there's only weekend touring with a few longer tours reserved for Black History Month and international travel. It is not just that the singers have other jobs and community involvements; it is that they have other parts of themselves.

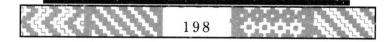

Some Factors in the Equation

In the early years, Bernice often reminded me that I too needed to be wary of finding my entire identity in my work with Sweet Honey. My path could encompass a wider course. It took me a long time to internalize this philosophy but eventually three major directions resulted. The first two directions, establishing Roadwork and creating the Sisterfire festival as a national experiment in multiracial coalition work, were public projects. The third direction was more internal and singular and farther from Sweet Honey and therefore more frightening.

Seven years into my work with Sweet Honey, Roadwork, and Sisterfire, I entered New York University's master's program in Jewish studies. Roadwork's activities had been steadily expanding, and I could not run the organization, represent Sweet Honey alone, and enter graduate school. I was not alone, Lucy DeBardelaben took over the day-to-day tasks of Sweet Honey booking in 1984 and she traveled with the group until early 1986.

It was a challenge to communicate the booking process to another human being since these steps had developed instinctively and by now were deeply internalized. It felt a little like analyzing my breathing or heartbeat. When Lucy took over on her own she was able to institutionalize systems that had existed in only an oral or improvised manner.

Three years later, in 1989, after a conversation with Dan Ben Amos, I entered the University of Pennsylvania's doctoral program in folklore. I wanted to look at the ideas I had developed as an activist through a scholarly lens. I discovered many literatures that reached to the heart of my own work with Sweet Honey. One of my professors, Roger Abrahams, offered a class called "The Folklore of Public Events" that especially drew out this connection. As I read Plato's words: "The crowd and masses have always been regarded as the enemy of culture and reason," I realized it was a thought by those who are in power; they define what culture and reason are. I then thought of Fannie Lou Hamer and the Freedom Riders and how they were received by the establishment. I remembered how the Echo Singers unleashed the spirit in the Smithsonian's Baird Auditorium, stretching the boundaries of establishment concepts of national treasures. I saw Sweet Honey concerts open up space in this racist culture. I saw how the process of producing the shows opens each person, whether a dentist from Orange County, a feminist study group, or a group of fishermen from the Highlands in Scotland, whether a group of Japanese factory workers in Hakodate or the Rape Crisis Center in Ames, Iowa. . . .

When I read Bakhtin's idea that each artistic achievement is a co-achievement between artist and audience resonating through time, I heard Bernice teaching "Run, Run, Mourner Run" in Brixton, knowing as the sound resonated through each person in the audience that they were not the same as before the show.

I read descriptions of public events that pointed to the inherent struggles in coalition work. Victor Turner said that "communitas (the consolidation of a group through shared experience) was the norm though quarrels sometimes arose and fighting took place. For people bring their conflicts with them to mass gatherings as

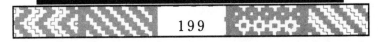

well as their desire to express fellow feelings." His words suggested that rupture of equilibrium might be an inevitable phase in the process.

Ronald Grimms said that "a public celebration is a rope bridge of knotted symbols strung across an abyss. We make our crossings hoping the chasm will echo our festive sounds for a moment as the bridge begins to sway from the rhythms of our dance . . ."

It is the second set in Varadero, Cuba, at the Popular Music Festival. I am listening to Bernice sing that she will stand by your side when you're down but she will not crumble if you fall. I am never bored, not after thousands of concerts, not after hearing these sounds for almost sixteen years. To work with Bernice and the Sweet Honey institution she fashioned out of the bedrock of her genius you have to be strong or you have to want to become strong. You have to want to grow. You learn about taking responsibility, you learn that even with a helping hand you run the race alone, you sharpen your skills at simultaneously visualizing the big picture and the tiny details of the moment, you learn about expressing commitment and holding and upholding political and human values despite the many opportunities that arise to withhold them. You learn about living through mistakes and living with success, you learn that nothing is more important than passing on what you have learned to other people. And this, all of this is Bernice's legacy. She teaches and learns from those she works closely with. In working closely with Bernice and the singing women of Sweet Honey, I have grown more fully into myself. Their beauty is contagious. I wish the whole world would get close enough to catch it.

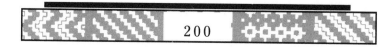

14

EXTENDING A VOCAL LINEAGE

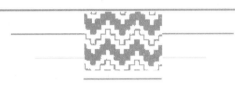

MCLEAN BOSFIELD

In November 1977, Bernice called and asked if I would serve as vocal producer of the album Sweet Honey was almost ready to take to the recording studio for Redwood Records. After the second rehearsal, I asked Bernice when they would give me a copy of the score to study. There was no score. All of the complex arrangements we have come to expect of Sweet Honey are in the minds and voices of these singers—indelibly so. So I adjusted my thinking and my way of working to fit that of Sweet Honey.

The winter of 1977 was very snowy and getting up to the Omega Studio in Kensington, Maryland, for recording sessions was scary because the roads were so icy. Evie had a very bad cold, which fortunately did not affect her voice. Yasmeen had one too and her upper voice was about to go. In the close quarters of the studio we were all eventually sneezing and clearing our throats and trying not to come down with anything that would upset the time schedule for the completion of the album.

Michelle Parkerson, the project coordinator/producer, kept the tea flowing. Evie had her paper cup and tissues. Yasmeen was sucking her lozenges. I used all of the skills of vocal production (physical and psychological) at my command and we finally came to the last session of *B'lieve I'll Run On, See What the End's Gonna Be* on schedule.

I learned a lot working with Sweet Honey and with the production staff on

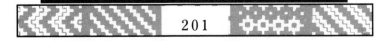

that album. I was in touch with women in the same place in their professions as I was in mine and that experience was one of the most rewarding of my career.

As far back as I can remember, I wanted to be a singer and travel the world singing to vast audiences. I was privileged to do just that. In addition, I have been a vocal role coach, rehearsal accompanist, and assistant to the conductor of the Everyman Opera Company's production of *Porgy and Bess,* minister of music of John Wesley African Methodist Episcopal Zion Church in Washington, D.C., and a voice teacher for the last twenty-five years of my career.

When I began vocal studies in the 1940s, and for many years before and after, there were almost as many ways to teach voice as there were voice teachers. Many vocal coaches (whose domain is repertoire—style and traditional presentation) took on the role of voice teachers (concerned with the health and development of the voice as instrument) with no real knowledge of the physiological functions of the instrument. (That is not to say there were not excellent vocal technicians in the world. There were quite a few of these technicians in Europe but not as many in the United States.) Those coaches had a sound in their mind's ear that they wanted reproduced by a given student, having heard famous so-and-so sing that song or that aria, and they would try to impose that sound on the student.

The teachers all wanted seamless singing, from the highest to the lowest notes. They knew they wanted resonance and supported tone, but had little idea as to how they were going to get it.

Within the last twenty years or so, I have seen a change in the whole field of vocal training. There is more understanding of and reliance on the physiological approach to the voice, allowing correct physiological use of the anatomy and physical laws of acoustics to determine what a singer's sound will be.

The lineage of the physiological approach in my vocal life comes through William Thorner, who taught Rosa Ponselle. He also taught Elizabeth Loguen, who taught my teacher Frederick Wilkerson.

My first voice "teacher" was a coach and a good one. But early on in my professional career, because of a lack of technique, I lost a sixth of my voice, from C in the staff to E above middle C. In 1952 a physician in England recommended Frederick Wilkerson to a colleague of mine who needed vocal rehabilitation after lapsed vocal cords. I accompanied my friend to his first voice lesson and Wilkerson became my voice builder for the rest of his life. He repaired my middle voice and taught me the physiological/anatomical approach to vocal production which I use and which I have taught to my students.

Frederick Wilkerson, whom we all called "Wilkie" or "Papa," master vocal clinician, and my lifelong friend, sang under the name Gilbert Adams in Europe in the 1940s, when he studied with Maestro Armand Crabbe of the Royal Conservatory of Brussels, Belgium. He had a brief career as a singer. In 1946, Mme. Raymonde Delannois, of the Paris Opéra, formerly of the Metropolitan Opera, wrote, "[Gilbert Adams] . . . has a voice rich in expressive tonal quality. He is a

splendid interpreter of song." Wilkerson taught me. From my personal view, the best vocal teachers have to have performing experience since the performance is the object of study.

In 1959, Wilkie gave me my first voice pupil. (I had been coaching by then for quite a few years.) He said, "Her problem is the same as yours was." He felt that if I had responded to the exercises which had healed my voice, I should be able to pass the knowledge on. Then, in 1962, he asked me to come to Washington to coach his voice pupils and to teach voice students of my own in his studio. Years of teaching his technique in the same studio with him and having my weekly voice lesson have cemented the technique within me.

My association with Sweet Honey started during the summer of 1977. Wilkie was going to New York to help Maya Angelou audition singers for a musical she was writing for the Shuberts. He was leaving his studio in my care in his absence. Bernice came in one memorable afternoon with Evie Harris, Yasmeen Williams, and Pat Johnson. Wilkie had them sit in a semicircle and we auditioned Sweet Honey. Bernice was already studying with him. Yasmeen was about to have surgery for the removal of nodules. Evie's neck posture needed attention, as did Pat's. Bernice was to continue her own vocal development.

After Sweet Honey's audition, Wilkie prescribed specific exercises for Yasmeen to use before and after her surgery. We agreed that Evie needed to go to the "Siberian Salt Mines" for her neck. I so named that most uncomfortable of exercises and positions—neck flat on the wall, hands akimbo to align the torso with the neck, and walk a few steps from the wall. I'd learned the technique in the studio of Madame Thorner (Thorner's widow) the summer of my first voice lessons with Wilkie. It was so hot that perspiration ran down my back and face; when I came off the wall I said simply, "Siberian Salt Mines," and went back on the wall.

Wilkie left D.C. The lessons continued.

As the Sweet Honey personnel changed over the years, I came to know most of the singers. I was glad to be there when Tulani learned she had a soft nodule. She elected a period of silence rather than surgery and worked diligently through a series of therapeutic exercises to rebuild her instrument.

It was good to see her singing on the *Live at Carnegie Hall* album some ten or more years later.

Ysaye came when she felt the need to develop more vocalization skills, to explore her lower as well as her upper voice, and to further secure her technique. Evie knew my studio door was open to her whenever she had a need—and that was when she came. By the time Aisha and Nitanju became a part of Sweet Honey, I was about to make a move into another part of my life. Bernice carried on in the Wilkie tradition.

Bernice was the most dedicated student of all. From 1977, when Wilkie gave her voice to me, we worked weekly until 1985, when I closed my studio in Washington and retired to Mexico. Our weekly sessions are still clear and sharp in my

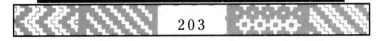

mind. Bernice was so physically drained after a full day at the Smithsonian, where she worked, that when she would arrive for her 5 P.M. lesson, she needed a special routine. I would prepare a light snack, a bit of salad, or a little codfish and cuckoo, her favorite, or whatever. (Cuckoo is a Guyanese version of polenta but the water to which the cornmeal is added has been previously boiled with okra. Cuckoo is only served as an accompaniment to salt codfish stew.) Then we would chat while she ate and unwound. After that we would work. Although I don't recommend eating immediately before singing, in Bernice's case it was imperative or she would not have had the energy to have a lesson.

Wilkie had the following statement among his memorabilia in our studios. These words, written so long ago by Charles Burney in his *General History of Music,* unqualifiedly apply to Señora Doctora Bernice Johnson Reagon, as I fondly called her when she was in the beginning stages of her work with the singers who were to become Sweet Honey In The Rock as we know them today.

TO OUR RISING ARTISTS

They must arm themselves with courage, fortitude,
And above all, with honest artistic principles;
For if our artists are unconvinced
Of the nobleness of their mission,
The sanctity of their profession,
And the great duties which they owe to it
And to themselves,
Then with what hope shall they as a class
Expect justice and recognition from the general public?

Truly the recognition from the public is unquestionable. No longer rising artists, the members of Sweet Honey are now well-established artists.

When Wilkie was killed (Sweet Honey sang "They Are Falling All Around Me" at the Washington memorial service), there were only two of us teaching his technique: Inez Matthews Jackson in his New York studio and me in Washington in mine. As I prepared to retire, Charles Williams was in the Washington area teaching (as much as his performing schedule would allow) at the Levine School of Music. There was no better teacher, I felt, with whom I could leave my professional performing students. I asked Charles if he would take Bernice, among others. And now I understand there are some Sweet Honey voice sessions with him on the books.

I retired to Chapala, Mexico, and Bernice still comes to me there whenever she can. I look for news of Sweet Honey in *The New Yorker* and other Stateside publications. And when my partner, and friend, Bill Jackson moved on to the other side, I reached for Sweet Honey and she was there. Via recordings, Sweet Honey In

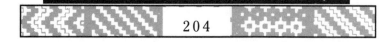

The Rock offered the blessing "Beatitudes" at the "Celebration of the Life of Bill Jackson" service.

Wilkie had another quotation framed in his studios, this one from Frederick Douglass. I believe Bernice and Sweet Honey illustrate this intellectual strength in their work.

> Man learns from the past, improves upon the past and looks back upon the past,
> and hands down his knowledge of the past to after-coming generations of men
> that they may carry their achievements to a still higher point.

It is said that to sing well, one must sing so that the sensation comes to the heart of the listener. We certainly get that when Sweet Honey sings, don't we? More power to Bernice and more power to Sweet Honey In The Rock.

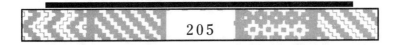

LEFT: TULANI JORDAN KINARD. NUBIAN LOCKS WITH BEADS.

RIGHT: EARLY TULANI HAIR SCULPTURE FOR SWEET HONEY: EVELYN MARIA HARRIS, MICROBRAIDS WITH MULTICOLORED WRAP.

(ALL PHOTOS COURTESY OF TULANI JORDAN-KINARD PERSONAL COLLECTION)

15

"SO GLAD I'M SAVED"

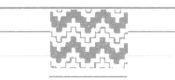

TULANI JORDAN KINARD

Being "saved" is a state of grace, an initiation. Within African American Pentecostal denominations the concept of being saved is usually based upon the Christian ceremony of baptism and speaking in other tongues as evidence of the experience of the spirit of God operating in one's life. The lifestyle of one who is saved is expected to be such that one is separated from worldly things and living in a spiritual consciousness.

Every Sunday the choir marched into the church singing "So Glad I'm Saved." This was the response to every life situation that challenged our spiritual foundation. Instead of "Hi, how are you?" Our greeting was "Praise the Lord . . ."

I once was blind and could not see
But the Lord—He saved me
Now I'm just glad to say
Since He washed my sins away—
So glad I'm saved today

My earliest memories of comfort and security were centered on my home and church—which were one and the same to me since every member of my immediate

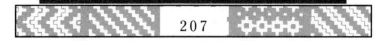

and extended family up to the fifth cousin on either side was a member of our church.

I was born Linda Catherine Jordan. My sister Valerie, my brother Stephen, and I are the offspring of two West Indian families. My mother's family is from Montserrat, which is located near St. Kitts; my father's family is from Barbados. My mother's uncle, the late William Weeks Sr. (Uncle Will), was from the island of Montserrat, and founded our family church, Emmanuel Temple Pentecostal Church in the Roxbury section of Boston, Massachusetts, in 1933. A few years later he turned the church over to Bishop Percyville Jordan, my paternal grandfather, who presided as pastor for over twenty years and as the presiding bishop in the state of Massachusetts within the PAW (Pentecostal Assemblies of the World) organization.

My mother and father were the union of the two "first" families of our church. Both my mother and my father sang in our church choir along with all my aunts and uncles, and my second cousins—William and Johnnie, Uncle Will's sons, who played for the choir.

My mother taught me how to sing, and by the age of three I was a soloist. Gospel music was the only music I knew and understood until I became a teenager. The giants of gospel—James Cleveland, Alex Bradford, and Roberta Martin—always sang in my house. Listening to the gospel records, listening intently to our church choir, and listening to my mother, who instilled in me the concept of my voice as a gift from the Lord, inspired *me* to sing for the glory of God.

Everyone in our family played the piano. To play for my maternal grandmother, you really had to study formally. She respected those who played by ear, but when she wanted to sing Hymn 109, she expected you to be able to really play it accurately—you had to practice extra to avoid any comments about your skill level on the keys.

As a teenager, I directed our adult choir and was the leader of a trio singing group. The group members, Earl Grant, Cinderella Williams, and I, believed that we could touch someone with our voices and give God praise at the same time. I played the piano and wrote a couple of the songs that we sang. We also arranged congregational songs and sang a few contemporary gospel songs. We all attended different churches—which made it hard for us to make a commitment to stay together.

As the director of our choir, I felt I had the ability to make a song live through other people, based upon my interpretation of the song. Many times the choir and I functioned as one voice—when the spirit hit we were able to move from a line rehearsed for weeks to a phrase inspired by the moment. Often I had to struggle to keep myself in control of the energy unleashed after a song. I would watch it ricochet off various choir members into the congregation and back. So many people being touched simultaneously by a spiritual experience from a song was, as I was

told often, something that could only happen as a result of having been baptized in Jesus' name and filled with the Holy Ghost (speaking in tongues)—being saved.

During my middle and high school years the glow of being saved began to tarnish upon the discovery of other music that I never listened to before. We were to shout, to do the holy dance, but we were not allowed to dance the popular secular street and social dances that constantly came up within the Black community. When I began to hear the music, R&B, soul, I wanted to dance to it, and sing it. I could not understand what was wrong with Stevie Wonder, Sarah Vaughan, Ella Fitzgerald, Nancy Wilson, Ahmad Jamal, Earth, Wind and Fire, Santana, Chick Corea, Herbie Hancock, Betty Carter, the Supremes, the Temps, Aretha, or Marvin Gaye—and who had not heard James Brown, "the Godfather of Soul," shout, "Say it loud . . . I'm Black and I'm Proud."

In 1976 I entered Simmons College in Boston as a freshman. I also began to sing with a talented jazz pianist, Ben Zine. After a few gigs in smoky, dark clubs, I knew that way of music would never be my calling.

In the spring of 1978, while visiting my best friend, Afi Saunders (then Pamela Benn), who was attending the University of Massachusetts in Amherst, I experienced a community of African American students who were very serious political activists, cultural intellectuals, artists, and musicians. It was incredible. The music was happening. The first weekend I visited her, Rahsaan Roland Kirk and Hilton Ruiz were performing at the School's Fine Arts Center. Afi's lover (Leon Sanders, "Kwaku," now her husband) was a jazz enthusiast and would take us on weekend trips up and down the East Coast to listen to music.

Afi was a dance/education major and she was living the culture. She shared many things with me, and ultimately because of my exposure to the culture via Amherst, my soul had been nourished in a way that demanded that my name should reflect what my soul was feeling—a deeper connection to African culture. I felt the need for a new name. I was growing spiritually, and not along the traditional path that I had grown up with. I had begun to change my diet—nothing too drastic but enough to feel the difference.

As I searched for my new name, I was drawn to the understanding that within the African tradition the name you carry and its meaning are reinforced within your persona every time it is sounded. Being the fire person I am, I instinctively knew that I needed a name that would provide grounding for me. I chose Tulani. It is a South African Bantu tribal name. It means Peaceful. The name change was intense. I felt like Linda was fighting for space with Tulani. I would tell people that I changed my name and then forget what the new name was. When Tulani sat on me firmly, a transformation inside took place. The external fire that was so apparent went internally to a quiet, deeper, more emotional fire—much more intense.

During the fall of 1979, while visiting in Washington, D.C., I met Andre Smith, a cultural promoter and organizer, who came from a similar background (his

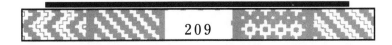

father was a Pentecostal minister). It was a relief to be able to talk to someone who understood my musical frustration. We talked about my inner sense of being born to sing and the intense way in which the musical expression of the church testified to and validated the spirit of God within my life. I was looking for the same type of music outside the worship/praise services and solo performances in church. We also talked about my not knowing how to define this music, what it consisted of, or who was singing it. What my soul was calling for—I felt very deeply, and it was about African people worldwide.

I never missed an opportunity to express my culture through performance. I had always included the work of an African American poet and composer whenever I performed outside the church, and within young people's discussion groups in our church organization I expressed concerns about our ability to connect with the community around the church. It didn't make sense to me to have spiritual power, enlightenment, and not use it for the upliftment of the surrounding community. Whatever I sang had to work on a personal empowerment level—"Prayer without work is in vain."

Midway through our first conversation, Andre remembered that a group called Sweet Honey In The Rock was performing that night at All Souls' Unitarian Church. It was their anniversary concert and they sang the kind of music that I probably would like to sing. He had a friend who performed with the group and he wanted me to meet her. I became very excited, and I wondered, while driving to the church, what and who these women were: they sing without music, they sing gospel and political music, and jazz and the blues too—I was *too* excited.

When we parked the car I was walking so fast my pace was almost a trot. As we walked in the church door, there was a sound of vocal music, the end of a chord, a second of silence, and then thunderous clapping—the concert was over. I was so disappointed. We waited around for a few minutes and he introduced me to his friend, Yasmeen Williams. Her energy was warm and receptive toward me; she sympathized with me for having missed the concert. Yasmeen extended an invitation to come to her house the following day.

That night I could not go to sleep. I wanted to hear their music. I couldn't wait to talk with her about it. The next day we went to Yasmeen's home. As I stepped in the door, I noticed that her living room was blue, incense was burning, and the vibration was peaceful. We began to talk, and immediately our souls connected. I knew her and she knew me. She told me that someone in the group was leaving and Bernice was auditioning people to replace her. She asked me if I wanted to audition. I remember feeling instantly hot; was this the opportunity of singing in a group and leaving Boston?! We sang together to see how well I harmonized. Seeming satisfied, she called Bernice Johnson Reagon and arranged the audition.

Things were moving fast and I was due to return home in a couple of days.

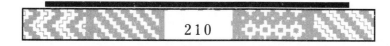

Bernice was the director of the Program in Black American Culture at the Smithsonian Institution. I was impressed. Yasmeen accompanied me to her office. As we got closer to the Smithsonian, the butterflies in my stomach increased, fluttering at a riotous intensity—but it was going to be okay. I was very nervous. Bernice was sitting at her desk, using the phone, surrounded by photographs of Black folks I had seen only in books. These pictures on her walls looked personal, like family pictures. Books were everywhere. She was dressed in an African outfit. When she turned to face me, she smiled. I thought of my mother, she too has an infectious smile that lights up her whole face.

We spoke briefly about my background, and then I sang a song for her. I don't even remember what it was—everything went so fast. After I sang, she asked me about my politics, and then she said she'd call me in a couple of days. I left feeling relieved that I made it through the audition without "messing up." When I went back to Boston the experience was in my mind but not at the forefront. When I got the call from Bernice I was very surprised. But within a week, I'd packed all of my things, quit my job, and moved to Washington, D.C.

My first concert was a first everything. I literally learned everything for that concert onstage. I sat between Yasmeen and Bernice, and I learned how to sing all over again. First, most of the songs were in the Baptist song style, which I knew nothing about. Baptists tend to lay back and build the song up, while the Pentecostal style is more like a song opening up like an explosion and going higher. Then there was the blues. And then there was rhythm and blues, most of it with political and historical poetry. Listening to their first record and tapes had not prepared me for the power and spiritual uplift that was felt by the singers onstage and by the audience.

Growing up believing that God served as a conduit for whatever spiritual upliftment one would feel, I had not had the experience of creating that energy outside a church environment, nor with songs that were not about Jesus. Whatever existed in each singer that knew about calling out that energy, it was manifested and exchanged among us, and then given to the audience. We weren't performing, we were testifying based upon life experience for some—Bernice and the Civil Rights Movement—and commitment to Black Nationalism for all of us. It felt as though we were the voice that many people did not have or the voice that was present but unable to speak because it had no support in their environment. So many emotional ranges were unleashed in each of us through the music that every day I contemplated how it had come to be that I could live this kind of life. It was all because of my work and experience with this group of women.

I kept meeting people whose reasons for living were more than a job, the weekend, or church. These people had intense political beliefs and/or spiritual commitments that they were ready to die for. Every time Bernice would call a song in concert or rehearsal the song became a living experience—a time and place in

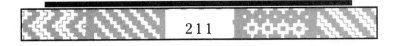

the history of our people. Bernice is a historian who brings history to life as a scholar and also brings that gift to her compositions. Singing with Sweet Honey was an African American history course through music.

From the fifth grade until my freshman year in college I attended predominantly White schools in the cities of Newton and Boston, Massachusetts. My consciousness as an African American student in this environment was high. I was the president of the Black Student Union in high school, and in junior high school I produced a program that dealt with Black awareness through the poetry of some of our political Black poets and gospel music. Given this level of work in my teenage years, I still felt awed when singing the songs Bernice wrote because she lived them, and every time we sang—we brought them to life not only for ourselves but for the audience as well.

When I began singing with Sweet Honey, the film *The Wilmington U.S.A. 10,000* had just been released. Bernice had composed the music and Sweet Honey performed the music sound track for the film. I will never forget seeing Ben Chavis (one of the Wilmington Ten) at one of our concerts and finding out that he had been released from jail to attend. After the concert he had to go back to jail. Songs like "Cape Fear River" and "If You Had Lived" made me feel like I never sang before but I was singing now.

If you had lived with Denmark Vesey
Would you take a stand?

I believed in Jesus and would sing my heart out any day or time for Him—and I believed in speaking and singing to these real issues, real people, real life. I could see and understand that what I was singing about had the power to inspire people to make a difference in the world. I was not only taking Black History 101, I was living it every time I opened my mouth.

When I first moved to Washington, I lived with a sister named Mudiwa Bolong. We had become friends while attending Simmons College in Boston. A friend of hers introduced me to Ramona Edelin, a sister who had an apartment in her home that she was willing to rent in exchange for the care of her newly born son, Ramad. I always loved babies and I needed a situation that would allow me the freedom during the week and weekends to study Sweet Honey's music. It was perfect. Dr. Edelin had recently moved to Washington from Boston to work with Carl Holman, president and founder of the National Urban Coalition. (Dr. Edelin is now president.) Every night our family dinner conversation was focused on politics, the struggle, and spiritual issues. The circle was now complete. I was surrounded by people who lived the Civil Rights Movement on some level, were committed politically, were now in positions to affect the next level of change.

The more I sang, the more open I became. I cared about what I ate and what I washed my hair with. I made sure that my hair was always braided. What had been

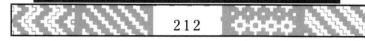

a slow process of metamorphosis was now moving one hundred miles an hour. Every time Sweet Honey sang about an issue it was as if we gave it life. Suddenly I had so much to think about. We were messengers singing about history, current events, sacred songs, and matters of the heart.

As a new member, my job was to learn the repertoire, so I really didn't have time for much else. But just as I was starting to feel okay about how I was doing, Bernice announced in rehearsal that she was going to dissolve Sweet Honey. For the first time I had a real voice in the decision-making process. I was the youngest member of the group, the baby (thirteen years later I'm still the baby). I remember feeling that this situation was like a dying person in need of a transfusion. In retrospect, today as a leader and business owner, I now know how Bernice felt being a group leader and feeling like you can't take another step without commitment from everyone. The commitment I had made to the group, as well as to the force, energy, and spirit that made Sweet Honey, had to stand strong in the face of what seemed to be its demise.

I spoke to the group about what Sweet Honey had come to mean to me and what it meant to the world. The importance of the work could not just die. Dissolving the group was not acceptable. I felt the issues that we were dealing with really couldn't compare with the injustices that were still happening in the world. We had a voice that was making a difference. Whatever it took to keep this voice alive, that's what we had to understand and move toward to resolve the internal problems Sweet Honey was experiencing. As a leader and individual, Bernice had to move from a total control space, because in essence the Sweet Honey "baby" had now become a toddler and the terrible twos were deep. Again and again I tried to say who Sweet Honey was and whatever my exact words were, somehow, the days passed and Sweet Honey sang another song.

At this time, there were only four of us: Bernice, Yasmeen, Evie, and myself. Bernice charted the course, Evie was the anchor, Yasmeen and I were the crew. Yasmeen and I were like sisters, spiritually and musically. It was a challenge to hold a line down and listen to her sing something when I just wanted to back up with a moan or yeah or some kind of accolade for what she had done.

I often wondered what was in store for me vocalizing with women whose real reason for being on the planet is to sing. Each concert was getting lighter for me—I knew my part and I began to feel at ease with some of the styling. I was taking voice lessons with McLean Bosfield. She looked like my Aunt Mary, but she was vastly different. A classical singer of world-renown stature, she initiated, with Sweet Honey, my process of learning my vocal instrument all over again.

One change that occurred as I learned more about my voice came while singing "Sitting on Top of the World." We were all surprised when at the peak of my lead I slid up vocally in a cry and a high thin reedlike note came out of my mouth—sustained and working. "All Praises Due to Love," "B'lieve I'll Run On" —the songs kept coming. The first blues I ever sang was "Stranger." The more I

sang the song, the more I understood the place I was in. Being a stranger—is what we are in this country.

The irony of it all was that I temporarily lost my voice in the fall of 1980. We were performing with Max Roach in a church near the Boston Common. I went to reach for my high note (Bernice called it a high "puppy dog") for "Sitting on Top of the World" and nothing came out. I knew then that I was in for a traumatic series of events. My voice, my salvation as I had come to know it, was not available for me in the way that I had been using it. Looking back on the whole experience to this point (knowing what I know now), I realize that the ancestors were dealing very deeply with me (charting my course); it was time for me to begin the next leg of my journey. Through my work with Sweet Honey, I was now infused with purpose for my creative expression in whatever form it would be.

Two months before that memorable Boston concert during which I lost my voice temporarily, I had met two phenomenal braiding artists, Nawili Ayo and her apprentice at that time, Fana Chisolm. They were in Washington, D.C., staying at Mudiwa's home on the last leg of what they called their Braiding Tour. D.C. was their last stop before returning home to Los Angeles. Six months prior to this, Mudiwa had been visiting friends in L.A. and she had her hair braided by Nawili. When she returned home, everyone who saw her hair had two responses: "By God, what a work of art—beauty and balance," and "Who did it? Where are they? I must have it." I had been wearing braids consistently from the time that I moved to D.C. The styles had been beautiful and I was satisfied. But when I saw Nawili's work, my spirit felt something. Nawili created the smallest braids I had ever seen, and she used small jewelry beads, semiprecious stones, glass beads, and traditional hair wrapping. All of the designs were traditional but with an African American expression. Little did I know then that Nawili would become my bridge over troubled water.

After my throat examination, the doctor's findings revealed two small polyps on my vocal cords. His recommendation was either to operate or, because they were small and soft, to maintain absolute vocal silence for at least a month, which would help them to dissolve. Having someone operate on my vocal cords was absolutely out of the question given that I had an alternative. I would not be singing for at least a month.

On the day I was given this information I also had an appointment to have my hair braided with Nawili. We had become friends during her stay and I had helped her find clients while she and Fana were in Washington. When I told Nawili what the doctor said, she invited me to come to L.A. to learn how to braid as well as to perform the complicated beading that was the signature of her hair designs. I had never really done anything with my hands before—I had certainly never considered learning how to braid—but my spirit was drawn to something about the beauty of her style of hair art. She further encouraged me by saying that I didn't have to talk while I was learning the art form.

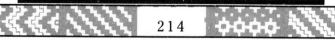

I had a few things to consider: Sweet Honey—what would they do without me? If I left the city, what would that feel like to the group? What would Ramona do about Ramad, the child I was taking care of? I'd never been to L.A. I had relatives there but it was a long way from home—in total silence. Things had a way of working in Divine Order, all of my issues were resolved, and everyone was comfortable with the resolutions. I went on medical leave with Sweet Honey, Ramad went to a woman who took care of children in the neighborhood, and by November 1980 I was in Los Angeles apprenticing with Nawili. Fana decided to stay in Washington, D.C., and acquired a Natural Hair Care Salon there and is a leading innovator in the art form. Nothing in my life up to this point had prepared me for this part of my journey.

Nawili was and has always been in great demand. We were working twenty hours a day—most days in her mom's living room. We sat on a couch (and clients sat on pillows on the floor) weaving intricate patterns with braids and beautiful colors and textures in the beadwork. I was driven. I had never worked so hard physically in my life, but I wasn't tired. The more there was to braid, the more I wanted to bead, and vice versa. All was done in total silence. I wrote a lot of notes but I never uttered a word. I was very comfortable with the silence and I noticed people forgot I was present. But more important, I was in a meditative state most of the time and this accelerated the process of learning. By the end of January, upon my return to Washington, I was a braider. I will always feel the deepest gratitude to Nawili for sharing her talent and life with me when I needed to heal, grow, and expand. Nawili's mom, who is called "Mommy" by everyone, showed love and kindness to me when I needed it, and never hesitated to open her home. My hands were now singing my song.

The politics of hair soon became my new mission. I quickly realized the cultural racism that exists. African Americans who wore their hair naturally, without changing the texture with heat or chemicals, were given a difficult time as they moved through the mainstream culture. I personally experienced the metamorphosis which takes place once a sister or brother makes a commitment to live in a natural state of being with respect to their hair. The transformation begins in the head, then it filters down to all the other parts of the body, affecting the eating habits, clothing, thought processes, lifestyles, etc. I observed over and over the level of empowerment and grounding that took place when one of my clients opened up enough to believe me when I told them how beautiful his or her hair was. In most cases, receiving this praise was a first-time experience. No other hairstyle worn by African American women, children, and men has ever been so empowering in that way. It all felt so natural, so connected to the spirit of Sweet Honey, taking on another manifestation within my person.

Upon returning to Washington, D.C., I began performing my new art form; everyone was surprised how quickly I had learned to braid. The braiding was all-consuming. I wanted to sing and braid, but my newfound love demanded almost all

of my energy. The process was healing. For the first time in my life, I was creating something new and different; each time I was braiding according to the individual and completing it. In essence, many of the challenges of my person were being addressed as directly as they had ever been. Sweet Honey addressed these kinds of issues as a group, but braiding was not a group process. It was truly personal. The depth of commitment, the creation, calling forth images that I'd never witnessed and placing them in a person's head, the implementation, the detail, the quest for beauty, balance, and perfection, the realization of the transformation—this was the healing. All of this happening every time I put my hands on someone's head. This was my hand song.

I had always traveled to New York on my weekends off with Sweet Honey and I began to spend more time there. Soon my braiding consumed most of my time and energy and I relinquished my full-time commitment to Sweet Honey. I moved to New York, though I also kept a Sweet Honey space in my life. To this day I sing in the group as a substitute whenever I get the call and can find a way to respond.

Upon my arrival in New York in the fall of 1981, I renewed a relationship that began at a Sweet Honey concert the previous year in Amherst, Massachusetts. Stanley Kinard had returned to his home in Brooklyn. For me it had been love at that first meeting, but because of time and distance it never really had the opportunity to grow until we lived in the same city. We became husband and wife and the proud parents of our daughter Sakeenah in 1983. Naazir Alade Kinard, our son, was born in 1989. Stanley always understood my commitment to Sweet Honey and my art form. When I would leave my family to go and sing, the length of time was never an issue. He too, even more than me, was committed to the struggle—the upliftment of Black people and the making of a better world—long before I realized who I was within this realm. He is a visionary, the creator of the Carter G. Woodson Cultural Literacy Project—the goal of which is to enlighten young people and their parents. He was and still is an activist within the Brooklyn community, having committed over twenty years of his life to this way. Yes, he understands.

I've stretched the limits of those around me and have been supported by my clients in ways that one can't even imagine. Bernice called me from Boston once; she needed me to be there to substitute for Evie. The concert was two hours away. I was in the middle of a hairstyle and I asked my client if she would mind delaying the process for four or five hours so I could do the concert. A client since I first started braiding in New York, Janelle Drone was also a devoted fan of Sweet Honey and took pleasure in knowing she could aid the process in whatever way she could. Kelly Walker, my assistant at the time, took over. Janelle was getting a twenty-four-hour hair sculpture which required two or more folks to complete it in that period. We were already fourteen hours into the sculpture.

I left to go to La Guardia in half an hour, arrived in Boston an hour after that, and made it from Logan Airport to the theater in half an hour. The concert was two hours, and I was back on the plane and back home all within six hours and we

finished Janelle that evening. After that experience, I felt I had earned a Sweet Honey cape: Go wherever, however.

My relationship with Bernice and Yasmeen remained close. Yasmeen and I, although separated by miles, became pregnant around the same time. We both went to the hospital the same night, Yasmeen for her birthing, me for complications. Her daughter Summer was born on July 29, 1983. Sakeenah, my daughter, was born twenty days later. Bernice went from being group leader to mentor, to mother (Mama B.), sister, and friend.

As I moved between the two worlds of music and hair sculpture, my objective has always been to present my art as a performance within a scholarly perspective. Once when we were on the road in the winter of 1981, I expressed frustration that major African American women's magazines were not treating our segment of the community with any attention or respect. The sisters who chose to wear their hair naturally or in African traditional styles—braids, locks, hair wrapping, etc.—were given minimal editorial exposure, if any. Many of my clients are women who present an empowered look because of their hair. I realized that it was not possible for African American magazines to push a natural-hair aesthetic on the same level as traditional cosmetology (featuring altered hair textures) because then their advertisers had no products to support the natural looks.

Out of that conversation came the "First Colloquium on Braiding: A Question of Aesthetics." This colloquium, conceived of by Bernice and produced by Marquette Folly from Bernice's Program in Black American Culture, brought braiders and scholars to the Smithsonian Institution. It was the first time we had gathered to discuss and share what was happening in this expanding new area of African American creative art. It was the first time an institution on the cultural level of the Smithsonian produced an event of this kind—bringing braiders and scholars together to present the history, discuss and share ideas, concepts, information, techniques, love, and support. Everyone who attended was fortified and charged at another level.

In 1987 I opened Tulani's Regal Movement—New York's first comprehensive braiding salon. My experience in group performance helped me to expand the development of team braiding—work done in concert—as a performance over a head, blending the talents, temperaments, and skills of braiders to create a hair sculpture.

From 1989 through 1992 I served as president of the National Braiders Guild, an organization formed around issues of support for braiders. In 1992 I became a co-founder of the International Braiders Network, a national not-for-profit organization committed to the preservation of the technique and the culture of the art of braiding. As president, I authored an amendment to the New York State Cosmetology Act which was adopted and legislated into law in July 1992, thus creating the first and only Natural Hair Care license in the United States. This legislation speaks to the needs of Braiders, Locktitians, and Natural Hairstylists. The impact on the

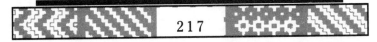

industry has been revolutionary. It is now possible to become a licensed professional without going through the existing system, which is dominated by a philosophy of changing the African hair texture as a way of beautifying the hair. We are now recognized professionally and charged with creating our own institutions to educate students who want to serve the community in the realm of beauty culture.

For me the Nguza/Saba, the guiding principles of Kwanzaa, which is celebrated in Bernice's composition "Seven Principles," is the force that drives me to organize on many levels. Sweet Honey as an institution has provided so much for me—most of all she has nurtured my ability to think and manifest my creativity.

My Ancestral Journey
The silence of my voice,
Made room for the hand-sung
Expressions of beauty from ancient places

In 1987 both Stan and I felt the need to grow more spiritually within our culture. We both felt the pull to know more; we both needed more energy from our ancestors to charge the work that we do.

The manifestation of this spiritual call was my initiation as a priestess of Sango in 1990 and Stanley's initiation as a priest of Obatala in the Yoruba religion in 1991. We are practicing the culture of the Yoruba peoples of Nigeria, West Africa. Yorubas are worshippers of nature. God is the supreme being, whom we call Olodumare. The realm of Olodumare is so vast that he has created deities, Orisas, energy forces that can be accessed through rituals of worship, belief, and initiation. Orisas are distinct forms of God and are the manifestation of nature. The voices of the Earth, Water, Wind, and Fire are clear in my head, as are my ancestors and the Orisas.

The New World Yorubas (which is the term scholars use for African Americans worshipping in the religion) have preserved the culture by way of Cuba. It is only a little over thirty years old in our communities. The most prevalent Orisas among the New World Yorubas are:

Orunmila: Orisa of Divination
Obatala: Orisa of the White Cloth/Wisdom, Expansion
Elegba: Orisa of Choices (a Warrior Orisa)
Ogun: Orisa of Energy—Creation of Motion, Sustenance of Life
            (a Warrior Orisa)
Ossosi: Orisa of an Idea at the Sound of Light (a Warrior Orisa)
Yemoja: Orisa of Motherhood/Oceans
Osun: Orisa of Beauty/the Rivers
Oya: Orisa of the Wind/Abrupt Change
Sango: Orisa of Lightning/Thunder/the King

Olokun:	Orisa of the Deepest Parts of the Ocean
Osanyin:	Orisa of Plants and Herbs
Babaluaiye:	Orisa of the Earth and Skin Diseases
Aganju:	Orisa of the Volcano
Ibeji:	Orisa of Twins/Protection of Priests/the Home

The preparation for my initiation into the Yoruba priesthood came from singing the songs of Sweet Honey and many other songs like these. While still in the womb, I marched with my mother from my uncle's storefront church to his new church. As a child my soul and spirit knew what it was to be in service. The need to acknowledge my ancestors, those who have prepared my ground, those who support my journey, those who provide help when I need it, whether I call for it or not, manifested through the music of Sweet Honey. The power of words, whether spoken or sung, is very real. Each time a prayer is said, a song is sung, and a thought is created, the universe provides an answer.

For me, spiritual energy that is used in the African American church song service, to call down the "Holy Spirit," is the same spiritual energy used in a Yoruba worship ceremony to call on Orisa. This was truly revealed to me the weekend following my initiation. I was on the road with Sweet Honey and we were onstage in New Jersey singing "Father I Stretch My Hand to Thee." In the middle of this song I felt an incredible surge of energy that was taking my breath—making it difficult to sing my line. I knew then as the tears were rushing down my face that Sango was all over me—just as he was in my crowning ceremony. But this was not a Yoruba sacred song to call Sango I was singing; this was an African American meter hymn charged by every ancestor who had sung this song as well as every voice in the present. I couldn't get to the dressing room fast enough. Bernice knew what was happening to me; I had not left—he had not taken full possession. It was just a touch—to let me know . . .

I've experienced baptism twice—the first time at the age of ten and the second at the age of thirty-two into the priesthood of the Yoruba religion. The feeling and the understanding that both rituals drew upon a sameness within me were so intense that I knew my grandfathers, my paternal grandmothers, and all of the deceased elders of my family (many of whom were founders of a Pentecostal denomination) were there and it was a homecoming. Someone in my family line had been through this process before.

I've experienced possession both in the Pentecostal church and as a Yoruba priestess, different levels of the same realm. I know the power of God and I've lived in a spiritual consciousness. Being "saved" in the African American Pentecostal experience is something that will never be denied or erased from my being. To me it is manifestation of our ancestors whose religious expression was altered because of the slavery experience. Every time we call Ella Baker, Fannie Lou Hamer, and many other ancestors in song their spirits are given voice. The inspiration, which is

felt from their songs, moves communities worldwide. Yes, it's the same. "Breaths" tells it all. Through the music, my role as a priestess unfolds as each year goes by. Mafefun Sango (All Praises to Sango).

> *My Independent Voice Is a Part of the Collective*
> *Voice of Sweet Honey In The Rock*
> *My musical history provides the vision*
> *Of my service to the Global Community*
> *I know that I belong to a Sisterhood that*
> *Supports who I am—they have given me tools*
> *To labor with in the world—I can call upon them*
> *When I Need, Whatever . . .*
> *It is a constant evolving process—For I see God*
> *everywhere—in everything—in every being.*

So in the tradition I say: Praise the Lord—Mojuba

Thank Ya!!—Modupe

So Glad I'm Saved!!!!!!!!!!!!!!!!!!!!!

Ase'o

(I salute the power within)

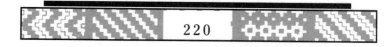

16

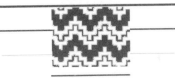

SWEETHONEYINTHEROCK
SONIA SANCHEZ

Set 1

What an honor it is for me to write a poem for some downhomeupsouth sweethoneyintherock women, keeping us alive, showing us how to be tough and soft as we walk towards love and liberation;

And i call out to Olukun to part the waters for these women, our sisters who made us look down the corridors of our birth;

What an honor to write a poem for some women who have loved us with their sweethoney breaths.

Set 2

I Say;

    A Love Poem:

        For Sweethoneyintherock
i Say who are these women who
call themselves sweethoneyintherock;
who are these sisters strutting on stage
like Amazons in tambourine laughter
Knees dignified with years,
infinite Knees, not bent on pavements
corporate teeth or genital grief;
who are these women singing in glass
in coal in flames in dust moving us

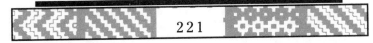

from eyes that circumvent God
from hands that beat women and children into worms;

i Say who are these compañeras
interrogating our days
waking us in the flesh alive
with our grandmother's quilts
with our mother's starched dreams
with our children scouting their birthplace
from our wombs;

i Say. i Say. i Sayyyyyyyy.
who are these women who call themselves
sweethoneyintherock?

SWEET HONEY IN THE ROCK: TWENTIETH ANNIVERSARY
ANGELA DAVIS

As one of the many celebrants of Sweet Honey In The Rock's twentieth anniversary, I count myself among the fortunate beneficiaries of the full twenty years of their cultural gifts. I also consider myself fortunate to be celebrating a twentieth anniversary in my own life as well—marking the year my trial on charges of murder, kidnapping, and conspiracy ended in an acquittal. These two decades of our history —the history of progressive, resisting communities—peacefully resonate in Sweet Honey's music.

The first time I heard Sweet Honey in person, it was at a rally in Washington, D.C. They were calling for the freedom of Joan Little and the Wilmington Ten. What is so astounding is not that they were on the front lines of cultural/political struggle then, but that they continue to position themselves in relation to struggles and issues—around ethnicity, class, gender, sexuality—that have become inordinately complex. And they are as much at ease singing a traditional spiritual as they are in entering the contemporary tradition of rap music.

The aesthetic and political passion that weaves the voices and gestures of the women in Sweet Honey In The Rock into new and constantly evolving combinations of music, movement, and messages is as fresh and contemporary in the 1990s as it felt to those of us who heard and saw them two decades ago.

Happy Anniversary, Bernice, Evelyn, Ysaye, Nitanju, Shirley, Aisha . . . and all the other women who have helped to make Sweet Honey such a magnificent cultural institution of our times.

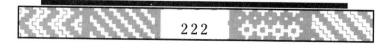

SISTERS IN SONG
BYRON HARRIS

The women of Sweet Honey In The Rock have been my "sisters in song" for my entire adulthood. Their wisdom, talents, and unfailing commitment to the truth have shaped me spiritually, politically, and culturally.

After each concert, I am more and more convinced that these women hold the key to the doors of life without racism, sexism, and oppression.

Sweet Honey In The Rock, you have a special place in my heart for all that you've been for me and all that you give to the world. Your song is eternal, as is my love for you.

Thanks for letting me be a part of your family and for never letting go of your dreams.

MUSIC IS ENERGY
CHARLES WILLIAMS

"Vocal coach for Sweet Honey?" you ask. Well, my dear friends, these are not only talented women, but intelligent and wise musicians who understand how important it is to keep their voices in peak condition.

For the past six years I have had the pleasure and honor of being vocal coach for Sweet Honey In The Rock. Bernice Johnson Reagon is a no-nonsense lady. She knew that to fulfill Sweet Honey's many and growing engagements, the group needed some vocal care and coaching. At that time, as co-chair of the Voice Department at the Levine School of Music, where I still teach voice and head its Music Theater Program, it occurred to me that a group like Sweet Honey might want a musical home and that having them at the Levine School in residence would be beneficial to both parties and to our shared communities. I brought Levine School executive director Joanne Hoover and Bernice together and it was done.

I am privileged to help train and direct Sweet Honey's wonderful warm and powerful voices. They come to me with individual or group vocal concerns. They come to get "pumped up" when preparing for a tour, an appearance in New York, or when putting a new repertoire together for one of their dynamic albums. In turn they give back in kind. Sweet Honey gives standing-room-only individual and group workshops sponsored by the Levine School of Music.

Dear Bernice, Evelyn, Ysaye, Aisha, and Nitanju, thank you for letting me be a part of your musical life. Sweet Honey is a gift to the world and makes life sweeter for us all.

Much love and hugs.

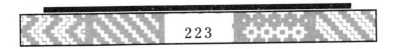

WE WHO BELIEVE IN FREEDOM

"THANK YOU, SWEET HONEY!"
WENDY ARMSTRONG

What is this feeling in my bones?
It's Bernice's voice with beautiful song.
It penetrates my bones.
From my arms to my thighs a great warmth inside.

Ysaye's voice is very deep,
I can tell by the vibrations of my diaphragm.
It shakes my stomach and rumbles my ribs,
oh my, it feels good.

Aisha, your voice I can feel in my head,
it massages my temples,
like the waves on the ocean's bed.

Evelyn's voice I cannot hear or feel,
but the expressions on your face
are more than enough,
full of emotions,
happiness,
sorrow and pain,
showing the depth and seriousness
of whatever you are saying.

Nitanju, your body shows how the music flows,
and your voice is so small it tingles my toes.

The interpreter is a very important part of the group.
She helps me to understand the lyrics
and where they start and stop.
Her fingers and hands as swiftly as they flow
take me everywhere Sweet Honey goes.

The whole group together moves my spirit and soul,
my heart starts to pound and tears fill my eyes.

The music "sounds" so good I hate to say goodbye.
So I'll continue to experience
Sweet Honey

and the healing sounds
that make my soul rock.

I am Wendy L. Armstrong. I am an African American. I was born and raised in the state of Kansas. I came to Washington, D.C., in 1984 to continue my education. I am a recent graduate of Gallaudet University's education program. I am also hearing-impaired. I started losing my hearing at the age of ten, and by the time I was in high school I was Deaf. I call myself hard-of-hearing because I can hear a few sounds in one ear.

Despite my hearing impairment, I have a deep love for the art of music. Before I lost my hearing I was a young musician and I wanted to be a conductor. I also wanted to sing and write my own music.

After I became hard-of-hearing I didn't want to go to concerts because I couldn't hear, feel, or understand the words. Imagine you are in a jar with the top on. When you look out you can see fine, mouths are moving, people are moving, but you can't hear anything. It's like you are in a silent movie.

A Sweet Honey In The Rock concert was the first concert I ever attended as a hearing-impaired person. Experiencing Sweet Honey is the most wonderful, uplifting, and exhausting experience I ever had. I can sit and look at the Sign language interpreter and understand the words. I can look at each singer to follow the beat and the flow of the music. Sometimes I can tell who is singing certain parts and sometimes I ask the interpreter. Sweet Honey has inspired me to ask other performers to make their concerts, plays, and lectures accessible for the hearing-impaired. By attending Sweet Honey concerts and events I have also learned so much about African American culture as well as African culture.

Living in a Deaf world, Black Deaf people are not exposed to the history and culture of our people. I was not aware of the ways Black people were being killed in Mississippi. I didn't know about the Burlington Mills of South Carolina or the way in which the clothes that we buy and wear are connected to the lives of workers all over the world ("Are My Hands Clean"); and that my people worked in the coal mines and babies were affected by radiation before they were born ("More Than a Paycheck"). I had never heard about Fannie Lou Hamer, Steven Biko, or any of the issues of that time. And as I attend Sweet Honey concerts today, I understand better some of today's issues, such as racism, women's issues, discrimination, etc. I can now recognize when these issues are affecting me and how I can help the Black Deaf community in dealing with them.

Thank you, Sweet Honey, for opening up a new world to me. Now I share this world with other Deaf people like myself.

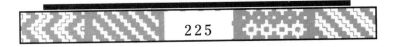

FAMILY
THE EARLYS

Miriam and James came together in Atlanta while in school during the late sixties, they met Bernice there, and as newlyweds they attended the first Sweet Honey concert. James Early gave Sweet Honey her first booking and he worked alongside Bernice at the Smithsonian Festival of American Folklife. Jah-Mir and JaBen heard the singing of Sweet Honey before they were born, and when they got here and looked around, they saw the family gathered . . . Momma, Daddy, Brother, Grands, and Sweet Honey singing . . .

MIRIAM STEWART-EARLY

The word "family" brings different images to each of us based on who we are and all the life experiences that have gone into shaping our sense of family.

Family has always been a very strong part of my life. To me, family initially meant parents, brothers, grandparents, aunts, uncles, and cousins. Then family grew to include husband, in-laws, sons, nieces, and nephews. As a young adult I formed friendships with women whom I began to see as the sisters I never had.

I began to make choices about who family was. Choices based on mutual understanding and a sense of respect that is deep and enhanced by unrestricted love and admiration.

Bernice Reagon is my sister, and the women of Sweet Honey are part of my family. I have been at each anniversary concert and look forward to them each fall as an emotional lift and affirmation. My two sons have been listening to the messages of Sweet Honey since before they saw light. They learned to sing the songs as they learned to speak. My youngest son wrote a book about his family when he was in first grade; he included his Aunt Bernice and Sweet Honey.

As incidents positive and negative have occurred in my life, I could always hear the sounds of Sweet Honey. When my father, brother, and mother passed it was the sound of Bernice singing—"You're not really going to leave me . . . It is your path I walk, it is your air I breathe . . . It's your strength that helps me stand . . ."—that helped me and strengthened me. As we plan our twentieth wedding anniversary, I hear Evie singin' "Seven Day Kiss." When I listen, and hear, the wisdom of my sons, I hear "Your children are not your children, they are the sons and the daughters of life longing for itself . . . They have their own thoughts."

It is not often that one gets to choose their family.

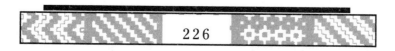

JAH-MIR TOUSSAINT EARLY

Family is "the path I walk";* the tree I sit under. It is the book I read, my family.

The path leads me further. The tree reaches to the heights that I must go.
The book is full of knowledge and time.
Family.
Family is the tree that points high, high, to where I must go.
Family is my rock, my support, my shield, my foundation.
I build upon family.
Family is there when all else has left you.
Family.
Family is the people that come to you and tell you they love you, and cry for you, and hope for you. They fight with you, and fight for you.
Family.
Family is the love that I feel in a room full of people, cousins, uncles, sisters, brothers. You may lose friends, you may even lose hope, but you have always got family.
Family.
Family is the tears that fall down my face when I lose one of them.
Family.
Family is "the path I walk"; that path leads to heaven.
Family.
Family is my beginning. Family will be my end. I love my family.
Family.
The hope, the dream, the knowledge, and the heights I must and can, above all, reach, is family.

JABEN AKUA EARLY

Family: People who love one another.
Family: Children, Brother and Brother.
Family: People who've raised me since I could crawl.
Family: We have a certain bond that nothing can break and our love is something no one can take. Our family stands firm and bold. Our love for each other isn't something you can hold. Yet we shall pass on this simple treasure to each

---

* "The path I walk" is an excerpt from the song "They Are Falling All Around Me," performed by Sweet Honey In The Rock, composed by Aunt Bernice.

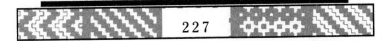

family member, this love you cannot measure. The strength that we hold shall never wander. Our united cause is for one thing—the people who make our family, you and me.

JAMES EARLY

I'm proud of me and mine, children, relatives, and all! I got some fine people in my family, just like we got some fine people in our race.

We've been all tangled up with Sweet Honey In The Rock—
Maillard, Louise, Evie, Yasmeen, and all of them.
Me, Miriam, Jah-Mir, and JaBen.

JaBen with a crying cold,
Bernice did lullaby and rock little JaBen.
Bernice talking with Momma Stewart
about teaching her son,
And me, Kwame, and the boys growing
into big and little brothers,
uncle and nephews, Black men!

Sisters consoling my love when her mother passed on,
Bernice and Adisa too . . .
Toshi stretching all of our minds:
comic strips, kites, movies,
and with the boys, growing-rites.

Jah-Mir and JaBen, "I hope the world is ready for you . . ."
"Here comes Steven Biko walking down the water . . ."

Thanksgiving space,
a family time,
extended from ancestral pasts to coming grace.

We celebrate the family of world cultures
and the race from Washington, D.C., to Moscow,
from the National Mall to Gorky Park.

Sweet Honey, my sister, me and you, and all of us,
in those deep and special consultations,

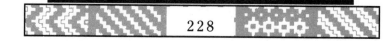

through those fierce and public times
we raise our voices,
frame our steps,
act on our future,
build our family.

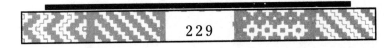

17

NATURAL WOMAN IN SEARCH OF THE ROCK
A SHORT FILM

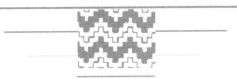

SAUNDRA SHARP

FADE IN:
EXT. [exterior], PARK—Day
CAM [camera] comes up on NATURAL WOMAN, crown slightly askew, a wilted Spirit tucked under her armpit, whose colorless toes are dragging her along. She sits down on a rock and begins to weep.

ANGLE ON:
NATURE, watching.

> BUSH
> Oh, no. Here comes another one.

> SPARROW
> Don't be hard on her, Bush. That's not why we're here.

> CAMOMILE WEED
> I could give her some herb, but she needs
> something stronger.

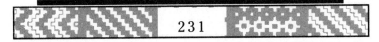

> RIVER
> Yeah, that Spirit is whipped! Definitely
> needs some Rock.

Natural Woman crosses to PINE TREE, and holds on to it for support. Tree whispers in her ear.

> TREE
> Get to The Rock, girlfriend, and you'll be healed.

> NATURAL WOMAN
> I just left a rock.

> TREE
> Unh-unh. You can't leave where you've never been. The Rock I'm talking of is a fortress for your Spirit. Just still yourself, and listen. And if you don't find The Rock, it'll find you.

CAM on Natural Woman. She is too excited about getting her Spirit healed to be still. She boogies out of the park, picks up momentum and becomes a whirlwind, moving toward the galaxy.

ANGLE ON:
Nature, watching her.

> BUSH
> See, I told you. We gonna be up all night with this one.

> WIND
> I'll keep an eye on her.

> BEES
> We'd better go also, to give you some backup, Wind.

CU [close-up] on WIND. When had it ever needed some backup?!

EXT., HARLEM—Night
Natural Woman lands, with a slide of the thigh, on a street corner in Harlem. Right off, BROTHER MAN flashes the inside of his jacket at her. It's lined with gold trinkets.

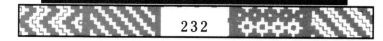

NATURAL WOMAN
No, thanks, Brother Man, but maybe you
could tell me where I can find The Rock?

BROTHER
You a long way from Alcatraz, Sis. But I can tell you how
to get there.

NATURAL WOMAN
Ummm, I don't think it's Alcatraz I want.

VOICE (off-camera)
I got what you want.

Natural Woman whirls around at the voice so close behind her. She sees WHITE
LADY, her arms open in welcome.

NATURAL WOMAN
You do?

WHITE LADY
I've got spirit mender, mind bender, grace, and forgiveness all packaged into one special rock. And it's got your
name on it.

NATURAL WOMAN
(a little suspicious)
You sure?

WHITE LADY
My sister, my sister. These things don't happen by accident. I mean, you, me, meeting like this in your time of
trouble. Here—
(pulls out a bag of cocaine)
—see how good it smells.

White Lady sprinkles some into her palm. As Natural Woman leans in to sniff,
Wind scatters the powder into the air. BACKUP BEES buzz White Lady as they
sing:

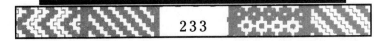

233

BACKUP BEES
(singing)
No, no, no, not that rock!
That white stuff will blow your top!

WHITE LADY
(threatening)
You know what you just cost me?!? Soon as I get these
damn bees off me, your ass is mine!

Frightened, Natural Woman dances backward and whirls back into the galaxy.
Brother Man calls after her.

BROTHER MAN
I like your moves.

EXT., GALAXY—Day
CAM pans the galaxy, following Natural Woman as she wings through space.
CU, the eye of a STORM. Pull back to see it's Natural Woman, a tornado out of
control. She crash-lands in Arizona.

ANGLE ON:
A SALESMAN, who rushes over, helps her to her feet.

SALESMAN
Looks like you could use "a piece of the rock."

NATURAL WOMAN
That's exactly what I'm looking for.

SALESMAN
(handing her his card)
I can set you up for life. We'll start with accident insurance, life insurance, fire in—

BACKUP BEES
(singing)
No, no, no, not that rock!
It can't cover what you've got.

Natural Woman scurries away, her Spirit still under her armpit, feeling even heavier
now.

LONG SHOT, Natural Woman walking, trying to clear her head.

> NATURAL WOMAN
> The tree's message . . . a rock . . . find a rock . . . a
> *fortress* for my—
> > (she lets out a groan)
> Yeah! Why didn't I think of it before?

Before Wind can stop her, Natural Woman has clicked her heels seven times and boogied off.

> BACKUP BEES
> Uh-oh! You don't think she's going to . . .

> WIND
> I'm afraid she is.

> BACKUP BEES
> We'll have to fax an alert to our associates.

EXT., STRAIT OF GIBRALTAR COASTLINE—DAY
A group of SPANISH FLIES patrol the shoreline, on the alert. A splashing sound is heard in the distance.

ANGLE ON:
Exhausted and wet, Natural Woman drags herself onto the Rock of Gibraltar, but the Flies prevent her from taking the hill.

> SPANISH FLIES
> (singing) ¡No, no, no esta roca, no!
> No esta un estación por espirito

> NATURAL WOMAN
> Run that past me again?

Natural Woman does not feel like dancing or searching anymore, and her Spirit is failing fast. She flags down a CLOUD and gets on board.

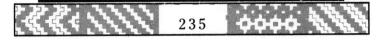

CU CLOUD

No cop copters, no ghetto blasters, no Scud missiles here. Natural Woman nestles into the cloud's silkiness, takes a deep breath, drops her head into the pure stillness.

In this still moment, she hears it. Her Spirit hears it. The music. The message.

SOUND TRACK

"Sweet honey in the rock . . .
Sweet honey in the rock . . .
Sweet honey in the rock . . ."

NATURAL WOMAN

Oh, *THAT* rock!!
(to driver)
Can you get me to that Music?

CLOUD DRIVER

That's not my route, but we have an out-of-body service that can get you there fast.

Driver places a call, and Wind lifts Natural Woman out of body, transporting her Spirit to the Music.

INT., WASHINGTON, D.C., THEATER—Day

The Music bursts out of the sound system and takes over the theater. It wraps itself around Natural Woman and transforms her. Opens her chakras and sets her crown aright. And her Spirit returns to her, healed. Healed by the Sweet Honey In The Rock.

FADE TO BLACK (always)

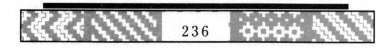

18

"WE HAD A GREAT TIME FOR A LONG TIME"

VIRGINIA GIORDANO

The choice seemed to be, in the words of Ralph Ellison, "to live with music or die with noise." Sweet Honey In The Rock chose song. And tonight, at Town Hall, the group of five black women singers will celebrate its 10th anniversary with a program of new and traditional music.

—JENNIFER DUNNING, *THE NEW YORK TIMES,* DECEMBER 2, 1983

I began working with Sweet Honey In The Rock in 1980 during their seventh year together. Now I am working on their twentieth-year concerts. Whenever I am producing a Sweet Honey show, that show is my favorite. I'm in love with producing, and in particular with producing this group. My name is Virginia Giordano.

> Sweet Honey aims for more than entertainment. "We want to engage audiences in a way that they have a visceral experience, raising questions not just about us and how we sound but also about themselves," Miss Reagon said.
>
> —*THE NEW YORK TIMES,* DECEMBER 2, 1983.

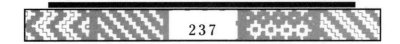

WE WHO BELIEVE IN FREEDOM

For Immediate Release

October 1, 1985

SWEET HONEY IN THE ROCK AT CARNEGIE HALL

SWEET HONEY IN THE ROCK, a quintet of Black women singers, will perform at Carnegie Hall on Sunday, November 17, at 8:30 P.M.

This concert is a special occasion for Sweet Honey In The Rock—this is their first appearance at Carnegie Hall.

Sweet Honey In The Rock sings fiercely of being fighters, of being women, taking their ever growing audiences through the historic struggle that is the Black American experience. With dignity, warmth, determination—they sing, always moving to that place inside where we believe in ourselves.

They hurl their voices in resistance against racism, lynching, slavery, rape, occupational dangers, nuclear energy and weaponry, sexism, discrimination, hunger and unfair housing. Their repertoire expresses commitment.

At this concert they are releasing two new albums—"Feel Something Drawing Me On," a collection of sacred songs, and "The Other Side"—both recorded on Flying Fish Records. They have four other albums.

This concert is signed for the hearing-impaired.

Photos and interviews available:
CONTACT: Virginia Giordano

For the past thirteen years I have made my living in the world as a concert producer. It is what I love best, it is what I do best, it is the grace that has been given to me. Live performance is grand, the larger-than-life moment. As a concert producer, I feel that I am a transmitter, that I provide the medium where the audience and performer exchange their energy.

November 1, 1985

Amy Horowitz
Roadwork
Washington DC

Dear Amy,

This letter will confirm our conversation re: the schedule for the Carnegie date:

2:15:   Sweet Honey arrives at La Guardia shuttle, staff pick up
3:00:   Sound and lights load into Carnegie Hall, group checks into hotel

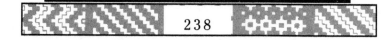

5:00: Sound check, all group members & technical staff (please use Stage Door entrance on 56th St.), light refreshments
6:00: Dinner break
7:30: Group returns to hall
8:00: Show starts
11:00: Curtain
11:15: Reception in Greenroom
11:45: Performers return to hotel

I am looking forward to our first concert at Carnegie Hall with enormous enthusiasm and great pride for all of us.
Sincerely,
Virginia Giordano

I don't specifically remember my first contact with Sweet Honey's music, but it was about the time that I was beginning to produce concerts independently. My feeling about working with them was instinctive. I didn't think about it; I did it. I produced them at Town Hall on Forty-third Street before moving to Carnegie Hall. Both halls were significant steps. Town Hall was the first professional concert hall for Sweet Honey in New York City and in Carnegie Hall they stand with a century of world-class singers, musicians, and performers. It is remarkable, a phenomenon, that a group whose foundation is political and who have never recorded on a major record label have growing audiences after twenty years. They have a devoted following with a commitment as strong as their own. Everyone that experiences Sweet Honey's power spreads the word. The press responds to them.

SWEET HONEY: UNCOMPROMISING POLITICS NEED NO ACCOMPANIMENT
Sweet Honey In The Rock refuses to make the compromise that haunts most musical groups, refusing to sacrifice its fierce political commitment or its carefully developed a cappella melodic style to create a more "mainstream" sound.

—MICHAEL S. KIMMEL, *THE GUARDIAN*, OCTOBER 1986

I have taken Sweet Honey to Boston and Philadelphia, and those shows have their own way of being fabulous, but the Carnegie Hall show is the most fabulous of all their shows that I produce. Our first Carnegie Hall, though, was, what can I say, the sweetest offering life makes.

My move from theatrical production to concert production surprised me. I'd found theater in college, then, during the mid-seventies, had worked as a lighting designer and production stage manager in and around Off Broadway. I was a talented lighting designer and considered making a go at becoming known for it, but it wasn't quite right for me—it satisfied me aesthetically but not fundamentally. By the late 1970s I didn't realize I was looking for something else to do, but I was.

That's when I found women's music, that small industry created by women, mostly lesbians, who made music from their experience as women freeing themselves from the limitations and constraints of the established music industry (for one thing).

I saw Margie Adam perform to a small gathering of women in a church. In characteristic style, I decided that if Margie could draw 300, I could probably sell twice that number of tickets. So I invited her to perform at Symphony Space, a converted movie theater on Manhattan's Upper West Side. I ran around town and got everyone I knew to help. Ars Pro Femina, a women's recording company, sponsored the show and sold soft drinks to raise money for their LP, *The Return of the Great Mother.* In the end we sold over 600 tickets, about two-thirds of the house, and it was by all accounts a success. At the end of the first set I was standing in the balcony alone when the audience gave Margie a very spontaneous standing ovation. That was it for me. A producer was born.

After that I created my own business and jumped in body and soul. I'm not even sure how I did this stuff then. I was producing, I didn't have any money, but I was doing it. Sheer nerve and passion. I loved it and I was doing lots of it. I've mostly been out there alone. Though as I look back I see that in each season, each phase, in each new place I arrived, there were companions to see me though— friends, lovers, helpers, staff, professional friends, co-promoters, bookers, managers, fans. People who share this feeling about this particular world as intensely as I do, and for a time share it with me.

From Symphony Space, I went to the other major halls, Carnegie Hall, Avery Fisher, the Beacon Theater, Town Hall, and even the Felt Forum (now the Paramount, beneath Madison Square Garden). And I got involved producing women's theater in little Off-Off-Broadway houses. One of my first big shows after Margie, was Cris Williamson with Jackie Robbins, June Millington, and Cam Davis at the Beacon Theater. The place was jammed with women; it was a scene, a coming of age in a way. I saw k. d. lang perform the other night and I was happily reminded of the fabulous female energy and scenes in those large concerts which I was producing ten years ago. The women's music network audience legitimized and created this "star system" for the completely independent, outrageously androgynous women performers today.

That music industry—that women made for themselves—was an emotional, difficult, and sweet place to learn. It gave me inspiration and independence which I had never experienced before. Women's music gave me an experience of my own talent and of myself succeeding on my own terms. I didn't have to remain a girl in eternal apprenticeship to the male ego. I have had the chance to return to the work principles I respect. It's been the best for me. And I know it. I am a good businesswoman, a teacher, a dependable partner, and a fair human being.

The concert music scene in New York City is fast-paced, expensive, exciting, and dangerous; it's for professionals. Gradually I got to know people who ran the halls, other promoters and people in the business—John Fernandez and Kimo

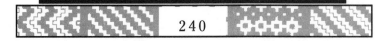

NINTH ANNIVERSARY CONCERT, GALLAUDET UNIVERSITY AUDITORIUM, NOVEMBER 1982. FRONT:
SHIRLEY CHILDRESS JOHNSON, SIGN LANGUAGE INTERPRETER (SLI), BERNICE JOHNSON REAGON.
BACK: YASMEEN WILLIAMS, EVELYN MARIA HARRIS, YSAYE MARIA BARNWELL, AISHA KAHLIL.
(PHOTOGRAPHER, SHARON FARMER)

Konzert anläßlich der Ausstellung DAS ANDERE AMERIKA
in der Staatlichen Kunsthalle Berlin vom 13.3. bis 24.4.83

Sonntag
13. März
20 Uhr
HdK Konzertsaal
Hardenbergstraße

Vorverkauf DM 12,–
Werbepalette
Detmolder Str. 65, 1 Berlin 31, Tel. 853 89 14
NGBK
Hardenbergstr. 12, 1 Berlin 12, Tel. 31 61 82
Büchergilde Gutenberg
Kleiststr. 19, 1 Berlin 30, Tel. 241 750
Elefanten Press Galerie
Zossener Str. 32, 1 Berlin 61, Tel. 693 70 26
und an allen anderen bekannten
Vorverkaufsstellen
Abendkasse DM 15,–

Donnerstag
17. März
21 Uhr
Passionskirche
Marheineckeplatz 1

U-Bahn Gneisenaustraße
Bus 24 und 28

Veranstalter:
Künstler für den Frieden
NGBK
Büchergilde Gutenberg

GIVE PEACE A CHANCE
SWEET HONEY IN THE ROCK
USA

Künstler
für den Frieden

TOP LEFT: 1982. FRONT: BERNICE JOHNSON REAGON, SHIRLEY CHILDRESS JOHNSON (SLI). BACK: YSAYE MARIA BARNWELL, YASMEEN WILLIAMS, EVELYN MARIA HARRIS, AISHA KAHLIL. (PHOTOGRAPHER, SHARON FARMER)

BOTTOM LEFT: "JOIN HANDS THE WHOLE WORLD ROUND," 1982. L TO R: YSAYE MARIA BARNWELL, EVELYN MARIA HARRIS, YASMEEN WILLIAMS, AISHA KAHLIL, BERNICE JOHNSON REAGON. (PHOTO COURTESY OF SWEET HONEY IN THE ROCK ARCHIVES)

ABOVE: SWEET HONEY IN THE ROCK OPENS MAJOR EXHIBITION OF AMERICAN LABOR HISTORY, "DAS ANDERE AMERIKA" ("THE OTHER AMERICA"), ON THEIR FIRST GERMAN TOUR, STATE ART HALL, BERLIN, MARCH 13–APRIL 24, 1983. POSTER: MARCH 1983. SPONSORED BY ARTISTS FOR PEACE AND BOOK GUILD GUTENBERG. (POSTER COURTESY OF SWEET HONEY IN THE ROCK ARCHIVES)

TOP LEFT: L TO R: SHIRLEY CHILDRESS JOHNSON (SLI), LOUISE ROBINSON, YASMEEN WILLIAMS, EVELYN MARIA HARRIS. FRONT: CAROL MAILLARD. (PHOTOGRAPHER, SHARON FARMER)

LEFT: L TO R: YASMEEN WILLIAMS, CAROL MAILLARD, AISHA KAHLIL, ROSIE LEE HOOKS, GERALDINE HARDIN, TULANI JORDAN. FRONT: BERNICE JOHNSON REAGON.
(PHOTOGRAPHER, SHARON FARMER)

BOTTOM : TENTH ANNIVERSARY REUNION CONCERTS, UNIVERSITY OF THE DISTRICT OF COLUMBIA AUDITORIUM, 1983. L TO R: YSAYE MARIA BARNWELL, YASMEEN WILLIAMS, CAROL MAILLARD, TULANI JORDAN, AISHA KAHLIL, SHIRLEY CHILDRESS JOHNSON (SLI), EVELYN MARIA HARRIS, HELENA COLEMAN, DIANARUTHE WHARTON, LOUISE ROBINSON, AYODELE HARRINGTON, ROSIE LEE HOOKS, TIA JUANA STARKS, BERNICE JOHNSON REAGON, GERALDINE HARDIN.
(PHOTOGRAPHER, ROY LEWIS)

RIGHT: L TO R: TIA JUANA STARKS, ROSIE LEE HOOKS, LOUISE ROBINSON, DIANARUTHE WHARTON. (PHOTOGRAPHER, SHARON FARMER)

LEFT: SMITHSONIAN EVENING OF CLASSIC GOSPEL SONG, FALL 1984. L TO R: EVELYN MARIA HARRIS, AISHA KAHLIL, YASMEEN WILLIAMS, YSAYE MARIA BARNWELL, BERNICE JOHNSON REAGON. (PHOTO COURTESY OF THE SMITHSONIAN INSTITUTION)

RIGHT: "FREE SOUTH AFRICA!" SWEET HONEY IN THE ROCK SINGING IN FRONT OF THE EMBASSY OF SOUTH AFRICA, WASHINGTON, D.C. L TO R: SHIRLEY CHILDRESS JOHNSON (SLI), AISHA KAHLIL, EVELYN HARRIS. AT THE MIKE: BERNICE JOHNSON REAGON, YSAYE MARIA BARNWELL, SUPPORTED BY DEMONSTRATION COORDINATOR, DR. SILVIA HILL. (PHOTOGRAPHER, SHARON FARMER)

LEFT: 1986, L TO R: BERNICE JOHNSON REAGON, AISHA KAHLIL, SHIRLEY CHILDRESS JOHNSON (SLI), EVELYN MARIA HARRIS, YSAYE MARIA BARNWELL. FRONT: NITANJU BOLADE CASEL. COSTUMES BY KEITH GOODMAN. (PHOTOGRAPHER, ROLAND FREEMAN)

TOP RIGHT: 1986. FRONT: BERNICE JOHNSON REAGON, YSAYE MARIA BARNWELL, EVELYN MARIA HARRIS. BACK: AISHA KAHLIL, SHIRLEY CHILDRESS JOHNSON, NITANJU BOLADE CASEL. COSTUMES BY AKIBA KIESMERA. (PHOTO COURTESY OF SWEET HONEY IN THE ROCK ARCHIVES)

BOTTOM RIGHT: USIA TOUR TO SOUTHERN AFRICA, WINDHOEK, 1990. L TO R: AISHA KAHLIL, CAROL MAILLARD, YSAYE MARIA BARNWELL, BERNICE JOHNSON REAGON, NITANJU BOLADE CASEL.

Sweet Honey In The Rock

SALUTE TO NAMIBIAN INDEPENDENCE

WINDHOEK
MAY 27—28, 1990

A Cultural Presentation of the United States of America

LEFT: BENEFIT CONCERT FOR CARIBBEAN CHILDREN'S HOSPITAL, LISNER AUDITORIUM, WASHINGTON, D.C., 1990. L TO R: SHIRLEY CHILDRESS JOHNSON (SLI), NITANJU BOLADE CASEL, YSAYE MARIA BARNWELL, JAMAICAN POET MUTABARUKA, JAMAICAN AMBASSADOR VAL MCCOMIE, CAROL MALLARD, AISHA KAHLIL, BERNICE JOHNSON REAGON. COSTUMES BY SEHAR. (PHOTOGRAPHER, EDWARD J. SHAW)

RIGHT: NEWPORT FOLK FESTIVAL, 1989. L TO R: SHIRLEY CHILDRESS JOHNSON (SLI), AISHA KAHLIL, EVELYN MARIA HARRIS, NITANJU BOLADE CASEL. FRONT: BERNICE JOHNSON REAGON. COSTUMES BY AKIBA KIESMERA. (PHOTOGRAPHER, JYM WILSON)

TOP LEFT: BLACK AND KENTE, OCTOBER 1991. L TO R: NITANJU BOLADE CASEL, EVELYN MARIA HARRIS, YSAYE MARIA BARNWELL, AISHA KAHLIL, BERNICE JOHNSON REAGON. (PHOTOGRAPHER, SHARON FARMER)

RIGHT: SINGING THE ANC NATIONAL ANTHEM AT THE 1991 MARTIN LUTHER KING, JR., COMMUNITY CONCERT. SWEET HONEY IN THE ROCK AND IN PROCESS . . . , FIRST CONGREGATIONAL CHURCH, WASHINGTON, D.C. (PHOTOGRAPHER, ROY LEWIS)

BOTTOM LEFT: MICHELE LANCHESTER OF IN PROCESS . . . AND BERNICE JOHNSON REAGON LEADING "I WANT TO THANK YOU—MARY MCLEOD BETHUNE AND IDA WELLS BARNETT." BACK: SHARON GREENE, CAROLYN SHUTTLESWORTH, NITANJU BOLADE CASEL, PAM ROGERS. (PHOTOGRAPHER, ROY LEWIS)

LEFT: VOICE IS ENERGY . . . STRETCH. STUDYING VOCAL SURVIVAL WITH CHARLES WILLIAMS AT THE LEVINE SCHOOL OF MUSIC, 1992. L TO R: BERNICE JOHNSON REAGON, NITANJU BOLADE CASEL, AISHA KAHLIL, CAROL MAILLARD, YSAYE MARIA BARNWELL. (PHOTOGRAPHER, SHARON FARMER)

RIGHT: TARRYTOWN MUSIC HALL, TARRYTOWN, N.Y., JULY 1992. PRODUCER, VIRGINIA GIORDANO. L TO R: AKUA OPUKUWAA (SLI), AISHA KAHLIL, CAROL MAILLARD, YSAYE MARIA BARNWELL, NITANJU BOLADE CASEL, BERNICE JOHNSON REAGON. (PHOTOGRAPHER, ROY LEWIS)

"WOMEN SHOULD BE A PRIORITY!" WASHINGTON, D.C., 1992. L TO R: AISHA KAHLIL, SHIRLEY CHILDRESS JOHNSON (SLI), NITANJU BOLADE CASEL, CAROL MAILLARD, YSAYE MARIA BARNWELL, BERNICE JOHNSON REAGON. (PHOTOGRAPHER, SHARON FARMER)

"We Had a Great Time for a Long Time"

Gerald—Carnegie Hall's managers, who make the hall feel like home; Erwin Frankel—a promoter, occasional co-promoter, always a helping hand and available with ideas; Harold Leventhal—Pete Seeger's manager, with whom I co-promoted Holly Near–Ronnie Gilbert; Linda Meier—one of the few other women working independently in the business in New York City; Allan Pepper and Stanley Snadowsky—owners of the Bottom Line, always open to new acts; Joe Taubman—my mentor in entertainment law; Gilda Weisberger—Carnegie Hall's wonderful booking manager; John Yates—from Washington, D.C., whom I co-promote with from time to time; Larry Zucker—manager at Town Hall, always challenging me to do more—their encouragement and respect for me and the performers were always there. And people from the audience who loved the concerts let me know it. I found my place in this larger-than-life world of New York City's concert and political life.

POLITICAL HARMONIES
Sweet Honey In The Rock, Carnegie Hall. Sweet Honey In The Rock raises the rafters with call-and-response gospel shouts and raises questions with songs like "Ode to the International Debt." They back up politically aware lyrics with five-woman harmonies that are a tribute to communal cooperation and joyful unity. Tonight at 8.

—*The New York Times*

Sweet Honey leapt to Carnegie Hall because it simply was time. For those who take part, the annual concert is a ritual of tremendous power. Sweet Honey understands the ritual use of music and its healing power for the audience. They play their audience like their instrument. They engage their audience emotionally in their own healing.

Sweet Honey audiences at Carnegie Hall arrive ecstatic. Maybe it's New York; maybe it's the cultural significance of this radical group holding court at Carnegie. Whatever it is, it's powerful. The audiences are wonderful; ages, colors, persuasions, ways of dressing, ways of being, put together for a grand stomp and shout.

SWEET HARMONY
Sweet Honey In The Rock can sound like a whole choir, a rock steady band or a sax, a drum and a flute. They are storytellers in the ancient tradition, proving that sometimes the sweetest sounds are born of the hardest situations.

—Soledad Santiago, *The Daily News*, November 17, 1985

Sweet Honey recorded a live album at the annual concert at Carnegie Hall.

November 7, 1987
Dear Amy,
An update; today, as you know, we are checking sound for the recording as well as live concert sound. We expect sound check to end after 6. Please let everyone

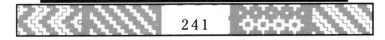

know that there will be a hot vegetarian meal ready for them, so that no one has to leave the hall for dinner.

Virginia

Sweet Honey In The Rock recently celebrated its 14th Anniversary with a show which was taped for a live album. You don't have to wait for the release of that record (which will be soon). You can catch Sweet Honey Sunday at 5 p.m. at the Apollo Theater, 253 West 125th St. in a one performance benefit for the Women's Center for Career and Educational Advancement.

—DAVID HINCKLEY, *NEW YORK DAILY NEWS,* MAY 3, 1988

Flying Fish released *Live at Carnegie Hall* later that year. Fans are always waiting for the next Sweet Honey album, and now the larger industry was taking a look.

They appear to be poised on the brink of wider acclaim. Last year, Sweet Honey In The Rock's anti-apartheid song "State of Emergency" released on the group's 1988 double LP *Live at Carnegie Hall* was nominated for a Grammy in the Contemporary Folk Music Category won by Tracy Chapman's "Fast Car." They did pick up a Grammy in the Traditional Folk Music category.

—LESLIE BARMAN, *NEW YORK NEWSDAY,* MAY 3, 1988

I was very interested in bringing Sweet Honey to the Apollo in Harlem and finally got to do so in 1988 with a fund-raiser concert for the Women's Center for Career and Educational Advancement. Ayodele Harrington, an early member of Sweet Honey, worked for the Center in downtown Manhattan and got me interested in their work—career education and training primarily for women of color. I was especially drawn to their philosophy of putting skills directly in women's hands. Ayodele has great energy and I enjoyed working with her (she and I did a live show together for WBAI radio to promote the concert). It was exciting working at the Apollo, another new theater, but more importantly, a cultural homecoming for Sweet Honey.

Some people, even when they are very young, have a sense of what they are born to do. I didn't; I found out later. Producing concerts and running my own business gave the focus and shape that had been missing in my life. A political and social foundation was buried deep inside me—nurtured during the 1960s, but not fully sprung. As I grew into my life, it discovered me.

Performers and audiences invent each other. The early women's music per-formers were a cultural expression of women's movement politics and there was an

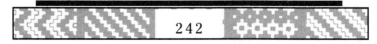

intensely personal audience involvement. This was a charged arena and I had to negotiate my way through a minefield of issues. Political correctness is a contextual idea, defined by the group that uses the concept at that moment. One idea held by some feminists involved in this scene then was that in a world where women have not gotten their fair share, we will create access within the world of women's music by seeing to it that all women get their fair share, equally—and somehow remain separate from the mainstream while doing this. Consequently, I was often criticized by the movement's self-appointed guardians of correctness for business practices which violated political ideas; like having two ticket prices, one for orchestra and one for balcony—elitism; or including men in "women's" music concerts; or using professional halls rather than school auditoriums—co-optation.

While I shared the idealism, in practice I often found these challenges difficult: difficult to listen to because I had a real purpose and direction and knew why I was doing things the way I did—and difficult to solve because there were many different and often conflicting views wanting demonstration. Finding a balance between personal aesthetics and politics and the practical pressures of doing work in the public arena, was in some ways my deepest political education, probably my Ph.D.

There is a national cultural network created by women and in those days I would spend hours in conversations with managers and promoters from other cities sorting out the politics—feminism, racism, sexism—from the commerce—capitalism, classism, socialism. We mentored each other. Barbara Edwards, who was manager of the jazz band Alive! was always present as a friend and first line of support. Jill Ferson has helped me with production from day one; I can't imagine a show without her. Carolyn Churchill is there first thing in the morning until the last of the flowers are swept off the stage and into my cab at night. Cynthia Frenz, general manager of Redwood Records, and Laurie Fuchs, founder of Ladyslipper Music, are solid business allies. Nona Gandalman from Boulder knows the ups and down as a promoter and we've promoted a few shows together in Santa Fe. Amy Horowitz, founder of Roadwork, supports my work with Sweet Honey and always opens the next door with me. Myrna Johnston from Boston is an extraordinary sound engineer. Denise Notzon is a great booking agent, she really cares about her producers and understands that they have to survive so that artists will survive. So too, Madeleine Remez, representing the next generation of cultural designers, and day-to-day contact with Sweet Honey. Penny Rosenwasser, who worked with me through Roadwork years ago, continues to help me understand some of the most complex issues. Jeanne Rizzo, formerly co-owner of the Great American Music Hall, taught me a few good tricks and brought me a great gig. Adrienne Torf, a most talented composer and keyboard artist, watches over me in her deliberate Taurian way. With Trudy Wood, Kate Clinton's manager, I can share the paradoxes and absurdities, all of them, often with a smile. Jo Lynne Worley of Redwood

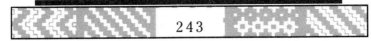

Records and Holly Near's manager has pushed me out there, dragged me out there, followed me out there, and been out there with me. These wonderful, visionary, powerfully life-giving women are my family in this business.

Through the 1980s I grew as a producer. Sweet Honey continued to reach larger and more diverse audiences. Women's music performers like folk singer Ferron and comedian Kate Clinton, became very popular. Holly Near shared the stage with Inti Illimani, Ronnie Gilbert, and other artists whom she recorded on the label she founded, Redwood Records. We all had our ways of contributing to each other's options. I branched out into other musical worlds. For years I promoted pianist George Winston, embraced by the New Age audience, and others in that genre like Liz Story, Andreas Vollenweider, and Paul Winter. I promoted jazz vocalist Cleo Laine and John Dankworth and occasionally co-promoted a show like that of the Argentinian diva Mercedes Sosa or guitarists Leo Kottke and Michael Hedges. I began touring performers to Boston, Washington, D.C., Philadelphia, and the small towns in between.

I like everyone I've ever presented more than once—I respect their music, their style, their values, and who they are in the world. Sometimes I'm asked, "What kind of music do you promote anyway?" I say, "I promote progressive people. The music has different sounds."

I define myself as a producer, and much of the work I do is community organizing. There is a world of difference between creating events from a situation where people are the energy and one—the commercial industry—in which money supports the energy for advertising, radio, clout, and access. If you grasp this difference, you understand how potent it is that another industry, created by women, multiracial women, with a political agenda, thrives.

Each city has its own approach for producing a concert. In Boston you do it the way Boston does it, in New York it's their game, Philadelphia is a whole other thing. Over the years I've been able to work with a variety of performers and reach their audiences in different ways at different times. Producing in another city can be tricky. I have to be present there even though I'm not.

Finding the Sweet Honey audience varies in different cities. In a place where conservatism is traditional, it is more difficult. These six African American women challenge every issue: racism, apartheid, misogyny, prison reform, rape, government, big business, poison, conspiracy, war. They challenge their audience to look deep within themselves.

December 1989
Virginia . . .

Once again, we would like to thank you for producing Sweet Honey In The Rock in Boston and New York . . . Symphony Hall and Carnegie Hall are incredible to perform in, and we hope you will extend our appreciation to all

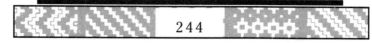

your staff who take such good care of us—from ironing our costumes to the delicious munchies (smile) and everything in between . . .

Wish you continued success and a meaningful holiday.

Sincerely,

Nitanju Bolade Casel

for Sweet Honey In The Rock

All for Freedom, Sweet Honey In The Rock's latest release, is a cultural gem for African American youth. This album reaches into the soul, strikes a chord of recognition in all whose collective unconscious contain memories of our journey from slavery to freedom.

—FREDERICA AFRIKA PAYNE, *THE NEW AMERICAN,* 1989

December 1989

Sweet Honey In The Rock

Washington, D.C.

Dear Members of Sweet Honey In The Rock,

Congratulations on the success of your New York and Boston shows. Your performance each year has become a ritual which nourishes our lives. We all continue to meet in a new place.

I am interested in expanding your audience here to those who don't go to Carnegie Hall—the children. *All for Freedom* is reaching out to the next generation, and I sense that a children's concert would be timely and important. By bringing the children into the concert hall, we are also bringing Sweet Honey further into the family.

I am proposing a children's matinee. I have reserved Washington Irving High School's 90-year-old auditorium for a concert on Monday, January 15, 1990, Martin Luther King Jr.'s birthday. The date itself is magnificent.

Let me know if you are available to play this date. I look forward to hearing from you.

My best,

Virginia Giordano

December 1989

To: Carolyn, Adrienne, Bruce

Please note: Sweet Honey Children's Matinee, January 15, 1990

Some people who are calling for tickets to this show don't realize it's for children. Sweet Honey is a ritual, a rite of passage, a healing. We keep Sweet Honey in our lives and they speak to us when we are crying, when we are healing, when we are praying, when we are laughing, when we are living, when we are dying.

This morning I went to a funeral, the service opened with "Breaths"—
"Those who have died have never never left, The dead have a pact with the
living, they are in the woman's breast, they are in the wailing child . . ."

Kids are near the other end of the spectrum. I want the next generation to
be touched by this great healing energy.

We tell them that Sweet Honey does this special show to celebrate Martin
Luther King Jr. Bring kids and share with them, kids need inspiration too.
V.G.

January 15, 1990, coincidentally, was exactly ten years to the day that I filed
business papers and declared myself a working producer. As I recall, things on the
personal front were a little grim for me this particular January, but the First Annual
Children's Concert was an outrageous success, the best anniversary celebration I
could have had.

I didn't know what to expect in the way of audience turnout. The first two
weeks in January are traditionally very slow in this business; everyone, having gone
to hell with themselves during Christmas and New Year's, is now broke and tired.
A few days before the show we hadn't sold many tickets and I was fretting. Even
though Sweet Honey's audience is notorious for buying tickets at the last minute,
I'm still never sure they will actually be there when the show starts (occupational
hazard).

Finally, the phone began ringing a few days before the concert with people
asking if the show was sold out (always an out-of-body-experience question when
you feel that you have more tickets to sell than you started with). We began telling
everyone who called that "no one will be turned away." This particular phrase
embodied the spirit of the King celebration and we stuck with it because I also felt
it was the most persuasive way to get the undecided ticket buyer to the box office.

Well, on the day of the show the floodgates opened up, and it was also raining.
Those people came from everywhere. Our usual mix of colors and styles, now with
kids, arm babies, walkers, groups, teenagers, grandmothers, everyone. Right before
the show started, when the house looked full, I went outside to check and found a
line two and three people deep, which stretched from the doors at Sixteenth Street
to Fourteenth Street, all of whom had been told that "no one will be turned away."

No one was turned away. Everyone cooperated, we found floor space and
standing room and packed the place to the rafters. The energy was amazing. The
kids were transformed. Their attention so fixed on Sweet Honey—watching these
women, singing with them, going up onstage to dance. At the end, we all held
hands and sang "We Shall Overcome." A lot of people wept from the pure emotion. I did.

"Sweet Honey is a community-based organization," says Evelyn Harris, "we do
all kinds of programs. This is our third children's concert in New York. We

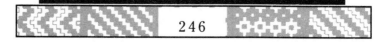

"We Had a Great Time for a Long Time"

always do it around Martin Luther King's birthday so that parents are able to bring their children."

Explained Harris, "Children have a different musical agenda than adults. It's completely different from what their parents look for. Their attention span is shorter. They don't like long songs. They like very lyrical music, something they can sing along with. And they like funny songs."

—THE DAILY NEWS, JANUARY 17, 1992

The Cathedral Church of St. John the Divine

Cathedral Heights
1047 Amsterdam Avenue
at 112th Street
New York, New York 10025

Office of the Dean
(212) 316-7493

November 25, 1991

Ms. Virginia Giordano
V.G. Productions
270 Lafayette Street Suite 907
New York, New York 10025

Dear Virginia:

I just wanted to include a quick note to express my long-standing gratitude to you for the work that you do and the contribution your concerts make to the life of the City of New York. I believe that for many folks out here trying to make a difference (advocate for a more humane city, a greater sense of "home", a healthier environment and a deeper sense of civic friendship) the music and leadership you bring provides a necessary sense of nourishment and hope.

The evenings I have spent over the last years at your concerts have been as close to a sense of community and fellowship as I have seen brought about these days. They are sustaining, emboldening and alive.

I am grateful for the fact that I can look forward to them as annual celebrations in my life and look forward to widening the circle each year. As an organizer I am aware of the complications involved in creating events which run as simply and elegantly as yours. I notice all the small touches.

I am enclosing a little information about what we do here at the Cathedral so that you and your staff might know that you are touching a lot of lives with your music.

Thank you for all you do and are.

Peace,

Amy Elizabeth Fox
Director of Advocacy

SWEET HONEY GROWS WILD

Sweet Honey In The Rock is a way of life, a way of being in the world with more than death, taxes and your personal problems. It's a way of life that has

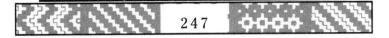

been torn down and beaten back like wild grass time and time again—by design and negligence. But it certainly has clarity that is life-breathing, celebratory. That it comes back is only as surprising as hearing ancient lyrics come out your mouth when people around you start to sing. Sweet Honey sings songs that have in different moments outlined the shape of divided towns or pieces of flesh shed from the body that has a will to be free. In the tradition of protest their songs give the details and hard facts; in the tradition of spirituals and gospel, they bury the dead and heal the living. Sweet Honey is what's growing in everybody's backyard today—news that never went way.

—THULANI DAVIS, *THE VILLAGE VOICE*, MARCH 30, 1982

Dear Sweet Honey
in the rock

Think you for letting
us sit in front seats
at your show

We liked your show

We had fun on stage
it was fun
We like your singgin
We had a great time
for a long time

We had a great time

from Lonnie

We have a great time, all of us . . .

VIRGINIA GIORDANO PRESENTS
Sweet Honey In The Rock
1980–Present
Apollo Theater, Avery Fisher Hall, Carnegie Hall, Town Hall, Washington Irving High School (New York City); Symphony Hall, Strand Theater, Opera House (Boston); Academy of Music (Philadelphia); Tarrytown Music Hall (Tarrytown)

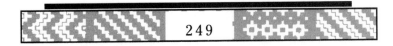

19

GOD IS GOOD

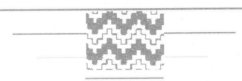

LAVERTE MATHIS

About twelve years ago I met Ysaye Barnwell. I had never heard of Sweet Honey In The Rock. Ysaye invited me to the anniversary concert that year, which was at All Souls' Unitarian Church. This experience made an indelible impression on my understanding of the power of music. It was an overwhelming experience on many dimensions: emotionally, spiritually, sociopolitically, culturally, and artistically. I had been emotionally moved by several forms of music in my life, long before my exposure to this group, but the one essential, compelling ingredient which Sweet Honey In The Rock provided in their music was an "all-encompassing" experience on an emotional and humanistic level. This was not entertainment! The breadth and depth of their artistic musical repertoire both touched and spoke to my soul.

Twelve years later my sentiments are the same! I have lost count of the number of concerts I have attended, but the number is not important. Every time I attend a Sweet Honey In The Rock concert, it's the first time. The concerts are always opportunities for new or renewed experiences. They are never the same. The concerts are living entities.

Through the years I have come to better understand and accept this musical group's effect upon the community at large and more specifically, the effect that the group has in my life.

Sweet Honey In The Rock is a perpetual reminder that "We Are the Ones

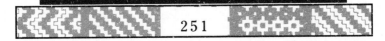

We've Been Waiting For." Sweet Honey is our alter ego, our superego, our conscience. The music motivates an acceptance of responsibility. She is a musical guru, a check and balance, a call to order, a unifying vehicle, a mirror, a journey, a broadcast, a symposium, forum, and platform. The group is a teacher of history and culture. Sweet Honey educates on the bio-psycho-social levels. She is every woman, man, and child. The group is us and we are the group. Sweet Honey is principled, honest, clear, concise, and beautiful. She is an institutional foundation opposing all forms of injustices, locally, nationally, and internationally. This ensemble of African American women singers represents professional mastery, integrity, and agents of change. Sweet Honey In The Rock offers hope.

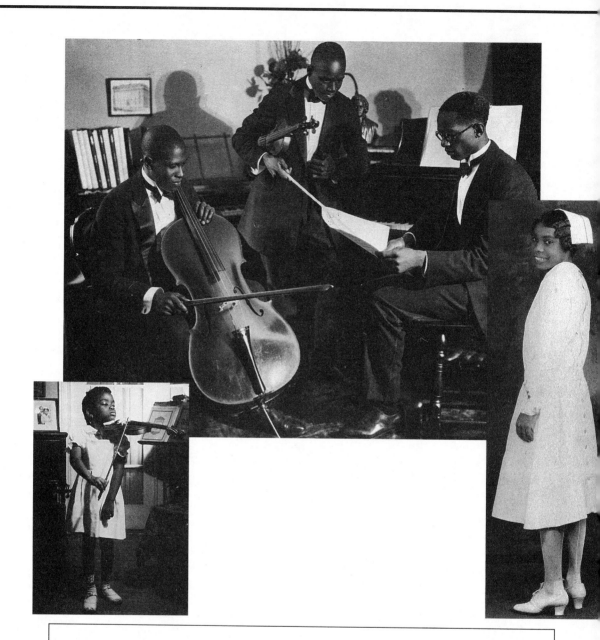

TOP: YSAYE MARIA BARNWELL'S FATHER IN THE IRVING F. BARNWELL [CENTER] TRIO, HARLEM, NEW YORK. (PHOTOGRAPHER, VAN DER ZEE, PHOTO COURTESY OF YSAYE MARIA BARNWELL PERSONAL COLLECTION)

BOTTOM LEFT: YSAYE MARIA BARNWELL, AGE FOUR, A VIOLIN STUDENT OF HER FATHER, IRVING F. BARNWELL. (PHOTO COURTESY OF YSAYE MARIA BARNWELL PERSONAL COLLECTION)

BOTTOM RIGHT: YSAYE MARIA BARNWELL'S MOTHER, MARCELLA ROBINSON (BARNWELL), GRADUATING FROM LINCOLN SCHOOL OF NURSING, NEW YORK, ONE OF THE TWO BLACK NURSING SCHOOLS IN THE UNITED STATES AT THE TIME. (PHOTO COURTESY OF YSAYE MARIA BARNWELL PERSONAL COLLECTION)

20

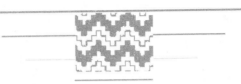

BECOMING A SINGER

YSAYE MARIA BARNWELL

When I joined Sweet Honey In The Rock in 1979, one door opened in my life as another closed. I am convinced that I had little, if anything, to do with my getting into Sweet Honey, although, in retrospect, I do know that this is where I belong. I had originally thought I would work with the group for one or two years; this is my fourteenth year with Sweet Honey. Joining a musical performing group was the last thing on my mind in 1979. I had in earlier years gone through the agony of deciding whether to be a musician or "something more stable." When I was a child, my father prepared me to be a concert violinist, but at thirteen, inspired by the play *The Miracle Worker,* I decided that I, like Annie Sullivan, would teach Deaf children to speak. This decision led to three academic degrees in the field of speech pathology. Destiny led me back to music.

My mother, Marcella Robinson Barnwell, was a registered nurse and was pleased by my decision to become a speech pathologist. She believed a woman always needed a profession to fall back on. Whatever I know about being independent and assertive in the world I learned (reluctantly) from my mother, who possessed those qualities and knew that as an only child, and a female child, I would need them. I watched her make her way in the world, speak her mind freely, contentedly do things alone if she couldn't get my father or anyone else to do them with her. It was she who encouraged me to choose a "stable" profession and pushed me from the nest by insisting that I go away to college. It was she who

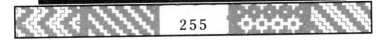

taught me that I (with God) am the only person that I could depend on and should therefore never be disappointed by others. These have been hard lessons for me to learn. Each time I step out I feel that I am being pushed, and difficult as it may be each time, I am grateful.

My mother and father began saving for my college education, probably from the day I was born. While I knew that there were many reasons that a college education was important, one reason conveyed by many Black women in my community was that if you were a dark-skinned and not necessarily attractive woman you would need a good education to carry you through life because you might not find a husband. (Years later at Howard University I would be told by a secretary that I might not receive a promotion to assistant professor because I was too dark.)

My father, Irving Frederick Barnwell, who named me after the Belgian violinist Eugène Ysaÿe, and who had instructed me in the violin for fifteen years (beginning at age two), was more than disappointed by my career decision. His dream was that I would become the first Black woman concert violinist that the Colored Race —that this country—had produced.

My father was an excellent musician and teacher. He played violin and viola in the Jim Van Houten Orchestra, was a member of the Samuel Coleridge Taylor String Quartet in Harlem during the renaissance, and played violin in the first production of Hubie Blake and Noble Sissle's *Shuffle Along.* He organized the Barnwell Trio—violin, piano, and drums—which played dance music at social functions. He began teaching during the 1920s and taught (over one hundred students) until two years before his death in 1990 at the age of ninety-two.

During my growing up I heard all kinds of live and recorded music. I observed all levels of performance proficiency, and internalized many years of my father's expert (old school) teaching methods. He selected his students carefully. He required that a parent be present at all lessons and during a child's practice. He trained the body, the mind, and the spirit. My father not only taught his students the techniques for playing their instrument (violin, viola, or piano); he gave them ear training and taught them theory and harmony. They could name the parts of the instrument they were studying and could describe how and of what materials it was constructed. His students learned both classical and popular repertoire and had to memorize everything. Under his instruction, my father's students excelled.

When I was twelve, my father was diagnosed with glaucoma and had a series of eye surgeries which left him functionally blind for three years while he recuperated. During that period, I not only became his eyes and his part-time nurse, but also taught, under his supervision, his beginning and intermediate students, and assisted with his advanced students. I could play much of what the violin students were learning to play. I could see whether a student's posture and technique were correct, and whether they were reading and playing scores accurately. I reviewed their written exercises. I kept my father's records, which included the dates of each lesson, what was accomplished, what was to be practiced, and what would be

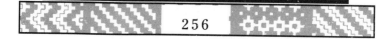

taught next. His records also included details of student payments and balances due. My father remained the disciplinarian, the fount of knowledge, the source of wisdom. He was the master teacher and he was allowing me to learn by doing. Although I would get two college degrees in education, most of what I know about teaching I learned from my father.

One of my father's mottoes was "You must be ten times better [than Whites] just to be considered their equal." He prepared me thoroughly to pass auditions at both Music and Art and Performing Arts high schools and to enter Newtown High School in Elmhurst, New York (closer to home), where I majored in music and graduated with honors.

I played in my high school string quartet and was concertmistress of the school orchestra. While in high school, I completed a special program at the Juilliard School of Music. I was also a member of the All-City High School Orchestra for three years. It was in that orchestra that I experienced a racism that went beyond being called a "nigga" by a White child or being excluded from a White friend's birthday party. Although I knew I was much better, I was put in the last row of the first violin section of the All-City Orchestra. I stayed there until Leopold Stokowski became our guest conductor. He asked each of us to play a difficult passage of the score we were rehearsing and after he heard me I was moved to the first row, next to the concertmaster. After his brief tenure, I was again banished to the back row. This lesson would repeat itself many times throughout my life.

Although Bernice first heard me singing (and saw me signing) during a church service at All Souls' in Washington, D.C., when I joined Sweet Honey In The Rock I did not think of myself as a singer. Because of my earlier training I thought of myself as a fine musician, an instrumentalist. Actually, I was afraid of my voice, of its sound and power. My voice was an untrained instrument.

When I was four, a "reader" told my mother that I would be a singer. My father wouldn't hear of it, and so Mother dismissed it and told me this only after I joined Sweet Honey almost thirty years later.

While I spent years studying first to be a violinist and then a speech pathologist, I knew others who had devoted their time, energy, and resources to becoming singers. They were developing their instrument, the voice, and their technique, so that their voice could respond effortlessly, seamlessly, and beautifully to every command. They had developed and were expanding a repertoire, and envisioned themselves either performing (in some capacity) or teaching for the rest of their lives. There was a difference between being a career singer and having singing as a part of your everyday life. These were professionally trained singers.

When I was growing up, everybody sang. My friends and I sang—playing games, jumping rope, and hanging out on the stoop, or on the block. Four girls in my neighborhood made a record before they were fifteen years old. My mother sang in the Chancel Choir of Calvary Baptist Church, Jamaica, New York, for many years; and we sang together around the house. My father and I sang bass lines to

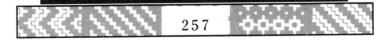

the hymns on Sundays as part of the congregation at Calvary. While in junior high school I sang in a Black community youth choir which performed spirituals under the direction of S. Carroll Buchannon. In college I sang with the Geneseo Chamber Singers, a college madrigal group under the direction of Dr. Robert Isgro.

I taught myself to sing "full out," using my whole voice, by listening to the albums of Nina Simone, Miriam Makeba, Odetta, Richie Havens, and Buffy Sainte-Marie through college during the 1960s. My repertoire of freedom songs came from these singers, from church meetings, and the SNCC Freedom Singers (Bernice was a member), which I must have heard on the nightly news, as well as from Joan Baez, Peter, Paul and Mary, Pete Seeger, Judy Collins, and Bob Dylan.

Through imitation (especially of Odetta) I discovered that my voice could cover a fairly wide range, from bass to soprano. I practiced this range by singing all the harmony parts to all the songs I would hear. To the consternation of some of my friends, I could sing harmony lines even if there was no audible melody. One friend once asked if I knew the melody to any songs, while another wondered if there were any songs which I did not know since I seemed to be able to harmonize anything I heard. I believe my range and ability to hear and sing harmonies easily helped me to successfully complete the monthlong Sweet Honey audition workshop, in August 1979, at Evelyn Harris' home in N.W. Washington, D.C. In the audition workshop, Lucy Murphy (a local community activist and singer) and I participated with the regular members of Sweet Honey in learning the words and parts to at least forty of Sweet Honey's songs.

The song "As Long As I Have Breath" was not one of the forty that I learned during that month. However, it was one of the three called during my very first performance with the group, at a political rally of 250,000 people held in September 1979 at Battery Park on the tip of Manhattan Island in New York. I got through it, and since then have always loved the challenge of performing, onstage, a song which I may never have heard before in my life. I listen to determine whether the structure of the song is familiar or predictable. Is it traditional or contemporary? Should I enhance the harmony or the rhythm or both? Am I the first to add something? Is anyone else singing and if so where are they? I begin to follow the melody with a harmonic and/or rhythmic line and look for musical and visual feedback that says I'm on the right track. I've learned the technique of either looking into the song leader's mouth to pull out the words or echoing the words as I hear them while humming or vamping to keep a harmony or rhythm going. This is risk behavior that I would never have allowed myself in my other walks of life. Ironically, after a few years in Sweet Honey, it would become the way of living my life and would feel much less dangerous.

I entered the State University of New York, upstate in Geneseo, in 1963. I went there because state universities had affordable tuition and because this one had an excellent reputation for its Speech and Hearing Department. There were eight Black students and faculty on campus that year, including me. By the time I

had completed my master's degree in 1968 that population had almost doubled to fifteen. A year later open enrollment brought 150 Black students—too late to be a source of support to me.

Three things characterized the whiteness of that campus for me: White people, many of whom had never personally associated with Blacks and resisted every opportunity to do so; sheep, which I never expected to see grazing in the state of New York; and snow, feet and feet of snow, which accumulated between October and May of each year and never completely melted until June.

Few things in my upbringing had prepared me for this cold, rural, racist environment. Blacks were essentially confined to the campus or to towns and larger cities outside Geneseo, or to the migrant labor camps three miles from campus. I was shocked to learn that in 1963 Dr. Jay Walker, the Black faculty member, could not live in the town of Geneseo, could not even get his hair cut there. In the dormitory I found myself trying to determine the difference between the ignorance and the racism of fellow students. One of my preassigned roommates was withdrawn from the school by her parents when I wrote saying among other things that I was a Black student. Another girl had been sent to private schools all her life to keep her away from Blacks and was arguing with her father about staying as I was moving in. She stayed and we enjoyed our time together as roommates.

As Black students during the early 1960s, we were caught in the struggle for integration. We did not want to intimidate Whites by appearing to be separatists, so we did not socialize together. Black male students could and did socialize with liberal White females but few White males chose to socialize with Black females. We had a very restricted and compartmentalized social life. The racially distorted atmosphere also had an impact on my academic experiences. In some classes where I had earned an A or B, I was given a C; there were no viable means of redress.

My college years were in general depressing, but in most ways, I excelled. I excelled because of the foundation my parents had laid for me. First, there was no question but that I would go to college. Second, I would finish. Third, my parents had provided me a grounding in God, and in the history and culture of Black people, which I began to draw from both literally and figuratively while I was in college. I brought from home every Black book (meaning books by Black authors or about Black or African peoples and culture) that I had ever been given or had purchased.

Those books became the core of my dormitory library on Blacks and minorities. My collection sparked student interest and discussion and soon involved the faculty in both the English and Sociology departments. Intense relationships developed among those of us who involved ourselves in these reading/discussion groups. In it were the seeds of a greater discussion in a sociology class and of a faculty/ student writing group led by faculty member Joe (and Molly) Lonero, and two other groups which I was instrumental in organizing: a tutorial program for migrant workers and the Northern Students Movement (a national organization of civil

rights student activists) at SUNY, Geneseo. In it were also the seeds of my own radicalism.

My most enjoyable experience at Geneseo was the time spent rehearsing and performing with the Chamber Singers. Relationships were formed through a love of music. The director, Dr. Robert Isgro, supported me in many ways. He included spirituals and other Black folk songs in our repertoire of madrigals, motets, and chorales. In his American folk music class I learned my first chords and strums on the guitar, and finally mastered Elizabeth (Libba) Cotton's "Freight Train." An accomplished songwriter, guitarist, and banjo picker, Cotton created songs in a gentle personal style with wonderful instrumental lines. My first recorded vocal solo lead was on a Chamber Singers album.

Before I graduated from Geneseo I had begun to perform solo from time to time in coffeehouses and folk clubs. I received encouraging reviews and good audience response, but I hated competing with conversation in clubs and hated performing alone. It was not for me.

In April 1968, as I was completing work on my second degree (the master's) at Geneseo and wondering what my life's work would be, Martin Luther King Jr. was killed. I remember singing "Precious Lord" at an assembly of mostly White, stunned, and grieving faculty and students. I decided that night that I wanted to teach at a Black college or university, and wrote to every one that I had ever heard of. To my great disappointment, most never responded to my letter. However, it was my great good fortune that Howard University responded favorably. That August, I was interviewed and hired by the College of Liberal Arts at Howard University. I joined the part-time faculty of (then) Federal City College and the full-time faculty of the College of Dentistry at Howard in 1969, and remained on the Howard faculty (with only a two-year leave, during which I obtained the Ph.D. degree) until June 1980. This was the door that was closing as I joined Sweet Honey in the Rock in September 1979.

It is probably obvious by now that I have strayed far from my original goal at age thirteen of teaching the Deaf to speak. I have never worked clinically with Deaf persons or persons with hearing loss. Each academic degree in speech pathology led me further and further from deafness. As a student, I was exposed to and fascinated by a vast array of speech and language problems as well as structural and functional problems which could be treated by a speech pathologist. I also began to realize that deafness was not simply a clinical and/or educational problem to be handled with specialized methods and materials. Deafness presented clinicians, educators, and others, with linguistic, cultural, social, and political issues which were not effectively challenged before the mid-1970s.

In 1976, after completing my doctorate and returning to the Dental School faculty at Howard, I realized I wanted to know Deaf people and to understand deafness. I had lost my inclination to teach them to speak but wanted to study Sign language. Through my personal relationships in the Deaf community I have learned

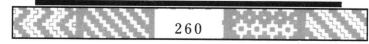

deafness. I have also learned that being Deaf can be as political as being Black, and that I could be an advocate for the Deaf and deafness issues as well as a speech pathologist.

In 1978 I took a six-month sabbatical from teaching at Howard University to study Sign language interpreting (for use primarily in medical settings) at Gallaudet University. I loved interpreting music and had done so as part of the Deaf awareness troupe at Gallaudet, but I had never sung *and* signed publicly until a Sunday in July 1979 when I reluctantly performed "He Ain't Heavy, He's My Brother" as part of a special service at All Souls' Church, Washington, D.C. Bernice did not usually attend All Souls' Church, but she did at the last minute on that Sunday. She found herself watching a Black woman who, it seemed, was a singer and a Sign language interpreter—just what Sweet Honey needed. She introduced herself at the end of the service, not remembering that we had met briefly during the early 1970s at a conference on African American history held at Howard University. I owned her solo albums and both of the Sweet Honey albums out at the time and I had seen the group perform. It never occurred to me that I could or would become a member of Sweet Honey. Bernice invited me to audition for the group at what would be a monthlong audition workshop.

The Sweet Honey workshop started the next day. In addition to learning new songs and teaching some of mine, I worked with the group throughout the month on the issues involved in making their concerts accessible, particularly to the Deaf. I had to help Sweet Honey understand that singing and signing simultaneously for myself was very different from singing my part in the group and interpreting for the entire group at the same time. The latter was impossible. At the end of August, I was invited to become a member of the group. I interpreted Sweet Honey's sixth-anniversary Harvest Fest Concert (at Howard University's Crampton Auditorium), but I had decided to be a full singing member and introduced the group to Shirley Childress Johnson, who has been our interpreter since 1980.

Although I feel I moved into the group easily, the truth is that I was in awe of every other voice in Sweet Honey and I couldn't really figure out how I had got to sing with them. I had listened to Bernice's voice often on early solo recordings and on the SNCC Freedom Singers and Sweet Honey recordings. She is a powerhouse of energy and resonant sound. Her voice is old, earthbound—a voice which rocks, excites, and calls you to action.

Evelyn's voice is like a razor's edge but would soften to wrap you in rich, lush, and sensual tones at any point she felt it appropriate. Tulani's voice is warm and familiar, with a Pentecostal shout energy and a jazzy flair. But most awesome is Yasmeen—the most effortless, seamless, and honest singer I have ever known. She sings from an incredible depth; sings runs as easily as we breathe; adds the perfect nuances to any line she sings; rarely, if ever, repeats what she has sung before; and can make anyone she sings with sound good, just by moanin', croonin', or hummin' in the background. One of her best leads is on the song "My Way" by Bernice

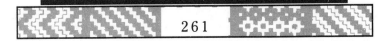

Johnson Reagon. In that song Yasmeen soars to a note which I find breathtaking. Lawd, let me near that note just once!

Was I expected to match these voices? Lawd, there's no way! It took over a year for me to understand that the group had seen *my* strengths—or had anticipated what they might become—and that the group was not trying to replace anyone but was creating a new position for me to find my own niche. It took about five years of being in Sweet Honey for me to find my position in the group, to feel comfortable with my voice, and to include "singer" as part of my description of myself.

After being in the group for several months, I began taking voice lessons for the first time. In many ways, a voice teacher is like a therapist. He or she works with an instrument which speech pathology literature refers to as "the barometer of the soul." The voice (whether speaking or singing) expresses your identity and can be read like a book by those trained to listen. I had learned this as a speech pathologist and knew a great deal about voice production, vocal pathology, and vocal rehabilitation. I needed a voice teacher who could help me apply my knowledge of voice production to the art and science of singing and could assist me in developing my voice for the rigors of singing with Sweet Honey. I also needed to deal with my broadening of my identity. I was becoming a professional musician after all. I was becoming a singer.

WORDS AND MUSIC BY . . .

I am not a prolific songwriter/composer; in fact, I've written relatively few works. Some have been written for and recorded by Sweet Honey. Some of these have stories . . .

"More Than a Paycheck"

For twelve years at Howard University I had struggled against three phenomena which I believe to be common at Black universities: chromatism ("You won't get that promotion because you are too dark"), sexism (try being a woman on the faculty of any school which produces predominantly male professionals—e.g., physicians, dentists, lawyers, etc.), and conservatism (outsiders are generally tolerated only if they bring prestige and/or [research] money, but don't try to change things). When I left the faculty of Howard University—a full professor, without tenure—in June 1980, I was devastated. A huge door had slammed, and it took five years for me to realize how many doors had opened.

In September 1980, a year after joining Sweet Honey, I entered a nine-month postdoctoral program in public health at Howard University College of Medicine. Sweet Honey was planning her first international tour to Japan for the month of December. Before leaving on the tour I had spent weeks trying to decide on a research topic which could be studied when I returned, and ran into obstacle after

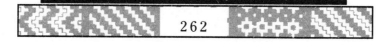

obstacle. It was the first of many times that I would have to negotiate a major leave of absence to travel with the group. I had pinpointed that I wanted to do research in the area of worker health, working conditions, and industrial disasters. So, in my favor was that among the eleven cities we would tour was Minimata, a Japanese city which had been the site of major industrial environmental dumping resulting in mercury poisoning of the ecological chain, including water, fish, and humans.

The research that I conducted for the public-health degree was inspired by being in Sweet Honey and resulted in the song "More Than a Paycheck." In Minimata, I remember asking if any songs had ever been written about their environmental devastation. No one knew. I began then to think about the songs I knew which described industrial or occupational conditions, illnesses, and disasters. Oddly, many of them had to do with the coal-mining and textile industries. I had grown up with Tennessee Ernie Ford singing "Sixteen Tons." In college I had learned "The Bells of Rhymney," a song that names ten of the major mining disasters which had occurred in southern Wales before 1950. In 1980 I heard a beautiful song called "The Mill Worker" recorded by Emmy Lou Harris.

These and many other songs became the catalyst for my research. I decided to collect and analyze the songs of these two occupations for their information about working conditions, disasters, mishaps, illnesses, etc. What I found was that the writers of the songs—all workers themselves for the most part—knew and described with great accuracy the working conditions which produced particular diseases or resulted in injuries or death from accidents or disasters. The songs are a form of primary data overlooked by workers who have tried to argue the ways that work has devastated their lives. I became convinced in the process of this research that almost all work produces either disease, injury, or stress. We bring these things home in forms as concrete as cancer-causing particulate or fibrous matter on our clothes or as nebulous as weekend alcoholic binges which result in spouse or child abuse. Each of us who works needs to assess to what degree that work endangers our lives and the lives of those we love. Ultimately, we need to make work more healthy: physically, mentally, and spiritually. The song "More Than a Paycheck" tries to sound the alarm on this issue.

We bring more than a paycheck
to our loved ones and families . . .

I wanted more pay,
but what I've got here today
is more than I bargained for
when I walked through this door.

I bring home asbestosis, silicosis,
brown lung, black lung disease

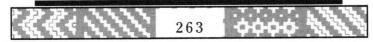

And radiation hits the children
before they've even been conceived.

"When I Die"

I am an only child and have always thought that if I died before my parents there would be a "proper" funeral and that I would be put away in fine form no matter what my wishes. That is, at least in part, because that is how it is done by people of my parents' generation, and because funerals are for the living even as they honor the dead. So I have not articulated any wishes other than to have my organs donated so that life may have another chance. When my best friend and potential life partner died of a severe asthmatic attack in 1981, only some of his wishes were acknowledged. He was cremated as desired but his ashes were contained rather than dispersed among the hills which he had loved and in which he had lived.

For years he had been an atheist. In spite of my search for a religion which I could practice, my belief in God had never wavered but had deepened. So when my friend died, I grappled with where his soul would rest. "When I Die" is the result of the dialogue I have had with my friend since his death. I no longer feel bound by concepts of heaven and hell, "proper" methods of disposing of the body, why the good seem to die so young, etc., etc., etc. I believe that we will each find our way back to the source from whence we have come and will if necessary begin the life journey again.

When I die you can bury me up on mountain top.
But when I die let my spirit breathe
Let it soar like an eagle
to the highest peak when I die.

When I die you can toss me out on the winds of time.
But when I die let my ashes roam.
Let 'em blow here, blow there.
I know they're going to find their true home
when I die, oh when I die . . .

"Breaths"

I have come to understand that it is the living which keep the dead alive long after they have gone. "Breaths" was the first song that I wrote for Sweet Honey In The Rock. I had heard the poem by the Senegalese poet Birago Diop years ago and it had sung to me when I heard it although I hadn't really listened. In the African worldview, the invisible world of spirit, humans, and the visible world of nature exist on a continuum and form an organic reality. The same is true of the relationship between past, present, and future. In Diop's poem "Breaths" we are reminded

of this continuum. In writing the music I tried to create a continuous melody line, rhythms that represent the relationship between human rhythmic functions and the laws of nature, and breath sounds representing the breath of life and the presence of spirit in air around us.

"No Images"

I became aware of Waring Cuney's poem "No Images" during the mid-1960s when I was first wrestling with self-concept and self-image within a political context. I was one of very few Blacks on a White campus; I supported SNCC and later the Panthers rather than SCLC; I was letting my " 'fro" grow; I was contemplating whether to change my name from that of a Belgian violinist (Eugène Ysaye) and an Irish slave owner (Barnwell) to that of a proud daughter of Africa with the memory of Belgium's and Britain's colonialization in my collective conscious and unconscious. I was pained by having to be ten times better than Whites at everything because I was Black, and because I was dark and not considered attractive by either White or Black standards. I was clearly in college for an education and not for a husband.

My college experiences forced me to create my own image, to discover myself. I lamented for all the young Black women (and men) who would not have an experience that would force them to confront themselves. I had heard Nina Simone sing this poem and her music was angry. In contrast, what I wanted to convey was a profound sadness. I sang my composition for the first time in either 1967 or 1968 and accompanied myself with a flamenco-style guitar. With Sweet Honey the song became a conversation among women almost as if sitting on a front porch talkin' about a young sistah who just passed by.

"On Children"

"On Children" was the first song that I wrote for a vocal ensemble. In 1978 I founded a choir, the All Souls' Unitarian Church Jubilee Singers. I created a musical setting for this Kahlil Gibran work in response to the Reverend David Eaton's monthly reading of Gibran's passage to mark the dedication of children. It has become a song of liberation for parents and children and has been performed by a number of choirs and ensembles around the country.

Your children are not your children
They are the sons and daughters of life's longing for itself
They come through you but they are not from you
And though they are with you
They belong not to you

"Song of the Exiled"

This poem was written by the Argentinian poet Alicia Partnoy, who for months was a "disappeared." I first heard the poem read at a Sisterfire festival in

1984 and asked for the words. Like each of the other poems which I have set to music, this poem sang itself to me as I read it. "They cut off my voice: I grew two voices . . ." When I heard it, it was read in Spanish and English. It was first a poem and now it is a song. It was first sung and recorded by Sweet Honey; now various choirs in the United States are singing it. Alicia's voice is doubling geometrically.

Song of the Exiled

For Sisterfire.
They cut off my voice:
I grew two voices
Into two different languages (tongues)
my song I pour.
They took away my suns:
Two brand-new suns
like resplendent drums
today I am playing.
Isolated I was
from all my people,
my twin songs are returning
like in an echo.
And despite the darkness
of this exile,
my poem sets fire
against a mirror.
They cut off my voice:
I grew two voices.
—translated from the Spanish by A. Partnoy and Sandra Wheaton

In 1991 another door opened for me. I was commissioned by the Glorious Rebirth Choir and the Dance Alloy, both of Pittsburgh, Pennsylvania, to write music for a dance piece to be choreographed by David Rousseve. David is a brilliant choreographer and writer, and is the director of the dance company Reality, based in New York.

I had never worked in this kind of collaboration before. David and I met and got to know each other by sharing personal stories. We eventually agreed on a concept and structure for the piece, *Crossings,* and the process for developing it. David would write the narrative text and send it to me in Washington, D.C.; I would write the music and send it to him in New York. When he was satisfied, he would begin choreographing the piece, and the music would be sent to the choir. We would then both do residencies in Pittsburgh, he with the Dance Alloy and I with the Glorious Rebirth Choir. Then we would all get together to stage and

perform the piece. The process worked very well (as it would for a subsequent collaboration, *Urban Scenes/Creole Dreams*).

One of the new songs is "No Mirrors," which Sweet Honey is now performing, was based on a conversation I had in 1969 with a friend who told me that the house she grew up in had no mirrors and that each day her mother or grandmother described in detail each of her features, how she looked, and how beautiful she was.

There were no mirrors in my nana's house
No mirrors in my nana's house
And the beauty that I saw in everything
the beauty in everything
was in her eyes.

. . . So I never knew that my skin was too Black
I never knew that my nose was too flat
I never knew that my clothes didn't fit
And I never knew there were things that I missed
and the beauty in everything was in her eyes

Child look deep into my eyes . . .

I will have come full circle in my musical evolution when I have completed my first work for voice and symphony.

In my travels with Sweet Honey, I have been to every continent on the globe. In her travels, Sweet Honey In The Rock has performed in some of the most prestigious halls in the world. I am a native New Yorker, so performing at Town Hall and Carnegie Hall was of major significance, but then there was the Apollo. I grew up going to shows there. I saw Frankie Lymon and the Teenagers, the Temptations, the Shirelles, Redd Foxx, and Moms Mabley. I saw the best and I saw some of the rest on amateur nights. The Apollo scared me more than Carnegie Hall, but it did not scare Sweet Honey, we had a great show there.

We have sung in the oldest and most beautiful cathedrals in Europe. Most of them were not designed for Sweet Honey's music. They tend to be cavernous, so that without a skilled sound engineer, the first song would still be echoing while we were doing the encore. We received rave reviews at the Royal Albert Hall in London. But for me, no hall will ever be as significant as singing on the stage of Central High School in Little Rock, Arkansas, looking at Daisy Bates, who was in the front row. Ms. Bates was a famed Black community leader, president of the NAACP, Civil Rights leader, and newspaper publisher, whom I had learned about at age eleven when I had watched on TV as nine Black children walked, terrified, toward the steps of this school amid the jeers, slurs, and threats of angry Whites. Now I sat

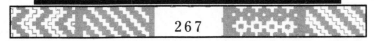

with Sweet Honey on the stage of this school, singing songs about freedom and justice to/with an integrated audience. It was my birthday and I couldn't imagine a more moving gift.

The most challenging trips, which gave me an opportunity to grow or to learn important lessons, were those I took to Africa and Japan. In 1985, Sweet Honey went to Africa for the first time, to the conference which closed the United Nations Decade for Women in Nairobi, Kenya. It was our first trip anywhere without Bernice. We were sponsored by Dame Nita Barrow of Barbados, whose mission for us was that we not only perform but organize a festival to end the conference. Traveling in Sweet Honey were Yasmeen, Aisha Kahlil, and Evelyn Harris besides me and Lucy DeBardelaben from Roadwork.

In five days, we accomplished quite a bit. We found several venues in which we could perform and booked them, chose performance dates and times, and prepared press releases which we had translated into several languages. We developed posters using photocopies of the *Good News* album cover to advertise the concerts. We rehearsed enough songs for two one-hour performances. (It was the first time Sweet Honey had traveled and performed concerts that were not programmed by and with Bernice, so we had to carefully select and rearrange our songs.) We collaborated with other artists from the United States (including Edwina Lee Tyler, master drummer and dancer, and Cheryl Byron, poet, dancer, actress). We also developed an article in several languages for the conference newspaper announcing auditions to be held for the festival and asking that dancers, musicians and singers, poets and storytellers please come to the auditions. We met with the proper officials to arrange for the festival to be held in an open area on the University of Nairobi campus, and gave them specifications for the required stage, sound, and lights. We selected thirty-eight acts from all over the world, designed a lineup, and had a festival. We interacted daily with Masai women in the markets where we shopped, managed to attend several conference sessions, and did get to a game reserve, where the animals must have been watching us looking for them. Maybe we were just too tired to see anything.

Our rehearsals and two performances before the festival were lots of fun. In the audience were both loyal fans and many, many women who had never heard of us before. We have met some of them again as we have continued our travels.

Sweet Honey performed for sixty to ninety minutes at each of these concerts. At one concert, Edwina Lee Tyler opened drumming as she entered through the audience. In one, Aisha instructed the audience and Sweet Honey in a children's song which taught Swahili words. The Kenyan women in the audience thought this was pretty funny. We also performed other standard Sweet Honey repertoire, including "Breaths," "On Children," "Ella's Song," "Study War No More," and "Biko."

The festival was a major success. Women singers, dancers, instrumentalists, and poets from about twenty-six countries, most dressed in their traditional cloth-

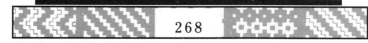

ing, creating the constant flow of colors and styles as awesome as the sounds and energies emanating from the stage. We had done it! For Sweet Honey In The Rock it was a triumphant experience!

Although this was Sweet Honey's first trip to East Africa, it was my second. However, it had been arranged so rapidly I hadn't remembered that as a person with the sickle-cell trait I had previously had an extreme reaction to the high altitude. On this trip I found myself becoming more and more ill but was driven by our mission, my personal sense of responsibility, and the internal dynamics of the group. I could not have stayed another day without seeking medical care.

In 1989, the next time Sweet Honey went to Africa (East and Southern—and mostly high in altitude), I was prepared. Over the years, I had developed a routine of checking the cities on our itinerary to see if they were in high-altitude areas (5,000 feet or more above sea level). I know now that cities like Denver, Boulder, Albuquerque, Mexico City, and Nairobi are problematic for me and require that I have oxygen available for intermittent use. Nonpressurized planes and skydiving are complete no-nos. Roadwork has been particularly helpful in working with sponsors to arrange for the prescribed medical equipment to be on hand when Sweet Honey arrives. Most sponsors who live in high-altitude regions understand that some people have difficulty and are eager to assist in any way.

The American sponsor for our second Africa tour needed to be sensitized. At one point it was said that if I had a medical problem requiring oxygen (and considerable advance planning as well as additional funds), perhaps I should not take the trip. The group was outraged and so was I. We said so! Besides the fact that such a statement violated laws protecting the rights of the handicapped, the reality was that the oxygen was a preventive measure which enabled me to function quite well throughout the tour. After we renegotiated (our sponsors deciding they wanted all of Sweet Honey and Sweet Honey deciding to accept their apologies for their insensitivity) we went on the tour. Our tour schedule was a sensible one which included performances and workshops as well as a bit of free time, and I had a glorious time.

None of us on that trip were quite prepared for the look and feel, the reality of Namibia, whose independence we were participating in celebrating. There, the official languages are German, Afrikaans, and English. The name of the capital city, Windhoek (pronounced Vind-hook), should have been instructive. Windhoek is a German city, with German architecture, German food, and German language set down in Africa. It was in Namibia that I saw the lay of the land defined by the apartheid system. Windhoek is the White city. Blacks who work or go to school there must be gone by 6 P.M. There is no transportation for them after that time. Just outside Windhoek proper is the Colored township, Khomasdal, which appears to be a nice middle-class suburb. Much farther outside Windhoek and beyond the Colored township is the Black township, Katutura. Rows of shacks with numbers painted in specific colors identify the location of the various tribes living there.

There is a street economy where items, especially cigarettes and liquor, are sold, and services such as a haircut or cooked food can be obtained. The people who live there have a community, but they are often without basic services like electricity, running water, good schools. Children skip across open sewage. I can only pray for what independence will bring.

Colonialization has taken a mighty hold in Africa, deep like an old tree which reaches out and grabs on to the earth with a vast system of spreading roots. In Zimbabwe, I talked with a director of the National Arts Council. During our conversation, he drew my attention to his very dapper (Western) suit with shirt and tie. He asked if I understood why he dressed this way and then explained that it was because traditional African dress had been deemed by legal regulation inappropriate for the conduct of business and public events during colonialism and the practice still continued even though Zimbabwe was now an independent country.

In Mozambique, a country of exquisite beauty, we experienced the terror of being in a country at war. We learned not to walk in restricted zones, and to hit the ground at the first sound of gunfire; we learned that after the electric pylons have been bombed yet again by RENAMO, there is a lottery that determines where power will be restored first; and we learned a new definition of the phrase ". . . if I can't have you, nobody will." The capital, Maputo, is a city of many cultural influences with a skyline of Western-looking office buildings, hotels, etc. Many of those buildings are vacant. When the Portuguese left, they tried to destroy everything. They not only killed cattle and broke machinery, they filled the elevator shafts of tall buildings with concrete, making them inoperable and uninhabitable. Now RENAMO (a military arm of the South African government) has picked up where the Portuguese left off by waging a war of destabilization against the country.

Our first Japan tour was in 1980. One experience I won't soon forget was meeting with a group of about ten Japanese radical feminists. They questioned us on many issues, and as we enjoyed a lengthy discussion with them, I realized that while they were fascinated with the power of our voices and the fact that we sang songs about women from the stage, they were all speaking to us in a whisper. I raised this as an issue for discussion and their discomfort was profound. Liberation has many levels and many forms.

With that trip to Japan, I brought back a koto, the first in a collection of instruments from other countries and cultures. I can now document my travels with my instrument collection. Since that trip I have added a chiranga from Mexico, bagpipes from Scotland, didjeridoos from Australia, a steel drum from St. Thomas, Virgin Islands, and drums from Uganda and Senegal. Other instruments acquired in the United States include a Celtic harp, violins, guitars, autoharp, mouth bow, electronic keyboard, drum machine, and shekeres.

Most of the time, my interest in bringing back an instrument is stimulated by dialogue with musicians in the country I am visiting. During our first Japan tour,

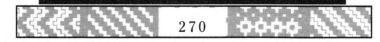

traditional Japanese musicians would perform for us following our concerts and we would then all go to dinner. While we struggled to communicate with words, much of the time our musics were more articulate. I loved the feathery sounds and textures of the koto and the samisen ensembles we heard, and cheered especially the women taiko drummers, who were incredibly fierce. I decided that I would buy a koto when a master player made finger picks for me and offered to help me secure an instrument.

BUILDING A VOCAL COMMUNITY

Sweet Honey In The Rock is like a tree which from its roots in Africa, the Caribbean, the experiences of slavery, Northern migration, the struggle for Civil Rights, and the institution of the Black church has grown strong, and is developing many branches. We initiated the workshop out of which was developed the group In Process . . . Other ensembles branching from the tree include: Street Sounds in San Francisco, Nanika in Philadelphia, Rafiki Na Dada in Baltimore, Revelations in New York, Wild Honee in the Virgin Islands, and Black Voices in Birmingham, England.

As we travel around to colleges, festivals, and various communities, other groups—Black, White, racially mixed as well as male and female—introduce themselves to us, often singing for us in the lobbies of halls where we have just performed. I have had the pleasure of working with some of these groups as a coach or consultant. And I, along with several other members of Sweet Honey, have discussed how wonderful it might be to have a conference or festival of women's a cappella groups. People everywhere want and need to sing.

During the mid-1980s, Sweet Honey received an invitation to conduct a vocal workshop for five days at the Omega Institute in Rhinebeck, New York. When the group decided not to attend, I decided to do it. That was the beginning of a wonderful path for me which in addition to Omega takes me to the Naropa Institute in Boulder, Colorado, the Agusta Heritage Center in Elkins, West Virginia, the Womancenter of Plainville, Massachusetts, the Multicultural Center of Cambridge, Massachusetts, the Washington School of the Institute for Policy Studies in Washington, D.C., as well as to England and Australia.

The workshop is designed to facilitate the development of a community through the vehicle of music from the African American vocal tradition. Musical forms include African rhythms, calls and chants, spirituals, ring shouts, hymns, gospels, songs of the Civil Rights Movement, and songs of contemporary struggle. The historical, social, and political contexts for the songs are provided as an introduction for each category of songs. Through participation in the songs and discussions of their contexts, the group (usually of fifty to sixty people) explores (from an African American worldview) the values embedded in the music, the role of cul-

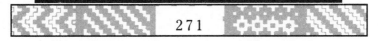

tural and spiritual traditions and rituals, ways in which leadership emerges and can be shared and supported by community members, the nature of cultural responses to and influences on political and social change, and finally the significance of a shared communal experience in one's personal life.

Most of the learners who attend these workshops are not singers. Many have been told that they should not or cannot sing and so they do not. Somehow, they manage to find themselves in the room with a lot of other people. Participants are specifically asked during the first day not to discuss their experiences with music, and despite what those experiences have been they find themselves singing, in harmony with others, in a matter of minutes. Students of the workshop and Happy Traum of Homespun Tapes of Woodstock, New York, encouraged me to produce an instructional kit, *Singing in the African American Tradition,* which through a set of tapes and a manual captures a great deal of the five-day workshop.

One of my greatest joys is hearing these voices raised together in glorious harmony. But an even greater joy is hearing the participants articulate how the experience of singing particular songs with other people in an accepting environment, after having gained an understanding of the source of the songs, has changed them. They have had to grapple with their feelings and behaviors related to differences, power, control, leadership, and risk taking among other things, all through the vehicle of performing the music of African American people.

STEPPING OUT ON FAITH

In 1985, after performing with Sweet Honey at an anti-apartheid street rally, I was arrested for demonstrating at the South African embassy. With that experience something major changed within me. I realized that I had just been arrested for supporting people I had never met and didn't know, yet I had been unable to act aggressively on my own behalf in an oppressive work environment. At the time I was working as a Training and Development Specialist at Washington, D.C., Children's Hospital National Medical Center. I decided to quit my job, and I literally stepped out on faith.

For the first time in my life I understood that nothing was promised and nothing was certain. I could not possibly know all the details of my life, nor could I hope to control them. With that concession, many more doors began to open. Each door that I have passed through has sent me down a wonderful path that I could never have anticipated. I began to understand that faith was not just believing that "things would work out." It was being centered and open, trusting that when the time was right, I would know what I was supposed to be doing in my life. I would know what was required of me and would have the energy and resources available to move through any situation. I understand now that faith is what conquers fear. I also understand that certain things were required of me: preparedness, patience,

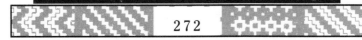

the willingness to "let go and let God," and finally acknowledgment and ownership of my talents, gifts, and power. When I realized this, I began to sing differently; I began to include the term "singer" in the description of myself.

I am learning to pay closer attention to what I have in the past called my intuitive voice. I have learned that if the voice says stop, I have to stop; if it says go, I have to go immediately. Most of the time I respond without having the vaguest idea of what is unfolding. Each time I respond I am blessed.

In September 1989, when we were beginning to plan our 1990 Black History Month tour, I announced to the group that I wanted to be at home on my birthday. This evoked some strange looks from other members of the group but they sort of let it pass. February 28 is always the last day of the tour, which typically begins on the fifteenth, so there's little chance of not working on that day and less chance of being at home. In October or November, I was pleasantly surprised by Madeleine Remez (our booking agent at Roadwork), who reported that I would be home on my birthday because we had a request from the University of Maryland. (Okay, I'll be home but I obviously can't plan anything because I'll be working.)

As I left on February 15 to begin the tour, I shook so badly I dropped my keys trying to lock my apartment door. I was the first to arrive at the airport and to discover that our flight had been canceled. The next flight meant a drive to Dulles Airport from National. When we were all safely on the next flight, I wondered if that had caused such anxiety. Although it had subsided, it increased slowly throughout the tour. I called my mother on the third day to find that my father, at ninety-two, had been hospitalized. He deteriorated daily. When I arrived home in D.C. at 11 A.M. on February 28, there was an astounding message on my machine. It was from my mother and she said, "Dad's worse. I think you had better come home." I did the Maryland concert and left for New York immediately afterward. I saw my father the next day, and on the following day he died.

He had given me so many things. My father was not only a musician; his curiosity was boundless. He was a passionate inventor with several patents on his innovations from the U.S. Patent Office. I've come by my fascination with gadgets quite naturally. Like him, I also like most those things that are functional. I move with ease and joy in this age of technology: ATMs, fax machines, voice mail, computers, buses with wheelchair lifts, CDs, camcorders, etc.

As my father taught music to so many, so have I searched for ways to encourage and train progressive and grass-roots people and organizations to use the available technology. That includes experiencing the impact that expanded communications and networking can have on their organizations, understanding that their research efforts on almost any issue can be cut at least in half by using on-line databases to obtain current information, and that disseminating information can be expanded by leaps and bounds with a computer and a modem.

My father was a bridge bringing the European-American classical music tradition to African American students for more than seventy years. I too struggle to

bridge the cultural and technical gaps to make a difference and to bring into my communities resources they need to compete in this information age.

I had insisted that my father come to hear Sweet Honey the first time we sang at Town Hall in New York in 1983. I remembered his disappointment when I decided to study something other than music, but I wanted him to know that his efforts had not been in vain. He came, and he loved Sweet Honey. He knew we were unique and hoped we would never change who we were.

So many things have come together for me. Things I could never have imagined when I was twelve or twenty-one or even thirty. Joining Sweet Honey In The Rock was the pivotal point. I have found my voice. I am told that it teaches, heals. The "reader" was right. Among many other things, I am a singer. But then too, aren't we all?

21

THE POWER OF SIGN

SHIRLEY CHILDRESS JOHNSON

My introduction to seeing the power of songs sung in American Sign Language came from my mother, a beautiful woman with a strong spirit. I was about ten and we were in church. She was singing "Swing Low, Sweet Chariot" in Sign so beautifully and with so much emotion that people were totally absorbed, so much so that one man was moved to tears. That was my first remembrance of seeing the power of Sign.

I grew up in Washington, D.C. During my youth, Mom and Dad were members of the Silent Mission at Shiloh Baptist Church, one of the earliest Deaf ministries in this country. At Shiloh the Deaf ministry has a separate sanctuary with a Deaf minister. Deaf people participated in church service, led the prayer and reading, and conducted the choir—all in Sign.

I move through my life as an African American, woman, hearing member of the Deaf community, and interpreter. Deaf people have a rich heritage and culture with a storytelling tradition in the same sense as the spoken language oral tradition. My mom has great stories. As an African American woman I am often responsible for passing on traditions. As a Sign language interpreter, I have the opportunity to participate in the sharing of both subcultures with larger communities.

I knew I had a God-given talent for interpreting music when during an interpreting assignment for a conference, I watched another interpreter's rendition of a

song. Hundreds of people were in attendance and there was a team of interpreters and a large number of Deaf people participating. The person started interpreting a song that was included as part of the opening ceremony. It was obviously challenging. However, I couldn't see the song! It looked like another speech being interpreted. There was no rhythm, no timing, no affect—all crucial for sign-interpreting song. It flows, it moves, it is poetic. That was when I recognized I had something special!

I am a part of the Deaf community, although I am not Deaf. Both my mom and dad are Deaf; my mom was born Deaf and my dad lost his hearing when he was a young child. As a hearing child born to Deaf parents, their language, American Sign Language, is my language. I grew up with direct access to Deaf people on a regular, daily basis in an intimate way. English was my second language.

I was blessed to grow up within a very proud independent family. I am Shirley Childress Johnson, Herbert and Thomasina Childress' daughter. My mom and dad had three daughters, Maxine Childress Brown, me, and Khaula Murtadha. I keep the Childress in my name. I cherish it especially since my dad passed. I am emphatic about my maiden name. The Childress is who I am.

My mother's family name is Brown. The Browns are from South Carolina and North Carolina. Edgefield County in South Carolina is where my grandfather Clarence Brown and my grandmother Martha began to raise their family.

My dad's family is in Tennessee, where he grew up. When he was about three, he became ill with spinal meningitis. A combination of the illness and the medication used to cure him caused the deafness. My dad left Tennessee as a child and ended up going to the Overlea School for the Black Deaf and Blind in Maryland. During the 1920s and 1930s when my parents were growing up in the South, residential schools for the Deaf were racially segregated.

My dad was a shoe repairman by trade. Young Deaf men were taught shoe repair, tailoring, or printing; young Deaf women were taught sewing. Everybody learned a trade of some kind.

My mom had attended the School for the Deaf in North Carolina. My mom tells a story about the day she enrolled—her father had a horse and buggy in those days and the family traveled with her to the school. She remembers entering a building and seeing all these strange people with her dad and her sisters Ruth, Della, and Mary. Her mom had created their own "home signs" within her family. However, my mother had not seen so many other people, all signing with unfamiliar signs. And then her family was leaving her; she was emotionally distraught. Months passed before she was reunited with her family. Today Deaf education has expanded so that it is now possible to attend a day school and thus eliminate the trauma of being separated from the family in order to be trained.

My mother was very successful in school. When she graduated, she was asked to become a teacher there. Her personality, and her caring, and her warmth with

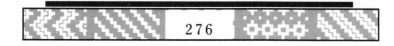

the children made her very effective and much loved by all. She taught school for approximately fourteen years. I often meet people who say, "Oh, your mom was my teacher." She is a brilliant woman. Her father and sisters moved here to Washington, D.C., in the 1930s. She was teaching school in North Carolina and she would come to Washington to visit the family during summer vacation. My parents met here in Washington, D.C.

People often ask me, "How did you learn how to talk?" Being born into a signing family where it was our normal way of communicating, I don't remember my exact age when I came to the understanding that there were ways to communicate other than signing. I could communicate using my voice—with or without my hands. My mom and my dad were born into families of hearing people, so at family gatherings there was voice conversation as well as Sign. We also had contacts with hearing friends and exposure to the sounds of radio and television.

It wasn't until I was about age seven that I realized that some people thought signing was unusual. I was out playing in the yard, while Mom and Dad were having a conversation in front of the home, when some hearing people came down the street making these gestures—not signing, but ridiculing. Dad became furious. I realized we were being ridiculed for communicating in a way that was natural for us.

The initial barrier to communication between Deaf and hearing people is attitudinal. If one has the attitude of a yes, I want to communicate with you, then the primary hurdle has been overcome. It is not so much whether one can sign or not; it is whether the attitude is positive. Once we overcome that attitudinal barrier, then the communication is easy. Learning to sign, writing back and forth, gesturing, pointing, using eye contact, hugs—all of that is communication.

Growing up, all of us signed. It was just something that was easy and natural within the family. When I was in my early twenties, I encountered—through my sister Maxine, who worked participating in a Deaf survey needs assessment for the state of Massachusetts—the family of a young Deaf man in which nobody signed. It astounded me that nobody in his family could easily and readily communicate with him. I had thought that if you had a Deaf person in your family, everybody—or at least somebody—signed. Even my two sons, Reginald and Deon, can sign with their grandmother.

Of course, not even every Deaf person signs. There is a great debate as to the best approach to Deaf education, including whether to use Sign language or oral speech and speech reading. I strongly support a visual mode of communication, using American Sign Language. It feels obvious and natural. If a person is not able to hear, then that person depends on sight—"strong eyes"—for information, for communication. American Sign Language is visual; it is language of the hand, the face, the body. The first language.

I began interpreting as a child, which is not uncommon in situations where

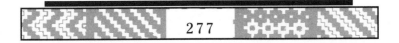

parents are Deaf and children are hearing. It doesn't happen as frequently now, but hearing children interpreted because there were few professional Sign language interpreters available. The profession of Sign language interpreting is still comparatively new. People came together in 1964 to organize Sign language professionals as interpreters. We had social workers or teachers who would sometimes function as interpreters. My first experience of interpreting was with my dad negotiating with a car salesman. I knew nothing about negotiating car sales. Dad wanted to pay a certain amount of money and the car salesman was talking about how great the car was and trying to convince him to buy the car at a higher price. I think Dad succeeded in getting the car at his price.

My parents were fiercely independent people and would not often use us children in interpreting situations. But sometimes there were circumstances, like interpreting phone conversations for them, which we, as children, were not always excited about getting involved with. An organization called Children of Deaf Adults (CODA) focuses on the unique experiences of growing up in a Deaf cultural environment, and provides a forum where feelings and frustrations can be expressed and worked through.

My parents were leaders. My dad was one of the first Black Deaf people to build and own his own home. He was president of a Deaf club. We often had club meetings at our home. In Deaf culture, people will often visit without advance warning. For a long time, telephones were not accessible to Deaf people. (Although Alexander Graham Bell, who invented the telephone, was a hearing man, it is interesting that his mom and his wife were Deaf.) So if two people were Deaf, even the seemingly simple task of visiting could be terribly complicated. I could send you a letter and it might get there a week later or I would just show up at your door. If you were home, great; if you weren't, I would leave a note and tell you I was there. (In 1964, Robert Weitbrecht, a Deaf electronics scientist, invented the acoustic coupler for use with the teletypewriter, creating telephone accessibility for the Deaf.)

Our home was open to Deaf folks. As in the African American tradition, we just put another potato in the pot. There is always another plate. And in the Deaf community, it is the very same way. You just welcome guests into your home.

My first professional interpreting assignment was in a mainstream high school program during the early 1970s. I interpreted the classroom discussions and the teachers' lectures. During that assignment I got excited and realized that I could do this work.

I graduated from Holyoke Community College and then transferred to the University of Massachusetts at Amherst. I first enrolled in the Media Specialist Program for the Deaf. Deaf education is visual, so we use a lot of media—film, overhead projectors, pictures, graphic displays, etc. However, I withdrew from that program and developed an individual concentration in Deaf education, taking courses in education, psychology, linguistics, and deafness.

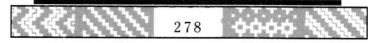

I received my certification and joined the local chapter of the Registry of Interpreters for the Deaf, the organization responsible for certification and professional development of interpreters. Through interpreting workshops, I try to keep current within the field.

To be an interpreter you have to first be fluent in the languages with which you are working, which in my case are American Sign Language and English. Good interpreters are people-oriented, they recognize that communication happens *between* people. Sign language interpreting facilitates and encourages that communication. To facilitate the message, which occurs not only in words or sign but also in human behavior, interpreters include not only a verbal text but also an attitude, the emotion involved.

My Sign-interpreting experiences cover situations A to Z. I have interpreted several births, weddings, and funerals. I have gone to job sites where Deaf people have hearing co-workers who don't sign, and I interpreted their staff meetings or training opportunities. I have interpreted in medical situations as well. Some interpreters will refuse a job if it is a medical assignment in a hospital setting because of their own difficulty in that environment. The medical terminology can be difficult, and sometimes you have to have a tough stomach to deal with the smells, the needles, and the people in pain.

Legal interpreting is another specialized area I've found challenging. I remember the first time I saw a man in handcuffs, and I had to go down into the cellblock. It was painful.

Interpreters abide by a code of ethics. For instance, interpreters have the responsibility of keeping information confidential. As interpreters, we take part in immensely intimate and personal exchanges that require developing a special place in our being to retain confidential material. Sometimes, even the fact that I have been on an interpreting assignment is confidential information. At those times, all that I know must be held within me and I have not always successfully found a way to ventilate my feelings. I continuously strive to increase my proficiency in the process that calls for maintaining confidentiality while unburdening myself of the stress created during a specific assignment.

I remember the first time I was contacted about working with Sweet Honey In The Rock. I was on an interpreting assignment for Ysaye Barnwell, who, then a member of the Dental School faculty at Howard University, was conducting a workshop. She actively incorporated Deaf people into the workshop and hired Sign language interpreters. We developed a friendship during the period when she had just begun her work with Sweet Honey In The Rock.

Ysaye talked about wanting to focus her energies on singing rather than attempting the complexities involved in the double job of interpreting and singing simultaneously. A person who interprets uses a separate mental process from the person who carries on a signed conversation representing themselves. A person participating in a signed conversation communicates ideas directly to another per-

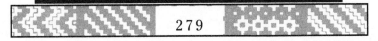

son who understands their language; the interpreter is required to submerge her or his own thoughts and become a medium through which other people's messages are taken in and transformed so that communication can take place between those who do not share the same language.

Ysaye invited me to try Sign-interpreting a concert. I remember writing the date in my appointment book, the event, and "SHIR" as the abbreviation for Sweet Honey In The Rock. I got excited recognizing that the first four letters of Shirley and the abbreviation of Sweet Honey In The Rock (SHIR) were the same. I thought: Oh, this fits, this is for me!

I have come to understand that other people have a real appreciation for my work and I am truly humbled by their enthusiastic responses. I have come to recognize my gift.

While interpreting Sweet Honey's music, I keep my focus on Deaf people. For many Deaf people, music is a foreign experience; it is not a daily, essential part of their lives. There are a lot of Deaf people who can more readily appreciate the experience of song. Some Deaf people who may have lost their hearing later in life have come to understand the impact a visual song can have. For other Deaf people, hearing family members or friends have influenced them. They see a friend or hearing family member really getting excited about a particular song or artist and they are stimulated to explore a new musical experience. Songs can be healing, informing, nurturing, and can be a solace to us during a time of depression.

I use the song's energy; I try to let go of Shirley the person and let the song claim its space and do its work. I continuously work to develop a more poetic style. It is the same concept as singers taking voice lessons; they are always trying to improve style and technique. It requires keeping focused on the message, on the person who is receiving the message, on the Deaf audience.

I am an extremely sensitive wear-my-emotions-on-my-sleeve kind of person. I cry at the drop of a hat. Once I felt my sensitivity was a disability. I have come to appreciate it now as being something special about me. Sign-interpreting Sweet Honey includes clear interpretation of the song true to its content, a poetic delivery, rhythmically in tune, emotionally sensitive to its nature, and timing commensurate with the singing!

Some of Sweet Honey's songs, like "Letter to Martin," by Sonia Sanchez, or "A Priority," a rap tune created by Aisha Kahlil and Nitanju Bolade Casel, are dense with text and performed as dialogue. There is a rhythm to that dialogue that I seek in sharing the song with the audience. My task is to deal with the translation— the meaning—and to try to come to an understanding of the song. When I am successful, I am delivering it in a way that is as rapturous and as powerful as the vocal rendition.

Sign-interpreting song has the feeling and power of sign poetry. There is a new sign for the word *poetry* that discards the old concept of visualizing a sheet of paper

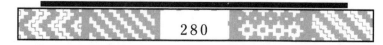

and the action of writing. The new sign has the hand coming out of the chest expressing an outpouring of feeling. Deaf people have come to a heightened sense of pride, fighting against biases against Deaf culture, fighting for the right to educate Deaf children in American Sign Language. Just as African Americans during the Civil Rights era declared Black pride, there is now the declaration of Deaf pride. That pride is reflected in the language, in the poetry.

During Sweet Honey concerts it is the Deaf audience that really energizes me. I am energized by seeing a Deaf person really reacting and responding to a song. The Sweet Honey message has connected with that Deaf person because that person has understood the song and is touched by it.

For most of this country's history, so many aspects of living have not been accessible to Deaf people. The doors were closed, the welcome mat not extended to attend concerts or church, to work in equal employment, or to participate fully in so much of what the society offers. Acts of discrimination have denied Deaf people their rights. Now, as a result of the Americans With Disabilities Act, it is against the law to discriminate on the basis of disability. But an opened door does not mean that the Deaf person feels welcome to come in. Sometimes it takes some active encouragement. For Sweet Honey concerts, it has taken sponsors who are willing to do the work of networking within the Deaf community. Putting an advertisement on a flyer is a start, at least it announces that an interpreted concert will take place, but more often than not, it takes an active reaching out to the community. Sometimes a hearing person who is excited about Sweet Honey will see that they have this dynamic interpreter, and practically twists the arm of the Deaf person. I have had Deaf people tell me, "She really forced me to come! I wasn't going to come, but I'm so glad I did!"

Within the Sweet Honey concert experience, it is crucial to see the faces of the artists, to see the body language, the expressions, especially for the Deaf audience, which is depending on sight to enjoy the concert. Also some Deaf people do read lips, so they do want to see clearly. The best seats (in my opinion and that of Deaf people I have talked with) are front row center. Here they can see the whole group and see the interpreter in the same viewing frame.

Sometimes you see interpreters far over in the corner, twenty feet or thirty feet away from where the action is. It means that a Deaf person has to turn away from the central action to see the text presented through the interpretation. I am not exactly sure where this practice of separation comes from. It is partly from the artist, who claims the stage as his or her individual space and feels the interpreter as an intrusion. That is one of the reasons why I really admire Sweet Honey for her bravery. These women include the interpreter as an integral part of the ensemble; thus, the Deaf audience is more fully included in the concert experience. One Deaf woman commented, "We could participate in the feelings and moods of the song." It takes courage to be all-inclusive. Not all artists will do that. On one occasion I

was interpreting for an artist who did not even want me to be on the same stage. I had to physically stand on a separate, small table. It made my job more difficult. It affected everybody adversely.

The most successful concert experiences happen when the artist, the interpreter, and the Deaf person are all part of the same intimate scene. If the artist is Deaf, such as a Deaf comedienne or a Deaf storyteller, I will Sign-to-voice interpret. It is important, again, for all of us to feel connected in the space so we don't miss the energy.

In some of Sweet Honey's workshops I try to convey to hearing people that the hazards of deafness within the predominant hearing culture can mean literally life or death. During the Detroit riots of the mid-1960s a citywide curfew was imposed. Roy Banks, an African American Deaf man and a personal friend of the family (as a child one of the thrills of my life was riding on the back of his motorcycle), was living there at the time. He had to travel in the early morning to work, but he did not know about the curfew. It had not been lifted. A policeman ordered him to halt. He did not hear. He was shot to death. Such tragic situations are far too numerous and show the insensitivity and unawareness of many hearing people. If the police handcuff a Deaf suspect, then that person is not able to communicate. Sometimes law-enforcement personnel misinterpret as aggressiveness the gestures a Deaf person makes and that misunderstanding has caused injury and death.

A Deaf friend and I were talking about the *People* magazine story on Sweet Honey; Sammy Davis is on the cover of that issue. I was referring to his death, and my friend asked, "Who is Sammy Davis?" I thought everybody in the world knew Sammy Davis. But he didn't know, because he had not heard his songs or seen any of his movies. I began to realize once again that there are so many things we take for granted, so-called household names are not familiar names within the Deaf community. That incident and so many others always remind me that information is power, and for many Deaf people, because so much of television is not accessible, radio is not accessible, neighboring conversations are not accessible, that power is denied. For many Deaf people, because English is a second language, reading English may be difficult. That further diminishes information resources. A Sign language interpreter, teletypewriter (TTY), and closed captioning devices can provide access to information.

We who communicate through Sign do have advantages. Deaf people have face-to-face conversation. Often hearing people will not look at each other when they communicate, or they will be doing something else and say, "Yeah, I did that yesterday," and keep on doing whatever it is they were doing. Visual language requires people to actively engage each other. This can also have its hazardous side. I remember a wonderful older Deaf gentleman, Harry Lee, who has passed away now. He and his friend, another Deaf man, were walking down the street and they were signing to each other. They were looking at each other, carrying on a conversation and walking. They came to the end of the sidewalk, and did not see the curb.

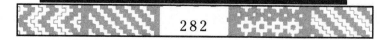

Mr. Lee fell and broke his hip. It took a long time for his hip to heal and it was difficult for him to fully recover.

Right now there is a real movement of Deaf people to clarify language pertaining to Deaf people and an increased self-identification. Many Deaf people have decided the term "hearing-impaired" is offensive. "Impaired" implies something that is broken, needing to be fixed. Many Deaf people proclaim, "There is nothing broken or needing to be fixed about me. I am Deaf, period. I am Deaf and I am fine." So the preferred language is Deaf and hard-of-hearing, or just Deaf.

Deafness has historically been viewed from the perspective of medical pathology. The Deaf artist creates work that celebrates Deaf culture and expresses the oppression of Deaf people. Hearing people and medical professionals have focused on the ear and not the person. One artist's painting has a big ear on a proportionately tiny person. It expresses the experience of growing up and being measured by the ability to hear and read lips. Some people are hard-of-hearing, and some people have a more profound hearing loss. Deaf and hard-of-hearing. Deaf and proud and using the power of Sign!

22

THE RANTINGS, RAVINGS, RAMBLINGS, AND RECOLLECTIONS OF A SOUND MAN

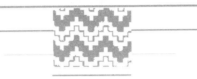

ART STEELE

"**H**ouse to half." The house lights dim. This is my cue. I'm on. I pick up the mike from the board, open the channel, and say, "Ladies and gentlemen, at the request of Sweet Honey In The Rock there will be no smoking, no photographs, or sound, or video recording of this evening's performance." The excited pre-show audience quiets magically and a Sweet Honey concert is about to begin.

Bernice leads the chorus into the opening of "Beatitudes," in which the group is the call and Evelyn Harris chants the response. "Blessed are—the poor in spirit . . ." Evelyn's voice is like clear blue ice on the response line set in lead position: "Blessed are the poor in spirit, for theirs is the kingdom of heaven." She's able to maintain a good distance from the mike yet sound like she's right up on it, something I've also experienced with blues "shouters" like B. B. King. The rest of the group is also well back . . . and quiet. As I boost the background vocal part to fill the hall, I get a sense of what the sound system de jure has to offer. The hall too, now full of people, is different acoustically from the afternoon sound check. The song is sung sotto voce, almost under the breath, without a lot of microphone energizing drive. I am listening as a sound man, a musician, and a human being.

Each Sweet Honey song presents unique sound challenges, and my role is to work the song musically and lyrically intact sometimes through the sound system and the hall's best efforts to capsize it. The experience can be a bit like shooting white-water rapids in a canoe. Each hall has its own story to tell, each sound system

its song to sing; I work to keep the story from being an adventure and the song from being the blues. To my joy, halls with long reverberation times caress every word of slower-paced, hymnlike text. To my sorrow, the same halls can garble text delivered in fast-paced and intricate ways. In "dead" halls (with no reverberation) the lyric clarity is dependent on the sound system. Each of the five singers is a dramatic and different soloist, and in ensemble work they often create vocal-accompaniment parts utilizing their bass, alto, and soprano ranges, sometimes in the same song. No static setting of the sound equipment is possible here. My contribution is dynamic, and my objective is to maintain the group's concept of ensemble unity through all their varying ranges as the music moves enhanced through the sound system.

"Beatitudes," also sometimes called "The Sermon on the Mount," serves as an intro for the group. This song is a statement of unity, community, and humility, and Sweet Honey often places the unfolding concert in perspective by starting with this "position."

"Denko." Nitanju uses a stunning African soprano-styled vocal timbre sounded in the top front nasal area when she intros this song. It has a strong buzz drone undercurrent and reminds me of a plucked banjo or an African kalimba "thumb piano." Sound gear tends to overemphasize the edge in these passages and I "ride" the tone controls carefully. I've found I must always pay close attention to Nitanju's voice in an ensemble mix. Her clear, silky-toned sweetness can sometimes be obscured when set among the denser-textured vocal timbres of the rest of the group, but here, leading in "Denko," she cuts like a knife.

"Denko" is another challenge dynamically—it starts hot and gets hotter. If I mix too loud at the outset, by the end of the song it can be too loud in the audience. Musically and creatively, Sweet Honey relies on a build of dynamic energy that they control. After committing to a volume level at the top of a song, I don't like to reconsider in the middle and "pull (turn) it down" at the mixer. When Sweet Honey steps on the gas I want the sound system to be there for them, fully responsive. They will also use shekeres (beaded gourd drums) on this song and during the percussion improv section, Bernice will thump her shekere, expecting the room to thump in reply. This is another test point/moment of truth for the sound system; it helps me define the type of bass response and pitch capabilities available in a given system.

"Wade in the Water." The opening line of this hypnotic song, which ebbs and flows like water itself, is in the skillful hands and voice of Evelyn, Yasmeen, or Carol Maillard—whoever is onstage this evening, but each of the other singers carries a lead in one of the verse sections.

Well you see, the children dresses up in blue,
You know God's gonna trouble the water,
You know it looks like my people coming through . . .

Ysaye's voice is a phenomenon. She sings the lowest and the highest ranges in the group, and performs a major portion of the bass work. When she enters the opening chorus of this song, the audience sighs, her bottom line grounds the song, and it is off to a great start. Ysaye's ability to jump ranges means her mike must be constantly checked for a linear (smooth) response without muddiness. How she hears on the stage and sounds in the audience depends on this. Much of my sound-check work with retuning any system we encounter, and the design work I have experimented with on my own system, is to make this linearity of low pitches and notes a reality. Though Ysaye has the lowest voice, in other songs each of the other singers will drop into the "Ysaye bass" territory and need corresponding attention. During the performance of "Wade in the Water" the lead by each singer gives me an overall mike-to-mike continuity check in a concert context. Bernice pitches her lead line well off mike here yet always punches through effortlessly. . . .

You know some say Peter and some say Paul
God's gonna trouble the water
But there ain' but the one God made us all . . .

The group *could* sometimes perform a song with *no* sound system. Bernice often walks off mike to sing acoustically in the hall, but this would be a limiting factor if they did it all the time. It would affect the audience response, which would have to go into a more reserved passive listening mode to hear the text, instead of the usual clapping and singing along while still hearing the music as it washes the hall from the stage via the sound system. The group would have to sing at full voice for the entire show, very demanding physically, and they would also have to give up the textures and power of lines delivered in some tunes almost at subliminal whispers. Although it makes my job harder, I like sound experiences that explore the full dynamic range—from the low extremes of what your ear can hear up to the full limit of what your ear can take, and Sweet Honey delivers this.

"See See Rider." For me, Aisha is the Jimi Hendrix of the group, and her intro to this song (à la Ma Rainey) epitomizes the feeling of the blues for me. Her primary intent in her singing is to reflect the feeling "behind" her voice . . . a feeling powerful enough to warp, change, and sometimes reshape the vocal quality itself. This is the sound I try to get in my blues guitar work. Emotions which overload the instrument itself sometimes can go "beyond" the instrument unleashing the feeling. "See See Rider" also offers dual bass work by Bernice and Ysaye done very softly—this use of deep soft notes takes away a lot of voice overtones and gives a very rich full sound. It's another sound challenge, however. So much mike sensitivity is required that the sound system usually rides on the edge of misbehavior during this song. I love listening to the strut of the chords through this song; it's one of my favorites.

Yasmeen is another Sweet Honey phenomenon. She opens with the softness

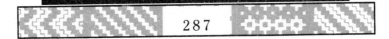

and sweetness of Nitanju or Evie and with the spine-tingling "growl" of Bernice in the same phrase. I've never heard a singer so able to occupy both singing styles as effortlessly and interchangeably as Yasmeen. The song's subject matter, the passing of time, youth and one's reaction to it, is universal and Yasmeen's delivery grabs me *every time.* When she sings I never question her connection to her subject matter, she wears a song like a cloak; it's hers.

On one English tour, in a medieval-style stone hall with a ceiling high enough to almost have weather, Yasmeen sang "Sweet Bird . . . why you fly so fast" and a bird flew from the stone pillars behind her above and through the audience. The song's expression is so powerful that this was experienced by us all as totally normal.

"Sometimes, day breaks in my life." Bernice, some singers sing to my ear or my brain, others to my body or heart, you sing to my soul. You "get up inside me" with your singing. It may not be comfortable what you say or sing but it feels right. The grit of sandpaper wears through old coverings, paints, or falsities to expose true wood beneath. "Sometime" is a masterwork created as a wedding song offering. The vocal cello-string talents of Ysaye create the framework for the ensemble of background lines that roll like ripples from a stone dropped in the water, and driven by the incredible soul of Bernice Johnson Reagon—not just my favorite, but that of everyone who has heard it. In Scotland, during a concert for the BBC, the entire audience, including me, was in tears. After a show in Hackney, England, a local a cappella singing group sang it impromptu to Bernice backstage. Powerful moments, powerful memories. At these times, being in the audience mixing, I am also in a prime seat, at the center of an audience being moved, strongly and deeply. There are involuntary cries, gasps, tears, tightly gripped partners' hands. . . .

She who sings with hands. Shirley is an advocate. The concerns of the Deaf community at Sweet Honey shows are presented to her and through her and she presents another view of the concert to them. Sweet Honey is a visual feast of movements and textures and a thought-provoking feast of ideas, words, and poetry. Shirley's work sets a place for those of different appetites to feast at the same table.

I gained a great respect and understanding for the Deaf community in 1972 when my blues band performed at Clark School for the Deaf in Northampton, Massachusetts. Going in, I asked, "Why? Why should we perform here?" I learned during the show. The connection Deaf people can have with music, vibration, and dancing is unique and precious. The entire band was changed, brought closer to our own music as we saw it retain its validity when perceived and enjoyed "vibra-tionally" by the Deaf audience. From then on we played at Clark as often as possible.

Who am I? I'm still trying to find out, but my name is Art Steele. I was born in New Hampshire in 1951 and I've been doing sound for concerts and playing music for over twenty-five years . . . a long time. In the "good old days" when I started, audio mixers only had four mike input channels (with volume controls only), sixty-

watt tube amps (not transistors) were the order of the day, and sound engineering was not a profession but a hobby. A few "snapshots" of my present and past life and sound (ha) advice offered buffet-style will serve as further introduction to the part of the extended Sweet Honey community I work in.

"DO YOU FEEL ALL RIGHT, BOB?"

"Do you feel all right, Bob?" The question is only partly rhetorical and directed at my "runnin' buddy," Bob Dwelley, who, among a select few others, provides my second pair of hands for the Sweet Honey sound production team when we travel with our own sound gear. (Bob is a graphics designer/concert promoter/DJ/gardener in addition to being a skillful sound man and representative of the cross-trained personnel I prefer to work with.) We're on a Sunderland, Massachusetts, to D.C. run. It is a thirteen-hour drive each way with eight hours of load-in, setup, sound check, and concert between, and limited sleep opportunities, which are folded in the truck passenger seat while the other drives. We have worked long enough together so that words are not usually necessary, a grunt or a monosyllable is all that's needed.

Over the years on the road I've learned what it takes to "jump-start" my body and have developed crazy formulas for what seems to work. Over the short term you can substitute eating, sleeping, and a shower/bath for each other and a small further driving increment (2 hours' sleep = 1 hot meal = 1 bath = 200 miles of driving).

"TURN DOWN YOUR BED, SIR?"

Sweet Honey does seventy-plus shows per year and these road trips are a part of them. On the other side (a Sweet Honey lyric) of the road I can often find myself in a swank hotel with pool, spa, exercise room, great restaurant, maids, bellmen, and TVs and phones *even in the bathroom!* But what you see is not what you get. The air travel, the grueling schedule (again with little sleep), van rides to and from sound checks, airports, and different hotels, can still wipe you out physically. My thrifty New England Yankee father would never understand, but I can state unequivocally that sometimes a good night's sleep is worth a $160 hotel bill.

"WELCOME TO WASHINGTON NATIONAL AIRPORT"

The typical air travel weekend starts with me leaving my house in Sunderland, Massachusetts, at about 4 A.M. for a one-hour drive to Bradley Airport in Windsor

Locks, Connecticut, to catch a 6 A.M. flight to meet Sweet Honey in D.C. Then we fly as a group usually two more legs, first to a hub airport, then on to the city of the concert. On our arrival (usually around noon) we are driven to the hotel (usually another half-hour drive), where the group checks in. I go directly to the venue to work with the sound and lighting crews to put up the show. Many venues have sufficient lighting for our show, but *very* few have adequate sound geared to Sweet Honey's stringent needs. This means a sound company had been hired (in some cases by me personally) and worked with weeks in advance by fax and phone to organize the show-day needs.

Now at the hall is the moment of truth: can this gear be put into shape for a 3 P.M. sound check? In most cases, there are major flaws to be corrected, hums or buzzes needing to be tracked and eliminated, or components to be fixed or replaced. I have walked London streets looking for a store to buy model airplane glue on a Sunday (I found it) and worked around the clock to resolder an entire sound system in war-torn Mozambique to the sound of military jets overhead.

"HEY, MADELEINE, CAN YOU BRING ME BACK A SANDWICH?"

The group's sound and light check at 3 P.M. takes about an hour. They will return to the hotel at 4 P.M. (more van rides) for a few hours and eat. I go with them for my first meal of the day if there isn't further work to do on the system. "Further work" means I might not be able to leave the hall for the ten to twelve hours until the concert is over. On these days, I lean on Madeleine Remez—Sweet Honey's artist representative and my partner on the road team—to forage for sustenance. Then it's a 6:45 P.M. callback at the venue for an 8 P.M. show (two one-hour sets with a twenty-minute intermission). After the equipment breakdown I make it back to the hotel by midnight for four or five hours' sleep. (I get up at four or five for a workout; I'm a running freak.) Then I am off to the airport for another day and more of the same. . . .

"ARTHUR! WHAT HAVE YOU DONE?"

I guess sound first started getting under my skin when I was fourteen or fifteen and wanted to put together a guitar amp. My parents didn't have much money but they *did* have an old Magnavox radio in a large wooden console cabinet. I took it apart without my parents' permission one weekend, to build a plywood speaker cabinet (with a door in the back, which I thought was very cool) and a separate enclosure for the electronics section. The whole setup wasn't much louder than the unamplified acoustic guitar itself, but I didn't care.

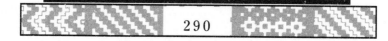

"THIS . . . IS . . . THE LORD!!!"

A second sound milestone was passed one Sunday several years later. That's when I hooked up all the speakers I owned, pointed them down a hill at my parents' house in Richmond, Massachusetts, and, inspired by the godlike tones of my own amplified voice, proceeded to intone, "THIS IS THE LORD—JUDGMENT DAY IS AT HAND." Pretty heady stuff for the neighborhood, I thought, but this is where I got one of my first acoustic lessons. The sound traveled down the hill to a railroad embankment, and, when carried into a valley by running water through a railway culvert, was clearly audible on Main Street of the town of West Stockbridge five miles away. Given that it was Sunday and people were coming out of church, a disembodied voice talking about Judgment Day caused considerable consternation! The "Steele" kid was talked about for many years, always with shaking heads and tsking.

"HEY, JOHN, ARE YOU USING YOUR FENDER TWIN GUITAR AMP TONIGHT?"

I never set out to be a sound man. I was just around with equipment whenever it was needed. I kept buying more and better gear, with the idea that other people renting my gear would enable me to purchase better equipment than I could normally afford for my own use. This led me in high school to form a collective of fellow musicians who would rent stage equipment to the Music Inn and Tanglewood in Lenox, Massachusetts. It would be used for such acts as Arlo Guthrie (a local), Kris Kristofferson, B. B. King, Ike and Tina Turner, Peter, Paul and Mary, Chet Atkins, Jefferson Airplane, Janis Joplin, and so on. To this day one of my favorite memories is that of B. B. King, head upraised, eyes closed, guitar uplifted, playing *into* a driving rainstorm as the canvas canopy over the stage would lift with each gust of wind and bent guitar note. Again, the right place, the right time. I was dealing with my childhood idols . . . I'd bring the gear home, still warm, to practice some of the guitar licks I had heard that night.

Not having money to buy new gear as fast as I would like, I started taking apart equipment to fix it—looking for parts that didn't look, feel, or in some cases smell right. Fueled by a love of mysticism and for science fiction, I think of sound equipment as having human traits and characteristics and needing to be made friends with. Thus a definition was generated which remains unchanged today:

A SOUND SYSTEM consists of *animate* bits of wire and parts with *individual* peculiarities, strengths, and weaknesses which when *introduced* by the system designer will operate as a *team* with the overall strengths canceling the collective

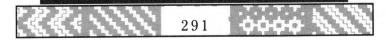

weakness which when used by an operator sensitive to this gestalt interrelationship becomes a good or great sound system.

And the corollary apropos sound systems you meet on the road. Many have been abused, traumatized, and "brutalized" by poor designers, uncaring operators, and inappropriate program sources. These systems must be treated with respect, care, and sensitivity. Only then do they seem to give their best, go that extra mile, and get you through the show.

"CALL ART"

I went away to college to attend the University of Massachusetts in 1970. I paid my way through a work-study program at (where else?) the UMass Campus Center audiovisual and media services. I quickly gained a reputation as the person to call for the "tough" sound jobs. I never turned down any chance to work on sound. This mania drove me to buy equipment with my own money (loans cosigned by parents and friends) to buttress the center's antique and often failing equipment. It also led me to bring my equipment to campus to use on university shows, not for extra money but to work with better tools. I'm talking about several trips with borrowed cars (I only owned a bicycle) moving 120-pound speakers and amps to the campus to work their shows for free. No wonder I began to be called "Crazy Art Steele." All through school I led my own blues band (Maelstrom Blues Group), saving enough money in the gallon pickle jar in my closet to buy a van. At last I could move my own equipment!

In 1974, I left the school and formed a sound company, Steele Sound Reinforcement Rentals. The school, however, became one of my best customers, using me and my gear for events featuring some of the greatest of the greats, like Count Basie, Duke Ellington, Dizzy Gillespie, Betty Carter, Sarah Vaughan, Roland Kirk, Woody Shaw, Ray Charles, and on and on.

It was at a show in the UMass Fine Arts Center in 1978 that I first met Sweet Honey. The group intrigued me on many levels. Musically, their power pulled from the places of two music styles I loved: R&B and blues from the golden years (1951–56) and from the improvisational "lyrical" clean styles of my earlier list of the greatest of the greats (mostly jazz). And yet Sweet Honey had elements of the rocking, multipart singing sound I was just getting into via a soul concert series I was doing in Springfield, Massachusetts, which was featuring such singers as the Dells, Dramatics, Stylistics, Delphonics, Unifics, and so on (all groups featured three to seven singers backed with a stripped-down, usually three-piece, rhythm section accompaniment). Intellectually, what intrigued me was that Sweet Honey was very political—and very vocal on all issues, especially Bernice Reagon.

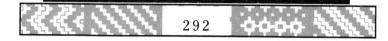

After doing all these concert series with world-renowned artists and getting rave reviews, I was, let's face it, getting "cocky" or at least perversely proud of my sound gear. However (and you can read a very big and humbling "however" here), Sweet Honey stressed my sound system dynamically and sonically in ways I never dreamed. I started seeing many, many ways I could improve my gear's handling of this most demanding of musical program sources . . . the unaccompanied human voice. This search for better sound and quality, this desire to go beyond current technological limits continues with me today and shows no sign of waning.

A SOUND PERSON'S MANUAL FOR GOOD SOUND

Sound is not a "hard" science but an art rationalized by "hard" science. When mixing a cappella sound I keep in mind that I am delivering art to the audience; it must be done artistically. The room is a cup to fill with sound completely, but without spilling a drop. If you attempt to "overfill" this cup, the room will speak and you might not like what it says. Sound systems likewise tend to show an ugly persona when overstressed. Sound as processed by the brain is nonlinear and very subjective. I therefore consider *each* audience member equally an "expert," and weigh the inputs and observations of nontechnicians heavily. Voices should live as 3-D images in the room, not as sounds violently spit from a speaker.

Mike working distances are very important, both for fidelity and for creating this sense of space. The distance the voice has to travel through the air to the mike should be between four inches and one foot. The performer should be able to hear the room and monitors at those distances for these reasons:

1. The performers can, with incremental moves, control their own sound mix.
2. The distance between the singer and the mike determines the audience's perception of a sound's origin in space (close to the mike and a quiet sound the ear interprets as "intimate," farther away and a louder sound the ear interprets as "intense"). Please note: greater intensity does not mean getting closer to the microphone.
3. The air between the voice and mike acts as a filter and tone control, taking the edge off hard consonant and "s" sounds and reducing "p" popping. It's these sounds which are necessary, without a mike, to propel the voice through the dense medium of air.
4. The singer-to-mike working distance can eliminate the need for sound effects, reverb, and echoes, devices which try to restore the sonics lost when you work mikes too close. The halls themselves have more reverb and echo modes than any digital electronic device. When you move back from a mike the room sound mixes with your vocal sound, preserving more of the natural relationship of the voice to the room.

5. In the mike working distance of four inches to one foot, the performer will also find several "sweet" spots at varying distances where the top and bottom vocal ranges seem in synch. Mikes don't pick up sound democratically. At the "sweet" spots the proper tonal relationships exist for a *natural* sound the performers *and* the audience hear better. To find this working distance (called "gain") the sound system speakers should be moved far enough ahead of the singers so as not to "feedback." I prefer the traditional two-way speaker systems popular about ten to fifteen years ago—a large (one-half to two-thirds the size of your refrigerator) bass cabinet (where the woofer is visible) and a large (one yard across) mid-range high-frequency horn.

I realize this last preference will be considered old-fashioned in light of modern trends toward small trapezoidal boxes with processors or outboard electronic compensator units (which I find very audible—read "unnatural"—in operation) or larger three- or four-component PA speaker boxes. The small speaker horns used in these new "modern" systems will always sound "pinched" and constricted; the multifrequency components will never reassemble the voice properly after it has been split into bass, mid-range, high, and tweeter ranges.

The older systems, with their larger horns, track *vocal* dynamics much more evenly and with fewer breaks in response than their modern counterparts—*and* cost one-fifth the price.

The same "older is better" thinking holds true with regard to amplifiers. I prefer working with the circa 1975–80 large and heavy power amplifiers (with strong, conservative power supplies), which can deliver more current and bass storage to give a more natural sound with crisp edge to consonants of words. Modern amps, in order to be smaller and lighter, primarily use "switching" power supplies and "draw power as needed," they don't store the current on board in capacitors but draw it from the wall electric outlets on demand. The problem, though, is that by the time they draw the power, the sound the extra power was needed for has come and gone (too much, too late, so to speak). The result is lack of clarity of text and unclear words.

Another factor in my never-ending battle for fidelity and intelligibility involves time travel. Often, due to system components alignment differences or electronic errors, low frequencies and high frequencies reach the ear at different times, and the brain "skips a beat" as it interprets the two different waveforms and "sews" them back together again. While this transaction takes place, *the ear stops listening* to new sounds. When five voices are singing, the translation is exponentially more difficult and longer, the group and the audience are struggling to hear, and much information is lost. Turning the monitors or sound system up will *not* solve this problem. Instead, the speaker components must be synched or "put in phase"—by reversing the wires at the terminals of the speakers, electronically changing the phase of the signals going into the amps, or by physically realigning the speakers in

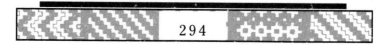

relationship to each other. Much of my Sweet Honey setup time is spent resolving or minimizing these problems.

To me, a speaker cabinet is a drum, the speaker cone is the head or skin, and the electronic impulse moving the speaker is the hand striking the drum. Technicians tend to mystify speakers, but *anyone* can tell if a drum is good. Most speaker cabinets are obviously *poor* drums and need retuning to restore an even, linear bass response. Most have a large boost in the *upper* bass frequencies with little usable response below. This means that bass singers will have trouble hearing pitch and placement in the "muddy" chords and even on middle register singing there will be a companion "ghost" bass note masking the true pitch. This can be alleviated on-site by retuning the cabinet by blocking at least one-half the "port" or air vent (the hole in the cabinet or drum which lets air out) with tape, cloth, wood, or foam. For a typical monitor cabinet of 2.5 cubic feet internal volume, I find that a port (air hole) about 3 inches in diameter and 3 inches deep into the cabinet (measured from the front of the baffle board) works well. After retuning in this fashion, bass and low bass notes will have pitch value and the bass drivers can respond faster, tracking the highs closer on dynamic passages. These phase and tuning tips, of course, hold true for the house main speakers as well as monitor speakers.

A good one-third octave equalizer is a painter's palette of the sound engineer. It offers three filters (tone controls) for each of the ten musical octaves, or thirty filters in all. The musical shape or width of these filters (how many notes they affect) and how they interact determines the unit's ability to create a 3-D sonic image at the listener's ear. Careful usage can help overcome poor room acoustics, poor speaker placement, and, in some cases, poorly designed or tuned systems. *It will not solve any of these problems,* but it can help. Use of the equalizer filters affects the phase problems discussed earlier.

Mikes are the paintbrushes. Your brush must be clean, "fine" enough so the brush strokes don't distract from the work and of good enough quality so as not to shed bristles in the paint.

Most of the mikes I like and respect have been marketed virtually unchanged for fifteen years. (Is this a recurring theme of "older is better"? Yes.) These oldie-but-goodie vocal mikes include the Sennheiser MD441, MD421, EV RE20, and BEYER M69 and M88.

I use BEYER M500 ribbon mikes for Sweet Honey on the road. These are my absolute favorite vocal mikes for singers who are not afraid; they reproduce vocal truth and many singers are not ready for this. The low-mass ribbon diaphragm element in the M500 can respond faster than an expensive studio condenser mike and offers smoothness through the vocal range (no peaks) and a very gentle proximity effect (added bass as you work the mike closer). However, they are very fragile, and expensive to fix. Keeping them in repair is a substantial expense and I've learned to travel with two extras.

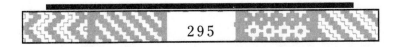

As for mixers, use your ears, not your eyes; bigger and more complicated is not better; the simpler and shorter the electronic path, the more "gain" and better sound for a cappella use. Every equalizer and auxiliary control on a large console mixer degrades the overall sonics, increases the noise level, and decreases the amount of sound possible before feedback. As in most of life, simpler is cleaner, better, and more effective. With complexity and added features also come serious sonic drawbacks and compromises. Beware, brother/sister, beware.

The quality of the mixer mike preamps is critical for vocal reinforcement. I often set the preamp input controls around "two o'clock." A cappella groups with the dynamic versatility of Sweet Honey require low noise with high gain levels (–60Db) for quiet passages and the ability to pass +20Db (on loud passages). This is a challenge for studio preamps costing hundreds of dollars, yet the preamps in most PA boards cost $10! For a year I traveled and mixed Sweet Honey on individual studio mike preamps which had been summed together, until I discovered two years ago the SONOSAX SX-6 (Swiss) mixer. It gave me excellent mike preamps, good channel EQ, individual limiters, and a very portable size. It's been my constant road companion ever since.

SWEET HONEY IS A TEAM

Sweet Honey is a team, and in many ways for me, it is a family that works to the highest standards and therefore allows massive opportunities for personal growth.

If there is an underlying commonality among the diversity of the Sweet Honey touring group, it is pride. No need for pep talks, mind games, or psych jobs, an objective is placed in the path of the team and it is leveled.

And they are generous—Nitanju and Aisha are in great part responsible for me starting my running regime. Also I've changed my diet after seeing them *cope* with the contradiction of finding good and "whole" foods on the road. Nitanju is a rock-steady humorous team partner. Aisha is a "wild child" who often sparks situations to new and exciting levels. Ysaye is my most frequent dinner/breakfast/shopping companion on the road. Her perceptions and technical bent often reflect my own and she's a welcome ear to share with.

Bernice and I don't talk as often as I would like, but when we do the thoughts and concepts fly fast and furious. I feel we draw things from each other. She is a voracious reader, as am I, and on tours when I travel with twenty to thirty books (the "road library") she is the most frequent borrower.

I am a highly motivated individual who expects credit for good work and original thoughts, I also take responsibility for failure. Many people are content to coast through life, "going with the flow." I don't mind crashing into a tree or two in my travels through life so long as it's my hands at the wheel directing my progress.

Often innovative thought and clues to right actions can be found lying on either side of the tree you crash into when you fail. Many people would give the tree a wide, cautious berth and so miss those treasures in the shadows. My personal motto is: "Who dares, wins."

In 1978, I crashed into Sweet Honey, and I have been exploring the treasures in the shadows ever since. I have become the person I am today: motivated, challenged, and privileged to be sharing space with these gifted Black women friends.

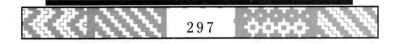

23

NOURISHMENT FOR THE SOUL

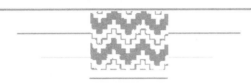

HENRI E. NORRIS

My involvement with Sweet Honey In The Rock has been described as an obsession by some, as an "adoring groupie" by others. But for those who know me best, it represents nothing less than active appreciation of a world treasure.

My active appreciation has included flights from St. Croix, Virgin Islands, where I lived for two years, to New York State, California, and Washington, D.C., to attend concerts. I've attended every concert I could. The commemorative poster of their 1984 University of California at Irvine concert hangs on the same wall as Nelson Mandela in my law office.

Sweet Honey In The Rock feeds and nourishes me to such a degree that I frequently attend all four concerts in an anniversary concert series. Sweet Honey has never bored me. I have always learned and been inspired to challenge myself even more because of the awesome creativity with which Sweet Honey speaks the truths of the day. The nourishment I receive sharing their space results in those trips and repeated concert attendance, which took place over the past eighteen years. They feed me!

I met Bernice Johnson Reagon while we were students at Spelman College in Atlanta. In 1968 we attended Stephen Henderson's class in Black literature at the Institute of the Black World. My political education grew tremendously through my exposure to Bernice, a courageous woman who, as an original Freedom Singer,

risked her life on the front lines of the battle to liberate our people. Bernice shared a wealth of experiences that helped shape my political thought and expanded my quest for justice against all oppression.

Of their early concerts, I remember best the concert at Crampton Auditorium at Howard University in the fall of 1979. During this time I was struggling with being actively involved in feminist organizing and finding the need to participate in forming Black caucuses in order to function within larger organizations like NOW. That night, Sweet Honey electrified the audience with political songs that touched my spirit. The women with whom I attended the concert retained a glow of pride and inspiration for weeks. Those incredibly talented Black women were our sisters. They were performing for us. They forced us to think about and challenge the status quo. They kept us honest. They made it easier for us to become a part of the solution and not the problem in our fight for freedom for all peoples. They spoke to us as Black women, not just as Black people. They honored those heroines who came before us and laid ground upon which we could build.

That evening was special also because it gave me the chance to give back to the group; I participated in it behind a camera. The concert was videotaped by my video production company, TransCultural Communications, Inc. In order for Sweet Honey to qualify to be showcased at the National Entertainment and Campus Activity Association (NECAA) convention, they were required to submit a videotape of their work. Our team of video editors (mostly me) worked with Bernice to put together a product which succeeded in getting them a showcase. This was significant because it provided them access to broader college markets and gave their college supporters more access to college funding. Thus their word spread. Word of mouth is still the main form of advertisement to promote this truthful treasure. So spread the word!!!!

I am honored to be a member of their extended family. Sweet Honey In The Rock is a Black institution which we must cherish, support, and share with the peoples of the world. Their work has always stood for the belief that none of us are free until all of us are free!

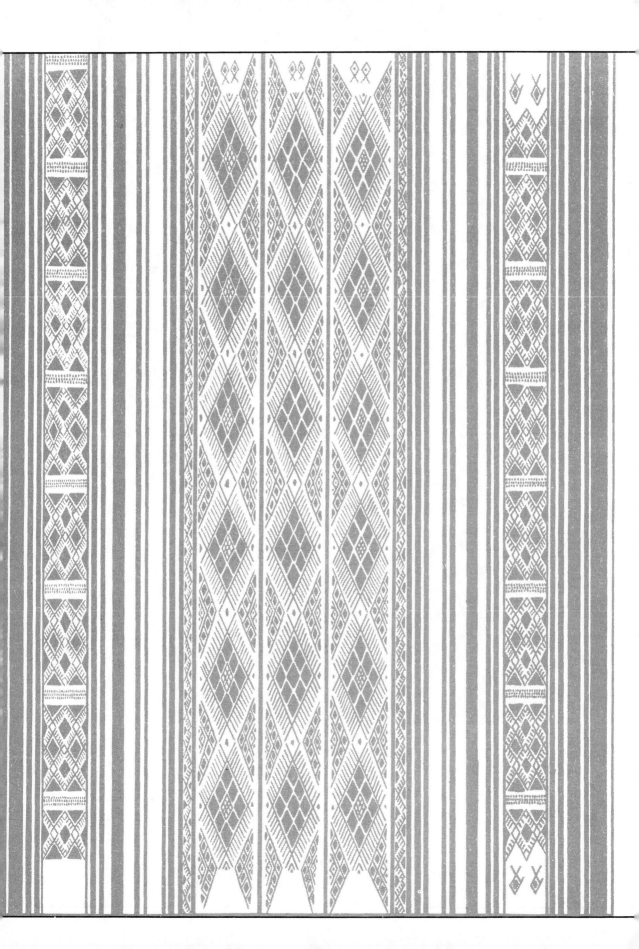

SCHEDULE OF CLASSES

WINTER 1978

INSTITUTE FOR CONTEMPORARY DANCE

TOP: AISHA KAHLIL—DANCE MASTER. (PHOTO COURTESY OF AISHA KAHLIL PERSONAL COLLECTION)

BOTTOM LEFT: MARVA JOHNSON (AISHA) IN THE EAST HIGH MADRIGAL GROUP WITH MR. HILLIARD. (PHOTO COURTESY OF AISHA KAHLIL PERSONAL COLLECTION)

BOTTOM RIGHT: SISTERS: (L) CLARICE (NITANJU AND (R) MARVA (AISHA) JOHNSON. (PHOTO COURTESY OF NITANJU BOLADE CASEL PERSONAL COLLECTION)

24

EVERYTHING WAS ARTS FOR ME

AISHA KAHLIL

I don't remember years. I remember I joined Sweet Honey In The Rock in 1981, but if you ask me about events or concert dates, I don't remember. I was very good in history, but I only remembered dates because I would study them. If I calculate it, I can tell you what year I graduated from high school. I remember my birth date, but the year I was married I would have to calculate. My life does not work very well with a calendar. I don't remember when, I remember what and how. I do have a good memory. Things exist in my mind as an unfolding, one thing happens and another thing happens. Things are in order, but not in calendar time measurements. I remember seasons, whether it was hot or cold, comfortable or uncomfortable, summer or winter.

Smells. The sweet delight of honeysuckle in early summer or the rich scent of earth and rain in deep summer. Smells and colors and feelings, unfolding like a vignette or bursting forth like an episode. These are things I remember, not years, or dates.

I was born in Buffalo, New York, in a hospital. That's what I am told, although my father, Stephen Coolidge Johnson, would constantly refute this. He would always tell me that I was not born; that I came here like him, on a beam from our home planet, Echo X. This story thrilled and delighted me, and I would ask him if my sister Nitanju, had also come in this way. He said, much to my mother's chagrin, that she was hatched from an egg. This story would not diminish as we

grew older, but, like us, it also grew and took on various dimensions. If Daddy was watching the news or reading the paper and some crisis was being reported, he would exclaim, "It's time to go home! I'm going to call my people and we'll all go back home to planet Echo X!" Even though I knew this story wasn't true, I found myself almost wishing it was, and believing in it a little, especially when I was very small, because it was a good explanation of why I seemed so different from my peers. I spent a lot of time reading, learning poetry and plays and rehearsing them, or I'd go in the closet to sing by myself for hours. I loved nature and the woods and would go off into the forest and wander by myself. I had few friends and was always a loner, especially in my younger years. "That's why I can't relate to them," I would proclaim to myself. "I'm from Echo X and one day I'm going back there!"

One of my earliest memories is that of flying. My sister and I used to share the same room and our two cribs were there. I would look over at Nitanju sleeping, and I would put my hands on the bars of the crib and start rocking back and forth and back and forth for I don't know how long, until it seemed I would go into a kind of trance. Then I would shoot out my arms and I would be flying, flying, up to the ceiling. Then I would be just floating there, and I would look down at my sister sleeping in her crib and I would look down at myself, standing there at the edge of my crib with my arms stretched out to me.

Another early memory was feeling frustration when my mother, Mary Magdelene Johnson, and her sister, Lucille Herring, would talk to me in baby gibberish. I understood what they were saying in English and wanted them to speak to me in "real talk," but I could not talk and explain this to them. It was intensely frustrating.

My memories of being into performance and theater are vivid. I remember from the second and third grade gravitating toward the stage. It was fascinating for me, a whole new world of possibilities. I especially loved going backstage, behind the rows of curtains. I would sneak into the auditorium between toilet and water breaks, go backstage and just be there, dreaming, for as long as I could. I began to see stories as plays. I would take a story and its characters and turn it into a play and make up what was said. The first one I did was a story about a princess and a butter churn. I turned it into a play and wrote down the lines and I persuaded my sister to play the maid with the churn and I played the princess. When we had it ready we performed it for my mother and father and then they brought their friends over and we performed it for them.

I was always the leader, the director. I would make up the play, the costumes, then convince my sister and friends to practice. Often they would get tired of practicing and would want to go outside and play, but I was adamant. Our shows were real events. We would do shows for birthdays, anniversaries, and holidays. My parents would have friends over for drinks and to see the show. One of my mother's best friends, Mr. Caldwell, who lived across the street, would always come; he used to call me his "Broadway star." He always made me feel that I could

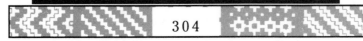

make it in theater from the time I was small till the time he died, by which time I was living in New York and performing Off Broadway. He was a dear and special man.

We attended the United Christ Church of Disciples. It was a family church. My uncle was the minister, my father and uncles were the deacons. There were always plays and presentations at Christmas and Easter. Every Christmas, it seemed, I would play the Virgin Mother, Mary. I loved the stage and becoming different characters.

My sister and I both sang in the choir and at times my mother would encourage us to do one of the duets we were constantly practicing around the house. I always loved to perform, no matter what the venue, although Nitanju was sometimes a little reluctant. I learned "The Creation" from *God's Trombones* by James Weldon Johnson, a work that was always in demand by the church congregation. I loved doing it each time, perfecting it, going deeper into the nuances of vocal inflection, commanding a response from the congregation.

In junior high school, I represented my school in the citywide Girls Declaration Contest by performing Ophelia's mad scene from *Hamlet.* I got through all the preliminaries and I was at the citywide finals, when I noticed this sister from another school. She was short, and dark-skinned, and she was too powerful! I knew she was going to be my main competition. She did the same James Weldon Johnson piece that I'd performed in church and she did it in a preaching style. When she spoke, the timbre of her voice shook the floor. Man, she was bad. When all the contestants had finished, I felt in my mind that we were the strongest. Then it came time to announce who won. First they called up the second-place winner, me, and I was sure she was first. But then they called the first-place winner and it was this White girl. She had had no kind of presence or feeling in her presentation at all! The judges picked her and I was devastated. I felt the tears begin, clouding my vision. Something hit me right then about how things could be, about how things were, and in that moment, everything changed for me. I walked off the stage numb. My eyes searched for, and found, the eyes of that sister and saw the hurt, confusion, shock. Then I went to my mother, who was waiting in the audience. I shared with her the pain she felt for me, and for herself, and for everyone who is Black, who must learn this lesson one day—young or old—of what it is to be Black and what it means to be Black in a White world. She hugged me, and as we turned to go, a White man, a teacher from another school, came up and said he wanted to talk to me. He took me aside and gave me a big hug and told me I had given a brilliant performance. He told me to never stop trying, that I could be a fine actress if I wanted to be, that I could go as far as I wanted to go, and that nothing should stop me, because what happened that day was not right.

Although I was greatly shaken by this event, I did go on. Next, I auditioned for and won a scholarship to the drama school of the Studio Arena Theater of Buffalo. Again, I did the monologue from *Hamlet.* After the competition, the offi-

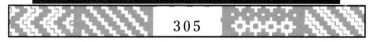

cials took me backstage and told me I was the only one in the history of the school ever to win a unanimous decision by the judges. This gave me a great deal of needed confidence. My father had come with me this time, and he was proud and happy. Twice a week I attended drama classes after school; we had acting, scene study and stage movement, and speech for the theater.

When I finished junior high school, I was offered a scholarship to go to the Park School, a predominantly White private school out in the far suburbs. The principal of my junior high school advised me not to go to that school. He said he thought I would be better off at East High, a Black school right there in the inner city. My parents didn't know what to do—on the one hand, they felt he might be racist and was trying to hold me back; on the other hand, they wondered what effect it would have on me to be isolated so far away, among Whites. They felt that sending me to the Park School would encourage me in the field of medicine, since I always had an avid interest in science, health, and the human body. I went to East High School in Buffalo. I know well now, as I didn't then, that that decision had a huge impact on the development of my life.

East High had the baddest choir in town—forty Black voices lifted in serious a cappella sound. My main ambition was to get into the choir. But I didn't audition the first year; I wanted to be ready, I was still quite shy about singing in school, around my peers. The last time I had auditioned for the school choir was in elementary school, in sixth grade, and I had been too shy to sing out, so I didn't get in. In the East High choir you had to be serious and committed, you had to have your grades up, and there was a lot required of you.

I was really into theater, so in my freshman year I auditioned and got the leading title role of Medea in a Drama Department production. This was considered quite an achievement for a freshman to be playing that part. I think the choir director became acquainted with me through that role, and it boosted my confidence, so when I auditioned for the choir the next year, I got in and I was ecstatic. When I joined the choir, I became one of the lead sopranos.

We rehearsed every morning at 7:30 for an hour and a half. Choir was a part of the curriculum every day, and there were also rehearsals after school. Mr. Hilliard, our director, was very strict, and a brilliant man. Through his work we became known as the best choir in Buffalo.

The workings of the choir became the central theme in my life. There were different branches of the choir; the large a cappella ensemble, smaller groups of madrigals, male and female ensembles, and I was singing in all of them—except the male ensemble, of course! When guest conductors would come to work with the Buffalo Philharmonic, they requested us. That way we learned what it was like to work on a professional level, and gained a lot of experience singing choir roles in *Carmen Jones, Porgy and Bess,* and *The Messiah.* We produced our own operas too, in which we got to sing the leads. I remember singing the role of Monica in *The*

Medium, by Gian-Carlo Menotti, for a WBEN-TV presentation. I was thrilled. I also sang the mother in Menotti's *Amahl and the Night Visitors.* I loved playing these operas, because it was singing and acting, costumes, scenery, lighting, movement—everything in one! This was great, I loved it, and knew even more what I wanted for my life.

In my senior year, ten of us from the choir performed at Carnegie Hall in New York, in Julius Eastman's production of *The Thruway.* This was quite a challenging experience for us, not only because of the prominence of Carnegie Hall and New York but because of the music itself. It was called avant-garde, and was something I had never heard before. It was so different—the way we were using our voices, like instruments—and the way we moved. It was like no other music I had ever heard of before and I'm not sure how much I liked it, but I loved the experience of singing it, and as I think back, I feel it opened places in my musical head for what was later to come.

Thanks to Mr. Hilliard, a whole new world was formed—opened. I think he had great hopes for me. He would coach me privately, at his home, and when it was time for me to graduate, he called me to his office and told me, in a serious tone, that I should consider music as a professional career. I was awed by his recommendation because of the deep respect I had for him, and I thought about it seriously, but in my heart, I had already made up my mind that the theater was my first love, and not the opera. I knew by then that I had to sing, but I knew it would be in a different context, for already there were other experiences shaping who I was to be.

East High also had a great band; we would sing and play together. It was directed by Mr. Ford, and was mostly composed of brothers. I was studying the flute with one of the members, but I finally had to teach myself because the brother, although extremely talented, was a dope addict, on heroin, and he missed many of the lessons. Nevertheless, I kept on and taught myself songs, mainly jazz tunes. Some of the most talented students of the band had a jazz combo and would rehearse and play professionally, and I used to hang out with them at their rehearsals. Buffalo used to be one of the jazz spots where all the major musicians would perform, and the jazz combo would get gigs as opening acts. So, although I was doing European classical music through my work with the choir, I was becoming more aware of Black artists like John Coltrane, Thelonious Monk, Yusef Lateef, and Miles Davis through my friends in the band.

My grades slipped in my senior year from the Honor Roll to the Merit Roll. No wonder, I was never there. I was always getting ready for some new show, some new production, so I didn't care, as long as I passed. I knew what I was becoming. Everything in my life revolved around the arts. I had always danced and always loved dancing. My sister and I used to have a ball whenever my mom and dad would go out to a party. We'd push back the rugs and tables; and we'd sing and dance, dance and sing, play piano and flute, and dance all over the house until we

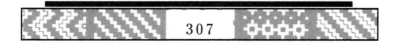

worked up a sweat. This would go on all night and we'd still be up when my parents came home about 2 or 3 A.M. I remember how much energy we had, how much energy we got from doing all that. We'd have a ball every time!

I also loved the discipline of dance, not just the social dances at parties, not just the free-form improvisations I used to make up around the house to all and any kind of music. I begged my mother for ballet lessons when I was twelve. She sacrificed, found the money from somewhere, and took me to Cora Tapson's ballet school. A little later, I studied African dance at the African Cultural Center in Buffalo with Kariamu Welsch, a great inspiration. When I was sixteen, I studied at the Ballet Center of Buffalo until I left home for college at seventeen. I loved dance, as I loved theater and music. When I was filling out my college applications, I would write in "performing arts" as a career goal, because I couldn't decide on any single endeavor, and I knew in my heart they were all equal parts of one whole.

While I was in my senior year of high school, I got to do a tour of New York with the Buffalo Black Drama Workshop. Ed Smith, the director of the workshop, was doing a production of a new play by Tony Preston called *Willus Way Is Not a Violent Man.* He came to our school looking for someone to play the part of Dottie, a twelve-year-old girl. He needed someone who looked young enough to play the part but was mature enough to go on the road for about three weeks, and who could take time out from school and studies to go on the tour. My teachers and the principal told him I was the one. I auditioned and got the role of Dottie, and I also served as assistant stage manager, so I learned quite a lot.

I vividly remember meeting Ed Smith. It was love at first sight. I mean the man was tall, jet black, and FINE. And thirty-plus years old. I knew it was hopeless. I knew it was what they call an adolescent crush. But it was my first crush, and it was real. I loved the sight of him, his smell, the timbre of his voice, his presence. I loved his knowledge of acting and of Black music and culture and history. And that awesome presence. I was in love. I was seventeen years old. It was just a crush, but it left me with a profound sense of love and respect for the man and the experience it gave me. And it was a new passage into womanhood. In many ways, that whole tour was like a rite of passage. I was in high school, I was on the road, and it was my first road experience. Hanging out with these older cats on the road—New York City, Greenwich woods—strolling after midnight, drinking wine and eating in late-night restaurants, listening to musicians, and partying, and just being with those cats made me know more about the life, the life of an artist and the sweet taste of it. I wanted more.

When the tour was over I stayed with the company through my last year of high school, studying and performing in several more productions. I stayed with them until I went away to college, and came back to them on summer breaks. They were a family to me. I learned a lot, not just about acting but about the freedom of my spirit and the beauty of my Blackness, of my nakedness, about the music, about

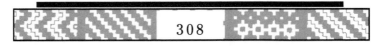

the integration of our great Black music as a liberating force from within. Trane and Pharaoh screamed louder, yet more gently. My soul exploded in outrage and swooned in understanding, as my body and mind sought expression. Leon Thomas' moans grew deeper, as the soft subtlety of those tones worked its sweet magic into the recesses of my soul. I was born again. And again. And again.

During this same year I started a small theater group in my high school. One of the productions I directed was *We Own the Night,* by Jimmy Garrett.

The play was scheduled to open the same night I was to leave town with the Drama Workshop for a one-month tour, so I was going to miss the premiere. But the play didn't go on. The principal stopped it from going on because of its content and its language; it was too political and had profanity. It addressed the inequality of the system and the racism of White people. The students rioted in protest to its cancellation. It was very hard for me to hear the news about the play and the protest and not be there in Buffalo. But at the same time I was learning so much and growing so much that I moved on.

This was also the period of the Attica prison uprising in New York and the imprisonment of Angela Davis in California. My sister had left for the South, going to college in North Carolina, and I was left as the only child at home. I became involved in the political struggle and went to the Angela Davis Defense Committee meetings. In trying to be an activist, I struggled constantly with my father. He didn't want me to go to these meetings at night, so I had to sneak out. He was very patriotic—totally into the land of the free and the home of the brave, not into the protests and the struggles. We used to have intense debates; it was not a pretty scene at that time. But it was something that I had to do, that I really had to be a part of.

At the same time students were fighting to get Black studies taught in school. We were tired of learning the White man's lies and trickery about our lives, our culture, our history. We wanted the truth, and we wanted it in abundance. We were searching. I was a seeker.

My lifestyle during this period was becoming more and more what felt like a natural style, what felt right for me as an adult learning to make her own decisions.

This questioning had begun early for me. I remember going to a predominantly White summer camp. I remember the White girls used to go swimming and let their hair just dry naturally and we always had to be so careful and wore swimming caps, afraid of our hair getting wet. Somehow something didn't seem right about that. I wondered why I should be ashamed of my hair because of the way it is? There was one sister there who let her hair just go natural. Some of my friends use to call her "nap" and that aggravated me; I really admired her.

I was the first one in my community to wear my hair natural. Many thought I was crazy. I just stopped pressing my hair. Next I stopped wearing a bra. My mother was starting to freak out, but once I explained the logic of it to her, she

acquiesced. My mom has always respected logic and good sense. Here I was, going around nappy-headed in a straight-haired world. Old folks just shook their heads, but some smiled. Young folks pointed.

While I was a senior in high school I started to change my diet; I became a vegetarian my freshman year in college. I had older friends who influenced me. One in particular, Yigal Joseph, was a teacher in my high school. He and his wife introduced me to vegetarianism, yoga, meditation, and Eastern philosophy. I began to study the books of Jung and Hesse, Gibran and Carlos Castaneda, to teach myself to meditate, and to open the doors of wonder.

I began to understand that the expression of artistic feeling could be greatly enhanced and liberated by the development of the spiritual self through these practices, and so I became quite serious about my search. All these books with their philosophies, although different on the exterior, spoke but one truth to me and that truth resonated loudly within my soul, into the center, the core of my being. "Seek ye first the kingdom of God and His righteousness, and all these things shall be added unto you."

I was also stimulated by my mother, who is very open-minded. We grew up eating a traditional Black people's diet until my mother began to study the teachings of the Black Muslims. She started bringing home their literature and the breads they made. She continued to cook pork for my father, who still wanted it, but she would not prepare it for us. I started to read their literature and became interested in the Black Muslims. What they had to say regarding diet, health, and discipline made a lot of sense to me. I began to see how so many of our people were virtually killing themselves with an attachment to greasy, non-life-giving mucus-forming foods—the legacy of slavery. These dietary practices seemed to me incompatible with the goal of spirituality. Was not the body a temple for the Divine? This truth was preached in both Muslim and Christian houses of worship. Yet how could the body be a temple if it was beset by wastes and poisons, clogged arteries, and mental and physical sluggishness from too much wrong food consumption. In this aspect, the Black Muslim path seemed superior to me.

Everything I did in regard to diet, dress, my hair, was from a freedom point of view. I had to free my own self and my own mind. It felt like a natural step for me to take; the more self-realized I became, the greater the outward manifestation and that manifestation was total liberation. I had no problem with going against the grain of Western society, because once I make up my mind that something is right for me, I just do it, that's how I have always been. My mother used to tell me often that she never worried that someone was going to influence me to do something I didn't want to do, because she always felt that if I did it, it would be something I really wanted to do.

In my senior year in high school, I applied and gained entrance to the American Academy of Dramatic Arts in New York, but all my counselors advised against that move. They thought I should attend an academic institution and get a liberal

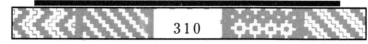

arts education, so I ended up at Northeastern University in Boston, where I majored in theater arts, and shared a dormitory room with my sister Nitanju, who was now also a student there.

Professor Kaplan, the head of the Acting Department when I got to Northeastern, was directing *The Baptism* by Amiri Baraka and I played the lead. It was a very strong role. I played an old woman whose character had a lot of sexual and religious undertones, and I gave it everything I had, and got very good reviews. Professor Kaplan encouraged me, and one reviewer for a local newspaper said that I was the only person he had seen in several productions of this play to do the role justice. I gained quite a bit of notoriety as a freshman from that play. But after *The Baptism* there were no more Black plays, and although I felt I was capable of doing the Eurocentric roles, I did not get the opportunity to participate. Several times I felt I was denied roles because I was Black. I started to stage-manage, and finally won a "thrilling" role as the dormouse in *Alice Again,* a remake of *Alice Through the Looking Glass.*

Disillusioned with Northeastern's Theater Department, I started a theater company at the Afro-American Student Center, and there I produced and directed several plays, among them *Where We At,* by Martie Charles, and Sonia Sanchez's *Sistah Sonji.* I wrote *"Om,"* an avant-garde theatrical montage of movement, and sounds. I was putting a lot more of my emphasis on directing during this period, and I was having a good time with it. But there were problems. My professors felt I was putting too much emphasis on working at the Afro-American Student Center and neglecting my work in the Theater Department. This was frustrating, to say the least. I began to wonder why I was there. The next year, I wasn't.

After I left Northeastern, I began to study music at the New England Conservatory of Music. I also got a job teaching theater at the Elma Lewis Center for the Performing Arts. At the Center I studied dance (modern, jazz, etc.) with Consuelo Atlas from the Alvin Ailey company. She was a beautiful dancer, and she inspired me greatly. I also worked in the resident mime company of the Center, directed by Fred Johnson, and he put together some really exciting works. While I was at the Conservatory, I met Lem Carroll, a brother who was exceptional. He had put together this band, Ebony Jua, and I became the vocalist. My voice flowered with that band. Free-formed African American celestial music. I began to advance, especially in terms of jazz and improvisation. I began hearing my own voice from within, as a singer.

This was a magical time for me, in terms of my vocal development; my sister and I had moved to Roxbury, and there was this really special place close to where we lived called Fort Hill. One day I climbed Fort Hill to meditate. At the end of my meditation, I began to hear this song, a beautiful, enchanting melody, and it seemed to come from inside me, and yet from around and above me simultaneously. I began to sing what I heard and the melody escalated, and became more entrancing, and I was thrilled by the wonder of it, that sound, and my voice singing it. It was

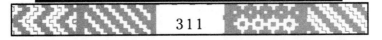

my first composition, and I still have it, although I have never performed it in public. To me it was and remains special, and was a very exciting beginning of musical awareness.

I would next begin to test this hearing, and this singing, in the context of other instruments, particularly African drums. I was very much a part of the local African cultural community and we used to get together quite often in the parks and in the streets, at different locales, and just jam all afternoon and evening. I would play percussion and dance at these events. My dancing was African-based, and free. Those jam sessions were like church, a spiritual coming together where we would praise the Most High and acknowledge and affirm our ancestors. It was not long after the experience on Fort Hill that I began to hear local melodies in the context of different rhythms; and from this base, I would begin to sing, first softly and then louder, as my courage and confidence increased. Some of the drummers and people standing around would begin to pick up the chants that I would start, and I would improvise on top of it. It was a great time of growth and freedom!

About this time, I had other experiences with racism and other prejudices. There was a group that held auditions for a singer that had gigs in hotels through-out the Boston area. I tried out—singing stuff like Tina Turner's version of "Rollin' on the River" and the Beatles' "Michelle, My Belle"—and got the slot. I was the only Black and the only woman in the band. We got a gig at this really nice hotel, a nice long run, and good money.

The first night on the gig I noticed the clientele was mostly White women. The fourth night I got a call to go to the manager's office. He told me he had been getting quite a few complaints from the clientele because I was Black and I was a woman and I was up there singing with all these White men. Plus, to make matters worse, I had natural/nappy hair and wore African-style clothing. He asked me if I would mind staying home from the gig. He said the band was really great and my singing was wonderful, but if I would stay home the band could keep the job. He was willing to pay my fee, even more if necessary, but would I please stay home. He was sorry, but that was the way it was. When I told the band, they got quite pissed, expressed their feelings to the manager, and quit that same night.

I was also dancing with a new company doing repertoire from West Africa, called Alldjenah, which means paradise. I learned that rejection could also come from within the group. Alldjenah was directed by Mountaga Sam, who seemed really uptight. He wouldn't let me dance in the front line during a performance, because, he said, I was "too skinny, don't look good—the costume." Hey, I was insulted. I knew I was thin, but I was also a bundle of African energy on the floor. So I took my energy and left the troupe.

At this time, I met Halifu, who was to become my mentor for many years. I knew from the first time I saw her dance that I would study with her. She was doing this dance piece with Stan Strickland, Bill Macke, and a host of other creative musicians and drummers, and it was wonderful! I had never *seen* anyone else dance

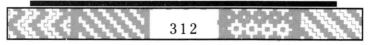

like that, but I had *felt* my spirit dance like that. So much energy, a movement explosion! It was as if she had actually *become* the music! Totally transcendental. I knew in my heart I had to be with her.

So I left Boston and moved to Oakland, California, to study with her company. Halifu became like a sister to me, and I have always loved her for the beauty of her spirit. I also started teaching on my own and cultivated a large following. I was developing my own teaching style, a synthesis of yoga, African dance, and aerobics—a movement that emanated from the center. I called it "a rhythm-yoga movement experience," and later "organic movement in African American dance." It was a great way to teach people, especially White people, many of whom had little sense of the African approach to rhythm, who flocked to my classes. I learned a lot about how to teach this from Halifu. She made a serious impact on me.

Being in California was quite a liberating experience, far-out and free. Sometimes a little too far-out. At times I longed for the stability of the East Coast. Then I heard Infinite Sound, Roland Young on horns and Glen Howell on bass. Their music was great—mostly free-formed improvisation which was very tight, rhythmic —and interesting. As soon as they finished playing, I knew I was going to sing with them, I could hear my voice with their music, so I went backstage and introduced myself. With Halifu's recommendation, I got an audition and became the third member—voice and percussion. It was the Cecil Taylor, Anthony Braxton, Chicago Art Ensemble school of music, and more. And less. We made a recording on Arch Street Records, entitled *Infinite Sound*.

California was a busy time. But it came time to move on—out of the Bay Area and back to the East Coast. I went back to Boston, and began teaching dance at the Joy of Movement Center at the Institute for Contemporary Dance, and at Leslie College. I began choreographing. Then I began performing with Stan Strickland and his band, Sundance. This repertoire featured many jazz standards. I learned how to control my voice to scat; I could use a great deal of the freedom I had gained working with Infinite Sound, but put it in a more contextual jazz base. There were also numerous original tunes, and a great degree of first world (African and other Eastern cultures) influence. We would often open a set with tambora (an East Indian stringed instrument, which I would play), flutes, percussion, then we would move into bass, drums, piano, and horn. We would never have a set list, but moved organically from one piece to the next, the band was so in tune. It was a hot ensemble. We had a great deal of work at various clubs and concerts. I was free to dance, and take the improvisation out as far as I wanted, and Stan was always right there with me with the horn.

I went to hear Abdullah Ibrahim (Dollar Brand) and my friend Adrienne had the band over for dinner and that's where I met my future husband, Talib. We started talking and right away discovered that we had many things in common, one of them being the music; we shared a love for our vegetarian diet, our love of things spiritual. We shared the desire to express that spirituality in terms of a creative,

313

artistic, and holistic lifestyle. Talib impressed me greatly because of his energy, his sincerity, his understanding and his righteous pursuit of the Most High, which at that time took the form of Islam. We had long talks about music, the Koran, nature —everything.

He came and heard me singing with Stan, got really excited, and invited me to do gigs in New York. From this we became even closer. We would make salat (prayer) together, go for long walks in the park and play flute and hand pianos (mbiras) together, transcending time and space. We began to envision together the potential beauty of a lifestyle lived in peace, harmony, spiritual accord, and total creativity. I moved to New York and we became husband and wife.

We were married by Abdullah Ibrahim, who performed the Islamic part of the ceremony, and Obara Wali, who performed the African traditional part—thereby uniting the best of our spiritual worlds. Abdullah Ibrahim was also our imam (spiritual leader), and it was from him that we learned more about the Sufi (mystical) branch of Islam. He had a jamaa (family) that was mostly comprised of other musicians. We would meet every Friday and read the Koran, hadith, and make dhikr (chanting the attributes of God). This was intense and rewarding, opening me up spiritually. It seemed to me that Sufism was the perfect form of Islam for the artist, in that it reached beyond convention and cultural imperialism to reveal the heart, the source, the center. Abdullah Ibrahim's music seemed greatly influenced by this religion; it was beyond beautiful. His wife, Sathima, was also a role model for me.

Talib is a musical genius; his sense of chords comes from a different place, an ancient place. We used to be up all night; he would play the piano and I would sing. He had his own group, and continued to work with Abdullah Ibrahim, while I sang and studied dance. I was studying with some of the greatest dancers at that time and I was really happy because I was really doing what I wanted to do. I studied ballet with Emiko and Yasuko Tokunaga, jazz dance with Fred Benjamin and Pepsi Bethel, West African dance with the International African American Ballet, who were the baddest people in African dance then and I started to work with Tito Sampa's company doing Congolese dance. I was primarily known in New York as a dancer. I was making a living teaching dance in elementary school and at the Henry Street Settlement for the Arts, and singing in the band with my husband.

I got a job at the Public Theater as a singer, but I had to also act and move. I got my Equity card. I got good reviews for my first show, *The Haggadah,* by Liz Swados. One of my best friends, at the time, Keith David, introduced me to agents who wanted to represent me, but at that point something broke in me and I realized I didn't want to be in the New York scene anymore. In a way it seemed like that would have been the prime opportunity for anyone—to be in theater in New York. I, however, turned them down and said no. I was tired of the whole theater environment—the cattle-call auditions with hundreds of dancers drinking coffee and nervously smoking cigarettes, the shows which seemed to express nothing *I*

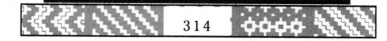

really cared about and which were not a part of me. This scene appeared harsh, abrasive, insensitive, and superficial, and I wanted out. I had set my feet on another path, a path that came from the heart, and I could not turn back. It seemed to me that theater, and art for art's sake, could not be for me in this lifetime. Creatively, I had to involve my total being on a much deeper level, in a manner that would reflect and embody my beliefs, my culture, religion—my very sense of living in the world. I realized that whatever I expressed as an artist had to come from inside me; it could not be a separate thing. My religious views had begun to evolve from Islam to ancient African (Khemetin) religion and philosophy. With all my being, I began to reach for the center, the core of my being, through prayer, much fasting, and a strict regime of discipline.

My best friend at the time, Anedra Shockley, was living with us and we would inspire each other on this path. We were preparing ourselves to become priestesses of the Most High. We would rise before dawn, and make ablutions, meditate, and pray. We would pray to the Most High and to the ancestors, fervently, joyfully, and things began to manifest.

It was around this time that we met Ankh Ra Semaj, a master jeweler and cultural historian and musician, specializing in the jewelry, history, and music of our ancient Khemetin (Egyptian) ancestors. He joined our ranks, and with great zeal we began to work together tirelessly to produce the show *Two Thousand Seasons—From Nile to Now* by Ayi Kwei Armah, which we performed throughout New York and in Washington, D.C. The production of this piece was more than a play for us. It was a way of life which absorbed our every breath, our total commitment—and our total search for union with the Most High.

I felt that everything I did had to come from my heart. It could not come just from what other people wanted me to do. It had to come from something I wanted to say, spiritually, and based on who I was as an African American person.

I joined Sweet Honey in 1981. Late summer. I had just come to D.C. to work with Brother Ah and the Sounds of Awareness, a band that was doing a tour to Europe and Africa. I had been living in Brooklyn, for a couple years, living the dance/music/married/religious/cultural life of the African American experience when I got the call. "Hey, Aisha, come on down to D.C. We've got a long tour lined up—Africa, Europe, the works!" Well, of course, I came. Left New York, husband, and everything, and came on down to D.C. and started rehearsing with the band.

. . . Loved it. So many trees—and Black folks—everywhere. Rock Creek Park was my favorite. Besides the music, Rock Creek Park was a big draw. If it wasn't the music from rehearsal in my ears, it was the music of the trees, or of the creek as it danced its way through one of the most beautiful parks I had been in—for a city, that is. Rock Creek Park. Lord, if I didn't run through that park! And Lord, if that park didn't run through me! A veritable wonderland of dreams, visions, and spirit, of quiet beauty, of subtle charm, of perfect ambience, of déjà vu. . . .

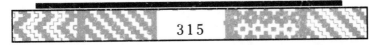

I loved the feeling of running through those trails. I had winged feet (Hermes didn't have nothin' on me), my breath falling and rising and falling to the steady cadence of Wolof mandiaani, or of sabar, or just a momentary rhythmic improvisation was played out by the syncopation of heartbeat, footfall, and breath. Breath. Running. Running. Never tired! Mesmerized by beauty, entranced by beauty, by the wonder of the perfect beauty of God's creation. And then to sit on a rock by the creek and listen, and meditate, close to the bosom of the mother, close to the heart of Allah.

The zoo was pretty hip too. When I first moved to D.C., I lived near the Washington Zoo, with some friends of my husband, Fred and Gloria Foss. I used to go running there at dusk. In Native American religion, in the medicine wheel, it is said that early dusk—that time of setting sun—is my power time, and I have always felt this to be so. Also, there were so few people there. And a great quietness would come upon the place and the animals would be more relaxed and open. I would spend big time with the wolves, who traveled in a pack, and would come near to the edge of their territory and stare into me. And I would stare into them, and together we would stand there, with no break in silence, our souls communicating through time. And I would think about the Native American and about how much of that blood runs in my veins, and of how much their spirits still occupy this land —so much of which was taken from them.

And then I would go and visit Najee—the black panther. And he would come close to the bars and gaze into me and I into him, and our silence would be unbroken. And I would be filled with the vision, the strength, and the beauty of my blackness, of my African ancestors. And I would drink from this vision my strength, my beauty, and my purpose. And then I would see the giraffe, one of the most graceful creatures on God's earth! How often would I delight in the mystic perfection of her dance. Watching her taught me more about movement than many dance instructors I have known. Then off I would run to see the gazelles, and I was in tune with the spirit of Tuareg, and of Fulani, whose blood runs so deep within me.

Then there was the creating music. Brother Ah. I had met Ah quite a few years before, back in Boston when I was with Stan Strickland and Sundance. For an older brother, he was one of the hippest cats I had met in my life. He must have been about twenty-some years older than me, but he had dreadlocks, and a consciousness to go with them. Far-out. Free. He told me of his days playing with Sun Ra and his Solar Arkstra, and I was really impressed. (I was later to perform with Sun Ra as a dancer.) He told me of his travels in Africa, in Kenya, and beyond, of playing flute for the monkeys in the Kenyan forest while they listened, entranced. I was entranced. His spirit spoke to me and I answered. I saw him as a benevolent father energy. He saw the boundlessness of my spirit, and encouraged me as an artist. He respected me as a musician, as a dancer, percussionist, singer, flutist. Artist. Spirit energy unleashed upon the world. To me Ah was freedom, in the greatest sense that an artist needs—permission to let go and be all that you are in

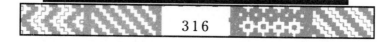

the moment of creative expression. And I loved him for it. And I loved the music of that band. It was the sound of the earth, of nature, of the sun and stars. It was dance. Dance all the way through rehearsal on a Wednesday night or a Sunday afternoon. Dance with your feet and your heart and your limbs stretching, dance with your voice and with your song. Dance with the rhythm of your life. Dance all the way home through the tree-laden, brownstone-lined, lamplit streets of D.C. on a hot summer night, with the sweat still glistening on your skin, and the melody of that dance still ringing in your soul. Life was a song.

. . . That song quickly changed to the blues, though, when I got another call. "Oh, Aisha, I'm very sorry. The tour has fallen through. Sorry." That's it. No Africa. No Europe. No tour. No gig. No money. *No money?* So what was I going to do now? I had left everything. Didn't even squabble with my husband for the TV and came to D.C. to be gainfully employed and now—no employment. Things were getting thin where I had been staying, and I needed to find a home of my own. A gig and a home.

An interesting challenge. But I was young, and I believed that life was a song; a continuous energy flow—things would work out. I would make them work out. I had no skills, other than those of a performing artist, and since I had left my native home of Buffalo, New York, I had always earned my living as an artist. But this time, things were going to have to be different. I needed cash immediately. The thought never occurred to me to return to New York, because by this time I was in love with D.C. So I would have to do something—and quick. Plus, whatever I did would have to be in tune with my karma—my cosmic vocation—and aid in my progression toward the Most High. So with that in mind, and with my best rags on, I left Fred and Gloria's house one bright sunny afternoon and headed down Eighteenth Street in search of a gig. I don't know what I thought I was looking for. Anything I could do, I guess. But as I was walking down Eighteenth Street I saw this sign in the window of the Kalorama Cafe: HELP WANTED. I went in, and came out gainfully employed as a kitchen assistant and a bus person putting silver and napkins on the tables and picking up dishes. I felt cool about it because it was a health food/vegetarian restaurant, so it fit in with my lifestyle. Besides, I could get food there.

About a week later, I got a gig at the D.C. Black Repertory Theater, teaching dance and vocal workshops. Life was great. It was summertime in D.C., in Rock Creek Park, and the zoo with its panther and the wolves. And my new home. A good friend of mine, Ameil Walker, recommended me to the members of the group house she was staying in. It was a beautiful home. Called Ananda Shanti. It was a spiritual abode housing a group of Black folks who were striving toward spiritual, physical, and mental balance through various disciplines—particularly Eastern-influenced disciplines—which included fasting, vegetarian diet, martial arts, and such. A great house, nice yard and trees, and a real peaceful, growing atmosphere for the most part. I was too thrilled. I gave thanks to the Most High. This was the

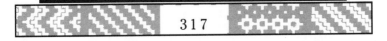

perfect space for me to be in. I could run down to Rock Creek Park in about five minutes. Life was great. Then I met Rip.

Rip was the dog of the house. He was beautiful to me. Part collie and part akita. Rip and I became fast friends. You might say it was love at first sight. He would run down to the park with me and stay all morning, running through the trails, and waiting patiently while I practiced my Tai Chi and Kung Fu. He was a real intelligent, independent kind of dog. The winos across the street used to call him the Hustler. They loved him too, and respected his personality. And how I loved Rip. How we loved each other. Aisha and Rip. Tim and Lassie didn't have nothin' on us!

I got another job teaching African-style aerobics at the Shaolin Martial Arts Academy on Georgia Avenue. I wanted to continue martial arts because I had studied Capoeira (a Brazilian martial art) in New York. As much as I loved to roam the woods, I needed to know a form of self-defense that would also boost my spiritual and physical discipline. So I studied Wu Shu and Tai Chi. I practiced, and ran through the woods with Rip, taught African aerobics, taught dance and vocal workshops at the Rep, and grubbed and bused tables at the Kalorama Cafe. It was summer. Life was great.

One afternoon (I think it was a Sunday brunch), I was busing tables down at the Kalorama Cafe, when I met this woman. I had been working there for about two or three weeks, and this light-skinned Black woman with hazel eyes and a distinctive appearance came in. She was interesting to me, so we struck up a conversation. I told her my name, and for some reason she asked me if I was a singer. "Yes," I said. She said her name was Evelyn Harris and she sang with an a cappella group called Sweet Honey In The Rock. She asked if I knew who they were, and said that they were looking for a fifth member to join their group, and would I like to audition? I thought about it—it sounded like a great opportunity. Sweet Honey In The Rock. I had heard them before and had attended one of their concerts when I was living in Boston. They were an interesting group, and they sang good music. The main things that stood out in my mind about them were that they were all Black women, sang a cappella, and I remembered how emotionally open they were during their concert. One singer, I believe it was Evelyn, cried during one of the songs, and the other singers comforted her. It was real, and one of the most unique things I had seen yet on the stage. I wanted to audition for this group. I said, "Yeah." I bused Evelyn's table. I finished up at the Cafe. Left and went home, excited at the prospect of the audition.

Monday afternoon/evening, 6 P.M. The audition. I still remember it. Kennedy Street, upper N.W., at the home of the group's leader, Bernice Johnson Reagon. Early evening shade of the summer. Row house back.

I forget who let me in but I recall checking out the array of Black women in the living room, in a circle. Evelyn welcomes me. The air seems relaxed and familiar, yet pensive in some way. I meet Ysaye. Eeesay. An interesting name. I meet

Yasmeen, who wears a Betty Boop T-shirt, and does look astoundingly like a Black version of the cartoon character. I meet other women who were also there for the audition. Then Bernice enters, and Evelyn introduces me. Bernice seems stern and down-to-business, somewhat severe. She bids me take a seat in the circle, and begins the singing process. We are doing some vocal warm-ups. Then we are singing and harmonizing together. I was no stranger to a cappella vocalizing, having sung in the choir in high school, but I had not experienced this type of singing for quite some time. Not only had I been singing with bands for the past seven years, but I had been singing jazz/free-form/avant-garde music. This music was heavy, down-to-earth, and earthy. It reminded me of the way the old people sang back in my church. We sang and harmonized for a good while together, and then Bernice asked us to sing something on our own. I forgot what I sang exactly, but I think it was something from the Doug and Jean Carn repertoire. My voice seemed wrong for this group. My voice, my style, everything seemed not to fit. . . . But the next thing you know, I was singing with the group.

When I attended that first Sweet Honey session, I had been many places and most of them had music and dance and acting together. I didn't decide to be in Sweet Honey, it was the next thing that came up. I found myself in the group initially wondering what was I doing there, especially when I got on the stage and people weren't even moving or anything, just sitting in chairs. I was not at all sure why I was in this group.

Bernice says that from the first day she thought that I would be in the group, but she had no idea why; she thought I was sent, and Sweet Honey was to be obedient. Singing in the group was a real challenge for me. I found that Sweet Honey required a certain sound, and wanted me to blend into that sound. I managed being in the group by just doing that, giving her what she asked of me. Once Sweet Honey made it clear that they wanted me to be in the group, and they thought that my voice could fit in, I also found that a part of me *was* that sound, that I could find myself in that space and could move with it.

I was introduced to blues in this group, and found that I understood the feelings beneath that repertoire created to circle and lance boils created by life's struggle and pain. I now carry the lead for most of the group's repertoire for blues.

My time with Sweet Honey has definitely been and continues to be a major test and an instrument for my journey. Maybe I have been sent back to learn the grounding that comes from singing the blues before truly being able to create and sustain the Music of the Spheres.

I taught the group the song "Meyango" and developed a vocal choral interpretation with "Mandiacappella." This is based on the Mandiani rhythm of Senegal. Performed with dance and singing, this piece was featured on the 1983 Sweet Honey recording *We All . . . Everyone of us.*

When Sweet Honey did a collaboration with the Dayton Contemporary Dance Company, Mike Malone was selected as the choreographer. Bernice sent him the

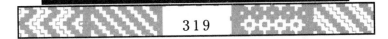

group's recordings and he selected several pieces to build the score for the suite. Included was my arrangement "Meyango" and "Mandiacappella" as well as several songs I led, "When I Die Tomorrow" and "Feel Something Drawing Me On," a gospel composition by William Herbert Brewster, the title song of Sweet Honey's album of sacred songs.

I find the most artistic satisfaction when I can balance what I get from and give to Sweet Honey with other dimensions of my talents. This is also true of other members of the group, especially Bernice, who has her own work with film and video, and as a soloist and scholar; and Ysaye, who has developed a network of choral workshops with another colleague, as well as several new ventures creating music for new works in dance choreography. We all find that Sweet Honey In The Rock is *one* of the important things we try to offer to the world.

With my sister, Nitanju Bolade Casel, I organized a production company, First World Productions, which houses the Fulani performance ensemble and First World Theater, which features lecture demonstrations and educational theater. It was while working on a performance production for Fulani that I wrote the composition "Fulani Chant." I heard that piece within as an ancestral energy creating a meditation. I called it "Fulani Chant" because it is the ancient Fulani who as a people and a culture call to me as one of them. We opened the performance with it. Later I brought it to Sweet Honey and we began to perform it. We recorded it for our first record on the Earthbeat label and yet in performance, as with all jazz-based compositions, I continue to look for the piece, working with it to let my inner voice find its way.

Sweet Honey concerts are complex, they are actually conversations, and therefore we perform with a consciousness of the experience and exchange with the audience. Sometimes I am hesitant to explore ranges of sounds that might be harsh or irritable, although my experience tells me that sometimes it takes making those sounds to get to another stage. When I listen to Trane, sometimes the sounds he makes on his horn, it sounds like he's dying or something and then he follows with a sequence that seems like something straight from heaven. It's like he goes through a phrase where he's climbing up a mountain—climbing, climbing—and all of a sudden he just soars. . . . It feels as if he had to go through that to get up there. How to find the path to expressing unlimited freedom within the earth-based rooted sounds of Sweet Honey continues to be my search.

My primary work with First World Productions has been lecture demonstrations and educational theater work. I have been dealing with children and focusing on teaching and productions, which has brought me great joy. Our shows focus on the roots and development of Black music and Black dance. We perform for a lot of Black schools in the inner city and then we go out and perform for predominantly White audiences with two or three Black kids. The kids all seem to love it wherever we go.

Right now I am working on some new choreographic works with a small

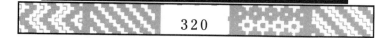

group of people. Although I don't think I want the headache of a company, I am thinking about having a small company trained to perform dance using multiple systems of movement. I have difficulty finding dancers who are versatile in ballet, African, modern, and jazz dance. The baddest dancers who can do African dance, who can really do it with the nuances it requires, usually don't have any other techniques. You find dancers who can do modern really well, and when you ask them to do African dance, they just look like a modern dancer trying to do African dance. It is very seldom that you can find dancers who can do both. The dance I create comes from a synthesis of both of these dance forms. I pray to be dancing all my life, for the rest of my life.

In Khemetin culture, the disciplines of dance and music were as doors of initiation into the mysteries of the Divine. The ancient Fulani people, the Woodabe, say that the meaning of life is to express truth, grace, and beauty in all things. For me this is the path to enlightenment. Imagine if this mission—the expression of truth, grace, and beauty in all things—was the guiding principle of every society. We'd truly have heaven on earth.

Dreams of love flow through the air,
Bright magic; love's magic is everywhere.
A soothing thought, a healing prayer,
Love's beauty, God's beauty beyond compare.

Dream songs of beauty;
True beauty flows from within
Love's timeless magic
Filling our hearts once again—forever!

Everything is arts for me; the story of my growth as an artist is the same as the unfolding of my soul as a Total Being. To master the art of life is a sacred mission. To be an artist is to seek that state of total surrender, of Divine grace, in as many places and times as you can in this world. We are singing and we are astounded by the beauty of the song; and our souls delight and take wing. This is to sing to the angels, to sing before the throne of God. We are dancing. We are dancing for the pleasure of the Queen and King of Heaven, and so we are dancing with boundless energy, creativity, grace, and joy. Simply to be an instrument of the Divine brings me the greatest joy.

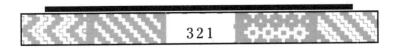

25

HEAR THE VOICES

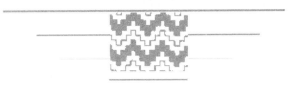

IN PROCESS . . .

The women of Sweet Honey In The Rock gave collective birth in Washington, D.C., to a song workshop for African American women. It was 1980. The workshop took the name In Process . . . Over the years, more than fifty African American women, of different political, economic, and social backgrounds, have embraced the opportunity to sing, learn, and share a space in the circle of Sweet Honey and In Process . . . Hear the voices.

Paula Pree: The workshop experience was a comfort zone. No matter how rushed your day, you were picked up by the Sweet Honey experience. From the beginning, the work was a catching hold to the music, getting a better understanding, keeping the culture and the form alive. Sweet Honey said its work was passing it on to others. And that became our work too. No matter what else is happening; you must get your work done.

Michelle Lanchester: Looking back now, I realize I was unconsciously seeking a safe place to reveal all of the voices, feelings, moods, and ancestors harbored within me. I am convinced that God Almighty guided me to the circle of In Process . . . and Sweet Honey In The Rock. The varied spirits within me found a resting place within the circle.

I was always told that my voice shook and trembled too much—too much vibrato, too old a sound. Finally the hiding, the fleeing, the shame shushed, and the healing, the layering, the nurturing—flourished. The circle invited, ignited the gen-

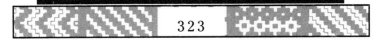

erations of ancient, ancestral voices to tremble, shake, twist, bend, stretch, somer-sault throughout the uninhibited workshop space. The workshop space served to soothe the African American vibrato sound. These voices, these spirits I had been blessed to carry within me, had been silenced by Western culture, by the music industry, but were crying for a resting place. And now they were free to come out and give voice to their many dimensions; to come out and visit with everyone, whether we were open to them or not, whether we acknowledged them or not.

But, ah, the moment the circle opened up the ancestral voices, the whole room became charged with inexplicable electricity. Here we were, all together, and the spirits took pleasure in dancing and soaring and expanding our vibratos, moans, wailings. Far too long they had been caught up in our souls, our throats, and they made their presence felt in our moments of facing them head-on. By facing them, we faced ourselves. Laughter. They hugged us with familiar embraces, they sur-rounded us, and we surrounded them. They danced in the middle of the circle and twirled us around and we each took turns jumping in and out, bathing in their warmth. The four- and five-part harmonies became layered with echoes, flutterings, and embellishments of ancestral croonings. There was a feeling and it sometimes felt like clapping, and it sometimes felt like rocking, and it sometimes felt like praying, and it was all over me.

Ivy Young: We thought In Process . . . was just a workshop. Then Bernice announced—and the members of Sweet Honey made it clear—that there was a need for us to share the music we had learned, maintaining our connection to the community. To prepare for our first concert, we had to commit to rehearsing three to four hours, five evenings a week. To get us physically prepared to perform, Sweet Honey put us on a regimen . . . no dairy products, water with lemon each morn-ing. We carried jugs of lemon water around with us everywhere we went. We were not allowed to drink anything cold . . . only tepid. We did push-ups, sit-ups, jumping jacks, and rolled around on the floor prior to vocal exercises and actual rehearsal. It displayed Sweet Honey's love and caring for us and showed us the discipline required for performing. Nine women performed in the first In Process . . . concert: Anita Brown, Paula Pree, Glenda Webb, Chi Hughes, Dyan McRae, Lee Hairston, Niani Kilkenny, A. Gale Robinson, and me. (Six of these nine women are native Washingtonians!)

Anita Brown: The first concert was kind of a big event. We really didn't have any desire to perform, but Dr. Reagon said, "Oh, you're all going to perform." We thought maybe we'd want to include an R&B medley, because we were from that era of music. That didn't go over very well at first, because Bernice didn't come from the urban, "colored" background that we did. So she told us we should bring her the names of some of the songs we thought we'd like to include. I remember the first couple of songs that came up and Bernice would say, "No, those words are sexist." I thought she was knockin' our history. But she was raising our conscious-

ness. So we ended up singing "Dancing in the Streets," "Searchin'," "What's Your Name?," "Try Me," and "In the Still of the Night." That was a big coup in a way, how we persuaded Sweet Honey to let us sing an R&B medley in the midst of "Chile Soweto" and "Abeyoyo."

Paula Pree: Although I had not auditioned, Anita Brown insisted that I come to the first Sweet Honey workshop, and Bernice drew me into the circle. My initial excitement at being there with the Honeys grew, as they brought to the circle history through harmonies from our past; they were good teachers whose methods informed us how to keep the culture moving forward through song. Today, still excited, In Process . . . continues widening the circle, still learning, still teaching.

Niani Kilkenny: What was fun was trying to get together costumes for the concert. And I remember that Chi and somebody else found some dollar-ninety-nine-cent plastic sandals from a vendor. And then Jasper, the vendor, had these printed things—sort of dashiki dresses—that cost about five dollars. They were wild—black, green, red, or something. They were really cheap but we could get them all looking alike. I guess it was the first stage in group design, group-coordinated costumes.

Pam Rogers: My sister Paula Pree insisted that I *needed* to hear her workshop's first performance in June 1980. At the concert, the women of In Process . . . sang together, while each woman of Sweet Honey read passages and poems about Black experiences. Lightning struck me when Bernice read about Birmingham, Alabama, and the cruelty and injustice against the children who were demonstrating for equal rights. I remembered my mother, holding Paula and me firmly by the hands, approaching a chanting crowd of White men, women, and children. We walked through the mob to integrate St. Joseph's Catholic school in Washington, D.C., in 1952. Hearing Bernice tell of other children who faced and survived the same struggle made me know all of our actions counted together and we were all connected. I had gone to the concert unconnected to anything, expecting to be entertained, to be an observer. But the voices speaking and singing our stories moved me from observer to participant. It was one of those significant experiences that change a life.

Carolyn Shuttlesworth: The first thing I did when I moved to D.C. in 1985 was to join In Process . . . It was during the first year in which Sweet Honey was not leading the workshop. But through the years, the women of Sweet Honey have cajoled, encouraged, and always believed in us and the music, and allowed the effort to become a truly communal one. Bringing the music of our past to audiences strengthened us and, hopefully, as we continue, we can bring new music to the circle and strengthen others.

Pam Rogers: Leadership of In Process . . . evolved from Sweet Honey to Ivy Young, Michelle Lanchester, and me. Then Ivy moved to the West Coast, leaving Michelle and me to carry on. We added a goal of creating our own music in the oral

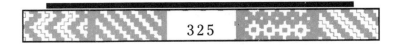

tradition. The growing AIDS epidemic inspired Michelle to write the first original In Process . . . song, "Another One." We first performed "Another One" in 1988, starting a new era for In Process . . . The following year, Michelle wrote "Patchwork Quilt." It's featured on our first recording, *In Process . . .* which Bernice produced. Sweet Honey regularly performs its own version of "Patchwork" and included it on their album released in 1992, *In This Land.*

Nketia Agyeman: There used to be a time I was so afraid to sing in front of anybody. The workshop helped me find that person within me I could share with the world. In Process . . . opened me up like a little flower. I had no idea we would be singing professionally. I was so glad to just have that space to sing. I appreciate Sweet Honey having paved a road by which In Process . . . can travel and In Process . . . being wise enough to recognize the branch in the road. When I first came, the goal was to create the singing for our survival. We are now going our own direction. We are like birds in a nest with parachutes, spreading messages through the music.

Lateefah Crosson: In Process . . . provides a connection to my culture, to the struggle. People who wouldn't ordinarily listen to you when you talk will hear your message when you're singing. Each of us is passing on a blessing, a positive message to learn, live, and think about. The first blessing is that God gave Sweet Honey this gift. They received the blessing and passed it on. Now we have received it and we're passing it on. The freedom song "Fighting for my Rights," created in jail by Charles Neblett to the tune of Ray Charles's "Lonely Avenue," really moves me because it shows that we still have a long struggle to go. We need to heal from drugs, from killing each other, from making slaves of ourselves.

Sharon Green: Pam Rogers had put me on the In Process . . . mailing list years earlier, but it wasn't until 1988 that I attended the Martin Luther King Community Concert they do with Sweet Honey every year. I was blown away! It was powerful music sung by all those powerful women. But I never even thought about being part of it until Pam invited me to an In Process . . . workshop. Four nights a week for three weeks in a non-air-conditioned space in July! We were sweating women in a circle, learning harmony. "Follow the Drinking Gourd" . . . How wonderful! We were singing a song of the Underground Railroad. It is a song about hope born in the hopelessness of slavery, where you have to look up to find your way to freedom.

It's hard being In Process . . . singing, rehearsing, traveling while doing all the livelihood things. It's hard being In Process . . . learning to open up to the music, the history, learning to trust other Black women and myself. I have never attended a workshop with Sweet Honey, but the circle they drew for In Process . . . is healing my spirit, leading it home.

Michelle Lanchester: And the circle was complete. Once the voices, spirits were out, there was no convincing them that they had to go back into hiding. We had tilled out sacred ground and it was sweet like honey and remains In Process

. . . within my life, my circle, my voice. I claim these spirits, these voices, these ancestors—nameless, yet readily identifiable every time I sing, moan, wail, shout, croon. I am forever grateful to the women of Sweet Honey In The Rock for creating a sacred ground for the spirits within me to find rest and sprinkle their voices all around without fear, without shame.

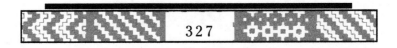

LEFT: NITANJU BOLADE DANCING DIONDONG ART OF BLACK DANCE AND MUSIC, BOSTON.
(PHOTO COURTESY OF NITANJU BOLADE CASEL PERSONAL COLLECTION)

TOP: PARENTS: YOUNG AND IN LOVE, STEPHEN AND MARY JOHNSON.
(PHOTO COURTESY OF NITANJU BOLADE CASEL PERSONAL COLLECTION)

RIGHT: MY HUSBAND, MFUNDISHI TAYARI CASEL.
(PHOTO COURTESY OF TAYARI CASEL PERSONAL COLLECTION)

BOTTOM: NITANJU BOLADE, DAKAR, REPUBLIQUE DU SENEGAL, AVEC "XALAM II," UN
ORCHESTRA DE DAKAR (NITANJU BOLADE, DAKAR, SENEGAL, SINGING WITH "XALAM," A LOCAL
DAKAR ORCHESTRA).
(PHOTO COURTESY OF NITANJU BOLADE CASEL PERSONAL COLLECTION)

26

CASSEROLE FOR LIFE

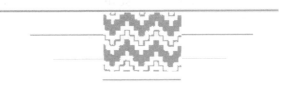

NITANJU BOLADE CASEL

Preheat your faith to 365°. Into an open mind, slowly mix the following ingredients:

 7 oz. of willpower
 1 lb. of patience
 3 heaping tb. of perseverance
 9 pinches of knowledge

Cover with love and let stand until it begins to rise beyond your expectations. In the meantime, stuff an open heart with equal parts of compassion and understanding until full. Take out your largest casserole dish and oil with all your ideas. Take the open mind and stuffed heart and place them side by side in the casserole. Bake forever inside your faith, and life's experiences will let you know when they are done . . . Bon appétit!

My name is Clarice Adelle Johnson Nitanju Bolade Casel. My parents, Stephen and Mary Johnson, gave me the first three names in preparation for this life, my experiences gave me the next two, and my husband, Tayari, gave me the last. This "name thing" is not even finished, as Tayari and I continue our search for a

traditional African family name which reflects our heritage to an even greater degree.

I was born in Buffalo, New York, on December 6 as a Sagittarian with a Moon in Leo and a Cancer rising. I have two sisters: Aisha, who appeared on the scene eleven months after I did; and Crystal, my sister in spirit, who never made it home from the hospital after my mother brought her into the world (although I have often wondered if she has reappeared in the form of one of my younger sister-friends, Konkou Keita). I remember our father having to tell us the news that not only had the baby passed during childbirth but our mother might not make it either because of all the complications that had affected her health. I am forever thankful that the Creator allowed her to come home to us, because it is her wisdom and unconditional love which have been the major factors in shaping me into the woman I am today. . . . Aisha and I must have been about ten or eleven, and it was the first (and last) time I saw my father cry. I will never forget that moment. It became a vital key, opening my door of understanding to the tenderness and love hidden beneath the overwhelming strength of this man I know:

> *Daddy . . .*
>> *quiet*
>> *Aquarian*
>> *family man*
>> *strong*
>> *seriously handsome*
>> *hardworking*
>> *bookworm (sci-fi!)*
>> *loving*
>> *proud*
>> *supportive*
>> *disciplinarian*
>> *clean and "fly"*
>> *protective*

This man, with a voice quality somewhere between Arthur Prysock and Billy Eckstine (the "crooners" of his day), met his match when he fell in love over forty years ago with Miss Mary Battle.

> *Mommy . . .*
>> *spiritual*
>> *absolutely beautiful*
>> *extremely giving*
>> *fun!*
>> *optimistic*
>> *Cancerian*

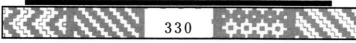

Casserole for Life

people-oriented
homemaker
organizer
motivator
gifted
"Don't take no stuff from nobody!"
visionary

My mom said when I was born I refused to open my eyes for the first few days. I'm sure I already sensed I would be facing a "mean world" and wanted to avoid that reality as long as possible. However, upon the discovery of whom my spirit had chosen as parents, I could relax—open my eyes—in the knowledge that I had been blessed in a very special way.

The first time I had my tarot cards read, I was living in Boston, Massachusetts. I remember the last card portraying a man walking with his head high, smiling in the sun, while simultaneously stepping off a cliff. Hmmm . . . my mom told me when I was around three years old, I was on the back porch playing, and when she and Aunt Lucille turned around to check on me, I was stepping off into space. There was absolutely no way they could reach me in time, so . . . boom! It was the first time my head established a serious relationship with concrete—and definitely not the last time I stepped off into space.

I joined Sweet Honey In The Rock in November 1985 and during those early years we used to dance Mandiani (a dance of celebration performed in Guinea, Senegal, the Ivory Coast, and Mali) at the end of our concerts. Aisha had arranged an a cappella version of the drum orchestration for this dance called "Mandiacappella," and one night in San Francisco at the Great American Music Hall, we had just finished dancing, and as I was leaving the stage, I stepped out . . . boom! I missed the stairs altogether. Being a dancer, I do believe in strong finales; however, this was a bit extreme. I went straight down on my ankle, which equaled crutches before the night was over. And should I mention deboarding a plane at National Airport? Fell down the steps, honey . . . boom! Once again, I had the sheer joy of finding out what life was like hopping around on crutches. *You* think this is weird? Hey, I'm *still* trying to figure out what this fascination is I seem to have with space and concrete.

Actually, I think I just wanted to fly. I have always heard people talk about flying—leaving the grounded nature of the body. It sounds so fascinating, exciting, and in tune with another side of life. And I know folks who fly all the time—on a regular basis, and *tell* me about their adventures. . . . Marie Guinier (sisterfriend) and I would often discuss the mysteries of flying and would pray for the phenomenon to occur in our individual lives.

However, when you pray, it is very possible that your prayers will be answered and you will receive exactly what you asked for. So, as I get on board another

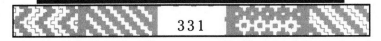

airplane to "fly" to my next Sweet Honey In The Rock performance . . . Hm-m-m-m-m.

. . . It's August 30, 1992, and we just returned last night from our third tour in Australia *(and a twenty-plus-hour "flight" experience)*. While I was talking with a member of Public Enemy's entourage (also touring Australia), he asked which group I performed with, and when I told him Sweet Honey In The Rock, he said, "Oh yeah . . . I heard yaw'll were *serious!*"

"Serious" is a good word to describe Sweet Honey. Within her nineteen years of maturation is the rock-solid foundation of strength and integrity nurtured and safeguarded by Bernice Johnson Reagon. Each of the twenty women who have stepped into the arms of this institution has added seasonings gathered from her own life's journeys; creating a musical message steeped in Afrocentric traditions and rich with the flavor of personal experiences. As the twentieth woman to be embraced by Sweet Honey, I have had the honor and privilege of sharing a very special creative space with seven of these singers . . . or should I say "forces."

Bernice . . .
 serious
 catchy laughter
 our fearless leader!
 wise
 maintains a child within
 focused
 intense
 disciplinarian
 innovator
 a force
 teacher/master
 radiantly beautiful

Evelyn . . .
 roots
 rockers
 fun
 willing to change
 strength within a unique frailty
 aware
 cutting if necessary
 buddy
 statuesque beauty
 elegant

homegirl
gritmaster!

Ysaye . . .
  friendly—extremely
  receptive and open
  caring
  sensitive
  explorative
  kind
  fun
  always willing to share
  fly
  a perfectionist
  not to be outdone, so don't even think about it
  Dr. Buywell!
  strikingly beautiful

Aisha . . .
  my sister
  intense
  sweet
  thunderhead
  spiritual
  fun
  disciplined
  grubmaster!
  nature woman
  strong
  exquisitely beautiful
  free
  innovator
  fashion queen

Yasmeen . . .
  luscious
  soothing
  soft
  serious
  playful
  sensuously beautiful
  air/breathy

Carol . . .
   intense
   fun
   open
   homegirl
   earthy
   spiritual
   genuinely beautiful

Tulani . . .
   ancient spirit
   calm
   spiritual
   innovator
   elegantly beautiful
   cultural
   centered

Each one of these "forces" is a role model for me; each one is so different, with her own unique energies to contribute to the group. They teach me by just being themselves.

Evie has helped me focus on improving my pitch. Lord, I thought the child was going to croak every time I sang an incorrect note (which was right regular while I was trying to learn the songs). Her entire body would shudder; her face would wince; she'd put her hands over her ears, and somehow try to survive the experience. I tried extra hard to get myself together as soon as possible for both our sakes. (I could imagine my picture up in every post office in the country: WANTED— FOR THE TORTURE OF EVELYN HARRIS! . . . I'm laughing about this now, but when I read this part to Tayari, he reminded me that I sho' wasn't laughin' before.)

Bernice. Where can I begin? I sit in awe of her onstage, listening with as much "wow" in me as the rest of the audience. She's taught me how to teach/educate through music, and how to turn a concert hall into a classroom and like a magician switch them again unnoticeably right before your eyes.

Ysaye helped me to understand that even though perfection may be unattainable, there's nothing wrong with constantly striving for it. Unofficially named our ambassador because of her outgoing personality, she has shown me how to step beyond my shyness to reach out to folks I don't know and embrace them.

Aisha and I are eleven months apart. For one month each year we're the same age, which would always be a strong point of contention for me during our younger years when I wanted to assert my powers as the older sister. ("You can't tell me

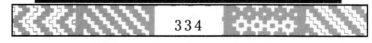

what to do; I'm the same age as you!" . . . Sigh.) I've been learning from this child all my life. She has found the secret of blending the strict discipline of regime into her lifestyle while simultaneously having a sense of freedom.

Yasmeen helped me to understand the uselessness of trying to "fill someone else's shoes." Sure, I knew intellectually that such a feat was not possible, but that information did little to negate the tremendous pressure I felt traveling from community to community with Sweet Honey immediately after she left the group. She has reassured me in so many ways about the spicy flavor my own unique seasonings have added to the dish of these twenty chefs.

Carol keeps me centered and aware of the innumerable possibilities of how to interpret and enjoy the forever unfolding scripts of life. Her natural talents as an actress accompanied by her spirituality and sense of humor are constant reminders of the world as a stage, with each of us playing her/his role.

Tulani possesses an inner resolve and wisdom that connect with the peace of my inner spirit whenever I share her space—moments so rare and extremely valuable to me.

Shirley opened my eyes and heart to a whole world of communication found in silence, and the sensitivity required to broaden my boundaries beyond what is narrowly deemed "normal" in this society.

> *Shirley . . .*
> *quiet*
> *sensitive*
> *expressively beautiful*
> *inner strength*
> *thoughtful*

So, with these "forces," I travel throughout the world accompanied by three "miracle workers" who, more often than not, must go far beyond their wildest dreams to help us survive on the road.

> *Art . . .*
> *informative*
> *extraordinarily witty*
> *fun*
> *soundmaster*
> *fruitman!*
> *easygoing*
> *bookworm*

What would we do without Art Steele on sound? Considering that we never use reverb or echoes and effects (no matter how tired and seemingly needy we may

be), if there is a way to create a unified sound with warmth and presence, Art will find it.

Sometimes with *great* equipment (his!) and ofttimes with stuff that has to be rebuilt/rewired and probably should be thrown away, he *Art*fully creates a sound we can live with. And it appears that if *he* can't do it, it couldn't be done.

Amy . . .
    dedicated
    spiritual
    focused
    kind
    thoughtful
    sensitive

Madeleine . . .
    caring
    the youngest, the smallest, yet trying to be the mother of us all
    fun
    seriously stylish

Madeleine and Amy are the backbone of Roadwork, Inc., and they not only arrange bookings for Sweet Honey but as the name implies, they often come on the road with us, pulling major traveling coups all along the way. From securing early check-ins at hotels to desired plane seating to personally delivered dinners after the concerts to whatever they feel will be helpful in keeping Sweet Honey strong, they are there, and sincerely appreciated.

Unfortunately, there are some things that are beyond the limitations of the "miracle workers," and travel conditions rank high on the list. For example, during one of our 1987 Black History Month tours, we were in Lynchburg, Virginia, on our way to Nashville, Tennessee. We had a ridiculously early flight—around 6 A.M. And believe me, after you've performed the night before and got back into your room by midnight; bathed/showered, repacked, and tried to get some sleep so you could have a decent voice for the concert the next night, and left your room before 6 A.M., after all that, that hour seems *quite* ridiculous, and much to my chagrin, necessary.

We arrive at the airport only to discover that due to fog (a traveler's archenemy—one of several) our flight was canceled. We waited . . . and waited . . . and waited. Eventually, we got a brainstorm idea to drive to the nearest airport—which was Roanoke, Virginia—and fly from there. We retrieved all of our luggage from the plane, rented a van, hired a driver, and off we went with new reservations and plenty of confidence. Child, do you know when we reached Roanoke the fog had followed us there and our flight was canceled once again! All we could do was

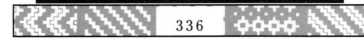

wait . . . and wait . . . and . . . (waiting is a whole entity in itself, completely depending on which airport one is either lucky or unlucky enough to find oneself in).

Our show in Nashville was scheduled for 8 P.M., and by the time we arrived it was about 8:30 P.M., but the hall was full of folks who were gracious enough to hang in there. (Thank you! You know who you are!)

There is nothing like a Sweet Honey audience. Nothing. The diversity of our audiences encompasses all ages, races, nationalities, and genders. Sometimes we'll walk onstage and there are folks who have already programmed the concert—the warmth, the love, and the expectations are already there. These folks know all the songs; they are ready to sing, dance, clap, chant, feel, and support us. I especially remember the brother who came with a slew of hand percussion instruments and sat in the front row. When we played, he played—and after we came back from intermission, he had expanded his collection with his *drums* in the room—ready to throw down!

Then there are the audiences who actually thought they had bought their tickets to come and watch this group like a television. It is exciting to watch them transcend their self-imposed boundaries and blossom like flowers before our eyes. Folded hands start to clap, feet tucked under the seats come out to pat, and once-silent voices not only sing but in multiple harmony lines. To meet/talk with people afterward and hear them express how they were touched by the music is truly a blessing. What more can a musician ask? This makes all the travel hassles worth their weight in gold, it's hard to even *remember* all of them—until you get back to your cruddy room. (Just playing! Just playing!)

Well, then again . . . there *are* those times when I wonder who was giving out those "star" ratings for some of those dives. To make matters even worse, it always seems that the beautiful, luxurious hotels with the elaborate health clubs and exquisite decor, twenty-four-hour room service, and terry-cloth robes hanging on the door are the ones we never seem to have a chance to spend any time in! Nine point ninety-nine times out of ten, if we have a hotel like that, the plane will be late and the day will be so jammed with activities that we barely see the room. But put us in a dive (as some folks do) where you can't even *think* about walking on the carpet without shoes because it's so dirty, or *entertain* the idea of taking a bath without catching something undesirable and you'd *best* have shoes for the shower, where there's a rickety TV with three local channels, and oh, we just have all *day* to stay there!

Don't even talk about food. Child, try being a halfway decent vegetarian on the road. There was a time when carrying everything but the kitchen sink seemed appropriate, but these days I don't even want to face the bags I *have* to carry (costumes, instruments, etc.), much less anything extra.

Now, there are those rare occasions when we are blessed to have producers who will prepare a feast that leaves us completely "tickified" (a state in which the

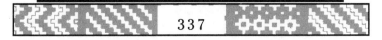

taste buds have been so delighted that one is forced to lean sideways due to the maximum stomach overload). However, we usually land in a town with a dedication and vigilance that would make a private investigator proud. Our goal: to hunt down any restaurant that may even *hint* of spice—Indian, Thai, Japanese, Ethiopian, etc. Ain't no tellin' *what* one might find. One afternoon we were directed to a restaurant for lunch, walked in, and lo and behold! A near-naked woman was doing some kind of burlesque act for a private party. As we stood there in momentary shock, the owner was encouraging us in: "Come on in! We have great lasagna!"

Unfortunately a lot of folks' interpretation of vegetarian cuisine equals *no* spice whatsoever, or in other words, removal of the joy of eating altogether. (Once someone served us a block of uncooked tofu with a piece of parsley on top— m-m-m-m-yummy!). Just another challenge to fit into a Sweet Honey day.

Some experiences stand out as truly unforgettable, and evidence of the cultural boundaries we have encountered on our musical journeys.

Like the poor woman in St. Olaf (yes, for those of you who watched *Golden Girls* on TV, there really *is* such a place) who came up to Madeleine inquiring about whether to completely fill the big "jug" with water, after so kindly filling the smaller one. To us they may have been shekeres (percussion instruments made from gourds and a woven net of beads), but to the eye of this beholder they were beautifully decorated water jugs. I just give thanks we found out *before* the concert. . . .

There are, too, those times when we are directly confronted with the issues we sing about.

Place . . . Holland, the Netherlands

Time . . . Spring 1990—early morning

Event . . . Racism everywhere

Aisha and I were getting ready for our morning jog. I was standing in the hotel hallway in my running attire waiting for her to come out of her room. We didn't have much time because I had a Sweet Honey emergency business meeting at 10:30 A.M. It seemed as if our sponsors had gotten the insane idea that they might be able to send us on our way home without our performance fee, which is a whole other story in itself. *Anyway* . . . as I was standing there, a middle-aged Caucasian man came up to me and in an extremely frustrated tone said, "Look! I am in room 1049 and I have a meeting at ten-thirty! Would you have my room ready by then!?" I looked dead into this man's face . . . Sigh . . . What a way to start a morning. I glanced into the next room at the housekeepers who were working diligently on my floor, and noticed that their uniforms resembled *nothing* I was wearing; however, we did share the same skin color (which, I supposed, to this particular character, *was* the uniform).

In a situation like this, one has several options for "reading" this individual— the only issue is deciding within a split second which route to follow: The calm, low, seething tones? The loud, obnoxious tones with attitude and maybe even a

338

finger snap? How about a defiant physical stance including all of the above? I decided to go with the calm, low, seething tones. "I also have a meeting at ten-thirty. I am a guest of this hotel just like you are, and I suggest you speak to one of the housekeepers about your room." In the next few humbling moments he realized that his foot needed to be removed from his mouth so that apologies could gush forward (and gush they did). I stood there listening to all that, yet somehow I didn't feel quite satisfied. Aisha came down, and while we jogged, I explained what had transpired; the more I talked about it, the angrier I became. I wondered if I should have used my loud, obnoxious tones? By the time we returned to the hotel, I realized something else had to be done on my part. Since I knew which room he was in, I decided to compose a letter informing him (1) that First World people hold just as many varied positions in life as anyone else, from presidents to lawyers to homemakers to factory workers; (2) that there is a golden rule as to why one should never ASS-U-ME (because it makes an ass out of you, not me), and (3) that it is the prevalence of unintelligent attitudes such as his that feeds racism and perpetuates the negative attitudes which continue to tear our societies apart on a global scale. After that was delivered, I felt only slightly better. Only one grain of sand removed from an entire beach.

So, how did I end up in Sweet Honey In The Rock?

i listen to the voice
that speaks to me each day . . .
i open up my mind
and hear what it has to say . . .
this voice is my guide,
keeping my life in tune . . .
with the melody of the sun,
and the harmony of the moon.
once i'm in tune with nature
like a river my life will flow . . .
leading me in all directions
the Creator wants me to go . . .

I've often wondered who this voice is: the Creator. An ancestral spirit? My own spirit? Or all of the above, plus some? Sometimes all of this spiritual wonderment gets displaced by a vivid image of the cartoon character Fred Flintstone. He always had that angel on one shoulder and a devil on the other, who were constantly giving him conflicting advice, and even battling with one another at times. Well, considering where I've ended up in certain situations, it's quite clear that my angelic messages were getting intercepted by another energy not exactly acting in my best interests. If I had an extra day of life on earth for every time I had to admit

to myself that "something *told* me to blah, blah, blah" . . . "I *know* I should have blah, blah, blahed," I would probably be hanging around forever and a day. So you'd think that by now I would just be a-listenin' and a-followin' that voice right regular, huh? So would I, but it hasn't quite worked out that way.

My father has always suffixed his suggestions/advice/orders to us with "you hear me?" which not only means by sound waves, but a discreet hint of a threat that we'd better do as he says. So there are clearly different ways to "listen" to *the voice* which has directed my life. One is to acknowledge its presence by hearing; two is to actually *follow* and do as it says. The latter has always proven to be the source of major positive changes in my life.

When I was sixteen years old, seemingly out of the clear blue sky, I contracted rheumatoid arthritis. (Don't worry, this is not going to be a big sob story, just hang in there for a minute—and quiet down those violins!) It started in one knee and by the time I was a freshman in college (North Carolina Central University, Raleigh-Durham, North Carolina) it had spread to basically all of my joints. The doctors had prescribed a host of medications, which included a dual marriage to Ben-Gay and Bayer aspirins (15 to 20 per day), and plenty of bed rest. I noticed, however, for some reason I wasn't getting any better. The straw that broke the camel's back was the day I woke up and my jaws were locked; I couldn't get the pills into my mouth. And as much as I love to laugh and be Ms. Optimistic about everything, search as I might I failed to discover the humor in this situation. *The voice* told me, "Throw away all of this medicine—forget about bed rest and just start *acting* like you don't have this problem." That is exactly what I did. I know my parents thought I was out of my mind when I came home that summer, but I had a "new attitude" (thank you, Patti LaBelle).

That fall, when I returned to school, I transferred to Northeastern University in Boston, Massachusetts, to reunite with Aisha, who was entering Northeastern as a freshman. I decided to change my diet to vegetarianism and start dancing—no matter the physical cost.

It was dance that started me down the cultural path of my ancestors. I couldn't begin to explain all that transpired during those years in Boston/New York in this brief chapter. However, I must admit that my experiences were indeed unique to a group of African Americans across the country who were determined to breathe traditional African culture into their lives "by any means necessary" (thank you, Malcolm X). For the most part, this was achieved through intimate contact with brothers/sisters from "home" (Africa), the Caribbean, and the United States, exchanging and sharing dance, music, religions, and folklore with one another. Oh no, I'm not trying to paint a perfectly rosy picture that everything was hunky-dory. There were rivalries, rip-offs, all the negatives one might experience in any group situation. However, this community-based culture not only survived but thrived in these United States and, I am happy to report, is still alive today.

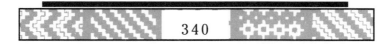

Casserole for Life

How in the world did I end up at that first big meeting called for the purpose of forming an authentic West African dance company? *The voice* urged me on over there even though she *knew* I had only been studying African dance for a year. It was in this meeting, November 4, 1972, that I connected with an international community of folks, an extended family, some of whom remain in my "intimasphere" today. "Intimasphere" is a word I got from my mom, which refers to that close space around an individual which is sacred—mine has been continually expanding over the years. I am surrounded by the best people life has to offer; all these folks have connected me to their spiritual networks and I am ever so thankful to Mother/Father God for putting me in tune with such a marvelous clan.

We called ourselves Boka N'Deye, a phrase from the Senegal/Gambia region of West Africa which means "of the same Mother" in the Wolof language . . . we were children of Mother Africa.

At one point there were over forty of us—we rehearsed four times per week, three or four hours per rehearsal. We were serious. We often rehearsed in the dead of winter with no heat. We danced on concrete, grass—you name it; there were no conditions too tough for us to conquer. We had teachers from all over Africa and the Caribbean—many of them students or professionals working in the area. At the end of each rehearsal we always formed a big circle and danced solos. There was no time limit on anyone—just continue until you felt satisfied and rest assured that we'd all be with you.

Time-honored traditions of Africa became our foundation for life. We made our own costumes; prepared and ate culinary delights; wore traditional clothes and hairstyles; spoke bits and pieces of different languages; sang chants and songs; played drums and other percussion instruments; sisters designed and strung shekeres while brothers made their own drums—carving the tree trunks into hollow shells, soaking animal skins in bathtubs for the heads of the drums and then stringing them onto the shells. We were determined. We had never set foot on the Motherland (not physically, anyway). We did benefit concerts for years—in jails, community centers, schools, festivals—and if by chance we did get paid, we always put the money aside for our dream to someday go to Africa. Sometimes I would sit and listen to tapes of the drumming after the concerts and would not believe there was *any* way *this* body was actually moving *that* fast for *that* long. You see, each ballet would be a good twenty minutes or so, and we'd do three or four in one night's concert (and that didn't include the musical interludes). Child, I guess that's part of the reason I'm tired right now.

But as the years passed, folks graduated from school and left the area, others decided to pursue different interests, and still others decided to abscond with all of the company costumes and contacts (I won't mention any names—you know who you are). Those of us who remained, who seemed to have an insatiable appetite for this lifestyle we'd tapped into, joined forces with De Ama Battle, founder and

director of Boston's Art of Black Dance and Music (ABDM). Not only did we incorporate the traditional African/Caribbean dance and music, but the repertoire broadened to include modern, jazz, and tap.

In 1981 I heard about auditions for a Haitian band in search of a vocalist. "Why not?" *the voice* said. I had learned so many different songs over the years in so many different languages (of which I spoke fluently absolutely none), but hey, I was confident that I could sing *anything* as long as someone could show me how to pronounce the words correctly. I went for it; I got it. The band was made up of musicians from the French-speaking islands (Haiti, Martinique, Guadeloupe, etc.) interspersed with several musicians from the Berkeley School of Music and ME! We rehearsed every day for about a month while Max, our manager, who was from Haiti, arranged a six-month tour for the group which included Paris and many of the French-speaking islands.

I rearranged my life. I had been teaching courses and workshops in dance at Boston University, Roxbury Community College, and the Joy of Movement Center, as well as directing my own company of young dancers (ages five to sixteen years) called Young Afrique (which had been initiated by Kofi Hennor from Ghana). So I turned over all my jobs teaching dance to my cronies and took a leave of absence from ABDM (where I'd become artistic director for De Ama Battle). Actually, I *had* started to wonder exactly how long I could continue dancing at the Ferrari level. My feet and the rest of my body started looking at cruise control in a nice Mercedes as a much more appealing method of living, and singing appeared to be a good way of accomplishing that goal. I bought myself a big ol' trunk and packed up what I conceived to be enough stuff to last me through this journey—which was considerably less in those days (smile). Max left for Haiti to make all the arrangements after having all of us sign contracts. There were over a dozen musicians in this band (or should I say orchestra?).

. . . Honey! Do you know we're *still* waiting for Max to return? Ain't that deep? *Now* what was I supposed to do? I had basically ended my life in Boston in preparation for the tour that was now *not* happening. What was I to do? . . . Mother/Father God is Great.

Raymond Sylla, a Senegalese dancer who had been working with ABDM, was on his way home to Dakar, and De Ama suggested, "Well, Nitanju, since you're all packed to go somewhere, and you are not going on the tour, why don't you go with Raymond and do some research for the company?" What did *I* say? Need you ask? Can birds fly? You know I jumped on that opportunity. What I didn't realize was that my six-week research project would turn into a four-year experience of living and working in Senegal, leading me down yet another path. *The voice* must be my God/Goddess, and I was sho' 'nuff taking heed to what she said. Finally. I'm so glad I did.

Excitement . . . Even though September 6, 1981, would be my second trip to Africa (the first time was in 1979), that did nothing to quell my feelings of elation

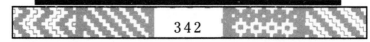

while leaving for the capital of Senegal from JFK Airport in New York . . . direct on Air Afrique with one of my teachers from Senegal and Marie Guinier—a student from my dance class who decided to go immediately after I told her about it. I didn't know her well then, but we hung in there through thick and thin to become sisterfriends. I asked myself, "How did I end up on this journey?" The Creator provides, and *the voice* guides . . .

I lived in West Africa from 1981 to 1985. Okay, okay. I confess. We did initially start out on a six-week visit, but going "home" really felt like "home" and we had no desire to leave. Meeting folks like Abubacar Africa Weaver, who left Boston to "visit" Dakar for one week over twelve years ago and *still* lives there, did not help matters any when it came time to return to the U.S.A. . . .

Marie and I worked to develop an organization we created called Artistes des Echanges Africains (ADEA). Based in Dakar, Senegal, we traveled to the Ivory Coast, Mali, Guinea-Bissau, and Gambia. Our experiences as Africans from the United States of America made it apparent to us that a medium was desperately needed to help bridge the gap between African people of the diaspora. We had so much to learn from one another. So much to unlearn. . . . We were frustrated from conversations with our sisters and brothers on the continent in which we had to argue that we too were African. The bottom-line question always came around to "Where were you born?" Once we answered, our fate was immediately sealed as being distinctly different and apart from our family, and we were determined to do everything we could to change that concept.

We combined the arts (music, dance, and folklore) with the ancient system of bartering (an extremely effective resource inspired by a zero-based budget) and began to work with organizations such as the University of Dakar, the American Cultural Center (American embassy), Radio ORTS, the Afro-American Dance Center, the New Experience Jazz Club, the National Theater Daniel Sorano, the Zoneta Club, the Schomburg Center for Research and Culture, the National Council for Negro Women, and Air Afrique in an attempt to broaden our understandings of one another.

This work (and the anger and frustration which created the need for it) was the inspiration behind "C'est le Temps" ("It Is Time")—an open thought to my brothers and sisters born on the continent from Nitanju, an African American Peulh (a sect of the Fulani ethnic group—a nomadic people found throughout West Africa).

C'est le temps to blend the musical experiences of African people living throughout the world. Let's create a new music, one which will captivate all listeners through the power of the truth it holds. Let's use all our experiences as tools to exchange—our rich cultures of music, dance, artwork, folklore and history, knowledge of sciences, math, medicine, agriculture, values, and morals —so that we will not waste time planting unfertile seeds in our life gardens.

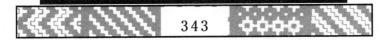

C'est le temps to extend our hands across the oceans of our pasts, grip firmly and hold tight—for between our palms lies the destiny of our future.

C'est le temps for all our music to teach and heal, strengthen character and rebuild nations. The same feeling that touches the soul during a rhythm from the Sabarr orchestra or a Baptist gospel song must prevail in all of our music which accompanies the circle of life . . .

C'est le temps for me to embrace you and learn from all the invaluable traditions you have been able to retain through the centuries. C'est le temps for you to embrace me and take advantage of my experiences as you move toward incorporating a Eurocentric culture of technological advances into your lives.

C'est le temps . . . it's time . . . You know it's time . . . I know it's time . . . Time knows it's time . . . to live.

By June 1985, I felt it was time to go back to the U.S.A. It was difficult to leave, though. Even as Marie and I were packing our bags, the manager of Youssou N'Dour (one of the most brilliant male vocalists in Senegal, whose international appeal grows each year) stopped by to offer a gig singing background vocals with his group. I began to think: Hmmm . . . *The voice* said, "No! Move your butt to D.C. YOU HEAR ME?" I listened . . . and left . . .

Well, I came on to D.C., moved in with Aisha, got an administration job at the World Bank, started performing with local musicians and studying traditional West African dance with Assane Konte, director of the Kankouran West African Dance Company. In August, Sweet Honey In The Rock (SHIR) had a monthlong vocal workshop during which each member invited someone and Aisha asked me. It was a wonderful moment in time.

By the fall, there was an opening for a full-time singer, and I was asked to consider the position. I had reservations because I was new in town and wasn't sure of making what appeared to be tremendous commitment; they also had reservations because they'd never had two sisters in the group before. (I can imagine—what if we were the kind who fought all the time?) I was honored that they would even consider me, yet I declined. Later, they asked me again, and although I was still undecided, *the voice* said, "Girl, how many times in yo' life do you think opportunity will knock twice for you?" Okay! Okay! I give thanks for what seemed to be another great time to be listening.

I sang my first concert in November 1985 and I was overwhelmed. I love the effort Sweet Honey makes to keep our traditions and history alive; whether through song styles (i.e., long- and short-meter hymns, spirituals, traditional African songs) or through song content (i.e., "Ballad of the Sit-ins," "Fannie Lou Hamer, If You Had Lived"). Often we learn the material for our repertoire in the oral tradition, which has many similarities to my experiences in dance. I recall two of my teachers, Rhonda Morman and Hazel Bryant of the International Afrikan American Ballet (New York), always stressing the importance of teaching and presenting our tradi-

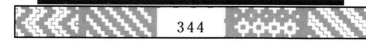

tions as close as possible to their origins. That way generations in the future will still be able to recognize a dance like Mandiani, for example, and know where it came from, what drum orchestra was used and for what purpose.

Imagine after all my years of dance . . . knowing *exactly* what I was going to do onstage (excluding a few solo steps—and even they were locked into a form that I knew well), here I find myself—onstage—with these *super*bad women, who expect me to sing a song to which I know not the words, the melody, much less a harmony, nor the form in some cases—IN FRONT OF A PAYING AUDIENCE! Oh, floor . . . why didn't you open up and swallow me like I prayed for so many times?

However, that is only one of many humbling life situations that has kept my head from ever getting big. These women would say to me (with such ease), "Look into someone's mouth and get the words." . . . Huh? My mind would try to compute exactly how this was going to transpire. When I looked into someone's mouth (while performing, of course), were the words going to travel so fast from their mouth to my brain that I would actually appear to be singing with the group? And let's not even mention a harmony line. I survived only through the support, love, and patience of the group, and I still suspect this phenomenon may rank right up there with the wonders of the world. Speaking of wonders, Sweet Honey wasn't the only positive experience happening at this time. Love was also in the air.

I was swinging on a swing in Adelphi Park, Maryland, when I first saw *Tayari Casel.*

Casel
He was/is . . .
   fine!
   strong
   aware
   talented
   a warrior
   sensitive
   dedicated
   fine!
   romatic
   fun
   spiritual
   serious
   disciplined
   fine!
   communicative
   supportive
   sincere

honest
straightforward
and let's not forget . . . FINE!

The voice said, "Hey, girlfriend . . ." Again, I listened.

On February 14, 1986, we were engaged to be married. And on October 3, 1987, we had the most beautiful wedding ceremony . . . blessed by our parents, Stephen and Mary Johnson; Gentle and Mary Casel; with my sisterfriends as bridemaids (Aisha, Marie, Ramatoulaye, Adenike, Rhonda, and Konkou) and Tayari's brotherfriends, our family and friends. The ceremony included Sweet Honey In The Rock singing, Assane Konte and members of the Kankouran West African Dance Company drumming, and Djimo Kouyate on kora (a string instrument traditionally played by the griots, or oral historians). All took place outside in Brookside Gardens in Silver Spring, Maryland.

I give thanks every day for this kind warrior spirit who has stepped into my intimasphere and challenged me to rise to trust the depths of love and all its shades/textures. I am so proud of his commitment to the African American community and in awe of his humbleness. His reputation in the martial arts as one of the leading innovators in the field spans over twenty years. His school, the African Martial Arts Academy, located in Washington, D.C., focuses on the development of the African origins of the art form rather than the Asian adaptations.

I also give thanks constantly for the discovery of that smokin' casserole recipe —an open mind and an open heart stuffed with a mixture of willpower, patience, perseverance, knowledge . . . Each time I sample a little, it amazes me how good it is; so good that it's hard to believe it's still cooking . . .

27

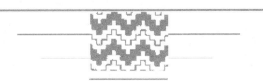

A BRIDGE BETWEEN CULTURES

AKUA KYEREWAA OPOKUWAA

We who believe in freedom cannot rest
We who believe in freedom cannot rest until it comes.

That which touches me most
is that I had a chance to work with people,
Passing on to others
that which was passed on to me . . .

Words spoken by Civil Rights Movement leader Ella Baker and set to poem and music by Bernice Johnson Reagon express my feelings about the work that I do as a performance Sign language interpreter. Ms. Baker expressed these words during the 1960s Civil Rights Movement against racism and injustice in the United States. In this chorus she talks about her commitment to working as an organizer for over fifty years. She helped people to understand how through organized efforts they had the power to break the chains of racism, exploitation, and injustice oppressing African Americans throughout the twentieth century.

The text of the song also deals with the cost of fighting for freedom even in the face of death. This time the murder of three Civil Rights workers in 1964 in Phila-

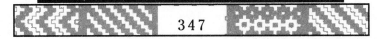

delphia, Mississippi, James Cheney, Michael Goodman, and Andrew Schwerner. However, for me, the words of "Ella's Song" transcend time and events to include the here and now. "That which touches me most . . . Passing on to others that which was passed on to me . . ." are concepts that speak directly to my efforts as a performance Sign language interpreter to pass on, define, clarify, and translate information that is transmitted onstage by the rhythmical lyrics and spoken words of Sweet Honey In The Rock.

From November 1991 to April 1992 I served as Sign language interpreter for Sweet Honey In The Rock. Although this was not my first time, it was my longest continuous experience working with them. I was in a position that Shirley Childress Johnson held as the primary interpreter for the group for a decade. Experiencing the Deaf audience participating in these concerts around the country by singing (signing) the songs, rocking with the audience, and giving the same kinds of messages as the hearing audience (i.e., "Go on, girl," "You got that right," "Right on," standing and screaming with hands raised, fingers wiggling, etc.) signaled to me that the "new" interpreter (as I was referred to by seasoned Sweet Honey audiences), her style and system, had been accepted and was appreciated in a way that only Deaf people can display.

There is a multitude of experiences within experiences that have made this journey with Sweet Honey rich and rewarding. One of my greatest enjoyments of life is that of observing, listening, analyzing, learning, and subsequently "passing on to others" (the Deaf audience) the music, the sound, the intensity, the fervor, the conviction, the history, the rhythms, and the excitement of the singing.

It is an education for me as Sign language interpreter to participate and share with the sage of the Civil Rights Movement (Bernice), the African song style expert (Nitanju), the jazz vocalist (Aisha), the best female bass (Ysaye), and their wide range of vocal sounds and energy designed to remind, educate, stimulate, motivate, and sustain those who attend a Sweet Honey In The Rock concert. The total experience causes me to examine very carefully my motives and commitment to the Deaf audiences. Further, the challenge to assist in disseminating information to the Deaf community becomes paramount in my mind. There are many who may not know about the educational and entertainment opportunity which Sweet Honey provides by incorporating a performance sign language interpreter in her concerts.

The willingness of the women of Sweet Honey to share themselves with diverse audiences makes them special. Members of Deaf audiences have noticed and commented to me about this choice. Some have asked, "Why does Sweet Honey provide an interpreter for the Deaf community when so many other artists just ignore them?" At some point, I too wondered about the commitment. After a season of constant contact, however, I realize that the group is committed not only in word (advertisement), in the showy part (an interpreter onstage), but also in deed.

One of those deeds occurred in response to an incident in Eugene, Oregon,

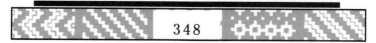

where members of the Deaf audience complained that their seats were so far from the stage that they could not possibly see the Sign language interpreter. The local sponsor had a section set aside for the Deaf audience but there were still members of the Deaf audience too far away from the stage. Sweet Honey responded to the problem without hesitation and urgently requested that the producer address it. The group asked that the situation be rectified before the concert began. Sweet Honey producers and audience members are often very special; upon being informed of the situation, audience members volunteered to exchange seats with members who needed visual access to the stage. The concert began—in that order. If I ever had any doubt as to Sweet Honey's commitment to providing accessibility to the Deaf community, this very action spoke for itself. By the way, this was a sold-out concert!

My commitment to the Deaf community evolved from growing up with a fervent passion to work for freedom, equality, and justice for all human beings. My first calling to the Deaf community, that of an advocate for the Deaf, began without my having a working knowledge of Sign language or of Deaf culture.

In 1978, a family with Deaf children joined the church where I was a member and officer. The pastor and members seemed to be at a loss regarding the actions required to accommodate that family and to make the services and church events accessible to them. Since the children were in my junior high Sunday school class, I explored the accessibility issues, developed a plan, and approached the pastor, the board of trustees, and the deacon board with the proposal.

In addition to the obvious communications need, seating arrangements were an issue. In the African American church setting there is a definite seating order, which is understood by all. The front pews are occupied by the pillars of the church —deacons, deaconesses, trustees, and missionaries. That proposal, and many discussions and one-on-one meetings later, resulted in the accessibility of all church services and events to the hard-of-hearing community. This included a front-row pew reserved for the Deaf community at all church events. Following the implementation of the Deaf ministry, I learned Sign language and interpreting and became the primary interpreter for the church, and also took on the responsibility of training a cadre of interpreters to provide the necessary services. That very program for the Deaf continues today, and was introduced and adapted by several others in Washington, D.C.

I believe, from my early experiences working with the Deaf ministry in my church through my travels with Sweet Honey, that Deaf audiences can experience as rich a range of excitement and cultural nourishing at a Sweet Honey concert (or any other concert) as the hearing audiences. The performance Sign language interpreter is the bridge between those cultures. Sweet Honey In The Rock continues to build and maintain that bridge.

For me, freedom for the members of the Deaf community is to be able to enter any concert hall, lecture hall, dance, or theater unannounced with the assurance

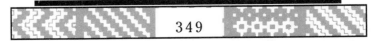

that the event is totally accessible to them. This is only achieved through under-standing and cooperation between the Deaf and hearing communities. Performance Sign language interpreters working with groups like Sweet Honey In The Rock (which is the vanguard for approaching the experience) will bring this dream to fruition.

"We who believe in freedom cannot rest until it comes."

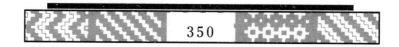

28

MORE! MORE! SWEET HONEY AUDIENCES ARE SPECIAL

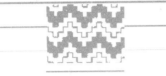

ADISA DOUGLAS

Her sounds stroke my spirit. They let me know that I am all right in the world. That is how I feel about the music of Sweet Honey In The Rock, a music that has been in my life for almost two decades. I have enjoyed Sweet Honey's music over the years through *all* of her recordings and as a cheering, singing, clapping member of many of her concert audiences throughout the United States and abroad.

Sweet Honey audiences are special. There is a unique interaction Sweet Honey has with her audience, and, for me, the more the audience and Sweet Honey spur each other on, the more exciting the concert. I remember the audiences as if the concerts took place yesterday. Sometimes the memory is a conversation I overhear or the blend of diverse faces, or the particular way in which the audience shows its approval, excitement, and appreciation.

Sweet Honey audiences are special, and for many Sweet Honey fans, the excitement begins well before the concert. I recall going to the outdoor Sweet Honey concert at Lincoln Center in New York City in August 1986. My longtime friend Patricia Rodney had come to visit from Barbados and had just arrived. We rushed in from the airport to my apartment to get dressed for the concert. Now, when you get dressed for a Sweet Honey concert, you open up your closet and reach for something special, something fun, something that makes a statement about who you are. It is an important ritual to go through if you are going to be in a Sweet

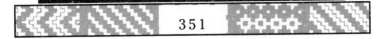

351

Honey audience. Pat and I tested this and that and finally settled on what we would wear—Pat, a soft cotton pants outfit with a beautiful pair of earrings made in Barbados, and me, a two-piece tie-dyed purple-and-turquoise dress made in Nigeria and my favorite jewelry, a pair of Navajo turquoise earrings. We didn't get too carried away because it was going to be a hot evening at an outdoor concert, but we did look sharp!

As we came up out of the subway, we immediately saw the crowd moving toward the mass of folding chairs, which were quickly filling up. This was one of those great, free New York City summer concerts that used to help keep me sane during the hot, humid days of New York City's July and August. We made our way through the crowd, and at last we chose two seats.

After we settled in, I checked out the audience. It was so exciting; there were so many people! There were people who seemed to have wandered into the crowd out of curiosity; there were others who had carefully followed the Lincoln Center summer performance series and had chosen this concert; and then there were, of course, the diehard Sweet Honey fans. The concert was thrilling, and it was great sitting in the midst of so many people experiencing their first Sweet Honey concert. Some began with hesitancy about all this clapping and singing "your part." After all, this was a concert, wasn't it? However, halfway through, they too were jumping up and down and clapping. For me, this was one of my most memorable concerts because its audience was New York City—welcomed in—anyone could come and enjoy. And they did.

Sweet Honey audiences are special. "Girl, Sisters Chapel will never be the same!" "Yeah, that was something else. This is the way the conference was supposed to end." So went a conversation I overheard two sisters having as they walked out of a June 1983 Sweet Honey concert at Sisters Chapel at Spelman College in Atlanta, Georgia. The concert was part of the founding conference of the National Black Women's Health Project, at which two thousand African American women had gathered. The project had made it a priority to ensure that women who normally would not have access to such an event could participate. President and founder Byllye Avery had raised scholarship funds, which were pooled to bring Black women from rural and urban communities all over the South to Atlanta. Together we networked and talked about health and the realities of being African American women.

The line to get into the concert formed early and soon was winding through the campus. Word got out that there was a Sweet Honey concert and folks from Atlanta were trying to get in as well as the women attending the conference (Sisters Chapel holds only 1,500). The chapel was packed; I mean packed! The concert was jumping from the very beginning, with clapping and singing starting right away. At one point, when Sweet Honey was singing Lucie E. Campbell's gospel song "In the Upper Room," the sisters seated in the balcony started stomping with so much zeal I thought the balcony was going to come down! The powerful voice of Yasmeen

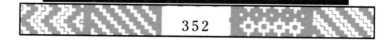

and the incredible bass of Ysaye Maria Barnwell created cross leads that moved the song higher and higher. The women in the audience were on their feet, clapping out a great rhythm that moved right with the song. The stomping in the balcony became louder and its intense rhythm moved to a head as the song ended. What a moment!

Then there was the moment when Yasmeen, who was then very pregnant, led "Crying for Freedom," written by Otis Williams and set to music by Bernice Johnson Reagon, the founder of the group and my friend for more than twenty years. Yasmeen was out front with the microphone and moving across the stage, and then up and down singing, "Crying for freedom, crying for freedom . . . I'm gonna take my freedom in the morning . . . Somewhere there's a child a-crying, somewhere there's a child a-crying, crying for freedom in South Africa." One sister in the audience shouted, "Oh Lord, Yasmeen's gonna have that baby right here!" Another yelled out, "Well, that's all right, this is the place to have it; this is the Black Women's Health Project!"

The concert ended, but the screaming only got louder. An encore later, the audience reluctantly calmed down and started moving toward an acceptance that, yes, the concert was over. But it really wasn't over, because for me and many of the sisters present that evening, it rests so easily in our memory. "Girl, wasn't that a great conference in '83? And the Sweet Honey concert . . . ! Yeah, Sisters Chapel will never be the same."

Sweet Honey audiences are special. My images of moments in them also rest easily in my memory. I recall:

◆ the audience's thunderous ovation of welcome that lasted a good five minutes when Sweet Honey came out onstage at the Zellerbach Theater in Berkeley, before the group sang one note.

◆ the hundreds of women sitting in the pouring rain for more than an hour, waiting and ready to hear Sweet Honey at the Michigan Womyn's Music Festival in Walhall, Michigan, in August 1990.

◆ the overwhelming sound of roars, whistles, screams, and clapping by the New York City Carnegie Hall audience in November 1987 upon first hearing "Emergency," a song about the state of emergency in South Africa, written by Evelyn Maria Harris.

◆ the thousands of people listening to a Sweet Honey performance at Clearwater's Hudson River Revival in Valhalla, New York, on June 16, 1991, one of the hottest days of that summer. Every spot on the beautiful slope of Westchester Community College was taken; and all during the concert, people stood up and sat down, clapping and dancing on their blankets.

◆ the excited audiences at one of Sweet Honey's Black History Month concerts in February 1991 at Bennett College, a small historically Black women's Methodist college in

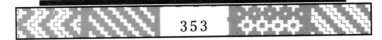

Greensboro, North Carolina, where students and people from the community packed Pfiefer Chapel, the adjacent Little Theater, set up as an overflow room, and a third room spontaneously set up as a second overflow room.

A wonderful development in Sweet Honey's work has been its concerts and workshops for young people. In celebration of *All for Freedom* (Music for Little People, 1989), the group's debut children's recording, Sweet Honey held its first children's concerts at the Children's Museum in Washington, D.C., in December 1989 and at Washington Irving High School in New York City on Martin Luther King Jr. Day in 1990. The New York City concert took place in the high school's auditorium, where approximately 1,500 children and their parents packed the place.

The concert began with "So Glad I'm Here," which, as Bernice Johnson Reagon describes it, is a powerful statement affirming one's presence in the universe.

So glad I'm here, so glad I'm here

I shout out my name
I shout out my name
I shout out my name, shout out my name

Everybody shouted out her or his name. The rhythmic song continued; clapping "upped" the ante. The bodies started moving. The concert had begun.

As Sweet Honey sang and told stories, some of the younger children got up and started moving around. Some of them came right up to the stage, some started dancing, some just looked in absolute amazement.

Sweet Honey also has participated in programs in which they become artists-in-residence in a community, which makes it possible for members of the group to conduct workshops for children as well as perform in their usual concert format. In March 1992 in Newark, New Jersey, Sweet Honey's artists-in-residence was part of a project sponsored by the Woodson Foundation and funded by the Victoria Foundation. The project made it possible for each member of Sweet Honey to conduct workshops with community-based projects in Newark that provide programs and services for children who often are underserved by or not a priority within the conventional educational system. The first day, each member went out to her assigned group and engaged in participatory activities. On the second day, there was a Sweet Honey concert for all of the groups, and additional programs serving children in the county were invited to participate. The third day, each Sweet Honey member went back to her group and did a follow-up workshop. What an incredible three days! The members reported not only on the children's responses but on how deeply moved they were by the experience.

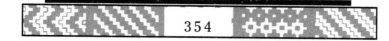

More! More! Sweet Honey Audiences Are Special

The concert was remarkable. The children were so excited and "ready"! As I watched the children and their teachers and leaders coming into the auditorium at Essex Community College (a perfect venue for the concert because of its size and warmth), I too got excited.

The lights blinked, then faded, and then Phillip Thomas, the executive director of the Woodson Foundation, came out onstage to introduce Sweet Honey. Sweet Honey came out onstage true to form in their beautiful bubas, magnificent hairstyles, and dramatic headpieces. "So glad I'm here, so glad I'm here," they sang. The clapping grew, the children shouted their names, and the concert began.

What made this concert so special for me was the children's involvement and appreciation of what was happening on the stage. In the front row, a boy who looked to be about eight or nine years old signed all of the words to just about all of the songs during the entire concert! He watched Akua Opokuwaa, Sweet Honey's Sign language interpreter, intensely as his hands gracefully moved through the air.

Bernice then introduced "A Priority," a rap song written and led by Nitanju Bolade Casel and Aisha Kahlil, saying, "I think women should be a priority," and there was a chorus of screams from the girls establishing firm agreement. Nitanju and Aisha began the song by taking their mikes and moving forward on the stage. Immediately, the children stood up, clapping their hands over their heads (many older audiences don't seem to get that this is a "stand-up" song). As Sweet Honey moved through the rhythmic sounds and words of women as contributors to history, literature, music . . . "the list is endless" and their contributions "are timeless," a chorus from the audience slid right under the rhythms and words coming from the stage. "Go, wo-men! Go, wo-men!" they sang. The children were ecstatic. They were hearing powerful messages in song forms and traditions from their culture, ones that were familiar and speak to them.

But there was also another kind of intensity in the concert. When Sweet Honey sang "No Images," a poem by Waring Cuney set to music by Ysaye, there was *intense silence.* Some children were literally sitting on the edge of their seats as they gazed at Ysaye, whose voice and stage presence can capture something very deep within yourself. Some seemed very pensive as they listened to the story of one who lived in a world that did not reflect the beauty of her brown body. Others seemed really wrapped up in listening to the song and watching the women in Sweet Honey gracefully dancing with their arms. . . .

As I watched the children, I thought about this being an audience of mainly African American and Latino children who were growing up in an urban environment that doesn't place too much hope in them, but who at that moment were hearing this declaration of their own beauty coming from six Black women, who themselves were a strong statement of beauty. Their colors, sizes, and shapes varied, but together the women of Sweet Honey formed a classical picture of the beauty of Black women.

At one of the follow-up workshops the next day, the children talked about

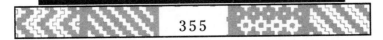

what the concert had meant to them and some things they especially liked. They liked the costumes and the hairstyles. They liked the group's rendition of Reverend William Herbert Brewster's "Old Landmark." They liked the power and resonance of Bernice's voice. They liked "Denko," a Bambara song from Mali arranged for Sweet Honey by Nitanju, and they liked the sounds of the shekeres. They liked Aisha Kahlil's composition "Fulani Chant," with its breathtaking sounds that don't easily slide off the tongue.

And what else did they like? They liked . . . no, they *loved* Sweet Honey! And with that statement went the question: "When is Sweet Honey coming back?"

I was deeply touched both by Sweet Honey's respect for and ease with children and by the children's innate ability to "get" the music. The children took the songs and "ran with them." They seemed to have taken hold of familiar sounds and new messages and placed them inside, and with that placement, there came an affirmation of themselves. Indeed, Sweet Honey came to Newark and into the lives of some of its children.

Sweet Honey audiences are special. I recall:

♦ the long line that wound its way around the beautiful historic wood-framed town hall in the center of Provincetown, Massachusetts, where Sweet Honey was performing one of its summer concerts in August 1989, and the sound of the wooden floors as the crowd rocked, swayed, and stomped its way through the concert.

♦ the circle of African Americans standing, surrounding the Sweet Honey stage at the June 1990 Odunde Festival in Philadelphia, and the row of elderly women in white sitting in chairs in the middle of the front of the circle, fanning, clapping, and nodding absolute approval.

♦ the building of excitement as Sweet Honey took the stage at the Newport Folk Festival in July 1989.

Sweet Honey audiences in the United States are special, but it also has been a fulfilling experience to be part of a Sweet Honey audience in other countries. I have sat in audiences abroad and have been amazed at the careful and quiet attention that is given to hearing the lyrics of the song, absorbing the sounds, and staying open to the experience by people who may never have heard this kind of traditional and contemporary African American music. As I witness this response, my chest is usually stuck out a mile, full of pride in being an African American woman. That pride emanates from the quality and care Sweet Honey gives to singing, to preserving the culture, and to rendering a message that often can be applied to whatever culture, society, or space she finds herself.

In Leverkusen, Germany, Sweet Honey participated in the Leverkusen Jazz Festival (Leverkusener Jazztage 1991). The performances were held in a huge room, but there were very few places to sit! People were standing everywhere and the

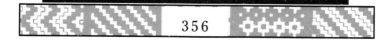

room was packed. The audience had listened to the Dave Brubeck Quartet and Dan Brubeck & the Dolphins and was now waiting for the Sweet Honey set to begin. There wasn't much coming and going because people did not want to lose their space! At last, Sweet Honey came out, and the crowd roared—what a great welcome! Then, as suddenly as the roars began, the silence hit the room. People listened intently, some leaned forward to get a better view, and others just looked on with great intensity. A woman behind me *gasped* when Sweet Honey began to sing. The first number ended, and the crowd roared again! And so it went until the end, most of the crowd was standing throughout the entire set!

At a concert in London, where Sweet Honey has a "serious" following, I recall rows of people standing up in the back of the hall. They were moving, swaying, waving their arms in the air, and singing "So Glad I'm Here." The song kept going on and on and got hotter and hotter. That was just the beginning of this concert!

At a concert in Bremen, Germany, a woman, sitting on one side of me in the front row, was experiencing her first Sweet Honey concert. At the intermission, she said, "My God, they are great!" At this point, I picked up the fact that an older couple directly behind me was speaking (in German, of course) about the concert to the other people around them. The man was waving his hands; and whatever he was saying he was saying it emphatically. I asked the woman beside me to tell me what he was saying. She let him know that I was interested in what he was saying about the concert. He looked at me and said (as translated), "My wife and I have been around for a while. We have seen many, many concerts. We love music. But we have never experienced anything like this. This is the best."

Sweet Honey audiences are special. There were some unforgettable audiences on Sweet Honey's third Australian tour, which took place August 8–28, 1992, and was sponsored by DISCURIO. At the Sydney concert, I recall a very special moment for me when Sweet Honey sang "Breaths" for a second encore. The audience had been on its feet applauding and screaming after the first encore. Sweet Honey came out amid the roars, sat in their chairs, and started singing—inviting us to listen to the air, the wind, the baby's cry for the voices of those who have passed thru the door we call death . . .

Ah . . . wsh! Ah . . . wsh!
Ah . . . wsh! Ah . . . wsh!

As Sweet Honey sang the soft whispers of "Ah . . . wsh!" some women who had been sitting on the floor in front of the first row moved quietly toward the stage. The only sound you could hear was the sound from the stage. Other people who had been dancing in the aisle during the encore moved in behind them, and very quickly people came from every direction toward the stage until the entire area (a huge space) between the stage and the audience was full. Bodies quietly swayed.

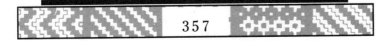

357

Some were still. Most of the remainder of the audience had sat down and was quietly absorbing the experience.

I sat in my seat and was deeply moved. I closed my eyes and let those harmonic, soft Sweet Honey sounds move through my body. I felt the presence of my twin brother, who had died in March, five months before, and I let the song not only allow me to have him there but also provide a comfort zone for my healing the pain of loss. I heard someone behind me crying, and I too let the tears fall.

In Alice Springs (located in Australia's Northern Territory, where the largest concentration of Aboriginal people live) the concert was held in a 500-seat hall, the smallest venue of the tour. This made for an intimate space, however, and the interaction between Sweet Honey and the audience was wonderful! For example, I watched a group of Aboriginal women pointing at Sweet Honey and talking to each other with much animation—they seemed struck by the women as they settled in their chairs to begin the concert.

This was the first Sweet Honey experience for most of the audience; so the concert also created lively conversations during the intermission. "They were great!" "Can you believe that song, the one that didn't have words? What was it called? Yes, 'Fulani Chant'!" Then, everyone was not comfortable with Bernice's monologue on racism. "What does she mean talking about White people are not pure!" and "Every country has their ugly history!" The audience was stimulated and the air was electric!

In Perth, a beautiful city in Western Australia located on the Indian Ocean and the Swan Sea, the concert was hot! Concert Hall, a large venue in the city center, was packed! The concert was put on during a week of demonstrations protesting a redevelopment plan that would create a huge complex of office buildings and restaurants on a beautiful location on the Swan Sea. The site was once a brewery but was being reclaimed as a sacred site by an Aboriginal group from the area. The unsuccessful four-year struggle of the Aboriginal people and their supporters to stop the construction came to a head the day before the Sweet Honey concert, and many of the people involved in the struggle were at the concert. The energy was so familiar—people fighting for their rights going to a Sweet Honey concert to get strengthened and affirmed.

The tribute and respect Aboriginal people gave to Sweet Honey throughout the tour were exemplified in this concert. Moments before Sweet Honey came out onstage to begin the concert, an Aboriginal woman jumped up onstage and placed an Aboriginal flag over the monitor. The flag, which had a black stripe, a red stripe, and a yellow sun in the middle, made a powerful statement of a people, their struggle and their hope for a new day. Some people in the audience immediately applauded; others seemed stunned. Sweet Honey came out, sat down in the space that had changed moments before, and began to sing.

Sweet Honey audiences are special. And so is Sweet Honey.

NOTES ON THE CONTRIBUTORS

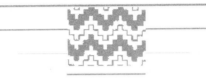

Wendy L. Armstrong is deaf, a graduate of Gallaudet University and a strong advocate for Deaf rights in Washington, D.C. She was introduced to Sweet Honey In The Rock by her mentor and friend Ysaye M. Barnwell.

Ysaye Maria Barnwell, singer, composer, actress, a native of New York, joined Sweet Honey In The Rock in 1979. A master choral director, she has developed a workshop designed as an introduction to choral singing. She holds a doctorate in speech pathology, a master of public health administration, and is an avid partici-pant in contemporary computer-information culture. She is currently working on her first full symphonic composition.

McLean Bosfield, former Sweet Honey voice consultant, is now retired and living in Chapala, Mexico, after a career as a classical singer, choral director, and vocal coach.

Nitanju Bolade Casel, singer, dancer, choreographer, cultural activist, is a native of Buffalo, New York, and sister to Aisha Kahlil, with whom she codirects First World Productions. She lives in Silver Springs, Maryland, with her husband, Tayari Casel.

Angela Davis has been teaching, writing, and lecturing about African Americans' and women's social theories and practices for the last twenty years, during which

she has also been active in a number of organizations concerned with issues of social justice. She presently teaches at the University of California at Santa Cruz.

Adisa Douglas is currently Program Officer at the Public Welfare Foundation in Washington, D.C. She is an active member of the National Network of Grantmakers and the National Black Women's Health Project.

The Earlys reside in Washington, D.C.: Miriam, teacher of children with learning disabilities; James, Smithsonian Institution Administrator and a leading voice in the national debate on cultural equity; Jah-Mir, twelfth grade; and JaBen, ninth grade.

Virginia Giordano, is an independent producer and president of Virginia Giordano Productons. Since 1980 she has been at the forefront in expanding audiences and opening access to formal establishment venues for her contemporary issue-driven cultural events and especially to women in the arts. She lives in the West Village in Manhattan and enjoys skydiving and sailing.

Byron Everette Harris, a serious music connoisseur and prolific recording collector, is the brother of Sweet Honey member Evelyn Harris and an avid fan of Sweet Honey for nineteen years. He lives in Washington, D.C.

Evelyn Maria Harris is an African American woman, parent, lesbian, singer, songwriter, arranger, teacher, choir director, playwright, student, proofreader, and singer in Sweet Honey In The Rock for eighteen years.

Michael Hodge is an actor living and working in New York. His degree in journalism brought him to Washington, D.C., for a position as a reporter for the *Washington Post,* for the D.C. Black Repertory Company, and of course, for Bernice Johnson Reagon.

Amy Horowitz, folklorist, cultural organizer, and activist, is founder of Roadwork, Inc., through which she developed Sweet Honey's national and international network. She is currently working at the Smithsonian Institution on a Jerusalem cross-cultural research and public-programs project and is a doctoral candidate in folklore at the University of Pennsylvania.

In Process . . . began as a Sweet Honey workshop and evolved into an a capella performance ensemble of African American women singers, and celebrated their thirteenth anniversary in June 1993.

Shirley Childress Johnson, a professional American Sign Language interpreter, joined the group as its official Sign Language interpreter in 1980. Since that time,

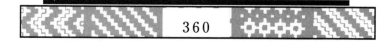

she has taken leadership in making the connection between Sweet Honey In The Rock and her national Deaf constituencies. She lives in Washington, D.C.

Aisha Kahlil, dancer, singer, composer, actress, cultural activist, and experienced singer in jazz, gospel, and African traditional styles, joined Sweet Honey In The Rock in 1981. She lives in Silver Spring, Maryland, where she codirects First World Productions with her sister, Nitanju Bolade Casel.

Niani Kilkenny, arts administrator, cultural programmer, and museum educator, is director of the Smithsonian Institution Program in African American Culture. A third generation Washingtonion, she and her husband Godfrey actively share its cultural treasures with their three granddaughters, Jasmine, Moya, and Naeema.

Tulani Jordan Kinard, singer, master braider, and African hair sculptor, joined Sweet Honey In The Rock in 1978. A native of Boston, as a master braider she pioneered the passage of legislation regulating natural hair care in the state of New York. She lives in Brooklyn, New York, with her husband Stanley and two children, Sakena and Najir.

Carol Maillard, a founding member of Sweet Honey In The Rock, an accomplished actress, choral director, and vocal therapist, was born and raised in Philadelphia Pennsylvania. Among her credits in theater on and off Broadway are: member of the D.C. Black Repertory Company, "For Colored Girls . . ." and "The Life of Bumpy Johnson." She lives in New York City with her son, Jordan Maillard Ware.

La Verte Mathis, a native Washingtonian and the proud father of three children, is a psychiatric social worker who serves as a consultant, educator, and advocate for mental health and AIDS-related issues. His advocational interests include interior and floral design.

E. Ethelbert Miller, poet and former vice president of the Associated Writing Programs and the PEN/Faulkner Foundation, is the director of the African American Resource Center at Howard University. In 1993 he was a visiting professor at the University of Nevada, Las Vegas.

Henri Norris, for more than twenty-five years an organizer and activist in the women's rights movement, lives in San Francisco, where she divides her professional time between her interests in film and video media projects and her work as a lawyer on women's health issues.

Akua Kyerewaa Opokuwaa is a Sign Language interpreter and longtime advocate for Deaf rights as well as other social justice causes. Now studying to be an Akan

priest, Akua is a mother, grandmother, sister, aunt, and cousin to a large family whose roots moved from Ghana to Georgia to North Carolina to New Jersey and to Washington, D.C., where she now resides.

Ann Rall is a graphic artist whose works have been an integral part of the women's cultural network in Washington, D.C., where she lives. She is currently a student in social work at Howard University.

Bernice Johnson Reagon, composer, singer, mother, historian, author, founder and artistic director of Sweet Honey In The Rock, lives in Washington, D.C., where she also works as a curator for the Smithsonian Institution. Her latest book is *We'll Understand It Better By and By: Pioneering African American Gospel Composers;* she is currently working on *Wade in the Water,* a Smithsonian Institution and National Public Radio production on the history of African American sacred music.

Toshi Reagon, daughter of Civil Rights Movement parents, is a singer, songwriter, and recording producer currently living in New York City. As a vocalist and a bass and guitarist, she fronts her own band and is currently working on her next recording project.

Madeleine Remez is a cultural worker in Washington, D.C., who has held down the business end of booking Sweet Honey In The Rock as a staff member of Roadwork Attractions.

Louise Robinson, singer, songwriter, and actress, is the founder and artistic director of an a capella ensemble, **Street Sounds.** She is an original member of Sweet Honey In The Rock, transitioning from the early years with the group and the Washington, D.C., Black Repertory Theatre to more than a decade of work in theater. She resides and works as a musician in San Francisco.

Sonio Sanchez, poet, mother, activist, and professor, is the author of thirteen books including *Homecoming, I've Been A Woman: New and Selected Poems,* and, most recently, *Under a Soprano Sky.* She received the 1985 American Book Award for *Homegirls and Handgrenades,* the Governor's Award for Excellence in the Humanities for 1988, and now holds the Laura Carnell Chair in English at Temple University.

Sandra Sharp is a poet, playwright, collector, and filmmaker who lives in Los Angeles, California. Her latest book of poetry is *Typing in the Dark.*

Art Steele, a musician and master sound engineer, currently divides his time between road/tour commitments as Sweet Honey's sound engineer, managing his

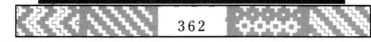

Audio Promedia sound company, and performing as guitar-vocalist/frontman for the Art Steele Blues Band. He lives in Sunderland, Massachusetts, with his wife of twenty years Carol, daughter Ilona, and son Ian.

Alice Walker has written numerous volumes of fiction, poetry, essays, and short stories. In 1983 she won both the Pulitzer Prize and the American Book Award for her novel *The Color Purple.* Her most recent novel is *Possessing the Secret of Joy.* She makes her home in Northern California.

Charles Williams, Sweet Honey's vocal consultant, made his Metropolitan Opera debut as Sportin' Life in "Porgy and Bess," has won international acclaim in theaters, opera houses, and on radio and television in Europe, and now balances a performing career between the United States and Europe.

Yasmeen, singer, songwriter, and producer, was born in Washington, D.C. She performs with her band and is a recording artist and is currently working on her next solo project.

Ivy Young is a native Washingtonian and a grass-roots activist and organizer in the human rights, advocacy media, international, and women's cultural movements for more than twenty-five years. Also a writer and singer, she is currently a project director at the National Gay and Lesbian Task Force Policy Institute.

ACKNOWLEDGMENTS

Armstrong, Wendy L: "Thank You Sweet Honey!" © 1993 by Wendy L. Armstrong. Printed by permission of the author.

Barnwell, Ysaye Maria: "Becoming a Singer" copyright © 1993 by Ysaye Maria Barnwell. Printed by permission of the author.

Bosfield, McLean: "Extending a Vocal Lineage" copyright © 1993 by McLean Bosfield. Printed by permission of the author.

Casel, Nitanju Bolade: "Casserole for Life" copyright © 1993 by Nitanju Bolade Casel. Printed by permission of the author.

Davis, Angela: "Sweet Honey in the Rock" copyright © 1993 by Angela Davis. Printed by permission of the author.

Douglas, Adisa: 'More! More! Sweet Honey Audiences Are Special" copyright © 1993 by Adisa Douglas. Printed by permission of the author.

Early Family (Miriam Stewart, James, Jah-Mir Toussaint, and JaBen Akua): "Family" copyright © 1993 by the Early family. Printed by permission of the authors.

Acknowledgments

Norris, Henri E.: "Nourishment for the Soul" copyright © 1993 by Henri E. Norris. Printed by permission of the author.

Opokuwaa, Akua Kyerewaa: "A Bridge Between Cultures" copyright © by Akua Kyerewaa Opokuwaa. Printed by permission of the author.

Reagon, Bernice Johnson: "Singing for My Life" and "Let Your Light Shine—Historical Notes" both copyright © 1993 by Bernice Johnson Reagon. Printed by permission of the author.

Reagon, Toshi: "Growing Up with Sweet Honey In The Rock" copyright © 1993 by Toshi Reagon. Printed by permission of the author.

Robinson, Louise: "Taking It to the Streets" copyright © 1993 by Louise Robinson. Printed by permission of the author.

Sanchez, Sonia: "sweethoneyintherock" copyright © 1993 by Sonia Sanchez. Printed by permission of the author.

Steele, Art: "The Rantings, Ravings, Ramblings, and Recollections of a Sound Man" copyright © 1993 by Art Steele. Printed by permission of the author.

Sharp, Saundra: "Natural Woman in Search of the Rock" copyright © 1993 by Saundra Sharp. Printed by permission of the author.

Walker, Alice: "Sweet Honey In The Rock—The Sound of Our Own Culture" copyright © 1993 by Alice Walker. Printed by permission of the author.

Williams, Charles: "Music is Energy" copyright © 1993 by Charles Williams. Printed by permission of the author.

Yasmeen: "Timeless" copyright © 1993 by Betty J. Williams, "Yasmeen." Printed by permission of the author.

Young, Ivy: "Sweet Honey In The Rock: A Few Memories" copyright © 1993 by Ivy Young. Printed by permission of the author.

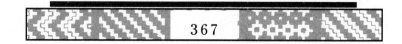